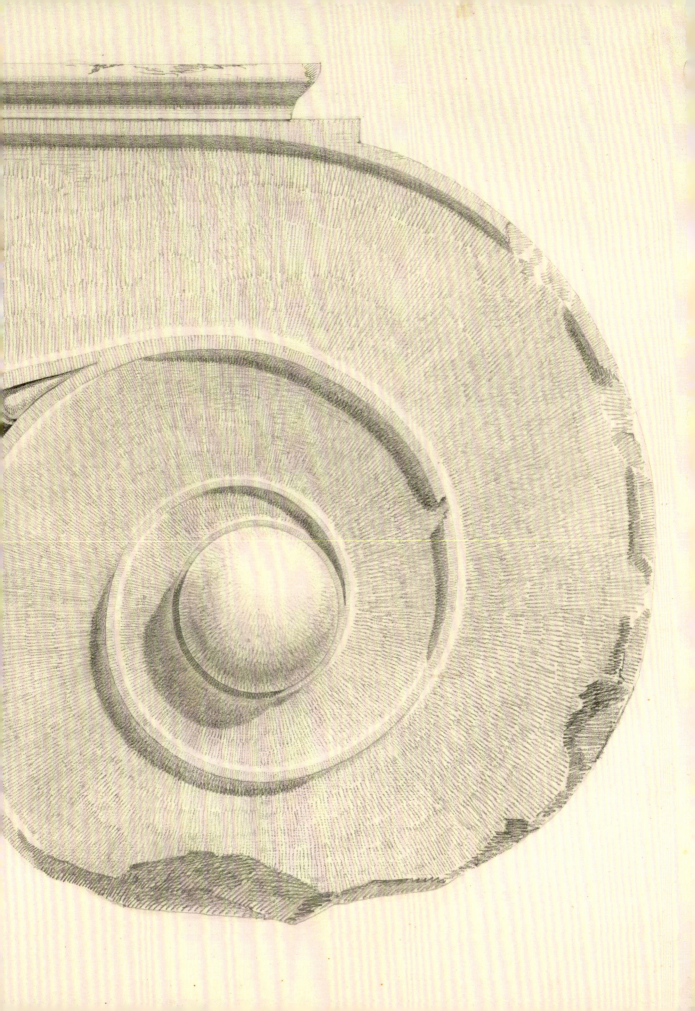

Retrospective Columns

Ionic Capitals and Perceptions of the Past in Greek Architecture

Samuel Holzman

PRINCETON UNIVERSITY PRESS
Princeton and Oxford

For my architects
Andy and Malcolm

You have, perhaps, heard of five orders; but there are only two real orders, and there never can be any more until doomsday. On one of these orders the ornament is convex ... On the other the ornament is concave ...

—John Ruskin, *The Stones of Venice*, vol. 1 (1851)

Copyright © 2025 by Samuel Holzman

Princeton University Press is committed to the protection of copyright and the intellectual property our authors entrust to us. Copyright promotes the progress and integrity of knowledge created by humans. By engaging with an authorized copy of this work, you are supporting creators and the global exchange of ideas. As this work is protected by copyright, any reproduction or distribution of it in any form for any purpose requires permission; permission requests should be sent to permissions@press.princeton.edu. Ingestion of any IP for any AI purposes is strictly prohibited.

Published by Princeton University Press, 41 William Street, Princeton, New Jersey 08540
In the United Kingdom: Princeton University Press, 99 Banbury Road, Oxford OX2 6JX
press.princeton.edu

Illustrations in front matter: p. ii, detail of fig. 5.5; pp. viii–ix, detail of fig. 2.3
Illustrations in back matter: p. 238, detail of fig. 5.3; p. 254, fig. 5.4; p. 271, fig. 2.3
Jacket images: Front (top): Ephesos, Ionic capital of the temple of Artemis, 6th century BCE. Front (bottom): Ephesos, Ionic capital of the temple of Artemis, late 4th century BCE. © The Trustees of the British Museum (both front images). Back: Ephesos, convex face of a capital from the temple of Athena Trecheia, late 4th century BCE (Ephesos Museum, Vienna).

All Rights Reserved
ISBN 9780691262550
ISBN (e-book) 9780691262567

British Library Cataloging-in-Publication Data is available

This publication is made possible in part by the Barr Ferree Foundation Fund for Publications, Department of Art and Archaeology, Princeton University.
Editorial: Michelle Komie and Annie Miller
Production Editorial: Sara Lerner
Text and Jacket Design: Jeff Wincapaw
Production: Steven Sears
Publicity: William Pagdatoon
Copyeditor: Lachlan Brooks
This book has been composed in Tiempos Text
Printed in China

10 9 8 7 6 5 4 3 2 1

Contents

- 1   Introduction

- 11   Chapter 1
  Bilingual Ionic Capitals in Context: How Buildings Tell Stories about the Past

- 42   Chapter 2
  Delos: Synthesis at the End of the Archaic Period

- 76   Chapter 3
  Oropos: Stone Carving and an Eye for Shadows

- 110   Chapter 4
  Neapolis and Thessaloniki: Stylistic Pluralism in *Apoikiai*

- 150   Chapter 5
  Athens and Eretria: The Influence of Painting on Stone Carving

- 198   Chapter 6
  Ephesos, Selinous, and Delphi: Retrospective Design in Ionia and Abroad

- 228   Chapter 7
  Conclusion

- 234   Appendix
- 236   Acknowledgments
- 239   Notes
- 255   Bibliography
- 272   Index Locorum
- 274   General Index
- 284   Image Credits

Introduction

A fame-seeking arsonist burned down the temple of Artemis at Ephesos in 356 BCE; it was one of the largest temples of the ancient Greek world and—supposedly—the first built in the Ionic order. The Ephesians confronted this trauma in three ways, two of which are well-known. First, the Ephesians rebuilt the temple on the same plan and footprint, but they traded the old, doughy style of carved decoration from the sixth-century temple for the rich, relief style that had become standard in the fourth century. Second, they tried to erase all memory of the arsonist by decreeing that anyone caught repeating his name would be put to death. The third response has not yet been understood: the creation of another new temple, which was dedicated to Athena at the spot where, according to local legend, Ephesos was founded. This new temple had Ionic column capitals that contrasted an outside face carved in contemporary style with an inside face that recreated the convex volutes of the ancient, burned temple (fig. 0.1). As a visitor entered the colonnade toward the spot of the city's beginning, she might have felt from the changing appearances that she was stepping back in time.

The temple of Athena Trecheia at Ephesos looked back to the past, and its juxtaposition of the old and new offered a narrative of resilience in the face of disaster. Indeed, this temple and its retrospective columns illustrate the power of architectural style, which could become a component of civic, religious, and ethnic identities. By reproducing obsolete elements from the old Artemision, Ephesian builders preserved destroyed physical testimonies of a local history of architecture that centered the city of Ephesos among the Ionians. The temple of Athena Trecheia at Ephesos, however, is not the only one of its kind: eight other Ionic monuments have Ionic column capitals juxtaposing the convex volutes characteristic of Archaic-period Ionia with the concave relief styles of later periods on opposite faces. These are discussed individually under names such as "convex-concave-capitals" and "capitals with hollow and solid volutes."[1] This type of Ionic capital appears on buildings and monuments at Oropos, Delos, Neapolis (Kavala), Thessaloniki (likely originating at ancient Therme), Eretria, Pallene in Attica, Ephesos, Delphi, and Selinous, ranging in date from about 550 BCE to about 250 BCE (fig. 0.2, fig. 0.3). They have a three-hundred-year chronological scope and a wide geographic range across the modern countries of Turkey, Greece, and Italy. Essential to understanding

these monuments, therefore, is documenting and presenting them all together, as this book does for the first time with original measured drawings and orthographic images based on photogrammetry.

The Ionic order is arguably the most complex of ancient Greek building traditions. Its early history is quite different from the other major Greek building tradition, Doric, which followed a rather linear pattern of early development and had most of its canonical features fixed by the first quarter of the sixth century BCE. Ionic buildings varied greatly by region, and developments rarely follow a strictly linear sequence. The Roman architect Vitruvius, in his *Ten Books on Architecture* (composed in Rome in the 20s BCE), relays a tidy origin story to explain the Ionic order, a system of columnar design to which he devoted the majority of book three. According to his account, the sons of the legendary hero Ion ventured to establish the Ionian cities on the coast of Asia Minor and built a temple to honor Artemis at Ephesos (Vitr. 4.1.4–8). Rejecting the manly Doric order of their mainland brethren as unsuitable for the goddess, the first Ionians crafted a temple with more delicate proportions and more elaborate ornamentation—establishing the model for the Ionic order. This account, relayed in the only surviving ancient architectural treatise, is a convenient, explanatory myth. Archaeological discoveries have shown that the conventions of the Ionic order as Vitruvius knew them took shape gradually over the course of the sixth and fifth centuries BCE.[2] Not only was there no one first Ionic temple, but temples alone were not the only place where this design idiom developed. Numerous freestanding Ionic columns used as pedestals for statues set up as dedications in sanctuaries show that votive columns were just as important as temple porticos in establishing the conventions of Ionic column design.[3] There were also other early columnar forms that never caught on, most notably capitals with volutes that rise vertically, dubbed "Aeolic" in modern scholarship because they are

0.1. Ephesos, Ionic capitals of the Archaic temple of Artemis, sixth century BCE (top left, British Museum, London), the late-Classical reconstruction of the temple of Artemis, late fourth century BCE (top right, British Museum, London), and the opposite convex and concave sides of a capital of the temple of Athena Trecheia, late fourth century BCE (bottom, Ephesos Museum, Vienna).

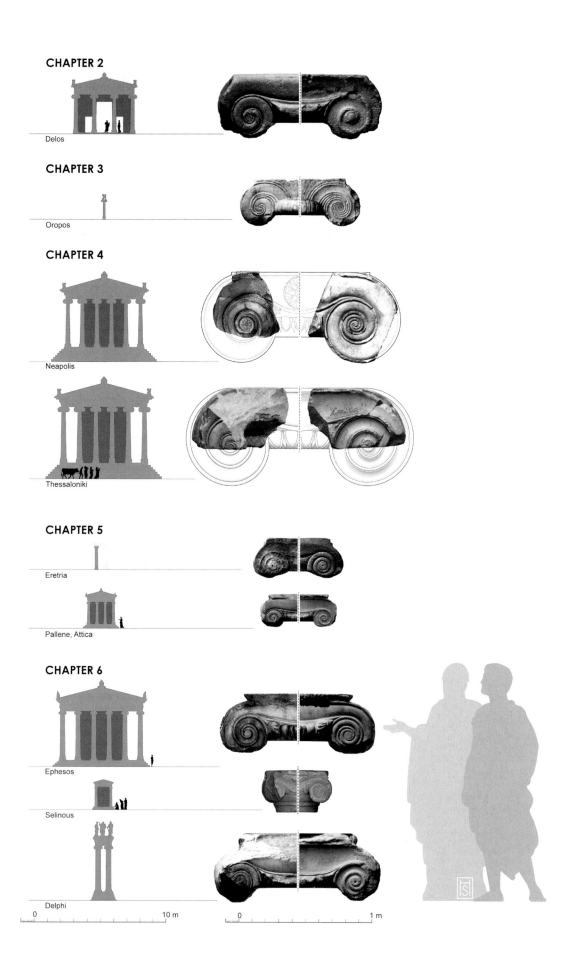

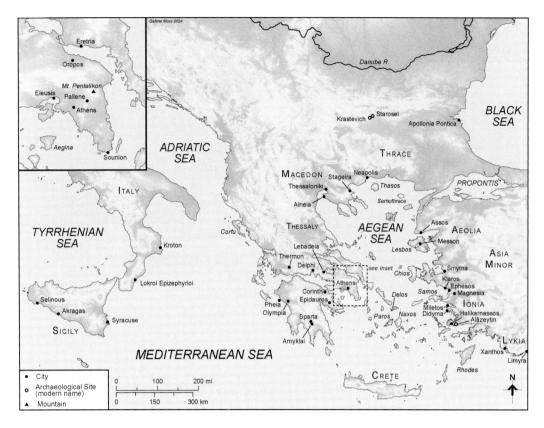

0.2. Bilingual Ionic capitals, arranged by chapter.

0.3. Map of sites discussed.

primarily known from the region of the Aeolian Greeks in the northeastern Aegean.[4] In the last two decades, it has become clear that the most important temples of Ionia had not just Ionic capitals with volutes, but a second type without volutes entirely, which topped off the column shaft with only the pillowy echinus (see, e.g., fig. 1.5).[5] Vitruvius also offered a second explanation for the origins of temple design, relating how the entablature of Doric and Ionic buildings originate in wood rather than stone (4.2.1–5). The triglyphs of the Doric frieze took the place of plaques at the ends of timber joists, and Doric mutules and Ionic dentils preserved in stone the ends of wooden rafters. This proposal of wooden origins has occasionally been extended to Ionic capitals, where the volutes were envisioned as a fossil of a horizontal wood bracket (*Sattelholz* in German) that reduced the span of the beam between columns. Scholarly consensus, however, now holds the Vitruvian doctrine of petrification to be legendary.[6] Doubt arises in large part from the Ionic evidence, which does not appear completely formed as a replication in stone of a preexisting manner of building in timber but takes shape gradually in stone over the course of the sixth century. A fixed architectural canon for the Ionic order only solidifies in the fourth century BCE. Much of the meaning of the Ionic order, therefore, lies not at a single point of origin—whether a primeval wooden prototype, a single exemplary temple, or a first inventor—but in the process of consolidation. As builders returned to and selected

Introduction   5

certain elements over others, they layered on meaning over time. Ionic capitals that plainly mix forms from different periods and places show the making of an architectural tradition in action.

Scholarship has understandably prioritized sorting buildings into a chronological sequence of styles to establish the dates of buildings and to present a larger historical narrative. Yet ancient builders were not oblivious to the persistence of older structures in their built environment. This book emphasizes that ancient builders revisited venerable old temples in new creations. It is tempting to borrow from the study of Greek sculpture the term "archaistic," but this term does not quite fit Ionic capitals that only half reproduce Archaic forms and that emerged at the tail end of the Archaic period. The archaistic style in relief sculpture is hard to miss. It is distinguished by rigid figures, mannered gestures, and geometric drapery folds, deployed in complete compositions. It first occurs for a full sculptural program on the frieze of the Hall of Choral Dancers on Samothrace (third quarter of the fourth century BCE).[7] Yet sculptors began to look back to stylistic features of early sculpture already in the fifth century, including in two metopes of the Parthenon where the stiff, frontal posture of older sculpture was borrowed to distinguish inanimate cult statues in mythological scenes where characters seek refuge in temples.[8] Long before the archaistic style was a full-blown sculptural model, elements of retrospective design crop up within specific, representational scenes, almost always in sanctuary contexts, mixed with other styles but always recognizable. In a similar way, archaism in architecture has generally been identified with bursts in specific historical contexts, such as Athens in the time of the statesman Lykourgos (338–322 BCE). Yet Ionic capitals with opposite convex and concave faces illustrate that retrospective design in architecture began at the end of the Archaic period and ran parallel to the wide-ranging pattern of retrospection in sculpture. These Ionic columns also parallel the repair and reconstruction of temples and altars, which sometimes called upon stonemasons to carve new pieces that matched older elements.[9] They also coincide with the symbolic reuse of older architectural members in new building contexts (i.e., spolia), a practice that took on particular importance in Athens in the aftermath of the city's destruction in the Persian invasion of 480–479 BCE.[10] Together this pattern of revisiting, reusing, and reinterpreting earlier monuments has been dubbed the "archaeology of the past," material evidence that shows a concern for the past and the shaping of memory independent from the writing of historical accounts.[11] Retrospective Ionic columns show patron communities embracing the pluralism of Ionic styles and juxtaposing elements from different places and times to embody histories and myths that were integral to community self-image.

The first chapter of this book frames how a set of heterogeneous buildings sharing a common anomaly tells stories about the past, who built them, and why. Many Greek temples are heterogeneous by circumstance, openly displaying histories of long construction, renovation, or repair. Others were heterogeneous by design, conspicuously combining different elements from scratch to engage in the same type of storytelling. The chapter then turns to the intentionality of retrospective design. Itinerant workshops of stone carvers, as well as traveling architects, were the primary agents for cross-pollinating architectural practices in antiquity, but these Ionic capitals warrant a model of agency distributed among carvers, architects, and their patrons to explain how features dependent on specific carving techniques were organized at a large scale to create buildings that changed appearance from different perspectives. This first chapter uses examples of heterogeneous and retrospective designs drawn from outside the realm of Ionic architecture—Doric temples, bilingual Attic vases, and incuse coins—to put the phenomenon of these Ionic capitals in their ancient cultural context and show their broader relevance to ancient Greek architecture and art.

The subsequent chapters explore where and when these capitals appear, presenting a diachronic overview of developments and regional adaptations in Ionic architecture. Chapter 2 examines the first fully formed examples, capitals which were carved for the sanctuary of Apollo on Delos, within the context of the sixth-century Cyclades, where there was much early experimentation with Ionic elements. Viewed from the perspective of late sixth-century Delos, this monument emerged as a response to the stylistic pluralism visible in sanctuaries after a century of rapid change. Chapter 3 steps back to a slightly older votive column, from Oropos at the edge of Attica, which blends Aeolic and Ionic elements, and combines the faintest traces of convex and concave volutes on opposite faces. Chapter 4 investigates how bilingual Ionic temples took hold in two colonies (*apoikiai*) in coastal Thrace, where syncretic cults were focal points for conceiving new identities and community histories between native populations and mother cities. In chapter 5, an Ionic temple at Pallene in Attica forms the basis for reconsidering how fifth-century Athens adapted and reinvented the Ionic order at a time when Athenians mobilized their Ionian ethnic identity in the service of empire. Chapter 6 returns to the temple of Athena Trecheia at Ephesos as a model of historic preservation and broader retrospective aspects of fourth-century Ionian architecture. Major retrospective Ionic cult buildings in cities and sanctuaries with Ionian roots drew upon historic elements to emphasize shared history to structure cohesive group identities. Yet chapter 6 also engages with exceptions that prove the rule: two private monuments from outside the Ionian sphere, an Aetolian dynastic monument at Delphi and a possible tomb monument at Dorian Selinous, are examples of heirloom Ionic elements mobilized to express the individual preeminence of elite families set apart from their communities.

Scholars have occasionally suggested that these capitals are simply cases of cutting corners, with less attention given to carving less visible faces.[12] The line of argument underlying this commonsensical interpretation has not been consistently articulated, but it has four main elements. First, the inward-facing sides of Ionic capitals were more difficult to see, and builders occasionally sought to save time and money when no one was looking, occasionally leaving one side of an Ionic capital completely uncarved, with blank volutes.[13] Second, reverting to an older, simpler way of carving could have labor savings that made the change in style economical. Third, this compromise suited lighting conditions as well as visibility, with more time-consuming relief carving placed in direct sunlight for maximum effect.[14] Fourth, Ionic capitals were originally painted, and this lost, multicolor layer of embellishment may have concealed shortcuts in the carving of capitals. This book casts doubts on this line of reasoning. The focused examination of each monument in the following chapters reveals that an explanation of frugality is premised on an incorrect assumption that all the capitals were oriented with the high-relief carving facing out. These monuments survive in scattered pieces (*disiecta membra*), and thus it is not always possible to reconstruct the exact position of each capital. Yet the position of some capitals can be ascertained with certainty based on dowel holes (Delphi), actual half-finished details (Pallene), and corner capitals, where the outer and inner sides are evident from overall shape (Delos, Ephesos). At fourth-century Ephesos, high-relief carving did face out, but the two earlier fixed cases (sixth-century Delos, fifth-century Pallene) were oriented in the opposite direction of what has generally been assumed. It is necessary to view these capitals as they once were, as part of larger buildings, set high above viewers, and with sculpted textures invigorated by the play of light and shadow—a mandate addressed here through perspective views of digital models, which capture the experience of seeing these dispersed elements as integral components of buildings. These monuments take different forms, including large temples encircled with colonnades, a propylon for entering a sanctuary, and freestanding columns supporting statues as votive gifts. To understand their internal contrast these capitals must be viewed contextually within buildings, within larger built environments, and within historical social settings.

Although this book sets aside the interpretation of frugality, because it is premised on an assumed reconstruction of the capitals that is not substantiated by the material evidence, it nevertheless considers the constitutive elements of this line of thought. At the root of each is a fundamental idea of much broader significance to the understanding of ancient Greek architecture: (1) builders grappled with the practical limitations of viewing their works, (2) the labor of carving stone was itself a central consideration of ancient building projects, (3) nascent aesthetic appreciation of light and shadow effects drove changes in carved ornament, and (4) the painted and gilded embellishment of stone, now largely deteriorated, substantially shaped the ancient perception of architecture. Thus, in chapter 2, the subsection "Conditional Visibility" addresses the constraints of viewing buildings, a subject that has long been a point of contention surrounding figural reliefs on temples that were impractical to look at directly, such as the frieze of the Parthenon, but that is a pertinent consideration to other forms of carved ornamentation. In chapter 3, the subsection "Carving Ionic Capitals" assesses the labor involved through experimental archaeology, recreating convex and concave volutes in marble with hammer, chisel, and stopwatch to determine empirically the differences in labor involved. Also in chapter 3, the subsections "The Interplay of Convex and Concave in Ornament" and "An Eye for Shadows" survey the popularity of variegated surface treatment in Ionic ornament and contextualize developments in chiaroscuro design in architecture in relationship to contemporary concerns for light and shadows in ancient art and thought. In chapter 5, the subsection "Ionic Polychromy" reviews the evidence for painting Ionic capitals. This survey draws attention to exceptional cases of capitals from the same colonnade painted differently, an underappreciated phenomenon that primed ancient audiences to look for differences in carved ornament as well.

0.4. Bilingual Attic amphora with the same scene in black-figure by the Lysippides Painter and red-figure by the Andokides Painter. Museum of Fine Arts, Boston [01.8037].

Instead of generalizing about visibility, labor, lighting, and painting to explain away this unusual corpus of Ionic capitals, this book argues that these exceptional artifacts offer insights about designing in accordance with vision, the craft of stone working, the refinement of chiaroscuro effects through surface modeling, and the original appearance of temples in more hues than marble white. A nonspecialist reader may wish to jump ahead from the focused discussion of specific Ionic monuments to these subsections in chapters 2, 3, and 5 to cut to the broader implications of this study.

    These Ionic monuments center the ways Ionic architecture often embraced internal variation, including the painting and sculpting of columns with different colors and patterns, features that are often absent from reconstruction drawings made without color or shading. Wilhelm Alzinger and Anton Bammer first compared the back-to-back pairing of convex and concave volutes on these Ionic capitals to the phenomenon of bilingual Attic vases, which juxtapose black-figure and red-figure painting techniques on opposite sides of vessels (fig. 0.4).[15] These are the creation of vase painters who were equally fluent in older and newer painting techniques and reveled in combinations that highlighted how each technique presented figures through opposite positive and negative shapes of added black slip and exposed orange clay. The capitals debut in roughly the same period, in the late sixth century BCE. Because the retrospective aspect of these capitals took on greater salience over time, this book relies on the more neutral coinage of *bilingual* Ionic capitals—emphasizing the striking visual contrast and the fluency of their carvers

0.5. Two non-joining fragments of Ionic capital volutes of similar size, one concave and one convex. Krastevich, Bulgaria.

in multiple approaches to carving—rather than on their associations with the past exclusively.

Bilingual Ionic capitals have been overlooked because they are anomalous, yet they appear as outliers because they have not been viewed synoptically nor integrated into the story of Ionic architecture. The overwhelming impression that Greek builders aimed for total homogeneity in their colonnades owes something to the modern practices of drawing reconstructions of ruined buildings by copying and pasting one standardized column that has been pieced together from many assorted fragments. Here is an inherent dilemma of archaeological illustration that warrants critical reexamination: the process of filling in the blanks with comparable material inadvertently propagates an image of uniformity.[16] Recent excavations of a fifth-century Ionic temple at Krastevich, Bulgaria, produced both fragments of convex capitals and one lone concave volute fragment of the same size (fig. 0.5).[17] Difference in the stone type means these fragment cannot be combined into a single bilingual capital, but the case illustrates how the chance survival of fragments could alter reconstructions. It is possible that additional bilingual capitals exist as fragments in excavation and museum storerooms.

Chapter 1

Bilingual Ionic Capitals in Context

How Buildings Tell Stories about the Past

In 1754–1755, the French architect Julien-David Le Roy traveled to Ottoman Greece on a mission to measure and draw the ruins of ancient architecture, many for the first time. He was struck by the variation of Doric columns that he observed. Until this point, the ancient columnar orders had been understood largely through the model of the "parallel" of five orders—the Greek orders of Doric, Ionic, and later Corinthian described by Vitruvius, and the Tuscan and Composite orders, which were formulated by Renaissance architects based on observation of Roman antiquities.[1] Le Roy observed that the Doric order itself was not static but seemed to change over time in phases. He set out a history of the Doric order in three stages by comparing plans, shaded elevations, and the sculpted profiles of column capitals.[2] Beginning with James Stuart and Nicholas Revett, Le Roy's contemporary rivals, subsequent investigators revealed errors in Le Roy's recording and interpretation that showed his initial Doric sequence was hopelessly muddled.[3] Measuring errors made the columns of the portico at Thorikos too squat on paper and the gateway to the Roman Agora in Athens too slender. Also, Le Roy was led astray by Doric columns that were not fluted. Ancient builders carved the channels on column shafts last because they were prone to breaking in the bustle of a construction site, preparing only the beginnings of the flutes at the top and bottom as guidelines. Le Roy mistook these unfinished columns as traces of a developmental phase before fluting was invented. Nevertheless, Le Roy's attempt to sort buildings into a chronological sequence based on formal and stylistic qualities was a revolutionary paradigm for the history of architecture and for archaeology.[4] When the London-based publisher Robert Sayer produced an unauthorized, cut-rate, English translation, he halved the price of the volume by compressing together Le Roy's figures—putting the Doric plans, elevations, and capital profiles side by side in a single diagram (fig. 1.1).[5] This distillation of drawings also set a lasting graphic model for subsequent research.

It seemed self-evident to Le Roy that the history of Greek architecture was written on temple facades, which only needed to be sorted by the discerning eye. His whiggish history of Doric architectural progress bares the distinctive imprint of his own mid-eighteenth-century moment. A developmental model had already been applied to medieval paleography, and Johann Joachim Winckelmann's sorting of Greek painting and sculpture into phases—beginning with an "Archaic" phase of Greek art characterized by simple, rigid figures—was soon to follow.[6] Le Roy's graphic presentation of architectural evidence was also dependent on the conventions of architectural drawing and publishing of his own era. Yet the pith of his observation, as he himself noted at the outset of his discussion of Doric architecture, was rooted in the text of Vitruvius.[7] Vitruvius appealed to legends of progress in building from ephemeral to solid materials (2.1.1–7, 4.2.2). In his description of the origins of the Doric and Ionic orders, he notes that they changed over time, with bulky columns replaced by proportionally slimmer ones, "succeeding generations having made progress in taste and subtlety of judgement and delighting in more gracile proportions" (4.1.7–8).[8] This statement offered a structuring arc for Le Roy's initial sequence of Doric columns. This developmental model, however, was not the invention of Vitruvius either.

Two centuries before Vitruvius, the Hellenistic engineer Philo of Byzantion (*Bel.* 50.30) conjured a similar progression in architecture from rude to refined: "For instance, the correct proportions of buildings could not possibly have been determined right from the start and without the benefit of previous experience, as is clear from the fact that the old builders were extremely unskillful, not only in general building, but also in shaping the individual parts."[9] For Philo, the technological and aesthetic improvement in architecture apparent from observing older buildings was an example of the importance of experience (*peira*) in advancing art (*techne*)—a central principle for his conception of engineering.[10] A notion of architectural progress may even be sensed in the fifth-century historian Thucydides (1.10), who contrasts the modern image of the Athens of his day to the settlement "in the old manner of Greece" still evident in Sparta.[11] At the root of these statements lies a progressive model of human history, which was articulated already by the sixth-century Ionian philosopher Xenophanes of Kolophon, who remarked that "the gods have not revealed all things to men from the beginning, but by seeking they find in time what is better."[12] The opposite, lapsarian model of history as a story of decline was also attested in antiquity and was occasionally invoked to express admiration and nostalgia for early sculpture (echoed in archaistic sculpture), but was rarely attached to accounts of architecture.[13] The current consensus on the stylistic seriation of Greek architecture is indebted to the diligent work of many investigators improving upon the sequence sketched by Le Roy, but it would be a mistake to regard ancient viewers, especially ancient builders, as oblivious to changes visible in the edifices around them.

When it came to the Ionic order, it was the convex volute that stood out to early investigators as the most striking feature of Archaic capitals. It was an unmissable contradiction to the terminology recorded by Vitruvius, which assumed the

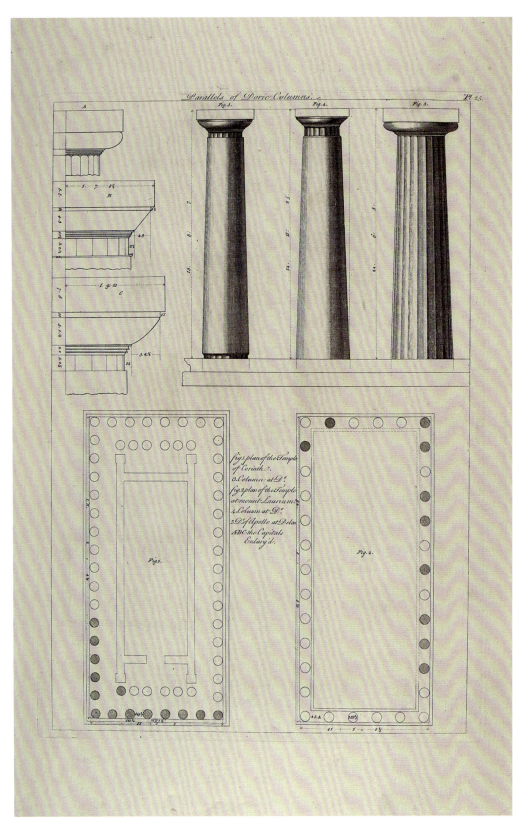

1.1. Robert Sayer after Julien-David Le Roy, comparison of Doric orders from Delos, Thorikos, and Corinth (Le Roy 1758b, plate 25).

volute "channel" (*canalis*) was by nature a sunken relief. This first impression of early capitals, however, became more complicated as more came to light, including numerous singletons from freestanding votive columns that could not be assigned a date as easily as whole buildings. Some of the very earliest capitals had a flat volute surface with an incised or painted helix, and some from the Cyclades had a shallow concave volute almost from the beginning. As Roland Martin put it in 1973: "We increasingly recognize that decoration is far from being the essential element that allows us to define the specific characteristics of a group; it sticks, often as an external addition, to very different structures and only these can provide the essential criteria for the classification of capitals."[14] Martin was part of a wave of studies of the proportions of Ionic capitals that looked beyond the surface to proportional ratios in the dimensions of capitals as the basis for chronological sequencing.[15] The specialist consensus that surface carving alone is not a dependable dating criterion, however, does not negate the signifying power of style to ancient viewers. In fact, it was precisely because sculptural style conjured earlier times and places that it was revisited—tangling up what might have been a tidy sequence of chronological markers.

Beginning with John Boardman, scholars have queried whether bilingual Ionic capitals are "transitional" between the convex type common in the sixth century and the concave type that became standard from the fifth century onward.[16] Anton Bammer, however, pointed out that these capitals have a long chronological span and cannot all mark a moment of sequential succession.[17] The contradiction between the place of these monuments within a sequence of styles and the actual chronology of their construction highlights how buildings tell stories about the past. Bilingual Ionic monuments are hardly alone in mixing disparate elements: many notable Greek temples change styles, either of architectural elements or architectural sculpture, from one side to another or from inside to outside. It is essential to distinguish between buildings that are heterogeneous *by circumstance* and heterogeneous *by design*. The former were built at periods of rapid change or were gradually built, renovated, or repaired over long periods of time, leaving inconsistencies that display each building's life story. The latter also tell stories about the past but were built with contrasting elements from scratch.

Two Doric temples, the temple of Aphaia at Aigina and Temple E at Selinous, are staples of Greek art history because their sculptural programs appear to change style from the west side to the east side. Scholars agree that the pediment figures at Aigina and the metopes at Selinous were carved during the rapid period of change between the late Archaic sculptural style and the Severe Style of the early Classical period, preserving this transformation in stone. There is, however, disagreement on the exact timing this change of style implies: Was there a hiatus in work or on-the-job innovation? For example, Brunilde Ridgway dated the west pediment of the Aphaia Temple to ca. 490 and the east pediment beginning a decade later, while Andrew Stewart dated the whole sculptural project to the decade of 480–470.[18] The sculpted metopes of Temple E at Selinous are even more puzzling because the start of construction, which was previously dated ca. 480 to accommodate the Archaic features of the western metopes, has been pushed down to ca. 460 by new analysis

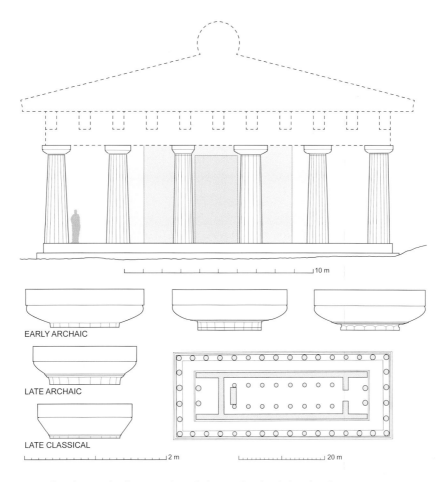

1.2. Olympia, temple of Hera, Doric capitals spanning the sixth to fourth centuries BCE (drawn after Curtius and Adler 1892, pl. 22).

of the foundation pottery.[19] Works of architectural sculpture exhibit great stylistic variation when viewed up close, but temples also present architectural forms that are visibly distinct from each other at a distance.

The temple of Hera at Olympia (fig. 1.2) is the most striking example of the build-up of columns in many styles, presenting a span of Doric architecture from ca. 600 through the fourth century BCE. When Wilhelm Dörpfeld first studied this temple, he proposed that the structure offered direct confirmation of Vitruvius's legendary account (4.2.2) that the first Doric temples were executed in wood and only later turned to stone. The absence of stone superstructure showed that all construction above the columns was executed in wood and terra-cotta. This inspired Dörpfeld to propose that the temple was much older, originally built all of wood and gradually petrified as rotting wood columns were replaced with more permanent stone ones, producing a transitional structure with a bricolage of historical styles.[20] Philip Sapirstein, however, has convincingly argued that this interpretation is untenable: the substantial stone foundation running continuously beneath all the columns shows that stone shafts were planned from the outset.[21] Instead Sapirstein proposes a scenario of a drawn-out initial construction phase that spanned the sixth century. Repairs were then conducted in the fourth century as part of a larger campaign of renovations at Olympia, which also left the temple of Zeus with heterogeneous columns (see fig. 3.30). The Heraion columns follow a general, stocky template, but they vary in diameter, the relief carving of the flutes, and the design of the capitals (fig. 1.3). The capitals range from early Archaic types with wide overhangs, pillowy profiles, and elaborate annulet patterns, to streamlined Classical capitals, which have narrower, conical profiles separated from the shaft by a more subdued necking band. Generations of stone-carvers worked on the temple of Hera uninhibited by expectations of conformity. Although the peppering of so many styles across the entire building prevents the reconstruction of the exact sequence of work, the general impression is of new and old standing side by side.

A spatial sequence of styles could be seen in the colossal Temple G at Selinous, which was begun ca. 530 and continued to be built until ca. 460 (fig. 1.4).[22] The temple's facade is in an Archaic style with pillowy capitals that significantly overhang their shafts. The west elevation, which faced the ancient city, had thicker columns with more conical capitals in a design approaching the forms of the early Classical period. Temple G was used as a temple, but the project was left in a visibly unfinished state.[23] The colossal task of channeling the flutes of the columns—put end-to-end the flutes would have stretched thirteen kilometers—never progressed beyond four of the eight columns of the facade. Temple G belongs to the league of colossal temples over 100 meters long, including the Doric temples of Zeus at Akragas and of Olympian Zeus at Athens, which were inspired by the three Ionian dipteral

1.3. Olympia, temple of Hera, Doric columns spanning the sixth to fourth centuries BCE (Curtius and Adler 1892, pl. 21).

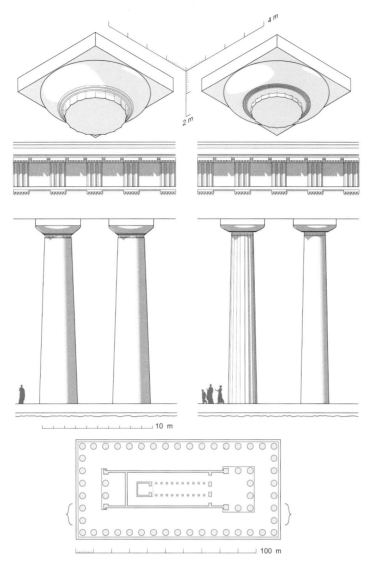

1.4. Selinous, Temple G, examples of the newer columns of the west elevation (left) and older columns of the east elevation (right), only half of which were fluted (after Koldewey and Puchstein 1899, figs. 103–6).

temples at Ephesos (Artemis), Samos (Hera), and Didyma (Apollo). All these ambitious undertakings stretched over many decades, and most remained unfinished to some degree. None are as well preserved today as Temple G, but many of them, particularly the temple of Artemis at Ephesos, must have given a similar impression of a long history of building revealed by dissimilar elevations.

The project to build the Archaic temple of Artemis at Ephesos took more than a century, as did the effort to rebuild it after the fire of 356. According to Pliny, who blurs the distinction between the first and second iteration, the temple "occupied all Asia Minor for 120 years."[24] In a treatise on botany (*Hist. pl.* 5.4.2), Theophrastus reports that the project put the exceptional shelf life of cypress wood to the test, when timber harvested for the temple's doors was stored for four generations before being used. Aenne Ohnesorg proposes that construction on the Archaic temple

Bilingual Ionic Capitals in Context

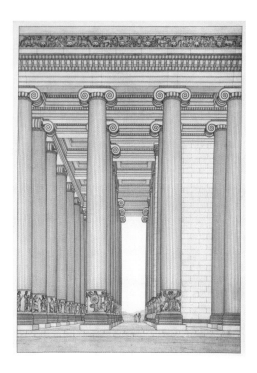 

1.5. Ephesos, Archaic temple of Artemis, reconstructed perspective by F. Krischen (left) (Krischen 1938, pl. 33) and updated by A. Ohnesorg (right) (Ohnesorg 2007, pl. 38).

began as early as ca. 575 / 570 BCE and continued down into the 450s.[25] Ulrike Muss has shown that the sculpture has a range of styles spanning the mid-sixth to mid-fifth century, progressing from the relief figures on the lowest column drums to the scenes on the sculpted sima at the building's roofline.[26]

Reconstruction illustrations of the Artemision, foremost among them the 1938 perspective drawing by Fritz Krischen (fig. 1.5) perennially reprinted with updates as scholars make corrections such as the presence of echinus capitals without volutes, gives a limited sense of the myriad textures of the actual surviving elements.[27] Fragments of column shafts, for example, show columns with thirty-two, thirty-six, forty, forty-four, and forty-eight flutes, with a range from shallow to deep carving, and at least one column with a rare design of alternating narrow and wide flutes (fig. 1.6).[28] The torus elements topping the column bases were even more dissimilar, with smooth profiles, or carved with convex rods, concave channels, convex and concave elements together, and occasionally sculpted with patterns of water-plant leaves (fig. 1.6).[29] The surviving fragments of capital volutes are all of the convex, Archaic, Ionian type, but there were at least three designs for the bolster sides of the capitals: a standard Archaic form of four large channels, a variant with channels subdivided into tongues, and interlaced leaf patterns that belong to later phases of construction dating from the Classical period (fig. 1.7).[30] Fragments of large rosettes were once mistakenly identified as a second capital type, but are now understood to be the inside angle of the corner capitals (fig. 1.8).[31] Smaller Ionic buildings usually combine two mitered half volutes or simply leave the two awkwardly intersecting interior volutes uncarved, but the colossal scale of the temple of Artemis required a

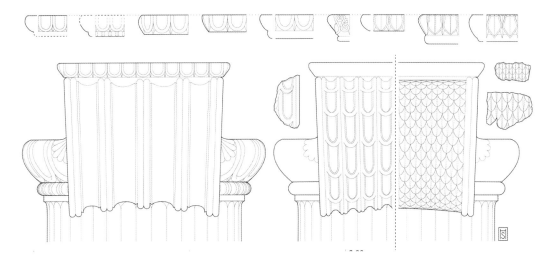

1.7. Ephesos, Archaic temple of Artemis, side view of capital showing the standard bolster design of four channels, as well as fragments with the interlaced leaf patterns and a selection of abacus moldings (drawn after Ohnesorg 2007).

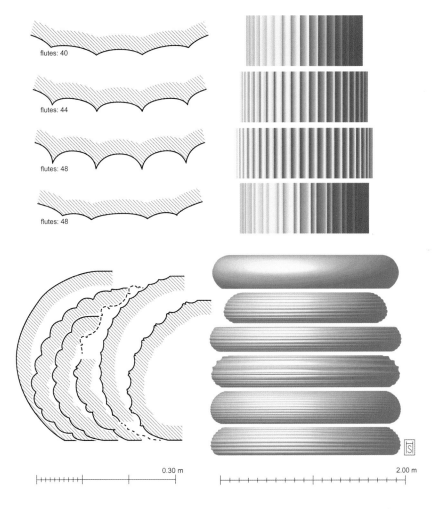

1.6. Ephesos, Archaic temple of Artemis, selection of column shafts and torus base profiles.

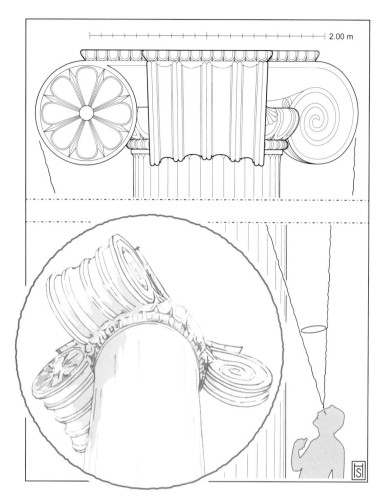

1.8. Ephesos, Archaic temple of Artemis, corner capital seen from below (drawn after Ohnesorg 2001, fig. 8).

better solution: the substitution of the volutes with two large rosettes, each almost one meter in diameter. Not only would a visitor see differences among the temple's columns, but looking up at the colossal colonnade from below it was possible to see in a single snapshot view that the corner capitals had convex volutes on one side and rosettes on the other. Simply put, variegation must have been one of the building's most striking features. Pliny cuts off his account of the construction of the temple (*HN* 36.97) by noting that "the other embellishments of the building are enough to fill many volumes."[32] No stranger to voluminous description—the comment falls midway through the thirty-sixth volume of his *Natural History*—Pliny hints that the opulence and variety of this temple's decoration were well-known. Pliny also hints at an explanation for the variety seen in the temple: each column was donated by a different king (*HN* 36.95). Pliny's comment is an embellishment of the statement of Herodotus (1.29) that the majority of the columns of the Archaic temple were donated by the Lydian king Kroisos, a claim that is substantiated by dedicatory inscriptions in Greek and Lydian found on fragments of its columns.[33] Occasionally, the piecemeal appearance of the columns in the temple of Hera at Olympia has been attributed to multiple donors, but inscriptions naming separate benefactors of individual columns are only known in the Hellenistic and Roman imperial periods.[34]

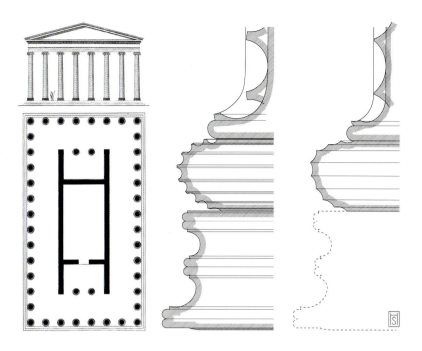

1.9. Lesbos, temple at Messon, late Classical profiles from the exterior columns (center) and archaistic profiles from the pronaos and opisthodomos columns (right) (plan and elevation adapted from Koldewey 1890, pl. 20).

1.10. Lesbos, temple at Messon, archaistic drums of rosy volcanic stone in the opisthodomos (foreground) and drums of white limestone in the peristyle (background).

While some Ionic temples, such as the three great Archaic Ionian dipteral temples, were heterogeneous *by circumstance*, others were heterogeneous *by design*. For example, the late fourth-century Ionic temple at Messon, Lesbos, mixed styles and materials in its colonnades: the columns encircling the temple were carved of fine white limestone and executed in the contemporary late Classical style (fig. 1.9, fig. 1.10).[35] The fluting of the column shafts and torus column bases takes the canonical Classical form of semicircular channels separated by flat fillets rather than sharp arrises. Within the colonnade, however, the columns of the pronaos and opisthodomos were of a different style and material. The fluting of the column shafts and torus bases are shallow and terminate in pointed arrises. Early travelers mistook the drums for Doric columns because pointed arrises became a canonical feature of Doric style, but the temple's builders were reverting to the style of sixth-century Ionian temples (compare with fig. 1.6 above).[36] The shallower carving could be a response to the harder stone used for these columns, but this choice—to use a rosy volcanic stone resembling the island's andesite bedrock—also seems to be a feature evoking a primeval past. Deploying different materials and period styles between the outer and inner rows of columns created a dramatic effect that made approaching the cella feel like returning to an earlier time in the island's history. Bilingual Ionic capitals engaged in the same staging of heterogeneity.

There are a few internal differences in bilingual Ionic monuments that are heterogeneous *by circumstance*. The temple in Thessaloniki (chapter 4) shows extensive recarving after it collapsed, and the temple of Athena Trecheia at Ephesos (chapter 6) had one of its capitals replaced in the Roman imperial period. Both cases of recarving and replacement, however, retained the bilingual design evident from the initial building phase. Everything, in fact, points to bilingual Ionic capitals as heterogeneous *by design*. To understand why they were made this way, it is helpful to consider another type of two-faced artifact that is also often dubbed "transitional" but has been reconsidered: bilingual Attic vases.

Bilingual Attic vases, which combine the black-figure and red-figure painting techniques on opposite sides, were long interpreted as stepping stones between the older and younger vase-painting techniques (see fig. 0.4). Because they so conveniently contrast the two techniques, Greek art textbooks typically use them to introduce the transition from one to the other.[37] Their transitional status, however, is generally disputed, as they are not the first with red-figure painting but rather fall within a generation-long overlap when both painting techniques were current.[38] The black-figure technique did not cease altogether. It continued to be used for a few decades more on Attic funerary *lekythoi*, and it persisted for a much longer period on Panathenaic prize amphorae—objects with ritual function and social currency, where the maintenance of consistent appearances was key to establishing the objects' identification and value.[39] Furthermore, bilingual vases are anything but incidental in their mixture of techniques. Their duality is bold and total, deploying duplication and mirroring to produce something polysemous, taken to its greatest elaboration on an eye cup where red-figure and black-figure warriors duel while their dying comrades collapse through the frame that separates their pictorial worlds (fig. 1.11).[40] Vases were inexpensive, portable, and personal objects not immediately comparable to architecture. Yet their striking visual effect and the scholarly attention to their change in style offers a useful model.

John Beazley coined the term "bilingual" for vases combining both the black-figure painting technique, in which figures are painted as black slip silhouettes with details incised through the slip, and the red-figure painting technique, in which a field of black slip is painted around figures left in reserve with details

1.11. Bilingual eye cup signed by Andokides as potter (adapted from Schneider 1889, pl. 4). Museo Archeologico Salinas, Palermo [V650].

added with a delicate brush.[41] Beazley tried to apply his method of connoisseurship, through which vases could be grouped by shared details marking the personal styles of mostly anonymous painters, but was ultimately of two minds about bilingual vases, vacillating over whether the black-figure hand of the Lysippides Painter and the red-figure hand of the Andokides Painter were connected to the same human body.[42] Beazley's successors continued this debate, sometimes veering toward psychoanalysis to present scenarios in which the Lysippides Painter and the Andokides Painter were mismatched coworkers grudgingly compelled to collaborate or a unified Lysippides-Andokides Painter struggling to break free from an overbearing teacher (Exekias) to find a personal outlet.[43] Bilingual vases pose a challenge to Beazley's method of connoisseurship because few of the personal markers of authorship can be reliably traced across the change in tools and techniques.

Richard Neer has done much to shift the discussion on the invention of the red-figure technique by reframing it, not within a developmental narrative where it stands as an inevitable step toward more naturalistic and mimetic art, but within a period that saw vase painters experimenting with many different techniques including added polychromy, where it was simply "one novelty among many."[44] From this short-term viewpoint, bilingual vases are not a "missing link" in an evolutionary sequence, but exhibition pieces:

> On these early vases, red-figure does not compete with black-figure: it complements it. Painters employ new and old in tandem, apparently operating on the logic that two techniques are better than one. Indeed, an emphasis on technique itself—on virtuosity and craft—is characteristic of bilingual pots. ... The point seems to be that to have both versions, positive and negative, is desirable. There is a virtual deadlock in such instances, as though technical extravagance—mere visual richness—were an end in itself. The Greek word for such lavishness is *poikilia* (literally, "adornment").[45]

Against a backdrop of many competing techniques, Neer proposes that bilingual vases fit an ancient aesthetic appreciation of visual diversity often expressed through the term *poikilia*. It is essential to understand a culture in its own terms, and *poikilos*, the adjective used to describe things that were multicolored, patterned, embroidered, gilded, shimmering, and even shapeshifting, could have been an ancient descriptor applied to bilingual Attic vases and bilingual Ionic capitals.[46]

Along similar lines, Gottfried Gruben saw the double-sided differences of bilingual capitals as a display of *Variationsfreude* ("delight in variety") on the part of carvers working "with artistic license."[47] The concept of *Variationsfreude* itself seems partly to belong to a renewed appreciation of ornament and historical styles in the German architecture academy that accompanied postmodernism.[48] The emphasis on joy as a quality of architecture also recalls the programmatic statement of Vitruvius (1.3.2) that sets "delight" (*venustas*) as one of the three tenets of the art of building. Gruben's impression that the multiform Ionic capital was a source of joy to its maker mirrors Neer's emphasis on *poikilia* as the ancient aesthetic concept of beauty in visual complexity that explains the emergence of bilingual vases. A subtle distinction can be drawn between the two parallel formulations. Gruben's *Variationsfreude* prioritizes the creative process and artistic liberty of the stone carver, while Neer's *poikilia* is in the eye of the consumer with vase painters keen to capitalize on market demand. The emphasis on market trends might go some way to explaining the shorter chronological range of bilingual vases compared to the capitals. The bilingual vases appear in a rapid burst, roughly simultaneous to the examples of bilingual capitals on Delos (chapter 2) and the northern Aegean (chapter 4), but they faded away quickly. The continued production of bilingual capitals in Athens in the mid-fifth century (chapter 5) and at Ephesos, Selinous, and Delphi in the fourth and third centuries (chapter 6), indicates a greater staying power.

Embracing variation could have a function in the construction process. Stone workers often had good reason to treat design specifications as elastic, by stretching, compressing, or changing patterns to fit stone blocks, rather than the other way around. The capitals of the temple of Artemis at Ephesos, for example, are topped off with a wide array of carved moldings, (see fig. 1.7), each seemingly composed on the spot to fit an abacus with a different height. The abacus at the top of an Ionic capital was the last area of wiggle-room when erecting a column; here any differences in the total heights of the columns, which inevitably resulted from the compounding of millimeter-level discrepancies among all the column drums, could be shaved off the top so that the architrave beams could be set level. The seemingly ad hoc molding designs on the abacus were an essential mask of ornament for a zone that was the literal margin for error in the total dimensioning of the column. More dramatically, in the case of the temple of Athena at Assos, Bonna Wescoat has shown how a flexible system based on simple proportional guidelines rather than fixed dimensions could lead to a heterogeneous appearance even within a rapidly built project.[49] Beginning from quarried blocks that were not always of exactly the same dimensions, carvers at Assos made capitals following a general scheme of proportional relationships, which was revised slightly as builders moved from the short ends of the temple to the sides.[50] Although the carvers used compasses and rotating templates to make

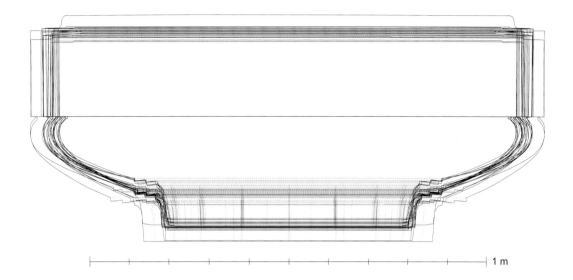

1.12. Assos, temple of Athena, superimposed profiles of the thirty-two surviving Doric capitals (drawn after Wescoat 2012).

individual capitals perfectly circular and symmetrical, they did not transfer the design of one capital to the next through templates. Superimposing the profiles of the surviving thirty-two capitals (fig. 1.12) produces a blurred silhouette, even when ignoring the capitals of the enlarged corner columns. Ancient builders depended upon a large box of tools for working with precision and consistency at large scale (straightedges, compasses, plumbs, levels, templates, jigs, etc.) and inscribed building accounts reference wax and plaster models used as guides for the standardization of carved ornaments, and even a complete Ionic capital used as a model.[51] Nevertheless, the simple fact that the Greek temple was a handmade building must not be forgotten.

Who Made Buildings This Way?

The first bilingual Ionic building was on Delos, and at least two subsequent monuments have Cycladic connections: the temple of Parthenos was built in Neapolis, which was a colony of Thasos, itself a colony of Paros, and the last bilingual Ionic monument was built at Delphi with imported Parian marble. From these connections, Elena Partida suggests that bilingual capitals may reveal Cycladic workshops or architects on the move.[52] The distinguishing feature of bilingual capitals, however, is the recreation of the old, east Ionian convex volute. Lucy Shoe Meritt interpreted bilingual Ionic capitals in Attica as proof of connections with Asia Minor, not the Cyclades.[53] Identifying the origins of artisans from the provenance of their style is slippery when the works are themselves stylistically multiform. Partida's and Shoe Meritt's proposals ask an essential question: Who made buildings this way?

Ancient temple building happened in fits and starts, and large projects depended on contracting many private entrepreneurs, especially itinerant workshops of skilled builders.[54] Thucydides twice mentions (4.69, 5.82) Athens sending stoneworkers to quickly fortify allied cities amid the Peloponnesian War, which gives a sense of the great mobility of workshops. The prevalence of Samian features on the Ionic temples in Syracuse and Lokroi Epizephyrioi in Sicily and South Italy has long suggested that itinerant workshops from the temple of Hera at Samos traveled west, probably during a period of turmoil after the assassination of Polykrates in 522 BCE, seeding a new school of Ionic architecture in Magna Graecia.[55] The inscribed building accounts for the Erechtheion on the Athenian Acropolis record that almost 40 percent of the workers were *metics*, free noncitizen residents, and a sizeable number of skilled workers were enslaved people.[56] Although most of the *metic* builders of the Erechtheion were likely freedmen or itinerant builders from Greek cities other than Athens, some *metic* and enslaved workers have names that could indicate Persian, Phrygian, Lydian, Karian, and Egyptian backgrounds (Medos, Manis, Kroisos, Karion, and Psammis respectively).[57] In contrast, J. J. Coulton pointed out that known ancient architects were most often locals to cities or regions, in no small part because patrons entrusted them with administrative and financial responsibilities as well as design oversight.[58] If the combination of different regional styles reflects human mobility, it is more likely the mobility of stone carvers than of architects.

The Throne of Apollo at Amyklai offers a definite reference for the amalgamation of regional practices by itinerant workshops.[59] In the mid-sixth century, a sculptor from Asia Minor, Bathykles of Magnesia, was commissioned to build a cult structure at Amyklai, just south of Sparta. Bathykles hailed from the wider region of Ionia (technically as a Magnesian he was ethnically Aeolian), and he added Ionic flourishes to the Doric colonnade, including volute brackets springing from some of the Doric capitals (fig. 1.13).[60] According to Pausanias (3.18.4), Bathykles used part of the money from the commission to dedicate a statue of his native city's patron, Artemis Leukophryene, and included a frieze depicting his team of Magnesian stone carvers dancing. The mixed Doric-Ionic scheme was the product of hiring a designer and team of craftspeople from the other side of the Aegean. Although a local Lakonian could not have imagined the startlingly inventive creation of Bathykles, it is implausible that this building's patrons sought out a design workshop from Asia Minor with the expectation of creating a conventional Doric structure. The Spartans, despite their insular reputation and stories of their gruff rejection of Ionian luxury (Hdt. 5.51), were adventurous patrons in the Archaic period, supposedly hiring Theodoros, one of the architects of the temple of Hera on Samos, to build the Skias, the covered meeting place of the Spartan assembly (Paus. 3.12.10).[61] The mixed Doric-Ionic capitals of the Throne of Apollo at Amyklai, therefore, offer a model of agency that takes into consideration not just Bathykles as an itinerant architect, but also his traveling team of Magnesian stone carvers and the Lakonian patrons who hired them. The same model applies to bilingual Ionic capitals.

Bilingual Ionic capitals may best be explained by a model of distributed agency resulting from a chain of decision-making, connecting patrons, architects, and stone carvers. Ancient accounts give mixed impressions about the autonomy of architects. At one extreme, Vitruvius (4.3.1) recounts that the architect Hermogenes

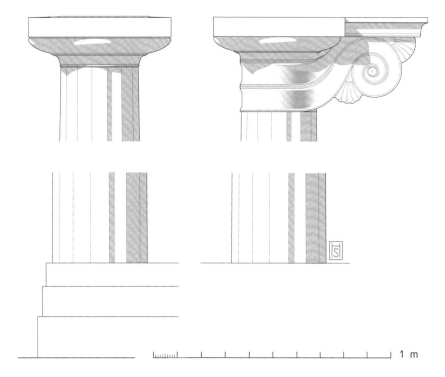

1.13. Amyklai, Throne of Apollo, Doric columns and Doric columns with volute brackets (after Fiechter 1918, pl. 6–9, 18).

took a commission from the city of Teos to design a Doric temple for Dionysos but duped his clients, who only discovered his plan to erect an Ionic temple when the blocks arrived from the quarry.[62] The Athenian decree authorizing "that the temple [of Athena Nike] be built in whatever way Kallikrates may specify" (*IG* I³ 35, ll. 11–12) seems at face value to give the architect carte blanche, though an amendment makes clear that he must report to and collaborate with a building committee.[63] An Athenian decree specifying additions to the Long Walls (*IG* II² 463) has so many added clauses that it has been taken to be the work of multiple authors offering alterations to an architect's design—that is, design by committee.[64] From the fifth century on, inscriptions describe temple building through public-private partnerships, where patron cities and sanctuaries appointed committees of building overseers (*epistatai* or *naopoioi*) to ensure that the architect's patron-approved specifications (*syngraphai*) were carried out to the letter by teams of stone workers operating as private contractors. Building contracts for the temple of Zeus Basileus at Lebadeia include provisions that overseers from the Boeotian League must witness the setting of every block and that blocks set without oversight must be removed even if positioned correctly (*IG* VII 3073, ll. 170–76).[65] It comes as no surprise that a project with such intense administrative surveillance was never completed. Architects who bucked their instructions could pay dearly. An inscription from Epidauros records that the fourth-century architect Perillos was fined 2,160 drachmas in connection with building the Abaton in the sanctuary of Asklepios and the springhouse behind it, effectively a fine of six years' salary.[66] The inscription does not say how Perillos erred as an architect, but it indicates that he appealed an initial fine of four years' salary imposed by the *epistatai* up to the ultimate project patron, the citizens of Epidauros, who voted in an assembly to uphold the decision of the building committee and increase the fine by half for wasting their time.[67] While it is convenient to speak of architects as visionary, autonomous designers (Vitruvius's Hermogenes certainly has a touch of Howard Roark), their design decisions were inherently a balancing act between the goals of patrons and the capabilities of craftspeople.

A rare glimpse of patron, architect, and stone carver convening to approve the production of an Ionic capital design comes from a building contract dated to the 350s BCE.[68] It orders the construction of an unidentified portico on Delos, which is now poorly preserved. In the inscription, the *naopoioi* of the sanctuary of Apollo accepted bids by private contractors from Athens to build the marble colonnade according to specifications drawn up by an appointed architect. The work was to be carried out to exacting standards, checked at several stages by the *naopoioi*, the architect, and an assistant architect (*hypoarchitekton*). Unlike the basic dimensional specifications for all the other blocks, the contract has special instructions for the production of the capitals (*IG* II² 1678, ll. 10–13): "As for the model (*paradeigma*) that will be made of the capital, it will be paid for in proportion to the money awarded for the work that the architect has ordered. The contractor for the work will also bring the model of the capital to Delos at his own expense, undamaged, and he will set it in place just as is specified for the others, after having received it undamaged in Athens."[69] In other words, one Ionic capital was to be carved in advance at a workshop in Athens, which was to serve as a model for carving the other capitals on site. The *naopoioi* seem most concerned to make explicit in writing that they would pay nothing extra for fabricating and transporting this model capital and expected it to be a functional piece that would be used in the final building. Because of its sculptural complexity, the design of the capital needed to be worked out at full scale, in the round, with the expertise of a stone-carving master. Producing one capital first to be approved and used as a model may have been a common practice that was elaborated only in this contract because it required an extra hand-off and transportation.[70] Importing a complete model capital from Athens is a scenario specific to a mid-fourth-century moment when Athens both exerted great control over Delos through the Delian Amphictyony and had eclipsed Ionia and the Cyclades as the major center for Ionic architectural design. This inscription thus does not provide an interpretative master key for other buildings. It does, however, illustrate the interchange between the parties involved, the balance of oversight and autonomy, and the formation and transmission of a design as it took shape in communication between building site, workshop, and quarry.

Bilingual Ionic capitals were the product of architects mediating between specialized marble carvers, who knew that convex and concave surface treatments could easily be alternated for striking visual effect, and patrons, who issued tall orders for new works that would both surpass present aesthetic expectations and possess all the stately authority of older buildings. In the case of bilingual Attic vases, it is easy to imagine the Lysippides / Andokides Painter(s) switching from black-figure to red-figure techniques in a moment of inspiration. Bilingual Ionic capitals, however, required a more considered process of collaborative decision-making.

1.14. Incuse coins from Metapontion, Kroton, and Kaulonia (top to bottom). Museum of Fine Arts, Boston [nos. 0102, 0177, 0169].

Each capital involved the work of many to quarry, transport, carve, hoist, set, and paint.[71] Another kind of two-faced artifact, incuse coins, can offer guidance because they were once attributed to a single designer but are now better understood through an act of negotiation between artisans and patrons.

Incuse coins appear in South Italy in the second half of the sixth century BCE (fig. 1.14). They have a distinctive reverse side that bears a concave, or incuse, mirrored version of the image from the obverse, although usually somewhat simplified and with the legend in relief. The incuse design gives the illusion that the image has been pushed through the silver flan from one side to emerge on the other, but their production is not more mechanically efficient than striking coins with two convex images. Experimental recreations and new scientific imaging have revealed that the blank flans were heated to make them ductile (i.e., annealed) before striking in an additional production step not required in other coin types.[72] In 1836, Duc de Luynes first connected incuse coins with Pythagoras of Samos, a speculation that

Bilingual Ionic Capitals in Context   29

perennially sparks curiosity.[73] Pythagoras spent his later career in South Italy at Kroton and Metapontion, cities that began minting incuse coins in his lifetime (ca. 560–480), though scholars now suggest that the first incuse coins minted by Sybaris date as early as ca. 550, certainly predating the arrival of Pythagoras.[74] The philosopher espoused a doctrine based around balanced opposites and found so many paired opposites at work in the world that he composed a "Table of Opposites."[75] Pythagoras's students applied his structuring theory of balanced opposites to a wide range of topics, including medicine, politics, and astronomy. Alkmaion of Kroton, for example, proposed that there are equilibria of opposite hot and cold, wet and dry, and sweet and bitter forces in the body, which when out of balance cause illness.[76] Similarly, Philolaos of Kroton explained eclipses by proposing the existence of a dark twin of the Earth, the Anti-Earth, which only becomes visible when it occludes the Moon.[77] The latest chronology rules out the possibility that Pythagoras or his students invented incuse coins, a proposal that was already tenuous. Yet, there are interpretative benefits to reading the opposite solid and void images juxtaposed on incuse coins within one contemporary mode of talking about the world in binary language, where equalized counterparts brought order to the human body, the body politic, and to the cosmos.

Rather than emerging from the mind of Pythagoras, the incuse coin developed from the glyptic art of die-cutters and gem-carvers, who labored over intaglio dies and seals in reverse to impress relief images on coins and seal impressions.[78] In a visual world where miniature images existed in parallel both as intaglios and reliefs, incuse coins capitalized on combining both techniques at the same time. The visual and tactile qualities of the coins aside, the type was widely adopted by the cities of South Italy, most of which were Achaean colonies, who used a shared Achaean weight standard, but who did not have an overarching economic union. The coins bear individualized images that identify their minting cities, but the incuse technique offered a second channel for communicating group belonging and regional affiliation without surrendering the unique identifying power of each city's insignia, or *parasemon*.[79] Incuse coins offer insight into the phenomenon of bilingual Ionic capitals. These two-technique objects spring primarily from the habits of artisans versed in both approaches to carving in miniature. Yet they were widely adopted because they could convey connections between the groups who commissioned the work. Resonances with the dualistic worldview propagated by the Pythagoreans may further have shaped how the coins were received.

Switching between convex and concave textures was a technique ancient stone carvers kept in reserve. Numerous Ionic monuments contrast convex and concave elements at a small scale, in molding profiles, geometric patterns, and particularly floral motifs (surveyed in chapter 3). The simple modeling of the convex volutes on bilingual Ionic capitals, however, is immediately evocative of the outmoded elements of early Ionic temples. Their large-scale revival of Archaic style and the contrasting pairing were part of larger design programs to signal continuity and venerate a history of temple building in Ionia. Bilingual Ionic capitals must therefore be seen in relation to local histories about buildings, the preservation of historic structures, and ancient cases of making architectural replicas.

Why Look at the Past through Buildings?

Bilingual Ionic capitals are part of a larger phenomenon of looking at the past through buildings, which is most prominently manifest in local histories about buildings and the preservation of historic structures. Temples were important landmarks of myth and history, and the catalogs of their many dedications sound like museum inventories. Josephine Shaya proposes that the museum analogy be taken seriously: as with the modern museum, the Greek temple should be understood "not as a storehouse but as a powerful cultural instrument that used collections of objects to substantiate, reinforce, and broadcast a particular view of the world."[80] She offers as a case study the Lindian Chronicle, an inscription set up in the sanctuary of Athena at Lindos in 99 BCE that enumerates forty-two dedications in chronological order, beginning with a dedication from the city's mythical founder, and continuing down to gifts from Alexander the Great and Philip V.[81] A fourth-century fire at the temple, which destroyed many of the earliest offerings, appears to have been the impetus to begin collating an indelible written record of the fleeting material evidence. Like the organized presentation of museum collections, which use a spatial itinerary from object to object to structure a narrative of history, Shaya proposes that the chronological catalog of artifacts presented a narrative in which the local patron goddess, Athena Lindia, was a power in world-historical events.[82] This model of understanding curated stores of votives within temples could be expanded to the buildings themselves. Bilingual Ionic capitals—by presenting old and new elements in spatial sequence—emphasized a direct relationship between the past and the present.

The replication of Archaic elements on bilingual Ionic capitals coincides with ancient cases of the preservation and veneration of fragments of lost buildings. This practice can be seen in the column of Oinomaos at Olympia, a monument that does not survive archaeologically but that was described by Pausanias (5.20.6–7).[83] His description of a decaying pillar of wood that was held together by metal bands is not difficult to picture: at Old Smyrna a late seventh-century stone column base survives with an iron ring corroded to its top, apparently added to prevent the wooden pillar above from splitting (fig. 1.15).[84] The column at Olympia was sheltered under a canopy and accompanied by a bronze tablet inscribed with an epigram identifying the pillar in Homeric language as the last remains of King Oinomaos's palace, which Zeus destroyed in a lightning strike:

> For I, too, Stranger, am a relic of a famous house
> A pillar, once, long ago, I stood in the house of Oinomaos
> But now, I lie with these bands on me, honored beside the son of Kronos
> Not even the fatal flame of fire received me.[85] (Paus. 5.20.7)

This column purported to be a relic from the myth that explained the existence of the sanctuary at Olympia and the Olympic festival of athletic competitions: when the suitors of the daughter of Oinomaos failed to beat him in a high-stakes chariot race, he nailed their severed heads to the columns of his palace. The treatment of the pillar foreshadows familiar practices of historic preservation: it was conserved with

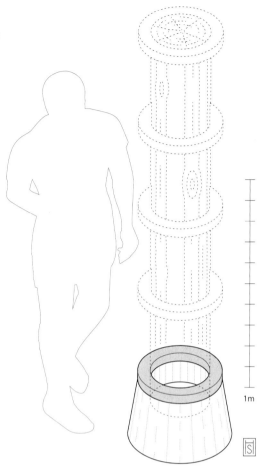

1.15. Old Smyrna, stone column base with a socket for a wood shaft and a corroded iron ring (gray) to prevent the wood from splitting.

stabilizing reinforcements, enclosed in a protective housing to prevent deterioration, and labeled with a sign explaining its historic and cultural value. Innumerable instances of architectural fragments from older buildings immured as visible spolia have come to light archaeologically, but in the absence of the interpretive label attached to the column of Oinomaos marking it as *timios* (an honored thing), the significance of their reuse and display is a matter for interpretation.

The perceived historical value of columns grew over time, layered on through restoration, reinterpretation, and recycling—processes also evident in the restoration of sacred sculpture.[86] An Ionic capital from Paros illustrates this process in action (fig. 1.16). It belongs to a freestanding column, with a cutting on top for a marble sculpture, probably a sphinx. An inscription cut across one side reads: "Archilochos the Parian, son of Telesikles, lies here / Dokimos, son of Neokreon, dedicates this monument."[87] The pillar purports to mark the grave of the celebrated lyric poet Archilochos, who accompanied his father Telesikles in settling Thasos, and who was later venerated as a hero on Paros (Arist. *Rh*. 1398b). A column no doubt seemed a fitting memorial for a poet, who likened dead heroes of Naxos to columns—a "pillars of the community" metaphor not uncommon in Archaic and Classical literature.[88] Yet Archilochos died around the third quarter of the seventh century. The capital, however, was carved around 550 BCE, belonging to a recognizable group of similar freestanding Ionic columns from Paros and Delos that are distinguished by an interruption in the volute channel at center (visible on the back of the Archilochos capital, but effaced by the inscription on the front).[89] Judging from the letter forms of the inscription, Dokimos's epigram was added in the mid-fourth century. The text's assertion that Archilochos is Parian presents another anachronism: authentic tombstones from Paros never identify locals as locals.[90] All together it appears that the fourth-century Dokimos reused a sixth-century Ionic column to mark a shrine for the seventh-century poet. The heirloom column was undoubtedly selected for reuse because it evoked the antiquity of the hometown hero, even though it fell short of his actual era by about one century. Dokimos was not shy about inserting himself into the monument, cutting into the capital to assert his piety and the bond of Parian co-patrimony that linked him to Archilochos. The reuse and reinterpretation of this capital shows how meaning was layered on over time, as an aging column took on new power to signify a legendary past.

The doctored column of Archilochos raises an additional question. Was it the obsolete style of convex volutes or simply the patina of the old capital that evoked the age of Archilochos? Alois Riegl argued that members of the general public perceive the "age value" (*Alterswert*) of monuments foremost in "signs of age" (*Altersspuren*) and not in outmoded architectural styles.[91] Style is too easily imitated, and its chronological interpretation is a form of specialist knowledge. Signs of aging, Riegl argued, trigger an immediate emotional response through sensory perception, while "historical value" (*historischer Wert*) represents a learned aesthetic system. The column of Oinomaos was an architectural relic that fits Riegl's model of age value. Its antiquity was not perceived in any stylistic features that distinguished the era of its creation. It was marked as an object of value by its state of deterioration

1.16. Paros, the Archilochos capital. Archaeological Museum of Paros.

Bilingual Ionic Capitals in Context

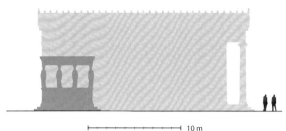
Athens, Erechtheion (south elevation, caryatid porch highlighted)

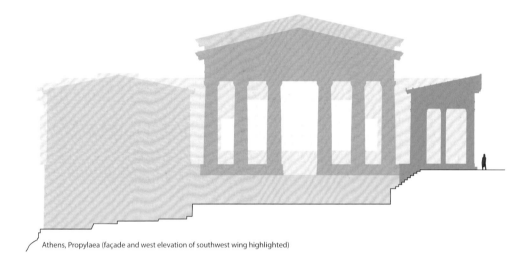
Athens, Propylaea (façade and west elevation of southwest wing highlighted)

and the rarity of its survival. After two centuries, the capital selected by Dokimos likely had signs of aging in weathered details, faded paint, and yellowed patina. Yet Dokimos's choice may also have been informed by an aesthetic appreciation of the capital's outdated stylistic features. The nascent appreciation of these features is evident in instances of imitation in architecture, which is a key feature of bilingual Ionic capitals.

The idea of imitation in architecture is not universally fixed and can change over time. In a seminal essay, Richard Krautheimer observed that ideas about copying in architecture changed noticeably between the thirteenth and fifteenth centuries CE.[92] Renaissance architects stand in contrast to their medieval predecessors, who replicated symbolic features of important churches (names, numbers of elements, plan geometry, etc.) without attempting to create visual simulacra. In *Architecture in the Age of Printing*, Mario Carpo carried this observation further, arguing that the proliferation of mechanically reproduced images with the printing press upended expectations for architecture with a new conception of visual fidelity.[93] Carpo's thesis has critics; Renaissance architecture is anything but homogenous, and hand-drawn architectural studies only proliferate in the era of widely available paper.[94] Nevertheless, the theory poses an essential caveat about identifying copying in premodern architecture when modern expectations about copying are shaped by new technologies. Roman writers lamented that the copying of manuscript

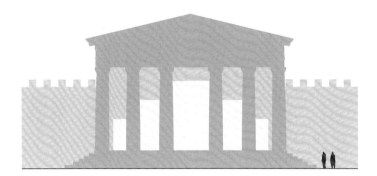

1.17. Scale comparison of quoted elevations from the Erechtheion, Athens, and the Heroon of Perikles, Limyra, and the Propylaia, Athens, the Thrassylos Monument, Athens, and the Greater Propylaia, Eleusis.

Limyra, Heroon of Perikles (façade)

Athens, Thrassylos Monument (façade)   Eleusis, Greater Propylaea (façade)

illustrations left them deceptively inaccurate, and there was some reticence in pairing easily copied texts with corruptible visual aids.[95] Vitruvius, for example, extolls the importance of plan, elevation, and perspective drawings as essential tools of the Roman architect (1.2.2), but his own text references accompanying figures that were only spare geometric diagrams, such as the geometric diagram for planning an Ionic capital's volute (mentioned at 3.5.8) rather than an Ionic capital itself. Changes in the notion of architectural imitation are apparent in antiquity as well.

Architectural allusions to the fifth-century monuments of the Acropolis of Athens began within a century of their construction. At Limyra in Lykia, for example, the heroon for the Lykian dynast Perikles (built ca. 370 BCE) quotes the south elevation of the caryatid porch of the Erechtheion (built ca. 421–404 BCE) with an elevation of four stone maidens taking the place of columns (fig. 1.17).[96] The rationale for this direct architectural reference is clear. The caryatid porch of the Erechtheion stood over the Kekropion, the purported tomb where Kekrops, the mythical first king of Athens, was worshiped as a hero. Therefore, this annex to the Erechtheion offered a model for the tomb of an ambitious ruler seeking to be venerated after death. Another fourth-century allusion appears in the choragic monument of Thrasyllos (built 320 / 319 BCE) above the theater of Dionysos on the south slope of the Acropolis, which reproduces the west elevation of the south wing of the Propylaia (built 437–432 BCE), creating a symmetrical composition around its thin central

Doric pier (fig. 1.17).[97] Yet, the heroon of Perikles and the Thrasyllos monument must be regarded as quotations rather than outright copies. Each excerpts a secondary elevation from a larger building, replicating many of the moldings and ornamental details, as the basis for developing a new facade composition that is a recognizable homage to the original.

In the Roman imperial period, attempts to replicate fifth-century Athenian monuments attain a new level of fidelity in their stylistic and formal details. At Eleusis, the Greater Propylaia and temple of Artemis Propylaia so closely replicate architectural elements from the Propylaia and Parthenon on the Acropolis, respectively, that the original monuments must have been surveyed to produce drawings, templates, and possibly even plaster casts (fig. 1.18).[98] A cache of ancient plaster casts from a Roman sculpture workshop has been discovered at Baiae, Italy, including fragments of at least twenty-four renowned Greek bronze statues of the fifth and fourth centuries.[99] This remarkable discovery, together with textual testimony, illustrates that the technology of plaster casts played an important role in the transmission of Greek statue types in the Roman sculpture trade. It has been estimated that making a mold for a plaster cast and carving a replica from it using a pointing machine took twice as long as carving a replica freehand, and these precision copies were undoubtedly prized in antiquity as feats of technical skill as well as faithful representations.[100] The technique may also have been applied to architectural ornament on rare occasions. The Ionic capitals of the Erechtheion inspired many loose imitations beginning in the fourth century BCE, but capitals from the Forum of Augustus in Rome (begun 20 BCE, dedicated 2 BCE) are such exact replicas (fig. 1.19) that they were undoubtedly carved using plaster casts of the originals as an intermediary for transmitting the design between Athens and Rome.[101] Making molds of statues for casts was not a simple or discrete task.[102] When it came to the Erechtheion, the production of casts of its architectural elements for Augustan building projects likely coincides with an ancient restoration project around 25 BCE that rehabilitated the temple in the aftermath of a disastrous fire.[103] These instances of precise replication aided by drawings, templates, and plaster casts are extraordinary instances that represent a new conception of visual fidelity facilitated by new technologies, but they are also the culmination of trends in architecture and sculpture that began centuries earlier. Bilingual Ionic capitals, produced between the second half of the sixth century and the first half of the third century, are products of an era when firsthand observation, personal memory, and oral accounts were the primary sources for transmitting architectural information.

This nascent interest in architectural imitation is first attested by Xenophon, who offers a personal account of building a small temple of Artemis Ephesia that he considered a copy of the great Archaic temple at Ephesos. When Xenophon returned safely from the ill-fated campaign of the Ten Thousand in 401 BCE, he dedicated on his estate at Skillous in the Peloponnese a small shrine to Artemis Ephesia, whom he credited with saving him (Xen. *An.* 5.3.7–13).[104] An oracle, Xenophon recounts, selected a spot with many environmental similarities to the sanctuary at Ephesos; both precincts had streams named Selinous with fish and mussels.[105] Xenophon commissioned a building and cult statue with intentional resemblances:

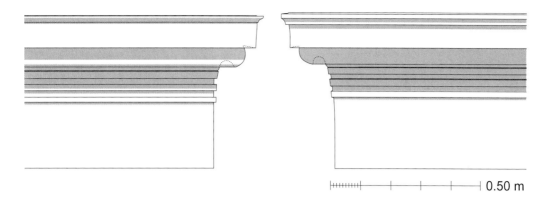

1.18. Scale comparison of anta capital profiles from the Propylaia, Athens, 437–432 BCE, and the Greater Propylaia, Eleusis, 170–176 CE (drawn after Giraud 1989, fig. 6).

1.19. Scale comparison of Ionic capital from the Erechtheion, Athens, 421–404 BCE, and an ancient replica from the Forum of Augustus, Rome, 20–2 BCE. The latter is thought to be carved with the aid of a plaster cast of the former.

"The temple, though small, *is made to look like* the great one at Ephesos, and the cult statue, though carved from cypress wood, *is like* the gold one at Ephesos" (*An.* 5.3.12).[106] Xenophon's emphasis on the contrast in scale and materials echoes the sentiment voiced by Plato that private individuals should avoid envy by making dedications of wood and stone and leave costly gifts of silver and gold to the state.[107] This individual offering on private land could never match the undertaking of one of the wealthiest city-states, but Xenophon sets up a rhetorical framework, whereby small scale and less costly materials are counterbalanced by faithfulness to both visual and symbolic aspects of the cult of Artemis as expressions of piety and continuity.

Xenophon's replica of the cult statue of Artemis Ephesia is easy to picture because there are around seventy surviving stone copies of the original, mostly from the Roman period.[108] In describing the Ionian colony of Massalia and its foundations, Strabo (4.1.4) mentions that copying the cult statue of Artemis Ephesia was a core element of their civic religion: "In all the colonies (of Massalia) they worship this goddess (Artemis Ephesia) foremost and they preserve the design of the cult statue and all the rites as they are practiced in the metropolis."[109] Extant and textually attested copies of cult statues occur in such variety and in such diverse contexts that Christopher Witcombe draws distinctions between *replacements* that substituted for lost, destroyed, or stolen originals, *replicas* used as cult statues at other sites (like Xenophon's and the Massalian colonies'), and *reproductions* set up as votives, some of which overshadowed the originals in scale, material richness, and workmanship.[110]

Similar trends are evident in architecture, but they are not as distinct as the reproduction of cult statues. A single, very large, late sixth-century Ionic capital with convex volutes was discovered by chance in the harbor of Marseille, the site of ancient Massalia.[111] It shows that at least one of ancient Massalia's temples hewed closely to the Ephesian model and aspired to ambitious scale. It has even been suggested that the maintenance of the form of Ionic capital with convex volutes in Magna Graecia into the fourth century, long after it was abandoned elsewhere, is not the product of provincial isolation but an embodiment of the conservatism with which the Massalian diaspora connected itself to the Ionia it had left behind.[112] It is much more difficult, however, to picture Xenophon's shrine actually resembling the Archaic temple of Artemis at Ephesos. The Ephesian temple had a dipteral plan with a double ring of 106 columns, which would have become an impassable cage of pillars when scaled down to any modest scale (fig. 1.20a). The temple had an exceedingly elaborate sculptural program that included a near life-size representation of a festival procession, complete with column drums and cubic bases sculpted with women bearing offerings, a priest clad in a panther skin, and bulls led in sacrifice—a profusion of images that even temples of the largest scale rarely sought to rival. This was, after all, the temple that Pliny would later refuse to describe on the grounds that a catalog of its ornaments would fill too many volumes. The probable small size of Xenophon's temple might be gauged by the comparative example of the temple of Artemis Aristoboule built by Themistokles near his home in Athens in the 470s BCE (fig. 1.20b).[113] Plutarch (*Vit. Them.* 22) reports that Themistokles's shrine was widely

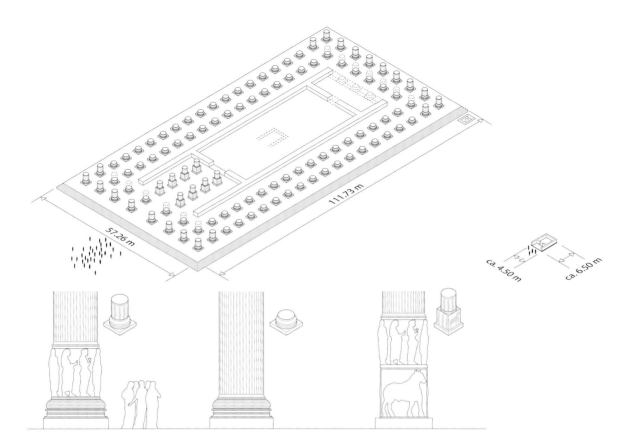

1.20. Scale comparison of the Archaic temple of Artemis, Ephesos, showing the arrangement of relief drums and cubic relief bases and the temple of Artemis Aristoboule, Athens.

deemed self-aggrandizing and accelerated the Athenian general's meteoric fall from public favor and his ostracism. The excavated remains of this temple, which was completely reconstructed in the fourth century when nostalgia for Athens's Persian War victories rehabilitated Themistokles's reputation, are anything but ostentatious. With this structure as a point of comparison, it would be generous to assume that Xenophon's temple had a facade of Ionic columns at all. Xenophon, however, in his own account as an ancient patron, conceived and presented his commission as a *likeness* of an Archaic Ionian temple despite admitted disparities in scale and materials as well as unspoken but probable dissimilarities in plan and decorative program. Xenophon's account offers an analogy for the intentions behind bilingual Ionic monuments as well as a model for their reception. Most Peloponnesian visitors to Xenophon's shrine had no reference for appreciating the visual fidelity to the Ionian prototype, but here the host was determined to point out the similarities both visual and symbolic. It is doubtful that many ancient viewers of bilingual Ionic capitals had the visual literacy of architecture to spot the connections, but residents of cities and priests at sanctuaries may have greeted visitors with proud accounts of their own temples, not unlike Xenophon's.

Heiner Knell starts *Die Anfänge des Archaismus in der griechischen Architektur* (1993) with a critique of the discipline's single-minded commitment to a model of developmental progress that has ignored elements of archaism as a widespread feature: "The idea of development ... largely determines the image of Greek architecture. There has hardly been any room for questions about different phenomena until now."[114] What Knell identified as the major examples of archaism, however, are primarily elements of continuity in the ground plans of temples. This includes fourth-century efforts to rebuild the destroyed temples of Artemis at Ephesos and the temple of Apollo at Delphi on the same plans as their predecessors, as well as the inclusion of engaged columns within the temples of Apollo at Bassai and Athena at Tegea, which evoke the dense interior structural supports of their Archaic predecessors.[115] These examples show builders asserting continuity between older and newer phases of the same buildings. These are Witcombe's *replacements*. Bilingual Ionic monuments emphasize a different strand of retrospective design in Greek architecture because they are in all cases *replicas* and *reproductions*.

Seen individually these quotations and replicas were discrete acts, undertaken by individual patrons for personal reasons, but together they reinforced and shaped traditions. In the field of literature, recent studies have emphasized that the formation of canons of classical texts in antiquity was no accident. For example, there were numerous playwrights in fifth-century Athens, who penned an estimated nine hundred tragedies for performance in the annual Dionysia, but the works of only three tragedians—Aischylos, Sophokles, and Euripides—have survived from antiquity intact.[116] Soon after their deaths, Aristophanes made clear that this triad stood head and shoulders above their contemporaries in his *Frogs* (405 BCE), in which the god Dionysos ventures to the underworld to revive one of the three to save Athens. Yet, the survival of a fixed canon of twenty-four of their tragedies rather than the works of others was not an incidental process of the cream rising to the surface. Johanna Hanink has argued that the canon of classical tragedy was largely created in Athens in the third quarter of the fourth century BCE, with the orator and politician Lykourgos taking a leading role. He leveraged the political rhetoric of nostalgia in the aftermath of Athens's defeat at Chaironeia in 338 by Philip II of Macedon. The process of creating a canon involved a constellation of informal actions, such as Lykourgos frequently quoting from these tragedians in speeches. But, the process also involved formal actions sponsored by the state: the annual reperformance of old plays was initiated in 386, bronze honorific statues of the trio were dedicated at the theater of Dionysos in 330 BCE, and the complete works of the three tragedians were copied and archived by the city.[117] To ensure fidelity, Lykourgos advanced a law that required reperformances to check their scripts against the official archive of original texts ([Plut.] *X orat*. 841f). The canon of Attic tragedy is easy to take for granted, but this received tradition was brought into being by a process of custodianship, editing, reproduction, quotation, and the creation of new civic monuments promoted by interested parties. The formation of the architectural canons of the Doric, Ionic, and Corinthian orders should also not be taken for granted. Analogous retrospective processes in architecture were also at work in Athens under Lykourgos, which saw the construction of the cyclopean-style retaining wall of the remodeled assembly on the Pnyx hill, a pair of archaistic Ionic capitals (see fig. 5.38), and the creation of a new fountain house by the Dipylon gate that reused sixth-century Ionic columns.[118] Fourth-century Athens furthermore saw the establishment of a new committee of ten officials, "the repairers of sanctuaries," who received an annual budget from which they contracted work for the maintenance of sacred buildings.[119] These are some of the small steps that contributed to the formation of architectural canons, a process that began taking shape before the fourth century and at sites beyond Athens. Bilingual Ionic capitals are important because they played a part in the formation of architectural traditions.

Bilingual Ionic column capitals have been overlooked in studies of Greek architecture because their contrasting combination of styles does not easily fit within interpretive models. These monuments, however, reveal something new about the societies that produced them precisely because they are different. Builders honed skills for high-relief carving that engendered the deeply cut Ionic volutes standard in later periods, but they revisited obsolete elements like convex Ionic capitals to emphasize the close relationship between contemporary practices and those of the past. Patrons often held double aspirations both to impress viewers according to the latest tastes and to assert historical ties with earlier buildings, tasking architects and stone carvers with harmonizing these dissonant ambitions. Bilingual capitals offer an untapped avenue for assessing the rules and meanings of the Ionic building tradition, but they also demonstrate the significance of this architectural tradition to religious, civic, and ethnic identities, especially as those identities transformed over time. In turn, these self-conscious explorations of sculptural style in architecture contributed to the distinctive aesthetics of Greek architecture.

Chapter 2

Delos
Synthesis at the End of the Archaic Period

Once upon a time, indeed, there was a great assemblage of the Ionians and the neighboring islanders at Delos, who used to come to the festival, as the Ionians now do to that of Ephesus, and athletic and poetical contests took place there, and the cities brought choirs of dancers. Nothing can be clearer on this point than the following verses of Homer, taken from a hymn to Apollo:
Phoebus, where'er thou strayest, far or near,
Delos was still of all thy haunts most dear.
Thither the robed Ionians take their way
With wife and child to keep thy holiday
Invoke thy favor on each manly game
And dance and sing in honor of thy name.

—Thucydides 3.104.3–4 (trans. Richard Crawley)[1]

When, where, and why were bilingual Ionic capitals initially carved? The first fully formed examples occur on the island of Delos, on the Propylon to the sanctuary of Apollo, built ca. 525–500 BCE (fig. 2.1). Sixth-century Delos sat at the center of a vortex of experimentation in the Ionic order in the Cyclades that was distinct from that of the Ionian cities on the coast of Asia Minor, regional styles that have been termed Island-Ionian and East-Ionian.[2] The pairing of convex and concave forms on the capitals of the Propylon held up a mirror to the architecture of Delos, which was filled with vestiges of a century of early experimentation and obsolescence in architectural forms and styles. Sixth-century Delos attracted major gifts from the wider Ionian world—most memorably Polykrates, the tyrant of Samos, donated the neighboring island of Rheneia, which he yoked to Delos

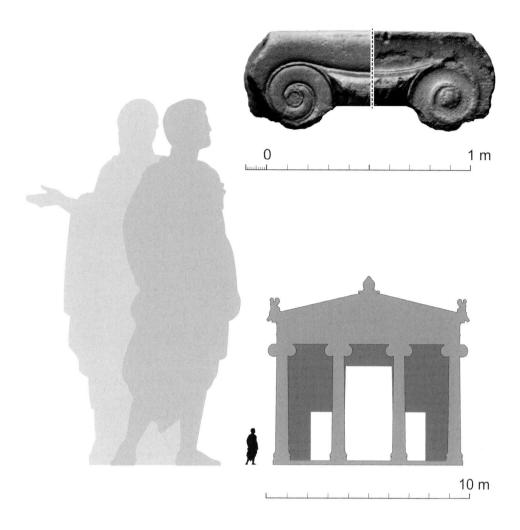

2.1. Delos, bilingual Ionic capital possibly from the Propylon to the Sanctuary of Apollo. National Museum of Warsaw.

with a chain. Delos could claim its festival of Apollo had a special pan-Ionian status accorded to it by the *Homeric Hymn to Apollo*, but as noted by Thucydides (3.104), its overall importance in this period was eclipsed by the preeminence of Ephesos and its festival of Artemis Ephesia. Although the *Delia* boasted a Homeric pedigree, it was only institutionalized as a recurring pentateric festival on the initiative of Peisistratos, the tyrant of Athens, shortly before the construction of the Propylon. Seen in this historical context, the Propylon brought together for comparison aspects of the two main regional Ionic styles in the Archaic period, the East-Ionian and the Island-Ionian traditions, and drew attention to the layered styles that attested to the sanctuary's history. There is a lexical paradox in labeling a building of the Archaic period "archaistic," but seen in its proximate context the Propylon engages retrospectively with its earlier neighbors. The Propylon is also a special case because the orientation of the capitals on the facade can be reconstructed with certainty (convex side out), and thus their visibility can be assessed as they confronted visitors entering and exiting the sanctuary with different visions of the Ionic order. The Propylon offers an introduction to the three-century phenomenon of bilingual capitals. It also holds the key to what later viewers found worth repeating. This chapter focuses first on the capitals and the reconstruction of the building itself before turning to the context that inspired their creation.

The Capitals from Delos, Nieborów, and Pheia

A corner capital from a major Ionic building of the late Archaic period—by far the largest Ionic colonnade from this period on Delos—emerged from the French archaeological excavations initiated in 1873 (fig. 2.2). Two additional capitals from the same building have come to light elsewhere, apparently removed from Delos prior to excavation. One was acquired by a collector of antiquities in Poland in the late eighteenth century. The other was pulled out of a harbor in the western Peloponnese at the site of ancient Pheia, where it was dumped as ballast. In 1997, Gottfried Gruben convincingly presented the connection of the three capitals, but the attribution has been overlooked in recent studies.[3] As a result, speculation about the Pheia capital attesting an otherwise unknown, large-scale, marble, Ionic building in the sixth-century Peloponnese, which would be a major historical and regional outlier, persists.[4] The case for their attribution to a single structure on Delos warrants reasserting.

The capital discovered on Delos emerged in the first decade of the French excavations, recorded first in a study of its design by architect Henri-Paul Nénot in 1882.[5] Its findspot was not recorded, but the hefty marble long sat just south of the Propylon until it was brought into the Delos Museum in 1963, a position that may have been close to its original findspot.[6] The capital belongs to the corner of a colonnade, with a projecting diagonal volute (now broken off) and two mitered half volutes at the interior corner. It is one of the best-preserved sixth-century examples of an Ionic corner capital and has thus occupied a special place in the understanding of the broader history of the Ionic order.[7]

The two-faced nature of the Ionic capital poses a challenge for designing an Ionic colonnade that turns a corner. The solutions ancient builders found for creating corner capitals with two adjacent volute faces were so varied that it is often difficult to reconstruct them when no fragments of the corner survive. Early Ionic constructions in the Cyclades did not have this problem, because the temples had only prostyle facades. These early columns, especially those connected with the Naxians, had elongated proportions with widely spaced volutes that call to mind simple wood brackets. Ionian temple builders in Asia Minor first encountered the problem in erecting rings of columns around temples, which required a capital to be viewed from two adjacent sides (see, e.g., fig. 1.8).[8] The solution, with a diagonal volute at the outside corner and two volutes at a mitered angle on the inside corner, although satisfactory, displaced the capital's center of gravity. This had not been a concern for the symmetrical design of normal capitals. Corner capitals drove builders toward more compact proportions.[9] The Delian corner capital is likely the first corner capital made in the Cyclades, borrowing from the east-Ionian model, and it illustrates how corners changed Ionic design.

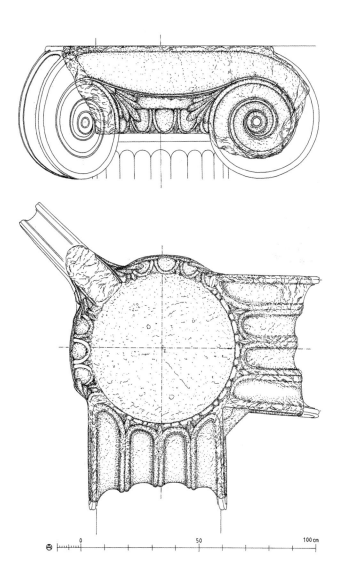

2.2. Delos, corner capital. Archaeological Museum of Delos. Study and drawing by A. Ohnesorg.

Henri-Paul Nénot, who participated in Homolle's Delos excavation in 1882 as the recipient of the Grand Prix de Rome of the École des Beaux-Arts, prepared a two-sheet study of six Ionic capitals from Delos (fig. 2.3).[10] In his accompanying report, Nénot remarked that the excavations had revealed a profusion of early Ionic capitals, which could not yet be associated with known monuments, but which had a bearing on the development of Ionic capitals, including possible connections with Asia Minor and Egypt.[11] The sheets are didactic in composition, presenting a sequential development of the form of the Ionic capital from an early uncarved capital with rising volutes to a Hellenistic example embellished with rich relief decoration. In order, the capitals are: (1) a votive capital with rising, Aeolic-type volutes,[12] (2) one of two votive capitals supporting sphinxes,[13] (3) the capital from the Stoa of the Naxians,[14] (4) the corner capital attributed to the Propylon, (5) the capital from the L-shaped portico of the Artemision (ca. 110 BCE), and (6) a capital attributed to

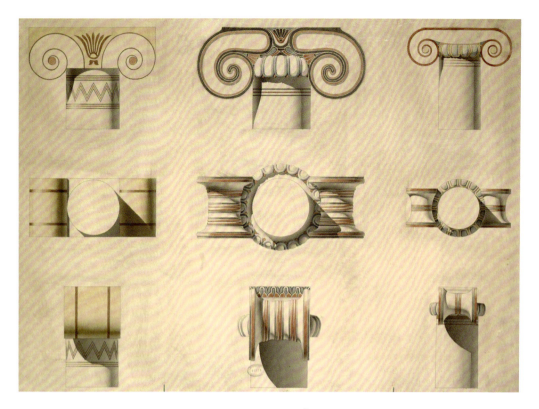

2.3. Henri-Paul Nénot, study of six Ionic capitals from Delos, 1882. École Nationale Supérieure des Beaux-Arts, Paris [AR823041, AR823042].

the southeast entrance to the sanctuary (second or third quarter of the third century).[15] This evolutionary "parallel" of Greek architectural orders had a long history, with sequences of Doric columns presented first in the late eighteenth century by Julien David Le Roy (see fig. 1.1).[16] Yet, Nénot applied a new archaeological approach to the special instance of Delos, which had produced so many varied early capitals to pose the opportunity of understanding development at a single site. These drawings were not simply documentary records of an excavation but highly polished restitutions to be displayed at the Académie des Beaux-Arts (ultimately exhibited at the Salon of 1884). Nénot took liberties in the reconstruction of all the ruined capitals, notably in the imaginative polychromy and the geometric decoration of the column shafts.[17] Significantly, Nénot disregarded the preserved state of the corner capital and produced an idealized reconstruction of a normal capital to better fit his presentation of a historical sequence. The judges of the Académie were critical of Nénot's work on Delos, concluding that he had done too little to justify his reconstructions or illustrate the underlying evidence.[18] In the case of the corner capital, however, Nénot's drawing presents a stunningly accurate prediction of the appearance of the normal capital from the same monument, two of which were removed from Delos long before Nénot's visit and only came to the attention of archaeologists long after.

Between 1779 and 1821, princess Hélèna Radziwiłłowa assembled a collection of Greek and Roman antiquities to decorate Arkadia, her elaborate English-style garden added to the Nieborów Palace (near Łowicz, about seventy-five kilometers

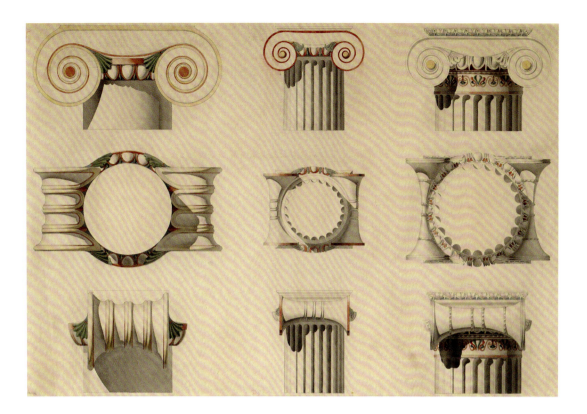

west of Warsaw).¹⁹ Arkadia draws on contemporary trends of Romanticism and Classicism in garden design, but Radziwiłłowa's garden was a distinctly personal project. She sought consolation for the early deaths of her three daughters in ancient Orphic religion and built for herself a reflective space that was not simply idyllic but was at turns mystical and Elysian. The highpoint of the collection of ancient sculpture, an over-life-size head of Niobe, which is said to be a personal gift from Catherine the Great of Russia, stands as a poignant avatar for the collector herself: a mother who turned to marble in grief at the loss of her children.²⁰ Arkadia surrounded Nieborów Lake with picturesque pavilions (a Palladian style temple of Diana, a gothic chapel, a ruined aqueduct, the spina of an imagined hippodrome, etc.) and repurposed architectural members—some reerected as pillars, others strewn in collagist lapidaria marking viewpoints around the garden. The most unusual of these repurposed stones was a bilingual Ionic column capital weighing about half of one ton (figs. 2.4, 2.5). It is first reported as displayed half-buried in the ground, but was later removed to the palace lawn and then to the archaeological collection of the National Museum in Warsaw, where it is displayed on permanent loan.²¹

    No surviving documents record how the capital was acquired around the turn of the eighteenth century, but two hypotheses have been put forward. It was initially suggested that Radziwiłłowa acquired the capital from Italian art dealers, the source of most of her antiquities, and that the capital may have come from a Greek city in south Italy.²² Tomasz Mikocki, however, put forward the more likely proposal that it

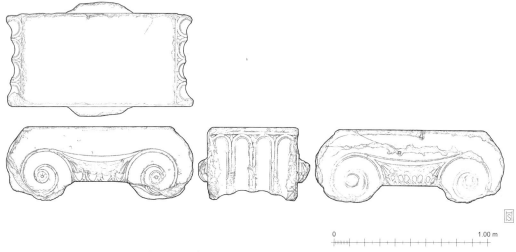

2.4. The Nieborów capital. National Museum of Warsaw.

2.5. The Nieborów capital, restored design.

came to Poland from the Aegean via St. Petersburg.[23] Although Western European collectors like Lord Elgin invariably take center stage in accounts of the early collecting of Greek antiquities, the Russian Empire was a major power in the Ottoman Aegean, with the courts of Catherine the Great, Paul I, and Alexander I amassing collections in St. Petersburg, whence Radziwiłłowa may have acquired the capital. When the defeat of the Ottoman navy at Çeşme in 1770 left the fleet of Admiral Orlov in control of the Aegean islands, a man from Mykonos named Kordias was contracted to dig for antiquities on Rheneia.[24] The Nieborów collection contains one Rheneian grave stele, which raises the possibility that several other pieces,

2.6. The Pheia capital. Archaeological Museum of Olympia.

including the Ionic capital, a large Hellenistic Corinthian capital, a bucrania altar, and an orthostate slab with a bucranium and garlands, all originate from the adjacent islands of Rheneia and Delos.[25]

A second bilingual Ionic capital (fig. 2.6) was dredged from the water at Katakolo, an important harbor on the west coast of the Peloponnese sheltered by the cape at the north of the Gulf of Kyparissia and the site of the ancient city of Pheia. A new museum at Pyrgos now houses underwater finds from Pheia, but the capital was taken to the Archaeological Museum of Olympia when it was discovered in 1974.[26] It was initially suggested that the capital originated in the Peloponnese, either part of a lost temple at Pheia or transported there from an inland Peloponnesian site like Olympia or Bassai.[27] Water and biological agents have pitted the whole surface of the stone, giving it an almost spongy texture, but a recent chip shows the bright white marble core with large crystals that is likely Cycladic marble. Also from Katokolo harbor are two Doric column capitals, now accepted as coming from the Stoa of Philip V on Delos.[28] All three capitals, Doric and Ionic, were probably dumped as ballast by a ship coming from Delos as it rounded the Peloponnese. This would hardly be the only instance of a cargo of antiquities from the Cyclades bound for European markets dumped as ballast: a group of thirty Rheneian grave stelai jettisoned on the island of Corfu are likely another shipment from the same period destined for a dealer in Italy.[29]

The two bilingual capitals from Nieborów and Pheia lack a documented provenance, but their connection to Delos seems assured based on their congruence with the corner capital. Gruben attributed the capitals based on the near exact correspondence of the main dimensions of all three capitals.[30] The most important concordance of their measurements is the alignment of their heights (ca. 36 centimeters) and lower diameters (ca. 58–52 centimeters), which show that the three capitals would sit seamlessly on column shafts of the same heights and diameters. The capitals have the same formal composition, including the unusual feature of a fillet above the echinus. The Delian corner capital and the Nieborów capital are nearly identical in their carving, but there are some small differences between this pair and the Pheia capital. These variances, however, are small by comparison to the shared contrasts between the opposite faces of each bilingual capital.

The bilingualism of the Nieborów and Pheia capitals is hardly a timid first experiment; it is bold and total. Alfred Mallwitz and photographer Gösta Hellner sought to capture the striking visual depth in the sculpting of the volutes by photographing both faces of the Pheia capital under identical, ideal studio lighting conditions (fig. 2.7).[31] This form of presentation (which is repeated elsewhere in this book in digital images) perhaps overemphasizes the effect of shadow contrast, especially under ideal conditions that were not those in the actual building. Gruben, who had only studied the Nieborów capital through Mikocki's photographs, concluded that the "artistic license" taken in the variance of its faces was the mark of a sculptor called in to help a team of masons with the most detailed elements.[32]

The alternation of the convex and concave volutes is echoed on each side by other features of the capitals. The convex side is paired with an egg-and-dart echinus, while the concave side is paired with an echinus elaborated with a Lesbian leaf

2.7. The Pheia capital. Archaeological Museum of Olympia.

or heart-and-dart molding. The pairing is deliberate: the simple curve of the ovolo profile matches the convex volutes while the S-curve of the *cyma reversa* adapts the concavity of the volutes of the other face. The designs of the volute eyes are also mismatched: the Nieborów capital has convex eyes on the concave side, and concave eyes on the convex side, while the Pheia capital has convex and concave paired. Each of these compositional inventions seems calculated to draw attention to the contrast. The choice to carve opposite faces almost completely differently was taken with no half measures, nor was it a small decision for a series of such large capitals. While there are more minor deviations, the shared differences between the faces seem part of a thought-out program of alternation.

There are small variances between the three capitals in the number of leaves on the echinus molding,[33] the presence of an astragal below the echinus,[34] the motif sculpted in the volute eyes,[35] the number of channels on the bolster,[36] and the termination of the bolster pattern at the echinus.[37] In total, these differences give the impression that the carver of the Nieborów and Delos capitals meticulously planned the geometry of the junction of the bolster and echinus on the underside of the capital, while in carving the Pheia capital this detail was eschewed to give the bolster a more swooping volume. Although the Nieborów and Delos capitals lack the astragal seen on the Pheia capital, this element was likely included at the top of the column shaft. Instead adding an astragal below the echinus on the Pheia capital allowed the carver to draw out the carved molding pattern in higher relief—opening a channel behind the darts. From these differences, it is tempting to spin a story about a carver becoming more daring and experimental while repeating the same capital design, or two carvers—one conservative, the other adventurous—tasked with producing capitals to the same basic specifications. Yet, there is a lesson here about the pitfalls of this sort of interpretation. If only one of the bilingual capitals survived, one might be inclined to see one side made by one carver and the other by another, but viewing both bilingual capitals together it is clear that their shared differences are the greatest aspect of consistency. The likeliest explanation of the differences, put forward by Gruben, is that the Nieborów capital and corner capital belong side by side in the colonnade on one facade, while the slightly different Pheia capital belongs to a colonnade elsewhere in the same building.

Finally, the Nieborów capital has two cuttings in the canalis of the concave side (see figs. 2.4, 2.5) that have not previously been observed. One socket (1.3 centimeters in diameter) is drilled into the canalis just below the fillet and is joined by a pour channel at the top of the capital, now half broken away. A second socket lower down still contains a broken metal stump embedded in the stone, an iron pin secured with lead that has chipped the surrounding stone when its projecting element was sheared off. Several antiquities in the Nieborów collection have been repurposed and repaired, which may have included iron pins, but these cuttings—particularly the drilled pour channel—are suited to the period of the capital's creation in the late sixth century BCE. The two attachments are placed at equal distance from the centerline of the capital, a symmetrical arrangement that suggests they secured a decorative embellishment in the form of a circular disk 17 centimeters in diameter. The two attachment points define a line 36 degrees from horizontal, or one tenth of

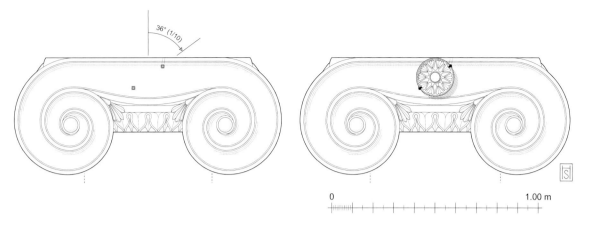

2.8. The Nieborów capital, attachment points on concave face, and tentative reconstruction of a phiale.

2.9. Comparison of volute eye designs of the Nieborów, Pheia, and Delos capitals.

2.10. Neapolis, temple of Parthenos, capital with an omphalos phiale carved in relief in the canalis. Archaeological Museum of Kavala.

a rotation of a circle, which suggests their placement may correspond to a circular ornament subdivided into ten or twenty radial elements (fig. 2.8). The attachment may have been a purpose-made metal ornament analogous to carved ornaments at the center of some Ionic and Aeolic capitals; in which case it may have followed the patterns seen in the volute eyes of the capitals: a rosette (the Nieborów capital), a crescent whorl (the Pheia capital), or an omphalos phiale (the Delos corner capital) (fig. 2.9). The placement of this attachment on only one of the three capitals, however, suggests that it was a secondary, votive attachment, probably a phiale. Phialai were among the most ubiquitous dedications in sanctuaries, and the inscribed inventories from Delos record hundreds of silver philalai, some of which are recorded as nailed to the walls and even the ceiling of cult buildings.[38] If this inference is correct, the Nieborów capital may be the direct source of inspiration for the design of the bilingual Ionic capitals on the temple of Parthenos at Neapolis (discussed in chapter 4), some of which were sculpted with an omphalos phiale in relief (fig. 2.10; and see figs. 4.2, 4.4, 4.5). The interpretation of the element is entangled in the identification and reconstruction of the building to which the capital belonged.

The Reconstruction of the Propylon

The sanctuary of Apollo on Delos was approached from the south along a grand processional route, the *dromos*, elaborated in the third and second centuries BCE by flanking stoas and culminating at the Propylon that marked the ceremonial entrance into the precinct. Shortly after gaining control of the island in 167 BCE, the Athenians erected a new gatehouse (Gruben's Propylon phase III) with a Doric prostyle facade facing south and two in-antis columns within the sanctuary, the ruins of which are substantially preserved today. This building, however, was wedged between two sixth-century BCE Ionic structures, the Oikos of the Naxians and the Stoa of the Naxians, structures whose ancient names are recorded in inscribed inventory lists (fig. 2.11). It is certain that the second-century Propylon is a replacement for an earlier gateway, the construction of which can be dated based on the sequence of abutting walls in the adjoining structures. The first phase of the propylon (Propylon I) was erected after the Oikos of the Naxians, overlying its steps at the southeast corner. In turn, Propylon I was built before the Stoa of the Naxians, which had no north wall but was built against the south wall of the gateway.[39] It was in the vicinity of the Propylon that early excavations uncovered the Ionic corner capital. The corner capital was initially attributed to the Propylon, a proposal reasserted by Gottfried Gruben.[40] The Ionic capital, however, has a discernibly later date than the Propylon's first phase, and if it is to be restored to the sanctuary's entrance, it must belong to a second phase (Gruben's Propylon II) from the last quarter of the sixth century, in which the initial gatehouse was significantly remodeled.[41] Recycled blocks in the second-century Propylon's foundations and sparse remnants of earlier in situ foundations indicate that there was an Archaic-period propylon, but regrettably they are difficult to interpret and do not independently attest a second Archaic phase (Propylon II). Excavations below the floor of Propylon III turned up fragments of marble Ionic architecture buried during the structure's second-century

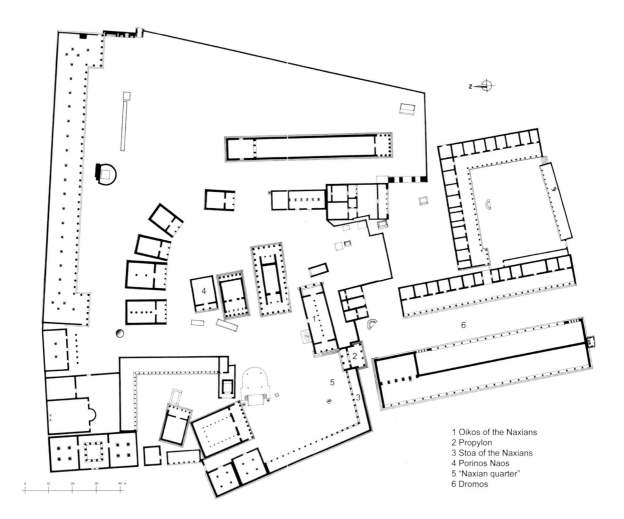

2.11. Delos, Plan of the Sanctuary of Apollo.

1 Oikos of the Naxians
2 Propylon
3 Stoa of the Naxians
4 Porinos Naos
5 "Naxian quarter"
6 Dromos

rebuilding, including a torus of a column base and a fragment of marble palmette, but a reexamination of Théophile Homolle's notebooks has ruled out the possibility that the capital was discovered beneath the floor, which might have clinched the attribution.[42] Gruben left out of his reconstruction a few fragments of carved Ionic moldings that belong to a ceiling, which he proposed might belong to the porch of the *porinos naos*.[43]

The Propylon bridged between the Oikos of the Naxians and the Stoa of the Naxians to the west, creating an enclosure ringed by colonnades on three sides. Sometimes dubbed the *Quartier Naxien*, this zone of Naxian benefactions became a locus for votive dedications.[44] The ancient account of a domino-like collapse of votives in this area—a bronze palm tree erected by the fifth-century Athenian general Nikias blew over and toppled the colossal kouros erected by the Naxians at the beginning of the sixth century (Plut. *Vit. Nic.* 3.4)—conveys the sense of dense display in this area. The *dromos* leading to the Propylon extended this zone for display with monuments spilling out of the sanctuary and piling up on the routes funneled between the South Stoa (mid-third century) and Stoa of Philip V (early second century). The Ionic corner capital dictates a prostyle facade, which on the Propylon can only have faced south; a colonnade on the north side must have been curtailed to an in-antis elevation by the adjoining corner of the Oikos of the Naxians. In plan, Propylon II was probably similar in overall layout to its second-century replacement, which had a tetrastyle prostyle facade facing south and a distyle in-antis elevation within the sanctuary. When viewed only in plan, the complex seems centuries ahead of its time, looking more like a Hellenistic or Roman-period peristyle gymnasium or agora entered through a propylon. Viewed from other angles, however, the jumble of elevations and rooflines put the piecemeal construction of the Naxian Quarter in the foreground.

Other scholars have endeavored to attribute the Ionic corner capital to the sixth-century temple of Apollo, which is called the *porinos naos* in inscribed accounts from the sanctuary. The marble Ionic capital belonged to the most impressive facade on the island for almost a century. It is logical to consider assigning it to the front of the main cult building, even if marble columns contradict the ancient appellation of the temple as a structure built of *poros* limestone. Although an elaborate, prostyle Ionic facade of marble would have been incongruous with the moniker, it is conceivable that the limestone walls of the temple still differentiated it from the two subsequent all-marble temples dedicated to Apollo, the temple of the Athenians and the temple of the Delians. Yet there are also architectural difficulties in assigning the prostyle Ionic colonnade to the temple's facade. The in situ foundations and parts of the limestone walls of this temple indicate that it had a porch with columns. The foundations, however, leave room for steps only to the front of the porch, the typical foundation arrangement for temples with columns in antis, and not a step wrapping around the sides as in prostyle temples.[45] On these grounds, Gruben proposed an in-antis rather than prostyle facade, which may well have been Doric like the other Apollo temples.

Roland Étienne has reasserted the attribution of the Ionic facade to the *porinos naos*.[46] Re-excavating the old trenches in the foundations of the Propylon confirmed that the scant sixth-century remains offered little in situ evidence to differentiate two separate Archaic phases (i.e., Gruben's Propylon I, Propylon II). If the plan of Propylon II mirrored the plan of its second-century BCE replacement as Gruben proposed, why were its foundations torn out root and branch when it was common practice to recycle foundations? While attributing the Ionic capitals to the *porinos naos*, Étienne also removed the marble ceiling elements that Gruben had attributed.[47] Inscribed accounts recording repairs to the *porinos naos* mention that the ceiling of the temple's porch was made of wood, so Étienne's reconstruction transfers the Ionic columns but has no more total marble elements.[48] Étienne offers rebuttals to many of Gruben's arguments, but conspicuously does not address the attribution of the Pheia and Nieborów capitals, which would multiply the number of columns in the building. The corner capital and the Nieborów capital fit well side by side in the same prostyle colonnade, but the slight differences of the Pheia capital suggest that the same building had a second colonnade, an arrangement that fits the reconstruction of Propylon II well. Squeezing the three capitals onto the four columns of the porch of the *porinos naos*, although workable in plan, is inelegant in elevation. Ultimately, Étienne has shown that Gruben's reconstruction of Propylon II is more tenuous than the polished reconstruction drawing, now frequently republished, suggests. Yet the alternative proposal of a marble, prostyle facade for the *porinos naos* is much less convincing. As is sometimes the case in archaeology, the fragmentary nature of the evidence makes it difficult to choose with certainty between two scenarios or to rule out the possibility of a third, as yet unappreciated.

Does the discovery of an attachment, likely a votive phiale, to the Nieborów capital incline the identification of the capital with the *porinos naos* over the Propylon? The inscribed inventory lists present a picture of the sanctuary's temples packed with dedications, including silver phialai nailed to the walls of the temple of Artemis and a gold crown nailed to a lintel or architrave of the Delian temple of Apollo.[49] Phialai are also among the items in the inventories of the *porinos naos*. However, the Stoa of the Naxians and Oikos of the Naxians on either side of the Propylon were also warehouses for votives, and dedications spilled out of the sanctuary, with monuments erected along the processional *dromos* leading up to the sanctuary. The Propylon was thus a conspicuous nexus for display in its own right. The discovery of an attachment for a votive dedication to the concave face of the Nieborów capital enriches the image of this structure, but it does not narrow the window of possible restitutions.

The contested reconstruction of the *porinos naos* has also been tied up with attempts to identify the temple's patron as one of the most important figures in the island's late sixth-century history, Peisistratos, the tyrant of Athens. Herodotus (1.64) and Thucydides (3.104) credit Peisistratos with inaugurating the quinquennial festival of Delian Apollo and for purifying the temenos by disinterring the dead buried within sight of the temple—an action that presupposes the presence of a temple, presumably the *porinos naos*. René Vallois and Fernand Courby proposed that blocks of limestone imported from the Akte quarry at Piraeus with cuttings for double-T clamps typical of Athenian builders could be restored to the *porinos naos*.[50] These telltale signs of Athenian masons at work on Delos would seem to link the first temple with Peisistratos. Yet this attribution is likely incorrect: the in situ blocks of the euthynteria of the *porinos naos* are of a different limestone and show no signs of double-T clamps. Adding the Ionic corner capital to the *porinos naos* lends the building a Cycladic stylistic connection, and Roland Étienne and Francis Prost use it to reinforce the conclusion that the Delians themselves rather than Peisistratos built the temple.[51] The capital itself, however, is not required to conclude that the attribution to Peisistratos is tenuous. Grouped together with the Oikos of the Naxians and the Stoa of the Naxians, it appears as a final major benefaction of Naxos.

The Architectural Context of the Delian Propylon

The emergence of bilingual Ionic capitals on Delos responds directly to their setting, particularly the Propylon's immediate context, appended to earlier Ionic structures, the Oikos of the Naxians and the Stoa of the Naxians. The Oikos of the Naxians, which was built of marble at the beginning of the sixth century, can claim many "firsts" of the Ionic order. The Oikos was built with an interior row of columns and porch at the west that contains the earliest surviving architectural use of the Ionic

2.12. Delos, Prostoon to the Oikos of the Naxians, Ionic capital and column base.

capital, the first marble column shaft with the twenty-four flutes of a canonical Ionic column, the earliest recognizable Ionic frieze course, the first Ionic geison, and the first marble roof tiles (carved with gorgon antefixes).[52] The one surviving capital from this phase has the recognizable silhouette of an Ionic capital but no carved volute or echinus decoration, details that were probably only added with paint.[53] The Prostoon, a porch added to the east of the building ca. 560, has the earliest known Ionic epistyle divided into fascia and initiates the use of a molding on the soffit of the Ionic geison, a canonical form. The capitals of the Prostoon (fig. 2.12; for the reconstruction by Nénot, see fig. 2.3, third capital) are similarly volumetric but have a faint inscribed line indicating a volute and volute eye. The echinus molding takes the form of a leaf pattern that was the predecessor to the later egg-and-dart form. After these renovations, the building had a distinctly heterogeneous appearance, with the interior cut in two by a screen of eight closely set columns running below the roof line, an in-antis west porch, and a tetrastyle prostyle east porch.

The original function of the structure, termed the Oikos of the Naxains in Hellenistic inventory lists, is a matter of scholarly disagreement. It seems to have been

Delos   57

the largest and most impressive building in the sanctuary until the construction of the Propylon and the *porinos naos*, and its plan, which includes spaces for dining couches, resembles the hestiatorion-temple type that predominate in the Cyclades of the Iron Age and Early Archaic Period rather than treasuries. Yet the Oikos of the Naxians differs from the three certain temples because it has no alignment with the *keraton* altar, and it may well have always been used as a treasury and clubhouse of the Naxians.[54] The expansion of the Oikos of the Naxians into a complex including the Propylon and the Stoa of the Naxians perpetuates the apparent double roles that frustrate efforts to typologize the core structure as either treasury or hestiatorion-temple: the complex of buildings served to showcase Naxian generosity at the front of the sanctuary but also shaped how Delian religion was practiced.

An L-shaped stoa was appended to the first phase of the Propylon in the third quarter of the sixth century, which was "the stoa which the Naxians dedicated" mentioned in an inscribed account.[55] If the Oikos of the Naxians had functioned as a treasury in the sixth century, the addition of a stoa fits a familiar pattern: at Delphi, the Athenians built a cluster of monuments, beginning with a small Doric treasury ca. 500, followed by a large base exhibiting the spoils from the battle of Marathon in 490, and then a small Ionic stoa for displaying "the weapons and ship-finials they seized from the enemies" in the second quarter of the fifth century.[56] The low colonnade of the Stoa of the Naxians reshaped the sanctuary by enclosing its south and west sides. This structure set the stage for the bilingual capitals on Propylon II because it already had a mixture of capitals with convex volutes and concave volutes, in each case the same on both sides.

No capitals were discovered while excavating the stoa, but six capitals found dispersed in the sanctuary probably belong to the building. These capitals are generally consistent with the stoa in their style, use of Naxian marble, and match the upper diameter of the one surviving column shaft at the stoa.[57] Five of the capitals are carved with convex volutes terminating in a whorl rather than an eye, although there are slight differences in the carving of their bolsters.[58] One of the five convex capitals has one face that is uncarved.[59] A sixth capital, which has the same dimensions and arrangement of a volute spiral terminating in a whorl, is carved differently: the volutes on both faces are concave, and the echinus is carved with heart-and-dart rather than egg-and-dart, as on the concave faces of the Pheia and Nieborów capitals.[60] The odd capital with concave faces has the same dimensions and a nearly indistinguishable bolster design from the others, but it has the addition of dowel holes on top and bottom, which may signal a replacement.[61] This pairing formed a precedent for Propylon II, which merges the convex and concave volutes with egg-and-dart and heart-and-dart in the same combinations.

Viewed in context, the Propylon was the hinge joining a complex of preexisting, remodeled buildings, and its bilingual capitals make distinct references to the hodgepodge of Ionic orders surrounding them (figs. 2.13, 2.14). The capitals borrow much of their modeling from the two types of capitals in the Stoa of the Naxians but add the volute eyes and weighty column diameter from the Prostoon. Just as the two faces of the bilingual capitals were diametric opposites, the thick pillars themselves could not have struck a greater contrast with the spindly shafts and undecorated

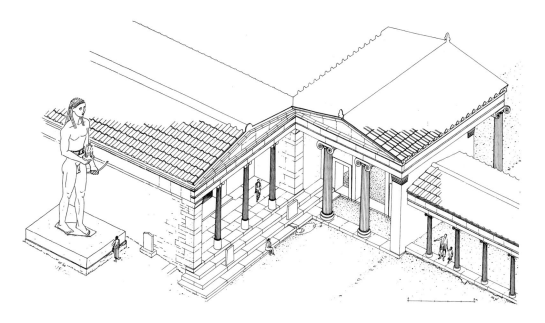

2.13. Delos, reconstruction of Propylon II proposed by G. Gruben.

2.14. Delos, Ionic columns (east to west, shown left to right) of the Oikos of the Naxians (Prostoon, interior colonnade with floor level altered, and east porch), the Propylon, and the Stoa of the Naxians at the same scale and relative elevation.

2.15. Samos, Heraion, column bases from the Rhoikos Temple (Dipteros I) in the foundations of the Polykratean Temple (Dipteros II).

capitals on the adjacent west elevation of the Oikos of the Naxians. The likely combination of prostyle and in-antis elevations on the Propylon reflects the combination seen on the east and west sides of the Oikos. The Propylon's intervention embraces the patchwork of pioneering Ionic columns that surrounded it, and the added bilingual capitals invite the viewer to reflect on the process of agglomeration.

At the time, the Naxian Quarter was not alone in its thoroughly heterogeneous appearance, but few other sanctuaries seem to have embraced it. Although the architecture of the Naxian Quarter charts a series of innovations in the Island-Ionic style that emerged in the Cyclades, it also responds to trends in East-Ionian temple building along the coast of Asia Minor. In particular, the decision to retrofit the Oikos of the Naxians around the middle of the century with a new, more impressive columnar facade, the Prostoon, responds to the trend in large temples ringed with columns, and the Prostoon column bases, with a simple, slightly concave drum topped with a torus, follow a type seen on the first dipteral temple of Hera on Samos (ca. 570–560). Dipteros I of the Samian Heraion initiated a metamorphosis in Ionic building, both in terms of its colossal scale and the textural elaboration of its limestone column bases. The experimentation with convex and concave forms on the column bases of Dipteros I, sometimes called the Rhoikos Temple after the sculptor mentioned by Herodotus and Vitruvius as the building's architect, set the context for competition in sculpted elaboration in Ionic building.

At the Heraion on Samos, Dipteros I was damaged by a fire ca. 530 and was demolished to make way for Dipteros II, also called the Polykratean Temple after the tyrant who initiated the new construction. The overall image of Dipteros I is cloudy because only small fragments of column drums, roof tiles, and acroteria survive, but there is a near perfect snapshot of the temple from the stylobate to about knee-height because builders recycled 102 column base fragments from the original 134 columns of Dipteros I in the foundations of Dipteros II (fig. 2.15).[62] The arrangement of bases, deduced from differences in diameter, shows a sequence of construction and experimentation, with shading and texture added to the bases as the project developed (fig. 2.16). The column bases within the cella are rough-hewn cylinders covered in toolmarks from shaping with adzes; they supported wooden columns that left traces of burning on top. To judge only from their bottom halves, the interior columns looked like the old-fashioned supports of the temples of earlier centuries enlarged to gigantic scale.[63] The column bases outside the cella, however, exhibit a wide array of sculptural treatment. One torus has very shallow concave facets meeting at sharp edges like the arrises of a Doric column shaft. Some bases have ten to thirteen concave bands separated by incised lines, while others have concave bands separated by flat fillets, like the fluting of later Ionic column shafts. A few bases have purely polygonal facets; some have convex bands separated by half rounds or flat fillets, and many mix concave and convex bands. Viewed by their spatial grouping, there is a sense of escalating complexity in their ornamentation progressing from interior to exterior. Visualized with shading, it is evident how the building presented—for a brief window of time—a pattern book of surface modeling that would become characteristic of bilingual capitals.

The column bases of Dipteros I have concentric toolmarks that have been

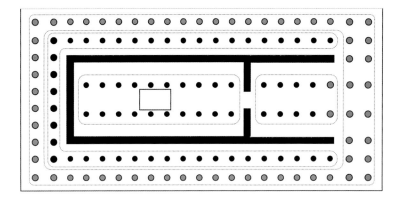

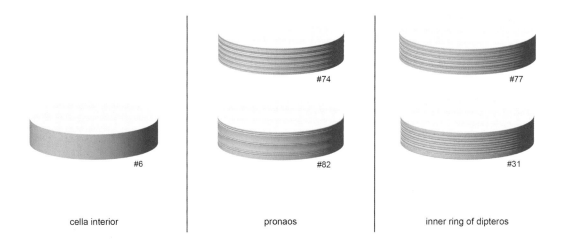

2.16. Samos, Heraion, Rhoikos Temple (Dipteros I), column base elements.

interpreted as evidence that the limestone was turned quickly and cut with a stationary chisel as one would in lathing wood. The invention of turning stone column bases at the Samian Heraion was identified as the feat referred to in Pliny's comment (*HN* 36.90) that the Samian sculptors-turned-architects Rhoikos and Theodoros designed columns that "when they were suspended in the workshop, were so well balanced that they could be turned on their axes by a boy."[64] This new carving technology, which was particularly effective on the soft limestone, opened up the possibility of adding shallow moldings to the bases through incision and abrasion, and the carvers tried many different types of shallow profiles only about 3 millimeters deep. In the first systematic study of the bases, Heinz Johannes formulated a narrative account of a new carving technique to explain a period of experimentation that produced this variety:

> In the varied, delicate shadings of the bases, the grooves, flutes, prisms and rounds, combined in the bases of [the pronaos and inner ring of the

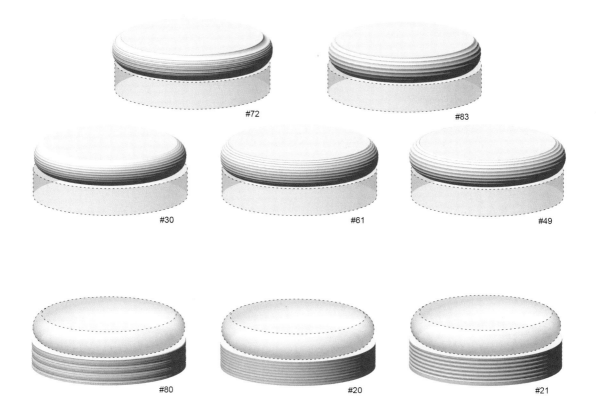

facade and outer ring of dipteros

dipteros] one still feels the first joy in the novel application to architecture of the invention of turning, which ignited the imagination of the workers to ever new variations. ... Then, from the shimmering richness of design, a harmonization of ornament forms was achieved, a tectonically refined standard of simple bands of shadow of six to eight flutes.[65]

Johannes drove home the point that the shallow channels were fundamentally bands of shadow by shading in his profile drawings (fig. 2.17). Subsequent research by Christoph Hendrich has streamlined Johannes's typological groupings of base fragments, but the general sense remains the same: a simple rusticated interior, an encircling ring of exuberant experimentation, and a facade in a canonical form, where larger, concave channels were chosen to lend shadow modeling to the geometric forms of the drum and torus.

Hendrich further observes that some of the fluted torus fragments from Dipteros I may not be bases, but capitals.[66] The inner ring of columns of Dipteros II had capitals with only an egg-and-dart echinus and no volutes, many of which survive well preserved. A similar scheme of capitals without volutes is proposed by Aenne Ohnesorg for the inner ring of columns in the Archaic dipteral temple of Artemis at

Delos 63

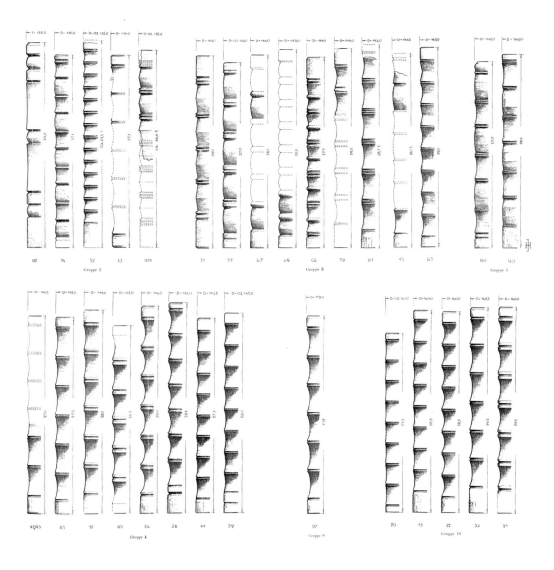

2.17. Samos, Heraion, Rhoikos Temple (Dipteros I) H. Johannes's drawings of the base profiles (Johannes 1937, pl. 18–21).

Ephesos (see fig. 1.5), and torus capitals adorning the flanks of the Archaic dipteral temple at Didyma.[67] There are no fragments of volutes from Dipteros I, and thus Hendrich suggests that spare fluted torus elements were used as capitals and that some may have even been topped with volutes made of wood, to produce an early form of the normal Ionic capital with a fluted echinus—a form known with convex volutes in two unusual examples from Didyma and one from Delphi (fig. 2.18).[68] The excavation of a temple at the site of Çatallar Tepe on the northern slope of Mt. Mykale, identified by Hans Lohmann as the Archaic site of the Panionion, produced sixty fragments of two types of capitals, including both a fluted torus echinus capital and capitals with a fluted torus echinus and lightly incised volute decoration (fig. 2.19).[69] The findspots of the capital fragments at Çatallar Tepe show that the torus capitals belonged to the inner chamber and the volute capitals to the pronaos.[70] Ceramic finds from the destruction deposit on the temple's floor suggest

64   Chapter 2

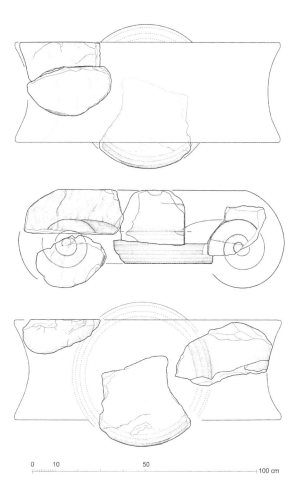

2.18. Delphi, Ionic capital with a fluted torus echinus, sixth century BCE. Archaeological Museum of Delphi.

2.19. Çatallar Tepe, Mt. Mykale, reconstruction of Ionic capital. Study and drawing by F. Hulek.

that the temple was built in the first half of the sixth century BCE and burned down around the middle of the century never to be rebuilt.[71] The Çatallar Tepe temple offers the most complete picture of the columnar design of an Ionian temple in the first half of the sixth century, when each of the dipteral temples was still underway. These fragments illustrate that some of the earliest experimentation with sculptural modeling on Ionic capitals was not in the treatment of the volutes but the echinus.

The Naxian Quarter in the sanctuary of Apollo on Delos and Dipteros I in the Heriaon on Samos were similarly heterogeneous *by circumstance*. Both give the impression of builders inventing the forms of the Ionic order as they worked. Samos, however, was markedly different because builders wiped the slate clean by burying their earlier experiments and starting over with a more homogenous scheme. On Delos, the mixture was embraced and provided a contextual impetus for the creation of the first bilingual capitals.

Conditional Visibility

Bilingual Ionic capitals raise obvious questions about visibility and perception because their opposite faces often corresponded to the interiors and exteriors of colonnades. Do their orientations convey a visual hierarchy in buildings? Do their faces respond to different visibility conditions? Given that they required viewing in the round, were their differences readily perceivable at all? The Propylon is a rare case where the orientation of the capitals can be restored with certainty and plainly assessed in a restitution. The result is the opposite of the common assumption that the concave faces of bilingual capitals faced outward because this profile creates more pronounced shadows in direct light.[72] Because the corner capital has convex faces on the exterior of the prostyle south-facing porch, it is assured that the normal capitals (the Nieborów capital) also had their convex sides facing outward and south for maximum visibility and direct sunlight.

Conditions of visibility are an important aspect of art and architecture, but their assessment and interpretation are not always as straightforward as they seem.[73] Questions about visibility and perception in Greek and Roman architecture have been directed mostly at narrative friezes sculpted in shallow bas reliefs like those of the Parthenon and the Column of Trajan.[74] This attention has been directed in part as a critique of dense iconographic readings facilitated by the close analysis of sculpture decontextualized for eye-level scrutiny by museum displays, plaster casts, drawings, and photographs. The architectural context of the Parthenon's frieze, its distance from the viewer, oblique viewing angle, indirect lighting, the obstruction of the interposed columns all interfere with a continuous reading, while the absence of paint and metal attachments pose the possibility of visual enhancement.[75] At stake is the question of whether narrative reliefs should be understood primarily as decor, communicating more through their presence, placement, overwhelming visual richness, and the value added by their labor-intensive creation, rather than through a sequentially legible story with ideological overtones.[76] Bilingual capitals faced many of the same conditional impediments to visibility, but were distinctly ornament in their communication of meaning.

The visual perception of architecture is conditioned by human field of vision, which is wider horizontally than vertically and especially limited upward because we tend to tilt our eyes about 10 degrees downward while walking.[77] The blinkered awareness of pedestrians was summarized by Jan Gehl in his 1971 manifesto to architects and urban planners *Life Between Buildings*: "A person walking down a street sees practically nothing but the ground floor of buildings, the pavement, and what is going on in the street space itself."[78] Gehl was writing in an era when advertising, merchandizing, and retail design ardently exploited principals of vision and behavioral psychology to maximize sales through impulse purchasing, notoriously distilled in the slogan of strategic product display "eye-level is buy level." At the very same time, however, Gehl criticized contemporary architects for putting the human-scale, street-level experience of buildings second, churning out public spaces that were stony and alienating. Gehl was not alone among theorists proposing that commercial advertising should serve as a source of inspiration for architecture, but while eye-level placement of chocolate bars might boost sales, architects in the past had used neck-craning perspectives—sights that would be in the periphery of vision to those walking with downcast eyes—for powerful effects.

For most of the seventh century BCE, the figural decoration on Greek temples was set mostly at eye level, in the form of wall painting and relief orthostates. Only

2.20. Selinous, Temple C, metope of Perseus and Medusa viewed frontally and from below. Museo Archeologico Salinas, Palermo.

in the last quarter of that century were images catapulted up to the entablature and roof in the form of friezes, antefixes, acroteria, and eventually pediment sculpture, in what Clemente Marconi has dubbed an underappreciated "revolution in Greek sacred architecture."[79] The change in altitude of figural decoration coincided with the crystallization of the columnar orders in stone, manifested in the many early Ionic columns that served as pedestals for statues, elevating sphinxes poised to invoke awe and terror.[80] Sixth-century temple builders were confronted by the imperfect, oblique views of newly elevated figures and sought out corrections, a learning process vividly preserved in the metope sculptures at Temple C at Selinous, which are set within frames that are larger at the bottom. The plinth at the bottom raised the figures so that their legs were not permanently obscured from view by the projecting taenia of the architrave below, a pragmatic correction that can be immediately perceived by lying down on the floor in front of the reconstruction in the Palermo Museum to approximate an original viewing angle (fig. 2.20).[81] As viewers approached the temple, the scenes remained fully in view up to around 11 meters from the temple's bottom step. The oversized plinth does not appear on the earlier metopes of Temple Y, the modest size of which did not produce viewing problems and was jettisoned on the later Temple E metopes, which swapped out the old sunken relief carving for high-relief figures projecting from the plane of the metope. The development of the Selinous metopes show a trial-and-error process of adjusting design to correct for the oblique views produced by increasingly taller edifices. This is an ad hoc forerunner to the rules offered by Vitruvius, such as the scalar system for proportionally enlarging capitals and entablatures with every five-foot increase in the height of columns (3.5.7–10), or the 40 percent enlargement of frieze courses with sculpted figures to lend them "distinction" (*auctoritas*) (3.5.10).

Visibility was a central concern frequently articulated in inscriptions. At least 150 Greek decrees, dating to the Hellenistic and Roman periods, contain a coda stipulating that the text be written down on stone and set up "in the most conspicuous spot" (ἐν τὸν ἐπιφανέστατον τόπον), sometimes qualifying that it be the most conspicuous spot of a city, of an agora, of a sanctuary, of a gymnasium, and, in one case, of the interior of a building.[82] Ioannis Mylonopoulos has cross-referenced the findspots of inscriptions with *epiphanestatos topos* clauses and observed that the actual spots chosen for the inscriptions ranged widely in sanctuaries, with some set up near entrances and others placed proximate to cult statues.[83] At least one honorific decree contains the provision that the most conspicuous spot be selected by the honoree, an acknowledgment that the assessment of maximum visibility was very much in the eye of the beholder.[84] Those who set up inscriptions, dedications, and buildings strove to achieve visual prominence, though their success may ultimately have been variable.

How visible were column capitals from within a building? There was plainly a difference in the conditions of viewing the inside face of capitals, which were inevitably seen from low, oblique angles, permanently in shadow, and often silhouetted against the brighter sky. Reduced visibility, however, should not be mistaken for invisibility or insignificance. The temple of Athena at Assos offers an insightful illustration. One Doric capital carries a large, now-fragmentary inscription on the abacus that reads in part " ... a bushel and forty ... ," which likely records an endowment providing a monthly grain ration and cash salary for a priestess of Athena (fig. 2.21).[85] Pry marks for setting the epistyle blocks on top of this capital show conclusively that the inscription was carved on the inward-facing side of the abacus, only to be seen from within the temple's peristyle.[86] Had the inscription been written on the temple's exterior as was more common, a viewer could step back to get a better look, but inside a viewer needed to look upward at an angle of at least 50 degrees to take in the text.[87] The size of the text was perfectly readable from the ground: taking into account foreshortening from the oblique view, the letters would still have appeared four times larger than the text of a Snellen Eye Chart that marks twenty-twenty vision. The "most conspicuous spot" this was not, but neither was it regarded as invisible. Evidently, the back of the capital was judged the perfect place for setting up one of the temple's founding institutional records. The Assos inscription illustrates that the inward-facing sides of capitals were not regarded as unseen—a principle also evident in the Delian Propylon.

The Delian capitals show a concerted attention to both faces. Only the inward-facing mitered volute halves of the corner capital were uncarved, a common choice at awkward junctions (e.g., the temple of Athena Nike). What work was saved by this omission seems to have been lavished on the normal capitals, where an alternative composition, complete with a heart-and-dart echinus, was crafted for the interior position that could be seen from a smaller range of views. It is counterintuitive that the more elaborately carved side of an Ionic capital should face inward, especially when the corner capitals in the same colonnade have an uncarved face on the

2.21. Assos, temple of Athena, column capital with inward-facing inscription seen from below.

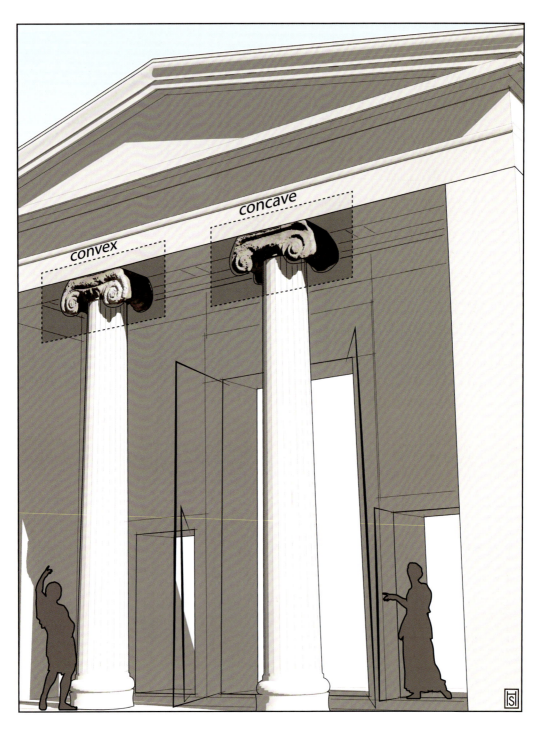

2.22. Delos, Propylon II, north colonnade with the Pheia capital restored alternately showing the possible convex and concave orientations.

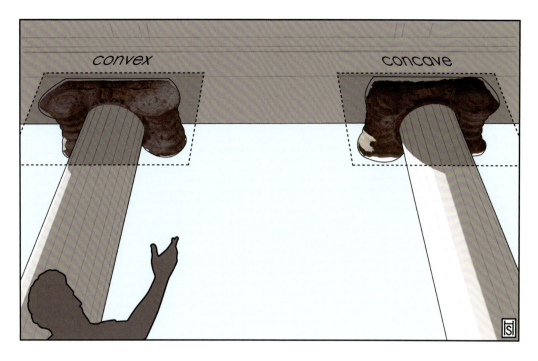

2.23. Delos, Propylon II, interior view of north colonnade with the Pheia capital restored, alternately showing the possible convex and concave orientations.

interior. Ancient builders and viewers may have considered the interior of a temple as the apex of a decorative program, elaborated with cult statues, textiles, and wall paintings now lost. A few gate buildings, notably the Propylaia to the Athenian Acropolis and the Propylon to the sanctuary of Asclepius at Epidauros, took a cue from temple design by introducing more elaborate columns to their interiors.

Although the orientation of the capitals on the facade is fixed, the orientation of the Pheia capital on the distyle elevation to the north is debatable. The capital might have the same orientation in relation to the building with the convex side facing out or in relation to the site with the concave side facing into the sanctuary. The Pheia capital has more sculptural definition generally and the unusual detail of complete undercutting behind the darts of the echinus molding on the concave side. Might the addition signal the exterior face? The two options of the orientation of the capitals in the distyle elevation are visualized in figure 2.22 (exterior) and figure 2.23 (interior). While it cannot be known with certainty if the concave side faced out toward the sanctuary, the decision was never about shadow effects, because the capitals on the north elevation were only in direct sunlight shortly before sunset, with the timing fluctuating throughout the year. Looking around in a digital model (fig. 2.23) offers a good sense of the visibility of the interior faces of the capitals as well as the range of viewpoints from which they can be seen. It does not fully do justice to the appearance of detailed marble elements silhouetted against the sky, especially in the bright sunlight. One may gather a sense of real lighting effects of a tetrastyle porch from the analogy of the temple of Athena Nike on the Athenian Acropolis seen from the inside (fig. 2.24). In antiquity, this viewpoint was the

privilege only of the cult statue of Athena Nike, but it simulates the sense of passing through the Propylon with doors open. The carved volutes of the capitals cannot be missed and would have been a special point of visual interest with the addition of painted decoration.

It is possible that the orientation of the capitals corresponded to the hierarchy of entering and exiting the sanctuary, rather than interior and exterior, with more elaborate capitals facing toward Apollo's sanctuary (and the general direction of the *keraton* altar) and the less elaborate faces oriented toward the city and harbor. A point of comparison is offered by the Propylon of Ptolemy II at the Sanctuary of the Great Gods on Samothrace, built ca. 285–281 BCE (fig. 2.25).[88] To those who approach the sanctuary from the west, the building presented a hexastyle Ionic facade toward the ancient city of Samothrace; at the east, a hexastyle Corinthian facade faced the sanctuary, and observers gathered in the Theatral Circle. The different elevations present a programmatic meaning for the sanctuary's mystery cult and its initiation ritual. First time visitors to the sanctuary entered through the Propylon's Ionic facade as noninitiates; after spending the night within the sanctuary they exited through the Corinthian facade of the propylon with new knowledge and the protection of the Samothracian gods.[89] The janiform propylon not only signaled the change between sacred and profane space separated by the ravine it bridges but mirrored the altered outlook of initiates.

In analyzing the function of the temple within Greek religion, Walter Burkert was a sceptic that architectural elements had intrinsic meanings, concluding it was "[not] of much avail to look for specific symbolic significance in the details of fluted columns."[90] Searching for a structuralist interpretation of Greek religion, he instead emphasized the importance of the colonnade in constructing the sense of the sacred by establishing one of several *permeable boundaries*, also including temenos walls, propylons, and doors that made palpable the access (*prosodos*) sanctuaries offered to the gods. As Burkert put it: "You are invited, even attracted to pass through the interstice, but there is an unmistakable distinction between outside and inside, especially as the columns come alive in Greek sunlight."[91] The design of the Delian propylon seems precisely calculated to represent this distinction.

Sites that were centers for early innovation in the Ionic order, such as the Heraion on Samos and the sanctuary of Apollo on Delos, hosted a cluttered collection of outdated iterations of Ionic columns by ca. 550. On Samos, a catastrophic fire and the ambitions of the tyrant Polykrates led to near total demolition and homogenized rebuilding. On Delos, however, Ionic buildings continued to agglomerate. When the second phase of the Delian Propylon connected the Oikos of the Naxians and the Stoa of the Naxians, its pioneering bilingual Ionic capitals collaged the mix of proportions, ovolo and cyma echinus patterns, and convex, concave, and uncarved volutes that existed in the Naxian complex after many phases of building and remodeling. The placement of the richly sculpted capitals contradicts expectations for their orientation: the convex side with a standard ovolo echinus faced

2.24. Athens, Acropolis, temple of Athena Nike, tetrastyle Ionic facade seen from the interior.

2.25. Samothrace, Sanctuary of the Great Gods, Propylon of Ptolemy II, split view of east (Ionic) and west (Corinthian) elevations (adapted from Frazer 1990, 83, 84, and Wescoat 2018, pl. 108).

outward on the south-facing prostyle porch, while the reverse sides of the normal capitals, which have shadow-catching concave volutes, an unusual heart-and-dart echinus, and at least one metal attachment, were relegated to the interior of the porch with the blank interior angles of the corner capitals. Chiaroscuro effects were less prominent, and it seems that the orientation of the capitals on the Propylon signaled the change of place in crossing between the city and the sanctuary on Delos. The semantic strategy of dividing places with a janiform building evident in the Delian Propylon was more elaborately developed in the contrasting Ionic and Corinthian facades of the Propylon of Ptolemy II on Samothrace.

Chapter 3

Oropos
Stone Carving and an Eye for Shadows

An individual capital from a free-standing column monument discovered near Oropos, from ca. 550 BCE (fig. 3.1), precedes the first bilingual Ionic capitals on Delos. Its design is noncanonical, Ionic in outline, but with the vertically rising volutes characteristic of Aeolic capitals. The pairing of convex and concave surfaces on opposite sides is incipient, carved no deeper than half a centimeter. It shows the early stages of juxtaposing visual textures in Ionic design, which became a perennial technique, particularly in carving lotus and palmette chains. The mixing of surface modeling must be understood in relation to the tools and techniques of stone carvers. Through the carving of a partial replica of one bilingual capital it is possible to regard attendant considerations, including the time and labor involved in the choices made by carvers. Modeled surfaces invite tactile interaction, but they ultimately serve to generate light and shadow effects. The development of shadow-rich modeling in Greek architectural carving runs parallel to developments in chiaroscuro painting and to scientific and philosophical exploration of light, shadow, and visual perception itself.

The Oropos Capital
Predating the first bilingual Ionic capitals from Delos is a capital now displayed in the National Archaeological Museum, Athens (fig. 3.2). It was found reused as the altar of the chapel of Agia Eleousa at Sykamino, near Oropos on the northern periphery of Attica.[1] The plinth cutting on top of the capital shows that it was originally a freestanding pillar serving as a statue base. Ionic columns supporting statues, usually sphinxes or sometimes kouroi, were a fashion of the sixth century, both as ex-voto dedications in sanctuaries and as roadside tomb markers.[2] Reused as spolia in a church near a port, it is difficult to ascertain whether this monument was originally votive or funerary, or even if it had been set up in this vicinity or if it had been brought by sea from elsewhere for reuse.

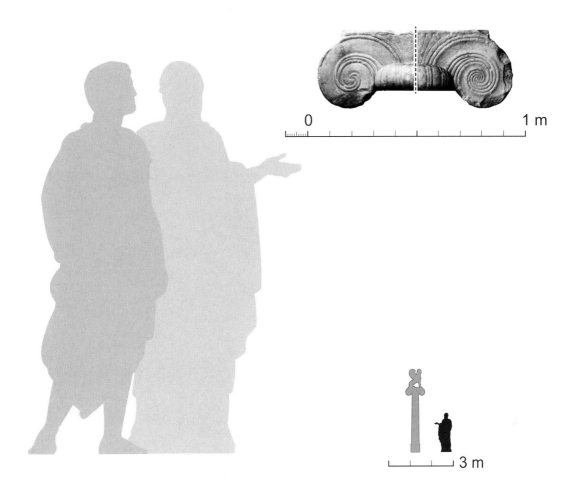

3.1. The Oropos Capital. National Archaeological Museum, Athens.

The lower surface of the capital has a square socket for anchoring the capital to a column shaft. The upper surface has a rectangular cavity and a central mortise hole for securing the plinth of a marble statue with an elongated rectangular plan, most likely a sphinx, though a lion or a figure of a striding Nike or Gorgon could also fit. The lost statue and column shaft were secured to the capital with a bonding system that included a pour channel cut straight through the center of the capital for adding lead to the socket of the lower dowel, a well-known Archaic system.[3] The builders were cautious in assembling the top-heavy monument, using doweling and hidden pour channels to bond the elements of the column and statue together (fig. 3.3). The capital has an orangey-yellow patina, but where the crust has been cracked recently the coarse crystalline structure of white Island marble shines through.[4] The majority of statue dedications set up in Attica in the sixth and fifth centuries were carved from imported Island marble, but their bases were rarely imports too.[5] The exception are Ionic and Aeolic columns used as statue bases, the majority of which are Cycladic marble. Votive columns blurred the line between sculpture and pedestal.

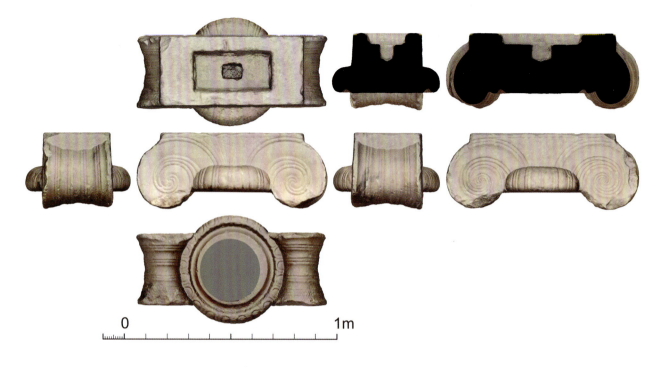

3.2. The Oropos Capital. National Archaeological Museum, Athens.

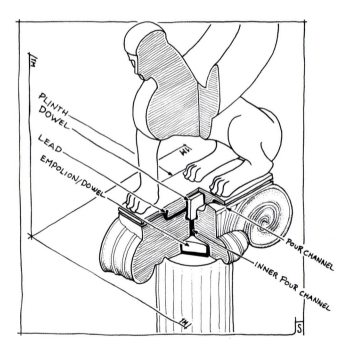

3.3. Schematic reconstruction of the bonding system of the Oropos capital.

The capital's connection to the Cyclades extends further than its material. The proportions of the capital resemble those of the early sixth-century Cyclades: the profile of the echinus is almost a semicircle, and the volutes are set high enough above it that the molding continues in abbreviated fashion under them.[6] The volutes follow the model seen on Aeolic capitals, rising vertically in two coils and divided by a central floral element. Between them is a fan of petals (eight on one side, nine on the other). The bolster sides are wrapped with five shallow flutes set off by fillets and an astragal. At the top of the capital, an incised line marks off a low abacus.[7]

One side has a convex channel, while the other side has a shallow concave profile set off by doughy fillets in the same pattern as the flutes on the bolster. The sculptural modeling of the volutes, however, should not be overstated: their greatest depth is only 0.5 centimeters into the relief plane, with much of the detail executed by shallow inscribed lines. Vitruvius formulated the depth of carving of the volutes of an Ionic capital as one twelfth the width of the volute (3.5.14). By comparison, the depth of carving of the Oropos capital is a trifling one fiftieth part of the volute width. The half rounds on either side of the volute channel double up after the first turn to make a dense whorl of lines at the center. The concave channel ends at a pinched point almost identical to the flanking half rounds, creating a coil of indistinguishable, intertwined tendrils. Where the volute emerges from the echinus, a triangular space is formed. This too is a borrowing from Aeolic capitals where a tapering negative space, either void or uncarved, separates the volute from the column shaft. These interstitial triangles vary greatly, an awkward leftover space after composing each volute with a compass and some liberty.

The capital has relatives in shape, design, and function. It is most similar to a pair of votive columns supporting sphinxes from the Sanctuary of Apollo on Delos (see fig. 2.2, second capital) and a similar example from Paros.[8] These capitals all have the familiar Ionic silhouette, but the volutes, which spring horizontally, do not meet in the middle, instead divided by a lotus flower or palmette. The division of volutes even without a carved filling ornament are also known on Paros and Naxos.[9] The doubling up of the helix around the volute channel predominates in the early sixth-century Cyclades, displayed prominently on the facade of the temple of Dionysos at Yria and the sphinx column dedicated by the Naxians at Delphi.[10] On the grounds that the capital resembles those of the second quarter of the sixth century Cyclades and has an echinus treated with a leaf pattern and drip profile rather than the later egg-and-dart molding, but has more compact proportions seen in later capitals, its date has been placed around 550 BCE.[11]

Although the capital was discovered near Oropos, it cannot be a spoliated votive from the Amphiareion at Oropos. Herodotus (1.49, 52) mentions that Kroisos offered precious gifts to the oracle of Amphiaraos as well as the Delphic oracle prior to his campaign against Cyrus in 547 BCE, and it is tempting to imagine a similar twin of the Naxian sphinx at Delphi set up at Oropos. Excavations at the Amphiareion, however, show no activity at the site prior to the last quarter of the fifth century, confirming the suspicion that the oracle consulted by Kroisos was in Boeotia and not yet at Oropos.[12] The capital could have been taken as spolia for the chapel from Eretria, just across the gulf of Euboea, where there was much sixth-century building

3.4. Hypothetical reconstruction of the Oropos capital as a freestanding monument.

3.5. Alâzeytin, Building 30, reconstruction of door pilasters (drawing after Cavalier and Mora 2011, fig. 8).

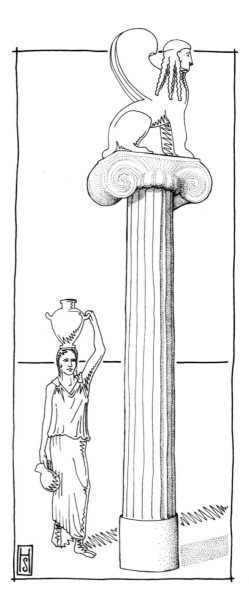

and another bilingual Ionic capital from the early fifth century (discussed in chapter 5). Instead, the column may have served as a tomb-marker for a prominent individual or elite family that lived near Oropos.

Without a known patron or context, one can still hazard some interpretations by viewing the capital in its position, topping a freestanding column and supporting a sphinx (fig. 3.4).[13] This capital is not "transitional" between Aeolic and Ionic, in that it is not a middle ancestor marking the halfway point in a transformation of one capital type into the other. Rather, it is a hybrid that mixes elements from two preexisting, distinct forms. Had the topping-off statue been a zoologically hybrid monster like a sphinx sculpted and painted to differentiate fur, feathers, and flesh, it would match the mixed capital below. The surprise combination of convex carving on one side and concave carving on the other would complement a statue that presents the figure of a woman from the front and something completely different at the rear.

Sphinxes on grave stelai swivel their heads to one side to confront a roadside viewer; sphinxes on Ionic columns set up as votives in sanctuaries (e.g., at Delphi, Delos, Aigina, Kyrene) are more aloof, facing frontally toward the bolster side of the capital. Other bilingual capitals must be considered in relation to hierarchies of building interiors and exteriors. The Oropos capital, however, may represent bilingualism conceived in the round, supporting a statue that ran lengthwise and gave no one side more prominence than the other. This is also the case for Aeolic-style doorframe pilaster capitals from the old Karian site of Alâzeytin on the Bodrum Peninsula not far from ancient Halikarnassos.[14] The volutes of the capitals protruded perpendicular to the facade (fig. 3.5), presenting their convex face toward the door and their concave volutes turned away. In both instances, surface variety seems to be embraced for its own sake without regard to the position of the viewer.

Carving Ionic Capitals

The Oropos capital appears rudimentary in its carving with almost no plasticity, yet all the essential tools for carving Ionic capitals are in evidence. This includes the drill in a simple form, used to tunnel out the pour channel that runs through the capital. It is the facility of technique rather than toolkit that is in progress. The blocky volumes of the Oropos capital invite us to envision the stone roughed out in the quarry as simple geometric solids (fig. 3.6). The slight abacus at the top of the capital offers a hint of the thickness of the protective mantle that surrounded the capital as it was transported from the quarry. Since capitals were carved upside down, this was one of the last parts of the capital to be defined.

3.6. Reconstruction of the stages in carving the Oropos capital from a roughed-out block. Study and drawing by M. Korres.

3.7. Reconstruction of tools used in finishing the convex and concave surfaces of the Oropos capital volutes. Study and drawing by M. Korres.

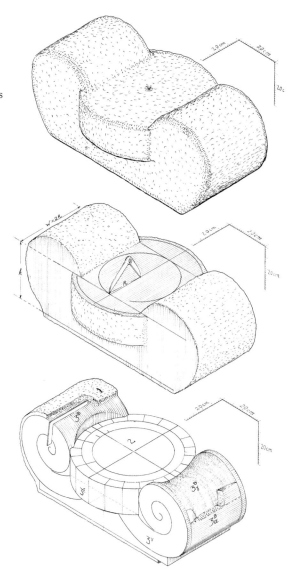

The carver first worked down the flat plane of the relief by removing excess material with a point chisel (fig. 3.7.4) and establishing the relief plane with a wide flat chisel (fig. 3.7.5). The design of the volute and its perimeter were marked out using a compass (fig. 3.7.1). With the perimeter of the volute composed, a marking gauge (fig. 3.7.2) could trace parallel bands on the bolster side of the capital to serve as guides for the pattern of channels and half rounds. The perimeter was worked out with fine flat chisels, first creating V-shaped channels, and then worked down to a curve. The petals at the center of each side of the capital show a switch from scored guidelines to V-shaped channels and then to smoothed forms. Smoothing the volutes may have entailed slightly larger chisels (fig. 3.7.7).

Carving convex and concave surfaces requires different tools. The V-shaped channel, made with a flat chisel in multiple passes to prevent breakage from undercutting, may be the basis for both forms (fig. 3.8).[15] Convex rounds are made by cutting down the sides at successively shallower angles to create a faceted surface that

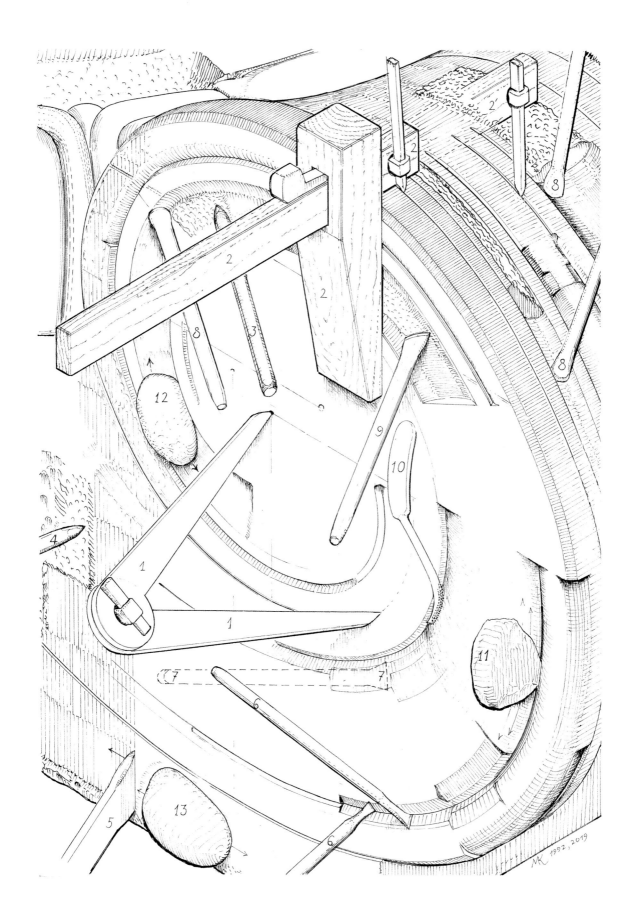

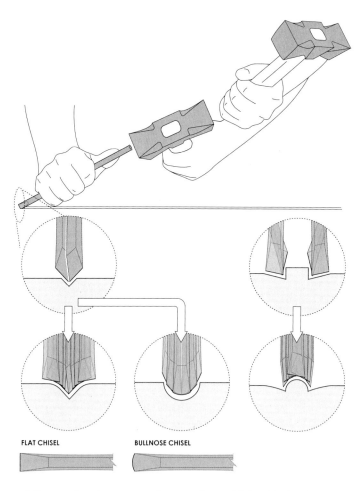

3.8. Process of carving convex and concave forms with flat chisels and bullnose chisels.

can be sanded smooth. The semicircular section of a half-round molding requires preliminary channels with almost vertical walls (fig. 3.8). A concave channel, however, cannot be created with a flat chisel. Instead, bullnose chisels with rounded ends were used, which create the final concave surface. Composite curves require bullnose chisels with different radii, as on the Oropos capital (see fig. 3.7.8, 3.7.9). To smooth the final surfaces, the carver may have used iron rasps (see fig. 3.7.10), but stone itself was always a handy tool, either special hard stones such as emery from Naxos or conveniently shaped marble chips to smooth flat, concave, or convex areas (see fig. 3.7.11, 12, 13). The difference between the convex and concave sides on the Oropos capital do not constitute more and less elaborate versions of the same operation but two branches in a sequence of operations.

From time to time, bilingual capitals have been likened to half-finished capitals, with convex volutes that require removing less marble substituted to save time on less visible sides of capitals.[16] To appreciate convex and concave relief carving as a primarily visual rather than economic choice, it is necessary to reckon with the tools, the greater volume of stone removed from a concave volute, and the differences in process. In addition to quantitative variances in time and labor, stone

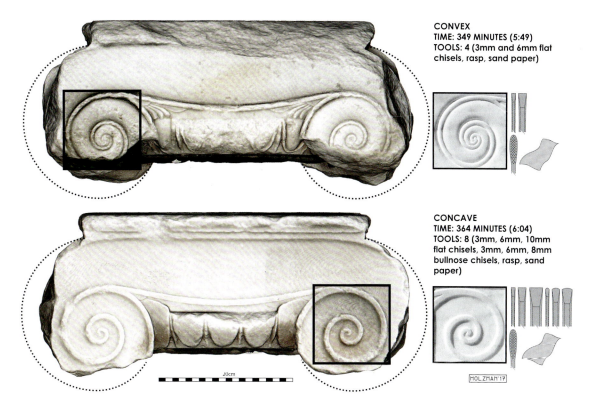

3.9. Marble carving experiment replicating 11 × 11 cm squares of the convex and concave volutes of the Stavro capital. Archaeological Museum of Piraeus [3773].

carvers have qualitative associations about relief carving—is one type of carving more difficult or easy, riskier and more prone to damage, more efficient, or more planning-intensive? Different types of work and technical complexity combine to give carving part of its price. For example, a 1904 mason's handbook listing prices for different types of work suggests similar prices for fluting and for carving convex moldings twice as large (i.e., concave carving was more costly by area).[17] Currently, marble carvers in Athens lettering tombstones by hand charge three times as much to carve relief letters as inscribed letters.[18] Ancient stone carvers undoubtedly attributed values to carving in a similar way.

To estimate the empirical and experiential differences of carving convex and concave volutes, I replicated part of the capital from ancient Pallene (Piraeus Museum 3773, discussed in chapter 5) in a marble carving test. I initially considered carving a replica of the Delos capitals at 1:5 scale, but a mock-up in clay showed the reduced scale thinned the depth of the relief and increased the density of linework to the point that it would not produce useful information.

I apprenticed with Petros Georgopoulos, Giorgos Desypris, and other marble carvers of the Parthenon Restoration Project while I was a volunteer draftsperson for the Acropolis Restoration Service (Υ.Σ.Μ.Α.) in September and October 2017, learning lettering and shallow relief carving.[19] After about twenty hours of stone carving experience, I undertook recreating two 11 × 11 cm square reliefs copying sections of the convex and concave volutes from the Ionic capital from Pallene at full scale (fig. 3.9).

Oropos   85

A slab of fine-grained Pentelic marble was used, oriented to be cut against the side grain, which is one of the inherent challenges of carving all Ionic capitals.[20] It is easiest to carve into the face grain of the stone, which loosely speaking is the horizontal face of the stone as it lies in the quarry. Statues, stelai, and other sculpted works whose only structural responsibility is to stand up, typically are flipped upright in relation to their quarry position (fig. 3.10). Yet stones with load-bearing duties, such as column capitals, are typically oriented in the same axis as they lie in the quarry to maximize strength and reduce the risk of splitting under pressure. Carving against the grain is more difficult work as the varying hardness of the layers can halt the progress of the chisel and cause unpredictable breaks. The end grain of marble can be especially knotty and even more difficult to work than the side grain. In undertaking the experiment, therefore, it seemed essential to replicate the experience of carving the side grain as in a real capital.

I used traditional hand tools made from modern materials (including fine chisels with synthetic diamond points) that cut marble more easily and require less frequent sharpening. An additional challenge to the validity of the experiment was my slow pace of work as a novice. Petros Georgopoulos estimated that the volute segments that took me twelve hours to complete would have taken him only three hours with the same hand tools and only two hours with the aid of a compressed-air hammer.[21] I have no doubt that, like Georgopoulos, an ancient stone carver worked many times faster than I did. The goal of the experiment, however, was not to

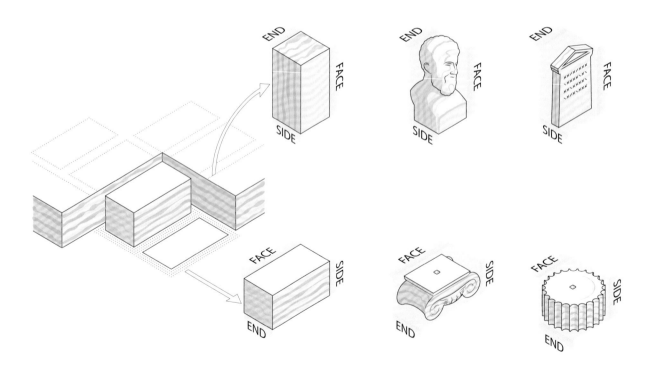

3.10. Typical orientation of stone grain in the quarry, in non-load-bearing carving such as sculpture and stelai, and load-bearing elements, such as column drums and capitals.

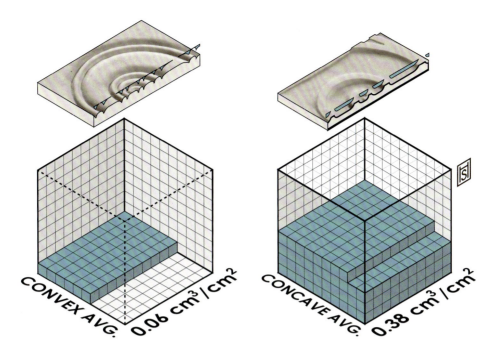

3.11. Average volume of stone removed from the convex and concave volutes of the stone-carving experiment.

determine the exact speed of an ancient stone carver, but to compare relative speed and other differences of convex and concave relief carving. The ratio of work between the convex and concave forms remains a valid datum for understanding ancient capitals because the modern differences (the material of my tools and my slow rate of work) are common factors for both carvings.

I expected that the concave volute would take more time to carve because it entailed cutting away a larger volume of stone (fig. 3.11). Petros Georgopoulos predicted the opposite: the convex volute would be more time consuming because the narrow V-shaped channels separating the convex elements require patience. The result of the experiment was not what either of us predicted. Although the concave volute required removing six times as much volume of stone (on average 0.38 cm^3/cm^2 for concave versus 0.06 cm^3/cm^2 for convex), it only took about 5 percent more time to carve. I spent five hours and forty-nine minutes on the convex side and six hours and four minutes on the concave side. The fifteen-minute difference seems a negligible variation. The convex volute took less time, but at a savings of only about three minutes per hour of work. The experiment suggests that the main parameters affecting carving time are the overall surface area covered, the level of pattern detail, and the maximum depth carved into the stone. Because these three major variables were uniform for the convex and concave volutes of the Pallene capital, the timing was nearly identical despite the sixfold difference of subtracted volume. This conclusion is likely limited to the bilingual capitals that have equal depth and detail on both sides (i.e., Oropos, Delos, Pallene, Eretria, and Selinous). Capitals with greater maximum depth on the concave side (Thessaloniki, Kavala, Delphi, Ephesos) surely had a greater asymmetry in carving times.

Replicating sections of convex and concave volutes took almost the same amount of time despite the difference in volume of stone removed because different tool sets and workflows were used (fig. 3.12). Besides the sanding tools for finishing the final surface, the concave side required three times as many chisels to carve (six flat and bullnose chisels versus just two flat chisels).[22] The concave side would take much more time to carve with only the same number of tools, but only because the work would be artificially inefficient. Stone carving is a physically strenuous task with little room for mistakes, and therefore good stone carvers switch tools and adjust techniques to balance speed and risk for greatest efficiency. The instinctual aspect of the craft is picked up through observation, imitation, and experience in a rote learning process by which an apprentice "steals the art" (κλέβει τέχνη), as modern Greek stone carvers put it.

I offer one anecdotal example of how knowledge about efficient work is learned and communicated among stone carvers. The first tool Petros Georgopoulos taught me to use was the punch (κοπίδι), a tool used to break large chips.[23] When I began using this unassuming tool and discovered that just a few forceful strikes could split a straight line through marble in a hailstorm of stone chips, I started laughing in amazement. Georgopoulos immediately cautioned me with a traditional rhyme of the marble carvers of Tinos: "The punch works wonders, but brings tears" (το κοπίδι κάνει θαύματα, αλλά φέρνει κλάματα). In other words, one mistake with this powerful tool can cause irreparable damage. This aphorism sums up a learned ethic about the careful equilibrium of efficient work and warns about the narrow window of usefulness of certain tools. The punch accomplishes one task in a workflow sequence very well, after which it is necessary to switch to increasingly delicate implements. Although not summed up so concisely in rhymes or even verbalized at all by stone carvers, every tool has a known range of use and roles within different sequences. Robert Sobak has emphasized that in classical Athens, craft (*techne*) was an important paradigm for understanding the acquisition of knowledge more generally. In the dialogues of Plato and Xenophon, Socrates frequently centers craftsmen as models for a discourse on how knowledge is attained.[24] A familiarity with craft techniques guided efficient work on capitals and must underlie many of the choices behind carvings.

The different toolsets for carving convex and concave forms require different workflows (see fig. 3.12.). The convex volute is undertaken with greater patience and attention to the initial v-cuts. Because very little stone is removed in carving the convex volute and there is no room for errors, one must work patiently. A mistake in the curve cannot be erased, so the spiral is first traced carefully with a fine flat chisel before working deeper (see fig. 3.12.*B'*). It is necessary to adjust the curving channels to ensure that the astragalus is of uniform width, but altering the vertical wall of the v-cut channel without chipping the stone by accidental undercutting is slow work (see fig. 3.12.*C'*). On the other hand, the concave volute can be roughed out quickly because the relief will be deeper, and each successive cut erases the one that came before it. The process begins by roughly cutting the spiral pattern with a medium flat chisel (see fig. 3.12.*B"*). Once the curving edges of the concave channel are cut exactly with bull-nosed chisels (see fig. 3.12.*C"*), the excess stone in the cavity

3.12. Stages in the process of carving the convex and concave volutes, with a representative cross section, tools, and time (blue circles represent one hour).

is removed quickly with large flat chisels—the bigger the better (see fig. 3.12.*D"*). Even the final sanding (see fig. 3.12.*E*) differs somewhat. Because all surfaces of the convex volute are rounded, the sanding tools may be rubbed back and forth quickly, irrespective of direction. But on the concave side, in order not to round down the sharp edge of the fillet by sanding against it, the sanding tool can only be dragged out and away from the edge in unidirectional movements (as one would in sharpening the blade of a chisel). The patient sanding of the concave volute therefore takes more time than the convex volute—in my experiment 26 percent more time. It was only at this final phase of work that carving the convex volute caught up and then outpaced the completion of the concave volute. Sanding concave volutes in antiquity was likely made more efficient with purpose-made rounded sanders (sanding jigs), which would add to the growing number of additional tools necessary for a concave volute.

The marble carving exercise demonstrated that although a concave volute does not take much more work to carve, it requires greater technical specialization and an enlarged toolset including bullnose chisels.[25] Sixth-century carvers in Asia Minor who produced only convex capitals did not lack these tools; bullnose chisels were required for carving the flutes on column shafts. Instead, they chose to use concavity sparingly. As the Oropos capital illustrates, a complete toolkit was available. The degree of technical specialization is only one part in a bundle of considerations—including subjective qualities like riskiness, patience required, and the degree of mental pre-visualization of volumes within the unworked marble—that a stone carver and architect weighed in deciding how to carve a capital.

When I began the marble carving experiment, I hoped to quantify the difference between convex and concave volutes as numerical estimates in the budget bottom line or schedule deadline of an ancient building project. But the experiment yielded nearly identical results when it came to assessing timing and labor (fig. 3.13). I removed six times as much stone to form the concave volute segment in almost

3.13. The completed marble carving experiment photographed in direct sunlight.

as much time as the convex volute segment because I used more tools in a different sequence. These separate tool sets and workflows in turn gave each relief its own subjective feeling: the convex volute required patience and the retracing of previous cuts with light blows, while the concave volute gave freedom to work quickly and strike forcefully. The final sanding gave almost the opposite experiences: the surface of the convex volute could be rounded down with rapid and free motions. Preserving the right-angle edges of the concave volute took focused, unidirectional sanding. If carving convex or concave volutes on Ionic capitals were simple, scalar construction tasks like building walls of different dimensions, then estimating the difference in time and labor involved would be a straightforward calculation and a good case study for architectural energetics analysis.[26] Appraising convex and concave relief carving, however, is a more approximate matter. It depends on multiple variables—some empirical, some subjective. The differences in process between convex and concave modeling were also easily interchanged. Approaching architectural forms first as a marble carver is an essential corrective to the tendency to consider the qualities of finished carving as inherently visual.

The Interplay of Convex and Concave in Ornament

The substitution of convex and concave forms was a technique that ancient marble carvers kept "in their back pocket"—in other words, a method not regularly required but always available when the need arose. Sometimes a decorative flourish alternating convex and concave elements could become a distinguishing scheme used by a local stone-carving workshop separate from temples altogether. In carving Ionic ornament, marble workers from time to time alternated convex and concave surfaces, frequently on the petals of floral motifs. The device was sometimes used in places as a solution to design problems, as on the treasury of the Siphnians at Delphi (ca. 525). The lavish sculptural embellishment of the Siphnian treasury included the addition of a relief lotus-and-palmette chain on the soffit of the geison, an area of the Ionic order usually left plain or only painted (fig. 3.14). At the corners, the pattern must stretch to turn the angle, but the carvers made a feature out of the enlarged palmette by switching the convex petals for concave ones, turning a kink in the pattern into a flourish. A similar alteration appears on a molding block from an as yet unidentified temple at the Milesian colony of Apollonia Pontica on the Black Sea coast of Bulgaria (fig. 3.15).[27] The molding terminated at the end of this block, and the pattern was precisely spaced to end between a lotus and a palmette, but the connecting scrollwork had to be cut. Here the switch between convex and concave surfaces was applied to the volutes, producing an effect reminiscent of bilingual capitals. As on the Siphnian treasury geison, the carvers at Apollonia have rebalanced an unavoidable misalignment with a splash of variety.

More often, however, carvers alternated convex and concave surfaces in regular sequences to add textural complexity to palmette friezes. The effect may debut on a necking drum from the temple of Hera at Samos (fig. 3.16), which is picked up by the Erechtheion.[28] The columns of the Erechtheion have necking drums with a carved anthemion, and a corresponding lotus-and-palmette frieze below the crown

3.14. Delphi, Siphnian Treasury, soffit of corner geison block.

molding of the exterior walls (fig. 3.17). The petals have alternating V-shaped and Λ-shaped sections, executed so crisply that it almost appears as if the central petals of the lotuses and palmettes were negative impressions of each other. Flipping convex and concave petals has some underlying basis in botanical observation, since the opposite sides of flower petals and plant leaves (the adaxial and abaxial sides) are often convex and concave or vice versa.[29] A marble palmette acroterion from the Ionic temple of Apollo at Naukratis, which has opposite convex and concave sides, is carved in marble to such an exceptional thinness that it comes quite close to evoking this three-dimensional quality of plants (fig. 3.18).[30] Yet, stone carvers also delighted in mixing convex and concave petals within the same flower element, exhibiting no concern for vegetal verisimilitude.

In sixth-century Ionia, marble stelai topped off with palmettes became the preferred form of grave marker. Most of these anthemion grave stelai had only painted or low-relief palmettes, but on Samos between ca. 560 and 500 there was a local

3.15. Apollonia Pontica, anthemion molding from unknown structure (pictured upside down from original orientation).

3.16. Samos, Polykratean Temple of Hera (Dipteros II), fragment of anthemion necking drum. Archaeological Museum of Pythagorion, Samos.

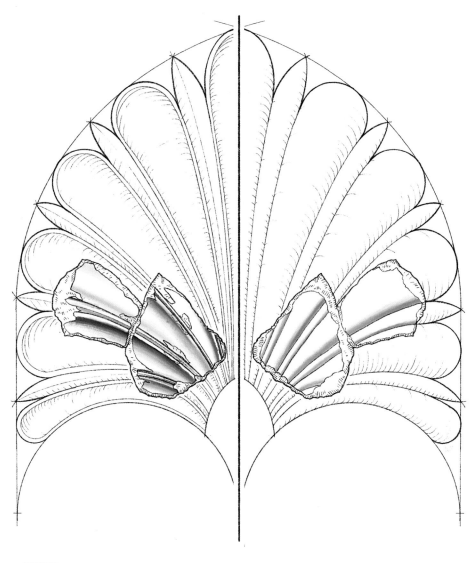

OPPOSITE
3.17. Athens, Erechtheion, anthemion wall crown.

3.18. Naukratis, Temple of Apollo, acroterion fragment with opposite convex and concave sides.

fashion for alternating petals with convex and concave profiles (fig. 3.19).[31] Luisa Balandat suggests that the varied sculptural treatment of the Samian grave stelai allowed for the individualization of tomb-markers that adhered to a single aniconic type.[32] Anton Bammer compared bilingual capitals to these Samian grave stelai, suggesting they were predecessors to "the effect of playing hollow and solid against each other."[33] The localization of the design may signal the trademark of a tombstone workshop on Samos, but it also crossed over to the columns of the Polykratean Temple of Hera, where they appear as corner palmettes on capitals as well as the anthemion necking drums (see fig. 3.16).[34] At the temple of Artemis at Ephesos as well, a single poorly preserved fragment attests to a palmette motif with alternating convex and concave petals in this Samian style (fig. 3.20).[35] It is not possible to reconstruct the position of such a small fragment: Aenne Ohnesorg suggests that it

Oropos 95

3.19. Samos, anthemion grave stele with convex and concave petals, ca. 550–530 BCE. Archaeological Museum of Pythagorion, Samos.

could be an anthemion frieze from the ceiling or roof of the Archaic temple, or that it could be part of an architectonic votive. Variations on the pattern of alternating convex and concave leaves continued to be used in Ionic design into the Hellenistic period, as on the bolster of the Ionic capitals of the Propylon of Ptolemy II on Samothrace. Wilhelm Burger's photograph from Alexander Conze's 1875 excavation publication (fig. 3.21), which was a pioneering work in the use of studio photography for an archaeological publication, is lit so that the convex and concave leaves present near photo-negative inversions of each other.[36] No paint survives on the Samothrace capital, but on the capitals of the Mausoleum at Halikarnassos, the interlaced leaves on the ionic capital bolster are painted in alternating rows of red and blue (see fig. 5.15). The alternation of convex and concave petals on palmettes and even interlaced leaf motifs seems an extension of the phenomenon of alternating light and dark or red and blue painted palmette petals. Here, surface texture achieves a coloristic effect.

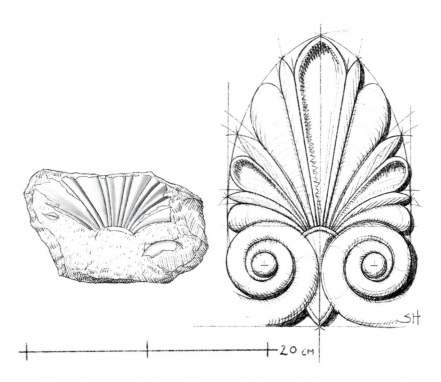

3.20. Ephesos, Archaic temple of Artemis, fragment of palmette with alternating convex and concave petals and sketch reconstruction.

3.21. Samothrace, Propylon of Ptolemy II, photograph of Ionic capital bolster with convex and concave leaves (Conze, Hauser, and Benndorf 1880, pl. 26).

3.22. Athens, Acropolis, Erechtheion, south wall base molding.

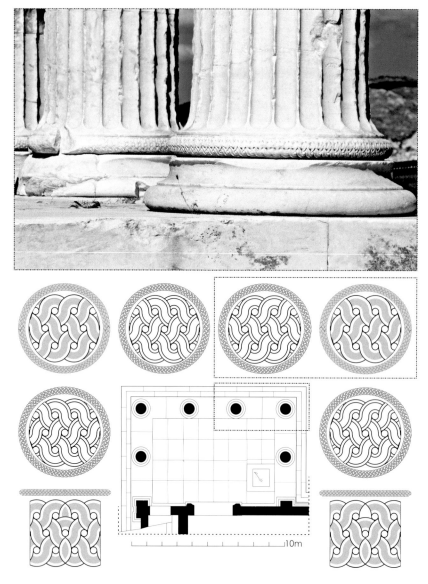

3.23. Athens, Acropolis, Erechtheion, alternating convex and concave guilloche patterns on the bases of the north porch.

The coloristic use of convex and concave surfaces is most pronounced in the Erechtheion, where it is deployed in many details. The south side wall base, which extends below the caryatid porch to the east facade, has an Attic base molding that combines a torus with four concave flutes and a torus with four convex half rounds (fig. 3.22). The scalloped edges of the two profiles are such close inversions of each other that it appears as if the convex and concave outlines might interlock like toothed gears. In the bright south-facing sunlight the two elements perfectly exhibit the shading difference of convex and concave sculptural forms. The column bases on the north porch, which are rarely in direct light, also alternate convex and concave profiles, albeit among adjacent bases. Each base of the north porch has a guilloche molding, but the columns alternate a convex and a concave profile for the knotwork ribbons and the clockwise or counterclockwise directions of the pattern (fig. 3.23). Here the variation in bases may well have been combined with differences in painting and gilding (discussed in chapter 5). The way the Erechtheion's design switches convex and concave surface carving with the freedom of a painter switching colors is a sign of a change in thinking about surface modeling in the Ionic order that was encouraged by bilingual Ionic capitals.

An Eye for Shadows

In *The Stones of Venice* (1851–1853), John Ruskin argued for a broad recategorization of columnar decoration, not classed into orders corresponding to historical and cultural styles but "divided into two great orders; in one of which the ornament is convex, and in the other concave."[37] In the overall silhouette of columns and their capitals, he argued for an expressive power communicating either the weightiness or lightness of a structure. The interplay of convex and concave modeling seen first on the Oropos capital and so many other Ionic ornaments raises an important question: Do we perceive convex and concave versions of the same patterns differently? Henri Mayeux, a professor of decorative arts at the École des Beaux-Arts, sought to elucidate a theory of perceptual effects in his design manual *La Composition Décorative* (1885).[38] For Mayeux, there were universal principles of pleasing design based on perception that could be taught through pairings of good and bad examples (his full compendium of didactic twins has a touch of Goofus and Gallant). He offered a pairing of lunettes, one drawing with sunken spandrels and another with relief spandrels, to illustrate that protruding forms have greater prominence (fig. 3.24). When correctly applied, the judicious use of concavities creates a visual hierarchy that gives definition to the whole form (fig. 3.24 top). Superfluous convexity robs a composition of cohesion and balance (fig. 3.24 bottom). Whether this principle is rightly applicable to ancient viewers or not, the overall trajectory of Ionic capital carving would have pleased Mayeux's sensibilities.

Mayeux's tidy system for good design based on a demonstrable perceptual hierarchy of convex and concave forms, however, found ready challengers among early cubist sculptors.[39] None was more confrontational than Alexander Archipenko. Taking a classical topos in *Woman Combing Her Hair* (1915), for example, Archipenko swaps convex and concave forms, mixing positive and negative shapes to produce

3.24. Henri Mayeux, examples of the correct and incorrect use of convex and concave design elements (Mayeux 1885, fig. 167).

3.25. Alexander Archipenko, *Woman Combing Her Hair*, 1915. Fitzwilliam Museum, Cambridge.

a figure at once fragmented and complete (fig. 3.25). Solids and voids are material antitheses, yet here they become perceptual analogs. Responding to unsettling announcements from the field of physics that categories as distinct as matter and energy were in fact interchangeable, Archipenko, as he put it, sought in sculpture "to liberate matter from its own shape."[40] The cubists were not alone in observing that convex and concave forms play tricks on our eyes, are easily mistaken for their opposite, and in combination produce a fluctuating ambiguity. In late sixth-century Ionia there was evidently a debate about the nature—and shape—of the Moon.[41] Perceiving the volume of the Moon is challenging because its distance subverts the expectations of binocular vision, and the unfiltered light of the sun produces a sharp division between zones in light and shadow with little gradation.[42] Herakleitos of Ephesos theorized that the phases of the Moon and eclipses could be explained if the Moon were a rotating, fire-filled bowl (σκάφη), with a luminous interior gradually occluded by its dark exterior.[43] As short-lived as Herakleitos's theory was, it was premised on the contingency and complications of distinguishing convex and concave forms.

For Vitruvius (1.2.2), it is not the architect's prerogative to make rendered drawings in a painterly way: of the three types of drawing, perspective (*scaenographia*) alone is to be "slightly shaded" (*modice picta*).[44] Yet the terminology of at least one molding, the concave channel of the Attic base called the *scotia* (from σκοτία, darkness), indicates a conception of the modeled surface primarily as the chiaroscuro effect it creates. Vitruvius praises the pleasing chiaroscuro effect of masonry walls with drafted margins (4.4.4), advising that "dressing the blocks so that they protrude around the bed and joints makes them *more painterly* and delightful to see."⁴⁵ Vitruvius's borrowing of the Greek comparative adjective γραφικότερος sets two-dimensional painting as the aesthetic standard by which to judge the shadow lines created by recesses in masonry.

Many features of the Ionic order seem implicitly to exist to create delineating shadows.⁴⁶ Figure 3.26 illustrates this by showing an Ionic colonnade in elevation in two ways: at left, in the conventions of an architectural drawing executed in outline with no shading, and at right only through the shadows that fall on the order with no drawn outlines. Except for the steps up to the colonnade, every element is defined and accentuated by shadow lines: the vertical shadow lines in the column flutes, the horizontal shadow lines of the fasciae of the architrave, the rhythm of the projecting dentils, and the curving shadows within the hollow volutes of the capitals. The shadow lines also mask the faint joint lines between the blocks making up continuous elements: the vertical shadow lines in the flutes conceal the horizontal joints between the column drums, and the horizontal shadow lines along the architrave

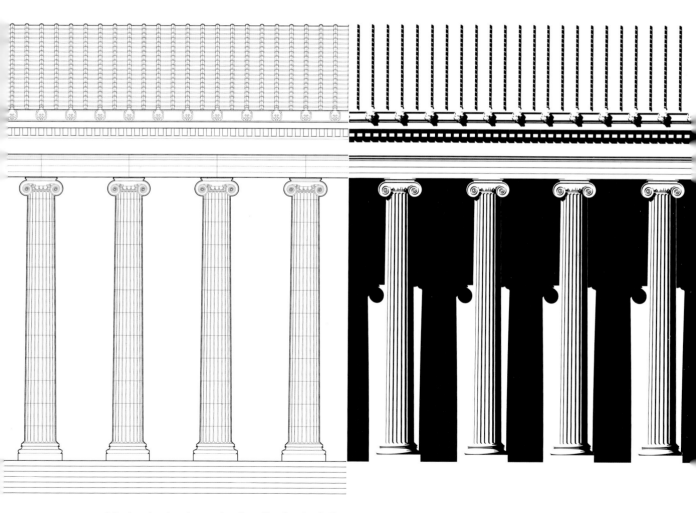

3.26. Ionic order elevation rendered as a line drawing (left) or only in cast shadows (right).

hide the vertical joint lines between the consecutive epistyle blocks. Through projections, setbacks, and sculpted concavities, the order creates shadows that emphasize and camouflage, directing attention to the edges and volumes of compositional elements rather than constituent blocks.

The eye relies on a host of depth cues (perspective, relative size, motion parallax, etc.) in order to perceive space and volume, and shadow gradient is among the most important depth cues for the perception of form.[47] Because flutes exaggerate the shading of a column shaft, they generate an optical illusion: the fluted column is perceived as rounder and more volumetric than a cylindrical column shaft of the same diameter. Vitruvius highlights this optical illusion as a reason for fluting columns. Awareness of this illusion must underlie the popularity of the form. Although fluting is primarily a chiaroscuro effect, Vitruvius searches for a geometric explanation (fig. 3.27):

> This [optical illusion] happens because the eye is compelled to make a longer journey where it encounters more numerous and more frequent stimuli (*plura et crebriora signa*). For if two columns of equal diameter are encircled by lines, and of these columns one is fluted and the other is not, one line makes contact with matter all along the hollows of the channels as well as the edges of the flutes. Thus, even if the columns are equal in diameter, the lines drawn around their perimeters will not be equal.[48]

Vitruvius's explanation that a fluted column appears more massive because it has greater surface area—inspired by the geometric conception of vision theorized in Euclid's *Optics* (ca. 300 BCE)—is jumbled and rather unsatisfactory in offering a geometric solution to a question in the realm of the phenomenology of vision.[49] But Vitruvius's reference to the eye being waylaid by "more numerous and more frequent stimuli" hints at the separate concept of visual fixation and suggests that relief carving makes an architectural element of greater visual interest.

One can see this difference on the half-fluted columns that became popular on stoas beginning in the third century BCE, but the comparison was also visible during the process of construction with some columns fluted and others unfinished (as was permanently the case in the unfinished Temple G at Selinous; see fig. 1.3).[50] Recent research in the neuroscience and psychology of vision has offered phenomenological explanations for the success of other well-known shadow effects in Greek architecture. A 2006 study, for example, showed that it is easier to visually identify objects that have shaded edges, with shadow lines creating "perceptual breaks" and "boundary enhancement" that aid the visual identification of objects.[51] While there is now a scientific grounding for understanding how these visual effects work, the ancient justification for chiaroscuro designs in architecture hinged upon a discourse of aesthetic assessment.

Greek architects developed and experimented with ways to enhance shadow lines and make their designs "more painterly." In a 1918 article, the visual artist and classicist Alfred Winslow Barker argued that Greek architecture preferred convex forms because they recall biological ones, going so far as to present plaster molds of

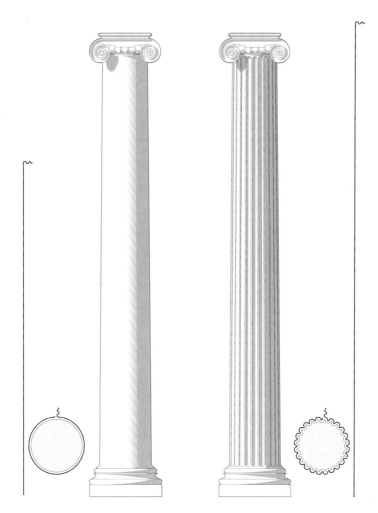

3.27. Columns with and without fluting and the circumferential line described by Vitruvius.

human body parts sliced to resemble the profiles of Greek architectural moldings.[52] Barker's claim that "in the Doric order there are few concave elements, and these are of small extent" holds true of the visually dominant lines.[53] Concave flutes, however, make up the majority of a Doric column's surface; by total area one of the Parthenon's Doric columns is 90 percent concave surfaces.[54] The concavities through shadow lines enhance the circular plan of the column and highlight the bulging entasis of the Doric shaft. The surface of a Doric column is in actuality predominantly concave, so that its *appearance* projects a strong sense of bulging convexity. As Kostas Zambas demonstrated in his methodical 2002 study of the columns of the Parthenon, Greek architects carefully refined the shadows cast in Doric column flutes to maximize chiaroscuro effects.

In the early fifth century, Doric architects began to move away from the early flute profile of a segment of a circle in preference for a segment of an ellipse (fig. 3.28).[55] Here, as often was the case, architecture served as the laboratory for mathematics: Doric builders, including the builders of the pre-Parthenon, were

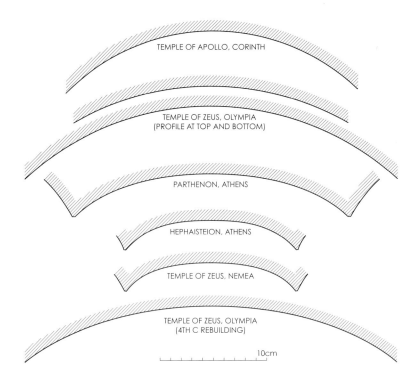

3.28. Doric column flute profiles from the sixth to fourth centuries BCE.

experimenting with applications of ellipses three centuries before Apollonios of Perge set out in writing an abstract explanation of the mathematical properties of ellipses as conic sections. Zambas illustrated the visible payoff of the elliptical profile of the flutes of the Parthenon.[56] If the Parthenon's column flutes had the form of an arc of a circle of equal breadth and depth to the elliptical flutes as built (dotted line in fig. 3.29), only two flutes would ever be in a state of half shadow at one time (fig. 3.29, second from left), and sometimes one lone flute would be in half shadow (fig. 3.29, right), whereas with the elliptical sections, up to three flutes are half in shadow simultaneously (fig. 3.29, left), and a minimum of two flutes are in half shadow (fig. 3.29, second from right). The elliptical profile of the Doric flute has a maximum difference from an arc segment of only 2 millimeters, but the elliptical profile produces a greater variety of shadow effects with more gradation of thick and thin shadow lines. This subtle refinement was executed along the Parthenon's almost nine kilometers of flutes because it made the building more painterly (i.e., γραφικότερος).

The temple of Zeus at Olympia preserves another important development in the shadow design of Doric flutes, recently revealed by Arnd Hennemeyer.[57] Built between ca. 472 and ca. 456 BCE, the early Classical temple has column flutes that follow the profile of a circle with a consistent radius (i.e., at the bottom of the column, the flute profile is an 81 degree arc of a circle with radius 26.8 centimeters, and just below the capital the flute profile is a 60 degree arc of the same circle; see fig. 3.30). As a result, shadows do not pass through the flutes uniformly but fall along a diagonal line as the flutes become deeper at the bottom. At some points during the day, the bottom of a flute may be one quarter in shadow while the top of the same flute has no shadow at all (fig. 3.30, left column, central flute). The temple underwent major renovation ca. 360 BCE, and the columns of the building's facade were rebuilt from a different limestone, but recreating the overall profile and proportions of the old columns.[58] The impetus for this renovation is debated, but the builders used the opportunity to implement fluting of consistent elliptical profile, evidently correcting for what had been judged a naive error of the initial construction.

In the Archaic period, Ionic columns began with a similar form of flutes to Doric columns, but Ionian architects in the late sixth century (perhaps first on Dipteros II of the Heraion on Samos) developed a different method for producing gradient effects. By inserting flat fillets to separate deeper concave flute channels with a half-circle profile, they created twice as many shadow lines as are possible on a Doric column. The change in the profile of the volutes of Ionic capitals from convex to concave was an important early step in the process of refining shadow effects in architecture that also happens in Doric order temples. Vitruvius emphasizes the importance of these features. While he generally glosses over relief designs and notoriously never describes the patterns of moldings, including the egg-and-dart echinus of Ionic capitals, he describes in great detail the profiles of Doric and Ionic column flutes, as well as the depth of relief carving of the channels of an Ionic capital's volutes.[59] These details are essential to his larger didactic mission and the aesthetic considerations of light effects, vision, and chiaroscuro design in architecture.[60]

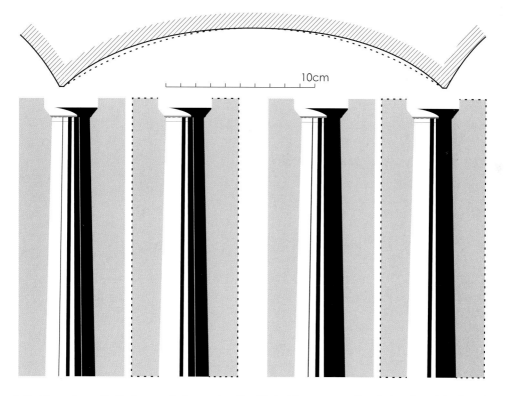

3.29. Athens, Acropolis, Parthenon, shadows cast on the elliptical flutes versus a flute design of equal depth with circle-segment profile (dotted outline). At left: three flutes in half shadow vs. two flutes in half shadow; at right: two flutes in half shadow vs. one flute in half shadow. Redrawn after Zambas 2002, fig. 66.

3.30. Olympia, Temple of Zeus, fifth-century (left) and fourth-century (right) columns with different flute profiles (drawing after Hennemeyer 2011, fig. 9).

Architectural refinements for chiaroscuro effects, such as the development of the concave profile of the Ionic volute or the development of the elliptical profile for the Doric flute, occurred simultaneously with rapid innovation in chiaroscuro painting. In the fifth century, Apollodoros of Athens, who acquired the moniker *Skiagraphos*, pioneered the illusionistic painting of shadows to convey form and pictorial space, a technique called *skiagraphia*.[61] In the early fourth century, Pausias of Sicyon, who was also known as the inventor of illusionistic paintings on ceilings, mastered the imitation of the subtleties of light within areas in shadow, such as reflected light. Pliny (*HN* 35.40) reports that Pausias demonstrated his technique in a virtuosic painting of a bull being led to a sacrifice, in which the bull was pictured frontally foreshortened and almost completely in darkness but with a palpable sense of the animal's mass that Pausias conveyed "by the shadow itself."[62] Pausias's pioneering observations about the subtleties of gradation within shaded areas no doubt inspired architects to think about the subtleties of surface modeling even within shadows. A third-century house at Amphipolis has a room painted with an

3.31. Amphipolis, wall painting, third century BCE, chiaroscuro rendering of an Ionic column with cast shadows in direct light and highlights in shaded area.

Ionic colonnade that employs Pausian chiaroscuro (fig. 3.31).[63] One half of each Ionic column is in direct light with dark shadows in the flutes, while the other half of the column is in shadow with painted highlights showing reflected light. The Amphipolis wall painting is hasty, but seeing how ancient painters depicted shadows and highlights on Ionic columns elucidates the chiaroscuro effects ancient architects may have had in mind when creating these designs.

The close observation and study of shadows was not the domain of artists and architects alone but was also the subject of inquiry on many intellectual fronts and reached a broad audience. In the allegory of the cave (*Resp.* 514a–520a), Plato uses the shadow as a symbol for the limits of human perception. The premise of the allegory, which involves prisoners in a cave who believe that the shadows of puppets are the extent of reality, assumes that the audience is well aware of the behavior of shadows spatially.[64] Plato's description of a shadow-puppet theater—the spatial position of the light source, the puppets, the wall that conceals the shadows of the puppeteers, the wall on which the shadows are cast, and the range of view of the cave's prisoners—depends on a good working knowledge of how shadows are cast. While notional shadows were rhetorically useful as synonyms for ignorance, illusion, falsehood, and powerlessness (including for Vitruvius at 1.1.2), shadows were also a subject of substantial empirical knowledge.[65] Because shadows predictably follow simple geometry that can be diagrammed by reckoning the position of the

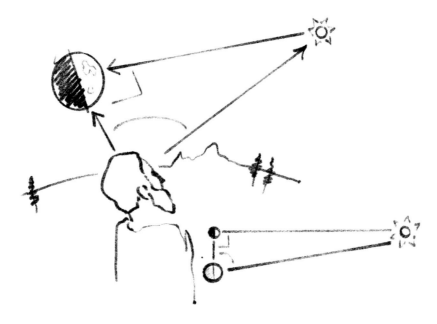

3.32. Sketch diagram of Aristarchos's observation that the half Moon signals a right triangle ("On the Sizes and Distances of the Sun and the Moon" Hypothesis 4) from which the relative distances of the Sun and Moon can be determined.

light source and the standpoint of the viewer, just as Plato sketches out, they were a useful way of investigating light and optics in antiquity with practical applications in fields as diverse as geodesy and horology.

One field that was fundamentally changed by the geometric study of shadows was astronomy. When Anaxagoras of Klazomenai (ca. 500–428 BCE) deduced that the Moon is not self-luminous as was previously thought (including by Thales of Miletos and Herakleitos of Ephesos) but instead reflects the light of the sun, it set off a new era of astronomy that investigated the Moon's phases and lunar eclipses by applying principles of light and shadow observed on terrestrial objects.[66] Aristotle (*Cael.* 298a2–10) is the first to record the observation that the circular shadow cast by the Earth on the Moon during a lunar eclipse implies that the Earth is spherical in shape.[67] Just as the legendary daughter of Boutedes of Corinth traced the shadow of her lover on a wall to create the first painting, Aristotle traced a shadow-portrait of Earth.[68] Aristarchos of Samos (ca. 310–230 BCE) applied astronomical shadow observation in an inventive way in his "On the Sizes and Distances of the Sun and Moon."[69] The half Moon signals that a terrestrial viewer sees the lunar sphere exactly perpendicular to the light of the Sun illuminating it, and Aristarchos deduced that measuring the angle in the sky between the Sun and the half Moon allows for the calculation of the relative distances of the Sun and Moon using an Earth-Moon-Sun right triangle (fig. 3.32). Aristarchos's calculation of the Sun's distance was based on thinking about celestial bodies in the way that a still life painter or an architect constructs the shading on a drawing, by observing how the shadows cast on three-dimensional objects vary depending on the relative position of the viewer and the light source.[70]

The geometric conception of light, shadow, and vision developed in painting, philosophy, and astronomy between the fifth and third centuries undoubtedly informed refinements in chiaroscuro design in architecture. In *Shadows and Enlightenment* (1995), Michael Baxandall showed how an interconnected group of mid-eighteenth-century French scientists and painters simultaneously shaped the understanding and representation of shadows with particular attention to the subtleties of how the hue and edge-definition of shadows convey the qualities of light sources and atmosphere.[71] Baxandall's portrait of a joint venture of scientists and artists investigating shadows is not specific to the Enlightenment; he compared it to joint developments in the understanding of light and shadows in the Renaissance, when polymaths like Leonardo da Vinci worked on both artistic and scientific fronts.[72] The interplay between scientific and artistic investigations of light and shadow in the ancient Greek world was similarly fruitful, and there is every reason to think that ancient architects were familiar with contemporary artistic and scientific breakthroughs. In his lost commentaries on architecture, the fourth-century architect Pytheos insisted that architects should attain a level of expertise in all arts and sciences to compete with those skilled in only one discipline (Vitr. 1.1.12). This was easy for Pytheos to say; as the architect of the Mausoleum at Halikarnassos, the sculptor of its crowning statue group, and the author of a book about the project, he must have had a surplus of talents. Vitruvius offers a more modest version of Pytheos's prescription: architects should have a workable understanding of a range of disciplines, including drawing, sculpture, music, and medicine.[73]

Once painters, astronomers, and architects began to observe the way in which shadows underlie the perception of forms, there was no going back. Cicero (*Academica* 2.7.20), who was interested in the way artists developed specifically attuned senses, remarked on the painterly eye for shadows: "How many things painters see in shadows and in the foreground which we do not see!"[74] The chiaroscuro effect on bilingual Ionic capitals is a sign that ancient architects and stone carvers were developing a "painter's eye" for shadow design.

When viewing the Oropos capital in isolation, pressed up against a wall in the corner of a gallery at the National Archaeological Museum, it is hard to appreciate the creative pairing of its two faces. Envisioned in its original setting, however, it emerges in relation to the tools and techniques of marble carving that became central to the application of chiaroscuro effects in architecture, part of the wide-ranging trials with sculptural treatment in the Ionic order in the sixth-century Cyclades and Ionia. The capital's presentation of shallow convex and concave modeling was to be seen in the round and explores the effects of shading. Sixth-century forays into surface modeling gave texture to and conveyed the volume of architectural members, which in turn established some of the most distinctive elements of the Ionic order: the capital with concave volutes, the Ionic column shafts with semicircular flutes, and the combination of convex torus and concave scotia in column bases. The juxtaposing of convex and concave surfaces was widely used by sculptors of Ionic ornament as a pattern element or coloristic effect, but bilingual Ionic capitals implemented this reversal at a large scale.

Chapter 4

Neapolis and Thessaloniki
Stylistic Pluralism in *Apoikiai*

The largest bilingual Ionic temples were produced in the region of the northern Aegean: one was dedicated to the goddess Parthenos at Neapolis (modern day Kavala), while the other was discovered in Thessaloniki, where it was transported in the Roman period, likely originating in the close-by polis of Therme (fig. 4.1). These temples stand out among monuments with bilingual Ionic capitals because they can be linked with known cults and belong to a specific historical moment, patron deities, and builders. The bilingual Ionic capitals on the temple of Parthenos at ancient Neapolis reflect the character of the unique local goddess, thought to be a syncretism between the Greek goddess Artemis and the Thracian goddess Bendis. Neapolis was a colony that crafted an identity independent from its metropolis through an ancient, aboriginal patron goddess. The temple's bilingual design, contrasting one contemporary face and one archaistic face, embody the self-contradiction of a new city (*nea polis*) with an ancient civic deity.

The temple discovered in Thessaloniki poses more questions. This "itinerant temple" had its blocks numbered, moved, and reassembled during the Roman period. Several hypotheses for the building's origin and new use have been proposed. A close look, however, reveals that the architectural members of the building itself have a story to tell. Traces of layered repairs over damage, most noticeably in the recutting of the volutes of all the bilingual capitals, strongly suggest that the temple collapsed before it was moved and rebuilt. Although the temple may well have come to serve the Imperial cult, its rebuilding in downtown Thessaloniki was first and foremost an act of restoration. The temple's possible original patron deity, Dionysos Thermaios at Therme or Aphrodite Aineias at Aineia, would also appear to have elements of syncretism (Greco-Thracian Dionysos and Greco-Anatolian Aphrodite), or at least prominent claims of an ancient foreign origin that may have inspired the temple's builders to choose a similar design to the temple of Parthenos at Neapolis. Here, too, architecture may have advertised a cult's eclecticism.

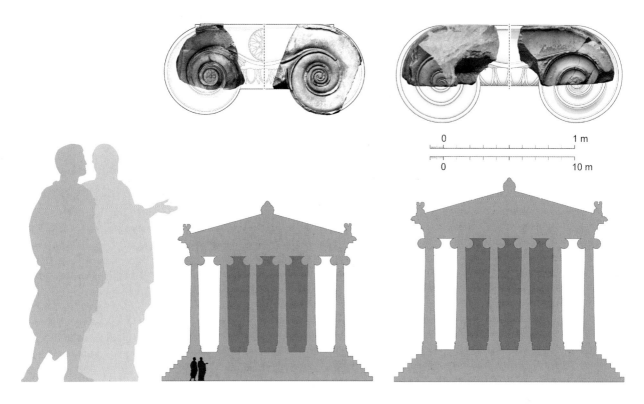

4.1. The bilingual Ionic temples from Neapolis and Thessaloniki.

It should come as no surprise that the largest bilingual Ionic monuments, which combine styles of different periods and regions, crop up at colonies. *Apoikiai*, or colonies, were new settlements that saw inhabitants arrive from throughout the Aegean, and they are important sites where Greekness itself was rethought through interaction with other groups and different religious practices.[1]

There is an unmistakable similarity between the two monuments that has been apparent since their initial publications, both by the archaeologist Giorgos Bakalakis. Although the opposite faces of each capital look strikingly different from each other, the convex and concave sides of the Thessaloniki and Kavala capitals share many similarities. The concave faces are deeply carved, with elaborate rosette patterns for the volute eyes. In contrast, the convex faces are doughy, with helices terminating in whorls—the model of Asia Minor. Their scale is different, and variances in total proportions lead to compositional adjustments in the details.[2] Overall, there is good reason to see workshop connections between the two buildings, as well as to a third fragmentary temple at Stageira, and a cluster of Ionic monuments on the island of Thasos.[3] The original foundations of the Neapolis and Thessaloniki temples have not yet been discovered, so the dating of both buildings rests on the sculptural treatment and proportions of the Ionic capitals.[4] Overall the design of the buildings should be understood as a group, probably as the output of a stone-carving workshop based on Thasos that specialized in Ionic design.

The Neapolis temple has more features canonical to the Ionic order of the Classical period than the Thessaloniki temple, and the conventional dates for the two—Thessaloniki / Therme ca. 500, Neapolis ca. 480—give a good sense of their stylistic sequence. At Kavala, however, there are signs of the long duration of building temples of this scale. Pits found packed with sixth-century votives and banqueting vessels show a major clearing of the Parthenos sanctuary before ca. 500 BCE to make way for the construction of the new temple.[5] The one surviving stylobate block of this structure shows that the finishing of the tread of the top step between the columns—one of the last stages in temple construction—was never completed.[6] Therefore, these dates at the beginning of and two decades into the fifth century must be understood merely as shorthand for projects whose planning and execution stretched on for more than a few years.

The Temple of Parthenos at Neapolis

The ancient city of Neapolis and the temple of its patron goddess, Parthenos, were situated on the rocky promontory at the center of modern-day Kavala. Léon Heuzey and Honoré Daumet, traveling to Kavala in the 1860s, observed an inscription naming the cult of Parthenos and one of the Ionic capitals of the temple.[7] Limited excavations by Bakalakis and Lazaridis within the historic center of Kavala discovered a part of the Parthenos sanctuary, securely marked by a large peribolos wall of marble and granite ashlars and numerous drinking cups marked as the goddess's property with the inscriptions "ΠΑΡ" and "ΠΑΡΘ."[8] They also recovered architectural elements from their excavations and from the walls of Medieval and Ottoman buildings that represent parts of a large late-Archaic temple in the Ionic order: one stylobate block,[9] one fragment of the spira of an Ionic base of Ephesian type,[10] two column drums with the canonical twenty-four flutes and Archaic pointed arrises,[11] seven Ionic capitals,[12] blocks of ovolo moldings representing four different courses,[13] a piece of an Ionic geison with bead-and-reel soffit molding, and the molded lintel of a door or window frame (1.3 meters wide).[14]

Without the discovery of its foundations, the temple's plan and dimensions can only be guessed at from the surviving elements (fig. 4.2). The stylobate block shows the steps had an imposing rise of 30 centimeters.[15] The capitals are the most impressive surviving remains, and their concave faces and overall compact proportions show strong similarities with three Ionic capital types from Thasos.[16] They were each originally about 1.5 meters in length and weighed close to one ton each. The temple is often identified as peripteral on the unwritten logic that the seven surviving capitals are too many for a hexastyle prostyle front. A peripteral plan would put it in the company of the Thessaloniki temple and the Thasian Herakles temple, which are also its siblings in style. It should, however, be cautioned that peripteral Ionic temples were rare in the Archaic period (with only one on Thasos and only one known in the Cyclades).[17] The seven extant columns could also be accommodated on a hexastyle amphiprostyle Ionic temple, like the temple of Athena on the acropolis of Paros and the planned temple of Athena on the acropolis of Thasos, which was only finished to the level of the stylobate.[18] Although Parthenos was a goddess

4.2. Neapolis, Temple of Parthenos, reconstructed columns. Archaeological Museum of Kavala.

of local significance for Neapolis, a hexastyle amphiprostyle temple on the slope of its acropolis would put her in dialogue with cults of Athena overlooking the cities from where Neapolis's settlers had set forth.

    The convex and concave faces of the Ionic capitals of the temple of Parthenos have a pronounced contrast (fig. 4.3). The convex side exhibits relatively shallow carving (one centimeter maximum depth) that lends a doughy softness to the whole. The ropy helix spirals around in four full rotations to terminate in a whorl. The concave side is more deeply carved (5.4 centimeters maximum depth), with a nearly semicircular channel set off by crisp fillets. After two and a half rotations (the canonical number), the helix terminates in a volute eye carved with a rosette (four petals and four darts). Based on the difference in depth of carving, about twenty times the volume of marble was worked away from the concave sides compared with the convex sides. The marble carving test presented in the previous chapter showed that convex and concave volutes of the same design and depth could be carved in the same amount of time despite a sixfold difference in volume of stone removed. The

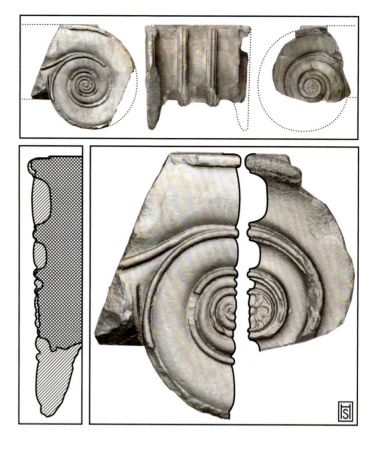

4.3. Neapolis, Temple of Parthenos, bilingual Ionic capital fragment and profile. Archaeological Museum of Kavala.

Kavala capitals, however, must certainly have taken longer to carve on the concave side given the increased depth of carving and the added complexity of the relief with fillets and volute eyes. The contrast of the carved volute eye and convex whorl, however, draws an intentional visual contrast between two different models of an Ionic capital, even if reasons of economy partly underlie the variance. The carvers seem particularly expert in carving deep relief with the use of the drill visible on the echinus. Added to the complexity of the concave sides and the overall contrast between the faces of the capitals are the central relief elements in the forms of a phiale and a rosette.

The capitals from Kavala have high-relief rosettes and a phiale carved in the center of the concave side of each capital. The sides have broken away due to substantial undercutting at left and right (figs. 4.4, 4.5). One capital has a well-preserved relief of a mesomphalos phiale, with a large convex boss at the center and a fan of alternating convex and concave lobes. The rosettes are less well preserved, and though previously reconstructed as simple flowers, a closer look reveals them to have an architectonic aspect (fig. 4.5): the outer petals are a heart-and-dart motif typical of Lesbian cyma, and the inner ring of petals follow the tongue-and-dart pattern known on metal vessels. At the center is a drilled hole for the attachment of a metal finial. The rosette fluidly blends a floral motif drawn from marble carving and metalwork. The phiale also has a blended character, with the concave lobes springing in bunches from sheaths like the corner palmettes of the capitals. The presence

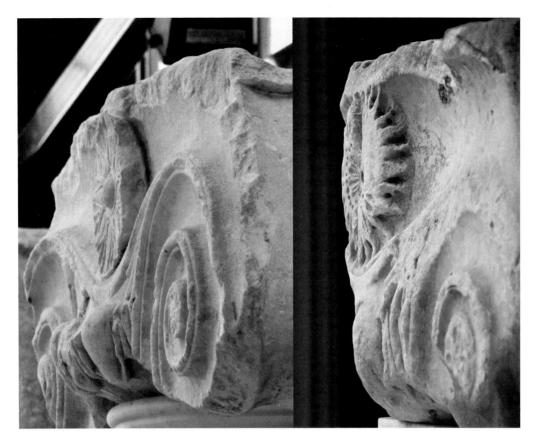

4.4. Neapolis, temple of Parthenos, oblique views of the phiale and rosette ornaments carved on the capitals. Archaeological Museum of Kavala.

4.5. Neapolis, temple of Parthenos, capitals with phiale and rosette carved in concave canalis and convex reverse (redrawn after Bakalakis 1936, figs. 13, 17).

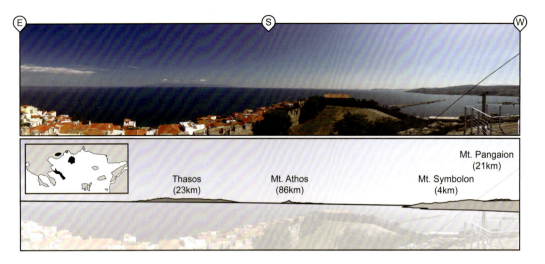

4.6. Kavala, east-west panorama from the Panagia peninsula.

of libation bowls and flowers as relief elements may have a direct bearing on the cult of Parthenos, as both elements appear as attributes of the goddess.

The augmented difference between the faces of the Kavala capitals highlights the importance of determining which side faced in and which out. It seems most likely—and has generally been assumed—that the labor-intensive high-relief concave sides should face out. Against this, however, is the model of the Nieborów capital, which had a metal attachment at the center of the capital on the side facing the inside of the building (see fig. 2.10). Similarly, on the temple at Messon on Lesbos, the capitals of the pronaos and opisthodomos have carved rosettes, while the capitals of the peristasis do not. Until the temple's foundations and more elements of its superstructure are uncovered, a conclusion on the orientation of the capitals should be reserved. Despite these open questions about the temple's design and the capitals' orientation, the building may be contextualized within the political setting of Neapolis and its cult of Parthenos.

"New city" was the quintessential name for a Greek colony, and the Neapolis founded by Thasos was usually identified further as the Neapolis "near Thasos" or "in Thrace" to differentiate it from other new cities with the same name, including two nearby in the Chalidike and in the Propontis.[19] Neapolis was the largest city of the Thasian peraia, the fan of mainland settlements established by Thasos, which was itself a colony of the Parians. Shortly after the arrival of the Parians on Thasos ca. 650, Greek pottery appears at Neapolis, and the other peraia settlements at Antissara and Oisyme.[20] Archilochos, who participated in the Parian expedition to Thasos, alludes to fighting and diplomacy with Thracians on the mainland in his poems.[21] No evidence has been discovered of inhabitation of the Panagia peninsula before the establishment of the colony of Neapolis, but this more likely represents the limited extent of excavation within the Old City of Kavala than the actual absence of Thracian settlement on the coastline.[22] Finds at the Cave of the Nymphs near Oisyme and the Artemision on Thasos show continuity of use of cult sites long before the arrival of Greek settlers.[23] Since the Panagia peninsula was the ideal location for a settlement and the syncretic cult of Parthenos seems to have been active from the city's foundation, a judgment about the absence of Early Iron Age Thracian activity near Kavala and the newness of Neapolis should be reserved.[24]

Unlike the other settlements of the Thasian peraia, Neapolis grew into a prosperous, autonomous city, in large part due to its strategic position. A well-fortified harbor and the nearby pass in the coastal chain of Mt. Symbolon gave the city particular control of traffic between the North Aegean and inland Thrace, particularly the mines on Mt. Pangaion (fig. 4.6).[25] Outside interest in the region of Thrace came from the area's resources: timber for shipbuilding, farmland, and especially silver and gold mines (from which Thasos collected 200–300 talents annually according to Herodotus).[26] An Athenian decree referencing the repayment of a loan of "monies, which belong to Neapolis from her harbor," gives a hint at the port duties the city levied on goods brought in and out of Thrace—and why Thasos, Athens, and the Kingdom of Macedon took a keen interest in controlling the city.[27] Undertaking the construction of the temple of Parthenos at a scale as large as any temple on Thasos signals the city's move toward autonomy and an identity as an independent polis preconditioned by confidence in their financial and political position.[28]

The first quarter of the fifth century, the period in which the Neapolitans built the large Ionic temple with bilingual capitals, was a turning point for Neapolis in its relations with Thasos, at least to judge from the souring relations that followed. In 465 BCE, the Thasians, resentful of Athens's intervention in Thrace and the Thasian peraia, revolted from the Delian League, but the Neapolitans allied with the Athenians, who conquered Thasos in a crushing two-year siege.[29] Thucydides pointed to Athenian meddling in the North Aegean and the siege of Thasos as damning evidence of Athens's turn toward overt imperialism, but Russell Meiggs and G.E.M. de Ste. Croix speculated that the Neapolitans were active partners in this affair, inviting Athenian intervention to distance themselves from Thasos.[30] The Thasians revolted again in 411 and unsuccessfully besieged Neapolis with Peloponnesian aid.[31] When the Athenians finally came to assist the Neapolitans in 409, they besieged and captured Thasos again together. An Athenian inscription (IG 1³ 101) from ca. 410 / 409 honors Neapolis for its alliance with Athens in this conflict. A second decree from ca. 407, which is inscribed on the same stone, affirms a Neapolitan proposal to erase a reference in the first decree calling Neapolis "a colony of Thasos." Not only did the Athenian Assembly approve the erasure and have the offending clause chiseled away, but the Athenians subtly shifted from referring to the Neapolitans "near Thasos" (παρὰ Θάσον) in the first decree to the the Neapolitans "from Thrace" (ἀπὸ Θράικες) in the second. By the closing decades of the fifth century, the Neapolitans had rethought their identity vis-à-vis Thasos and spoke up about how they preferred to be identified. Tensions eased in the early fourth century, when Paros brokered a peace treaty between Thasos and Neapolis and the Thasians decreed that sons born to a Neapolitan father and Thasian mother could be Thasian citizens.[32] How much earlier in the fifth century did this rift between Neapolis and Thasos begin?

It remains unclear exactly when and how quickly Neapolis slipped out of the control of Thasos.[33] Around 525–520 BCE, Neapolis started minting its own coins—decades before coins from any other Thasian colony.[34] Coining money—on the

4.7. Kavala / Neapolis, topographic sketch of the Panagia peninsula today and ca. 480 BCE, showing the likely position of the temple (using Google Earth satellite image).

Thasian weight standard—does not indicate autonomy, but it shows that the city's income and expenses exceeded what could be managed by relying on the mint on Thasos.[35] Chaido Koukouli-Chrysanthaki has suggested that the foundation of a new wave of Thasian colonies in the late sixth century just to the east and west of Neapolis represents Thasos's attempt to hem in an independent Neapolis.[36] The construction of a large marble temple for Parthenos surely represents an important change for the city.[37] The temple was not erected on the top of the acropolis of the city, where it might be expected, but occupied a prominent position on the steep western slope of the Panagia peninsula overlooking the city's harbor (fig. 4.7).[38] Athenian inscriptions mention the temple of Parthenos as the site where inscriptions should be erected and loans could be made, suggesting that besides its religious functions, the temple took on the roles of state archive and bank.[39] Whether the construction of the temple is proof of Neapolitan independence from Thasos, however, is not wholly conclusive: the building itself may rely on large quantities of marble and employed large teams of stone carvers, for which reliance on Thasos was essential. Another

4.8. Coin of Neapolis depicting Parthenos with bowl and flower (redrawn after Friedländer and von Sallet 1889, 103, no. 36).

4.9. Athens, Epigraphic Museum, cast of relief depicting Athena and Parthenos shaking hands (*IG* II² 128). Archaeological Museum of Kavala.

difficulty is the brief interlude of Achaemenid activity in the area. Although Herodotus (6.43–45) does not name Neapolis among the mainland settlements where Thasos hosted the Persian army, the army must have marched through Mt. Symbolon by the Neapolis-Krenides road. The monumentalization of several temples in the early fifth century has been linked to a rebuilding after the Persian Wars.[40] It is uncertain, however, whether the Persian army sacked the sanctuary of Parthenos as it did other Greek cities and sanctuaries.

Parthenos was a poliad goddess, the civic patron of the Neapolitans. When Neapolis began minting coins with a second die rather than an incuse punch, the mint added Parthenos to the reverse, hair tied in a bun, sometimes wearing a wreath, earring, or necklace.[41] A fourth-century bronze issue of Neapolis (fig. 4.8) shows Parthenos wearing a chiton and polos, and holding a libation bowl and a flower—either a poppy or a rose.[42] An Athenian inscription (*IG* II² 128; fig. 4.9), which reiterates the alliance between Neapolis and Athens, is crowned with a relief of the two cities' patron goddesses shaking hands.[43] Parthenos wears a long chiton and polos and clutches something to her chest with her left hand—perhaps a flower. She is represented as smaller than Athena and is set apart from the contrapposto goddess by a rigid posture. The relief and coins signal through the frontal and inflexible pose that they are representations of a cult statue in the form of an Archaic *xoanon*.[44] Finds from excavations within the sanctuary show that Parthenos was honored in typical fashion, with banqueting and dedications, including hundreds of terra-cotta figurines of types known from the sanctuaries of many goddesses in the eastern half of the Aegean. One element of the cult, however, stands out as an oddity: an inscription mentions a space dedicated to the goddess for the storage of meat from sacrifices, a practice at odds with the customary distribution of meat for immediate consumption.[45] The man who would salt and store meat from a sacrifice rather than distributing it for feasting was the ancient archetype of shameless behavior![46] Parthenos remains relatively enigmatic given that she lacks a clear correspondence with a common Olympian goddess. Athena Parthenos and Artemis Parthenos are well-attested divine epithets, but worship of the goddess named only "Parthenos" was less common.[47] The other major instance is in the Crimean Peninsula, where a cult of Parthenos—presumably an incarnation of Artemis Tauropolos—was worshiped in the form of a *xoanon*. Parthenos's role as a civic patron aligns her with Athena, who had major poliad cults on Thasos and Paros.[48] Collart first proposed that the Neapolitan Parthenos was a Hellenized version of the Thracian goddess Bendis, often worshipped in the Greek world as Artemis Tauropolos.[49] The worship of Parthenos at Neapolis may also indicate the port's importance as a hub of connection between the Aegean and Black Sea trade routes.[50]

Parthenos is paradoxical because she is at once largely generic and strikingly individual. The goddess's non-specificity may have been part of her power, embodying the city of Neapolis while being immediately relatable for Thasians, Athenians, and Thracians.[51] If Parthenos does not correspond as plainly to the canonical appearance of Bendis and Artemis Tauropolos adopted in Athens in the fifth century, it is because Greek settlers could often take considerable license in reinterpreting Thracian cult sites. On the acropolis of Thasos, for example, an eighth- or seventh-century Thracian monumental rock-cut tomb—of a type well-known in inland Thrace with associated hero / ancestor cults—was adapted into a shrine for Pan and the nymphs.[52] Syncretic gods take on greater significance as our impression of colonial sites in Thrace shifts to take into account the Thracian perspective—most notably since the discovery of the Pistiros Inscription at Vetren, Bulgaria, in 1990 (*SEG* 49, 911).[53] The Pistiros Inscription (dated ca. 359 BCE) recounts an oath sworn to Dionysos by three Thracian dynasts to uphold the rules established by the previous Thracian king, Kotys I, for hosting the Thasian trading colony Pistiros.[54] The document aims to incentivize trade and establish trust between Greeks and Thracians, including provisions like a promise not to forgive debts owed by Thracians to Greeks that would have given traders confidence in lending money or trading with credit abroad.[55] Dionysos is an unusual god to uphold an oath for Greeks, but there was a well-established equivalence to a Thracian god, sometimes named Sabazios by Greek sources.[56] For example, Herodotus (5.7) reports that the Thracians worshiped only Ares, Dionysos, and Artemis, by which we must understand that the most prominent Thracian gods had these Greek equivalents.[57] The Pistiros inscription shows that an important step for building the mutual trust that supported trading outposts was finding common ground among the gods, with gods like Dionysos and Artemis acting as "trans-cultural mediator."[58] The ability of Parthenos to stand on common ground between Greeks and Thracians may have been a crucial advantage for the Neapolitans during the early period of the settlement.

4.10. An imaginative impression of the cult statue of Parthenos.

The large Ionic temple of Parthenos and its unique column capitals, unusual in their relief decoration even by the noncanonical standards of bilingual Ionic capitals, fit in precisely with the geopolitical situation of Neapolis in the first quarter of the fifth century. As Neapolis gained financial security and autonomy, it centralized the cult of Parthenos as a patron deity, with the cult taking on an important part in civic identity as well as the city's administration. The syncretic goddess Parthenos may have had early importance as a source of common ground between colonists and Thracians, but the reason for her further elevation and centralization lay in her ability to embody civic identity separate from Thasos. A colony's appeal to ancient local history as a strategy for creating independence from a mother city is not without precedent. When Corinth went to war with its colony, Korkyra, Thucydides mentions as an aggravating issue the way the inhabitants of Korkyra boasted of having inherited their naval prowess not from the maritime giant of Corinth but from their island's ancient inhabitants, Homer's Phaeacians (1.25.4). The goddess's cult statue, presumably a *xoanon*, was represented as a small Archaic figure holding a libation bowl and a flower (fig. 4.10). The figure presents the model for the inspired elaboration of the temple's capitals, which seem to advertise the goddess, both with reliefs of her attributes and by embodying her ancient nature in the old Ionian type of convex volute. The temple's design is by no means a repudiation of Thasos—that would come later when the temple's coffers were emptied to fund the Athenian siege of the metropolis in 409. The carved volute eyes, for example, are a particularly Thasian characteristic, and the acquisition of the marble and the skilled carvers depended on Thasos. But the temple seems eager to mix many elements, including the Ephesian type base, the possible peripteral form more common in Ionia (probably preceding the Herakleion's peristasis), which was designed at a scale larger than at any Thasian temple except the unfinished temple of Athena. The bilingual Ionic capitals from Neapolis—though one example in a larger phenomenon—seem precisely positioned for a new city that prioritized an antique goddess with a syncretic aspect as the city turned away from its metropolis.

The Itinerant Temple in Thessaloniki

The second bilingual Ionic temple in the northern Aegean was discovered at the intersection of Karaoli ke Dimitriou ton Kiprion and Antigonidon Plateia in the northwest of the old city of Thessaloniki (fig. 4.11). It was first uncovered briefly in 1936 and then reburied by construction; the 1923 Exchange of Populations necessitated much improvised housing, and the rapid building that followed covered over and destroyed many archaeological remains that had only recently come to light in the aftermath of the great fire of 1917.[59] Giorgos Bakalakis began collecting the architectural elements associated with a large late Archaic Ionic temple that were

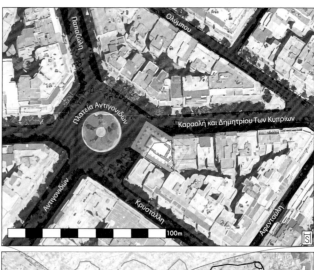

4.11. Thessaloniki, temple site below Antigonidon Plateia (author's map based on Google Earth satellite imagery and Tasia, Lola, and Peltekis 2000, fig. 2).

4.12. Thessaloniki, bilingual Ionic capital in the *kathedra* of the Panagouda church (Bakalakis 1963, pl. 17.4). Archaeological Museum of Thessaloniki [ΚΑΜΜΘ 4].

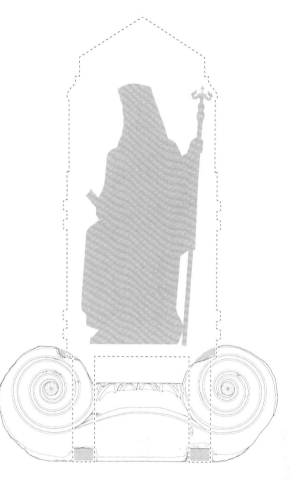

4.13. Detail of cuttings in capital that likely correspond to the chair rails of the *kathedra* of the Panagouda church. Archaeological Museum of Thessaloniki [ΚΑΜΜΘ 4].

scattered around the city. For example, one bilingual capital was removed from the Panagouda church (built 1818), where it formed part of the throne of the bishop, with cuttings that still mark the position of the chair rails (fig. 4.12, 4.13), while a second bilingual capital was recovered in the suburb of Polichni (three kilometers north of the city), where it had been hollowed out and pierced with drainage holes, presumably to serve as an olive press. A rescue excavation at Antigonidon Plateia in 2000 revealed again the southwest flank of the temple's krepis that had been found in 1936, including one Ionic column base in situ.[60] Test trenches dug alongside and within the foundation down to virgin soil (reaching 4.05 meters below the temple's paved floor) brought to light foundations composed of layers of stones and lime mortar that confirmed that the members of the Archaic Ionic temple had been moved and rebuilt at this site in the Roman period.[61] Inscribed letters related to reassembly that are visible on the surviving members collected by Bakalakis had always indicated that the building was moved and reconstructed, thereby explaining the appearance of a building two centuries older than the city of Thessalonikeia.

Rescue excavations carried out in 2010–2012 about 200 meters to the north of the temple site revealed more architectural members.[62] The excavations in the lot of 27–29 Douhioti St. exposed the remains of a grand peristyle square (ca. 23.5 × 22 meters) built in late Antiquity. Although the structure has only been partially unearthed, it was an impressive public space, with a square paved in large slabs of marble, a fountain, and an imposing colonnade on all sides. The colonnade seems to have been made entirely from spoliated columns from the temple at Antigonidon Plateia. The preliminary report on the excavation identifies two column bases, four column drums, and one bilingual Ionic column capital, with dimensions matching those associated with the Archaic Ionic temple reerected at Antigonidon Plateia.[63]

To date, the recovered elements of the temple in the Archaeological Museum of Thessaloniki include a spread of pieces from the krepis to the sima. There are five column base elements: two trochilos drums from a standard Ephesian base, and a third spira drum resembling the Samian-type base of similar proportions, as well as two fluted tori crowned with large bead-and-reel moldings.[64] Two further base elements were recovered at the Doubioti St. excavation.[65] Five column drums with a range of diameters from 80 to 58 centimeters and an assortment of numbers of flutes: one drum of the canonical twenty-four flutes, one twenty-six, two twenty-eight-flute drums, and one thirty.[66] This motley selection would be unusual for a single building, but it is known on many Ionic temples of the Archaic period, such as the temple of Artemis at Ephesos (see fig. 1.6).[67] Four column drums from the rescue excavation at Doubioti St. are all unfluted. There are four Ionic capitals in the Archaeological Museum of Thessaloniki, of which three are bilingual in design; the fourth is slightly smaller, with concave volutes on both sides.[68] This fourth capital certainly belonged to the same building despite the difference in size and design because it bears an inscribed "I" ("10") that puts it in the same series with the two inscribed bilingual capitals, which are inscribed "Δ" ("4") and "IΘ" ("19"). The third bilingual capital was also likely inscribed, but it is now such a small fragment that the inscription is lost. The rescue excavation at Doubioti St. produced an additional bilingual capital, inscribed "KZ" ("26").[69] From the entablature, no architraves survive, but fragments of a large ovolo course belong to the crown molding of the architrave, including both exterior and interior corners. This course combines original as well as archaizing replacement blocks. A low-relief head of a youth has been identified as part of an Ionic frieze, but the size of the fragment does not indicate if it belongs to a building or a sculpted relief. Regardless of whether the entablature had a frieze course or dentil course above the architrave, a second, smaller ovolo course likely represents the molding that crowned this course. One sima block with a lion-head waterspout belongs to the roof.[70] The enclosure of the temple cella is attested by a block of a wall base molding with a large bead-and-reel[71] and one dozen pieces of a doorframe.[72] The sculpting of the doorframe was especially elaborate, with a double ring of moldings, including heart-and-dart, egg-and-dart, and bead-and-reel, as well as a sculpted crown molding above the lintel.

The itinerant temple in Thessaloniki was slightly larger in scale than the Parthenos temple. Although the column and base diameters varied marginally, the bilingual capitals in Thessaloniki were markedly larger—originally ca. 1.8 meters long (1.5 meters at Kavala). The difference is most pronounced in their proportioning, with volutes more widely set in Thessaloniki. This difference in planning

4.14. Thessaloniki, orthographic views of opposite faces of two capitals. Archaeological Museum of Thessaloniki [ΚΑΜΜΘ 3 and 1].

reverberated in the details, with four rather than three eggs on the echinus, and five rather than three petals to the fan-shaped corner palmette (fig. 4.14; and see fig. 4.21). Because the scheme of eggs and darts typically aligned with flutes and arrises of the column shaft, the centered dart in the Thessaloniki capitals may indicate that the columns were set in the noncanonical arris-on-axis manner.[73] Additionally, there are some small stylistic differences from the Kavala capitals: the corner palmettes overlap the echinus, and the volute eyes have alternating pointed and rounded petals rather than a mix of petals and darts. As at Kavala, the convex face has a doughy helix terminating in a whorl rather than a volute eye. The concave face has a half-round helix offset with acute fillets. The volute eyes in Thessaloniki have a more elaborate design of sixteen thin petals, alternating pointed and rounded ends, each with a drilled hole at the center for a metal attachment (similar to the large relief rosette on the Kavala capitals). The difference in the depth of carving between the faces is pronounced, but the difference is not as great as on the Kavala capitals.[74] Some details of the capital like the molding of the echinus are difficult to picture because later repairs have obscured them. The Thessaloniki temple is undoubtedly the senior, with its more ungainly capital proportions and noncanonical features, such as the large numbers of flutes and the dart-on-center echinus design. The overall impression of the two buildings' capitals, however, is of close kinship, including the compositional feature of a gap between the canalis and the echinus (a commonality with early Athenian capitals and the bilingual capitals from Delos).

The capital that is not bilingual in design (*Catalog of Architectural Members of the Museum of Thessaloniki*, ΚΑΜΜΘ 2) associated with the temple is slightly smaller in scale and of a different design. Both faces have concave volutes and volute eyes. It has three eggs on the echinus and three channels on the bolster rather than the four seen on the bilingual capitals, and the helix of the volutes has a flat rather than rounded profile. The corner palmettes and the overall composition, however, are of the same design. The bolster too seems to nod to the bilingual Ionic capitals by interspersing a small concave channel in between the pairs of half rounds. Most

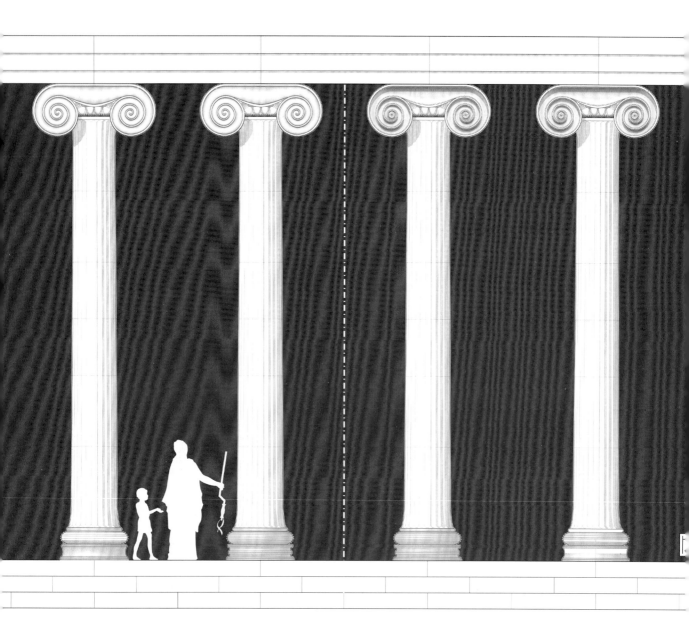

4.15. Thessaloniki, reconstruction of convex and concave faces of columns.

surprisingly, the volute eyes take the form of a plain mesomphalos phiale. The alternation of rosettes and phialai as the eye ornaments for the Thessaloniki capitals would seem to mirror the combination of rosettes and phialai as relief ornaments on the capitals of the temple of Parthenos at Neapolis. The findspot of the capital does not associate it with the temple: it was discovered on the other side of the city.[75] The capital, however, has an inscribed "I," the numeral 10, of the same size and placement as the "Δ" ("4") on ΚΑΜΜΘ 4, the "IΘ" ("19") on ΚΑΜΜΘ 3, and the "KZ" ("26") on the capital from Doubioti St., indicating that it was part of the same building program for the itinerant temple. The uncovered krepis of the temple under Antigonidon Plateia shows that the building—at least in its rebuilt form—had two in-antis columns in the pronaos, and Bakalakis proposed that this capital belongs to a slightly smaller order for the pronaos.[76] The excavation at Antigonidon Plateia revealed the breadth of the temple, which indicates that it had a hexastyle facade, but not the length, leaving the total number of columns in doubt. There were probably at least thirty columns in the outer ring.

The pronaos capital raises a problem in reconstructing the orientation of the bilingual capitals. It has often seemed self-evident that more deeply and elaborately carved concave faces of the bilingual column capitals should face outward to catch greater shadow contrast in direct light. The lower relief of the convex canalis would logically face inward where its rounded surfaces would capture more delicate aspects of chiaroscuro shading from reflected light (fig. 4.15). Additionally, the decision of the later builders to inscribe the letters on the convex sides also suggests that this was not the primary presentation side. But the logic that concave and convex faces correspond to outward- and inward-facing directionality to receive direct and indirect light, respectively, is frustrated by the pronaos capitals, which have two inward-facing sides, which are both concave. It is possible that the bilingual Ionic capitals were consistent and had their convex faces outward. This would place it in the company of the south facade of the Propylon to the Oikos of the Naxians on Delos (chapter 2) and the small Ionic building at Pallene in Attica (chapter 5). If the concave faces were directed inward toward the ornate doorframe of the cella, it would have created a sculptural crescendo. But if the convex faces were directed inward instead, it would have created a space for comparison within the colonnade, where a viewer could see the convex faces of the peristasis capitals and the concave faces of the pronaos columns at the same time. This arrangement would have created an even greater apparent contrast between the two designs.

It seems that the architect and stone carvers who worked on the itinerant temple delighted in eclecticism and contrast as a form of embellishment as much as those at work on the temple of Parthenos at Neapolis. Given the stylistic and formal similarities, many of the same craftspeople may have been involved in both projects.[77] The apparent joy in drawing visual contrasts and doubling embellishments by combining multiple models may also be detected in the temple's elaborate doorframe (fig. 4.16). It outshines even the most decorative doorframes of the Cycladic Ionic tradition, which is also evident on Thasos. There is a primary frame of egg-and-dart and heart-and-dart with two rows of bead-and-reel surrounding the portal, which is a near twin of the doorframe of the temple of Herakles on Thasos—the

4.16. Thessaloniki, detail of doorframe moldings. Archaeological Museum of Thessaloniki [ΚΑΜΜΘ 8].

4.17. Thasos, temple of Herakles, doorframe in situ.

Table 4.1. Proposed Identifications of the Itinerant Temple in Thessaloniki

Original site	Original deity	Second use	Date moved	Advocates
Therme	Dionysos	Imperial cult / Dionysos	reign of Augustus	Bakalakis 1963; Vitti 1996
sanctuary extramural to Therme [continuity of location]	Dionysos	Imperial cult / Dionysos	[continuity of location]	Tiverios 1990; Tasia, Lola, and Peltekis 2000; Boehm 2011; Boehm 2018; Palamidis 2017
Aineia	Aphrodite	Imperial cult, including Venus Genetrix	reign of Augustus	Voutiras 1999; Schmidt-Dounas 2004; Karadedos 2006a; Steimle 2008
_____	_____	Roma and Hadrian as Zeus Eleutherios	reign of Hadrian, specifically 131/132 CE	Stefanidou-Tiveriou 2012
Stageira	Zeus	_____	_____	Sismanidis 2021

main difference being the reversed sequence of moldings (fig. 4.17).[78] Noting the near mirror-image inversion, Jacques des Courtils suggests the two doorframes may be the work of masons working from a shared template.[79] At Thessaloniki, this first frame is then surrounded by a second frame, which is less elaborate (a plain cymation and half rounds) but adds tectonic complexity with mitered joints and intersections with the first frame. A heart-and-dart crown molding topped off the doorway, which was probably flanked by volute consoles, now lost. This door-within-a-door is a *mise-en-abyme* that combines the Cycladic tradition of molded doorframes with the east Ionian doorframe to produce a perspectival effect. The capitals embody this same reflexive attention to form, presenting alternative designs of the Ionic capital drawn from Asia Minor and the Cycladic tradition prominent on Thasos. The interpretation of this structure and its design combining different regional styles ultimately hinges on contextualizing it with its original location and cult.

Several interpretations have so far been offered for the original location of the temple, its original deity, its second use, and the date for its transference (summarized in Table 4.1). The presence of a late Archaic Ionic temple in Thessaloniki is unexpected because it predates the foundation of the city by almost two centuries. Cassander cemented his claim to the Macedonian segment of Alexander's empire by marrying the princess Thessalonike, daughter of Philip II and half-sister of Alexander, in 316 / 315 BCE. The wife that brought Cassander into the Argead Dynasty was an opportune choice for namesake when he founded a new metropolis on the Thermaic Gulf that linked Macedon more closely to the Aegean, Thessalonikeia.[80] Cassander was in part imitating his father-in-law Philip II, who had set the model for city-founding by establishing Philippoi at Krenides in 356 to mark his conquest of Aegean Thrace.

The region of the Thermaic Gulf had been home to the Thracian tribes of Mygdones and Krousaians with numerous Greek colonies and emporia founded along

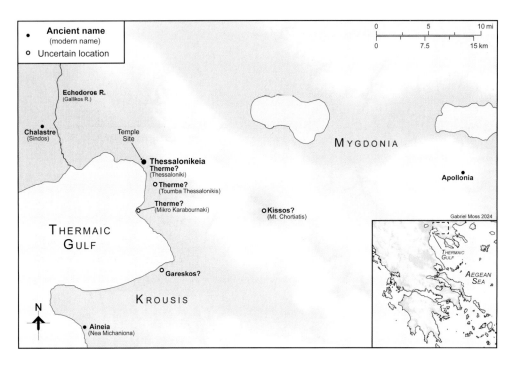

4.18. Map of the Thermaic Gulf and surrounding region.

the coast in the Archaic period (fig. 4.18), and had an early history of colonization similar to that seen in the Thasian peraia. In the fifth century, Hekataios of Miletos called Therme, the most prominent Classical city of the Thermaic Gulf, "a city of Greeks and Thracians."[81] In the Classical period, the area was contested between the spheres of Macedon and the Athenian Empire.[82] According to Strabo, Cassander razed twenty-six cities around the Thermaic Gulf to resettle their populations in the new foundation, although Strabo could only offer the names of six of them: Apollonia, Chalastre, Therme, Gareskos, Aineia, Kissos.[83] Ryan Boehm has recently raised serious doubts about the extent to which Cassander's *synoikismos* physically destroyed twenty-six cities, not least because several returned to prominence shortly after and others were already reported as destroyed in Philip's conquest of Thrace three decades earlier.[84] Apollonia, for example, is named by Demosthenes among the thirty-two cities in Thrace that Philip II destroyed "so ruthlessly that a traveler would find it hard to say whether they had ever been inhabited" (9.26).[85] The foundation of Thessalonikeia profoundly restructured a region of earlier cities, raising several possibilities for the original site of the itinerant temple. Among the Greek cities supposedly destroyed by Cassander, two with prominent cults have been proposed as the Archaic Ionic temple's original site: Therme with the cult of Dionysos Thermaios and Aineia with the cult of Aphrodite Aineias.

Bakalakis first proposed the identification of the temple as that of Dionysos Thermaios. Dionysos, as mentioned previously, was an essential point of syncretism for Greek colonists in Thrace, and Dionysos remained an important god in Thessalonikeia, with one of the city's tribes named Dionysos.[86] The itinerant temple was excavated in a modern neighborhood of Thessaloniki called *Omphalos*, which

Bakalakis suggested might be a corruption of a name of one of the city's ancient neighborhoods, *Phallos*, mentioned by Leo Mathematicus, Bishop of Thessaloniki, in a speech in 842 CE.[87] Phallic altars and votives were a common element of sanctuaries of Dionysos, and Bakalakis suggested that *phalloi* set up at the temple at Antigonidon Plateia may have been the landmark that gave rise to the name of the neighborhood.[88] Bakalakis's argument implicitly requires that the itinerant temple retained its cult connection with Dionysos after it was moved and was not exclusively rededicated for the imperial cult. In contrast, the itinerant temples in the Athenian Agora all show that their Roman-period iterations had only limited connections to their original dedicatees. Cults for Dionysos and Roman leaders could be combined, as in the instance of the temple of Dionysos at Yria on Naxos. Here an Archaic Ionic temple was refurbished in the Roman period, incorporating honors for Antony and then Augustus within the Dionysos cult in the form of a new cult statue of Dionysos with portrait head of the Roman general substituted with one of the first emperor.[89]

An alternative identification of the temple was proposed by Emmanuel Voutiras, who suggested that the itinerant temple belongs to a cult of Aphrodite Aineias from Aineia, which if moved in the time of Augustus, would coincide with pervasive ideology connecting the imperial family with Venus and Aeneas.[90] Although there is certain evidence that the temple was disassembled and rebuilt during the Roman imperial period, little of the speculation about the identification of the date of the building rests on the physical remains. Dating the transportation of the temple to the era of Augustus hinges on the association with the broader phenomenon of itinerant temples, namely the temple of Ares in the Athenian Agora, and the possible association with a temple of Julius Caesar ("Καίσαρος να[ός]") mentioned in an inscription from Thessaloniki dating to the Augustan period.[91] According to legend, the Trojan hero Aeneas established the city of Aineia and its cult of Aphrodite Aineias on the Pallene peninsula that encloses the Thermaic Gulf, while a minority ancient opinion held that the Trojan hero died there without ever traveling to Italy.[92] Though Aineia is reported as one of the cities destroyed by Cassander in the synoecism of Thessalonikeia, the annual festival for the hero Aeneas continued into the Roman period and drew an annual pilgrimage from Thessalonikeia, as described by Livy in the period of Augustus.[93] Cults of Aphrodite Aineias existed elsewhere in the Greek world, at Leukas in Thessaly and on Mt. Eryx in Sicily, although the association with Aeneas was likely enlarged during the Roman period by Greek cities to curry favor—and possibly even avoid taxation—by promoting associations with Rome's Trojan ancestry.[94] Prior to the Roman period, the association of Aphrodite with the wandering Trojan hero might have marked Aphrodite Aineias as a goddess of seafarers, like Aphrodite Euploia or Aphrodite Pelagia. Ludolf Malten, however, proposed that the goddess was a syncretic figure of Anatolian origin that combined Aphrodite with aspects of the Phrygian cult of Mater Idaea.[95] A series of second-century BCE coins of Leukas picture the cult statue of Aphrodite Aineias with eclectic attributes, including an aphlaston (ship's stern ornament), a headdress topped by a crescent moon, and accompanied by a stag and a dove.[96] These admittedly show strong divergence from canonical representations of Aphrodite, but do not prove an Anatolian origin (fig. 4.19). Connecting the temple with either Aphrodite Aineias

4.19. An imaginative impression of the cult statue of Aphrodite Aineias at Leukas from coin images.

or Dionysos Thermaios hinges on the interpretation of the site in Thessaloniki, and answers to the questions of when the temple was moved, if it was rededicated, and how far it seems to have been moved.

The preliminary publications of the 2000 rescue excavation and the architectural members have offered some clues to the questions of when and from where the temple was moved. Before the site was uncovered again, Bakalakis identified the letter forms inscribed on the architectural members, which come in two hands, as dating to the first century BCE.[97] This identification has been treated with some skepticism but never further substantiated or rebutted.[98] The rescue excavation revealed conspicuous signs of rebuilding. The floor pavers are of a much poorer quality of marble than the Archaic architectural members and appear to be completely replaced.[99] Below the six marble steps of the temple, the limestone euthynteria, and a limestone foundation course, the excavators discovered a foundation made of layers of stones and lime mortar. Within the foundations, Tasia, Lola, and Peltekis identified the wall of a previous structure built with limestone and recovered a fragment of an Ionic cymation (ovolo molding) carved from limestone, which they identified as part of an Archaic structure. They argued that the limestone foundation and molding fragment represent an Archaic predecessor to the temple at this very site, and proposed that the temple was not moved far and had long been in this sacred area.[100] Theodosia Stefanidou-Tiveriou has challenged the identification of the unpublished limestone molding, and Christopher Steimle has railed against the circularity of the argument that the temple should be expected in the "Area of Temples," a name coined because of the presence of the Roman-period temple.[101] The original foundations of so large a temple must have been substantial, and no traces have been found in the areas excavated at Antigonidon Plateia.

The Kavala and Thessaloniki temples were not the only marble Ionic structures on the coast with a Thasian connection. At Stageira, a 2006 excavation on the top of the city's northern hill revealed the foundations for a temple, either tetrastyle prostyle or distyle in antis.[102] Diogenes Laertius (5.16) mentions statues of Zeus and Athena set up at Stageira, and either might be the patron deity of the temple. Like the temple in Thessaloniki, it had large courses of ovolo moldings in two sizes, and an anthemion course. Three fragments of flutes reveal shafts with sharp arrises rather than fillets, and fragments of double astragals show bases of the Ephesian type, but most of the elements of the temple are absent. Konstantinos Sismanidis raised the question of whether the temple at Stageira was the source for the architectural members in Thessaloniki.[103] A comparison of dimensions, however, reveals no connection between comparable pieces. The two ovolo courses in Thessaloniki are of different heights (15.5–16 cm; 19.5–20 cm) than the two from Stageira (18 cm; 25 cm).[104] The block of an anthemion molding in Thessaloniki is also of a different height and pattern (18.5 cm tall, seven-petal palmettes) than the pieces from Stageira (21 cm, nine-petal palmettes).[105] The temple at Stageira offers a valuable illustration of the reach of an Ionic architectural workshop from Thasos building temples along the coastline in the late sixth century. It cannot, however, be the origin of the temple in Thessaloniki.

The rescue excavation at Antigonidon Plateia uncovered two fragmentary statues, one Zeus Aigiochos and a Roman emperor in a cuirass. Earlier finds of statues in this neighborhood include depictions of Augustus, Tiberius or Claudius, Hadrian, and an over-life-size female figure identified as Roma.[106] All suggest that the temple featured honors for the emperors, although the accrual of many statues of emperors over time at a major temple is well attested and may not indicate a center for the imperial cult per se. Stefanidou-Tiveriou proposes that the over-life-size statue of Zeus was fitted with a portrait head of Hadrian and together with the figure of Roma formed a pair of cult statues for the temple, depicting Roma and Hadrian as Zeus Eleutherios. In this guise, she proposes, Hadrian was honored for the establishment of the Panhellenion, granting special privileges to Greece in 131 / 132 CE.[107] This pastiche of historicizing figures—the Roma draws on the Lansdowne Amazon associated with Polykleitos and the Mattei Amazon associated with Pheidias while the the languid, youthful Zeus owes much to Lysippos—would certainly match the eclectic combination of Archaic forms in the temple itself.[108] An endeavor, however, to sketch out Stefanidou-Tiveriou's proposal (fig. 4.20) reveals that the Zeus inevitably measures up much shorter than Roma. The mismatch in the scale of the figures, not to mention the differences in their carving, makes it doubtful that they were initially created to be a pair.

4.20. Sketch reconstruction of Stefanidou-Tiveriou's proposal for cult statues of Roma and Hadrian as Zeus Eleutherios showing difference in scale. Archaeological Museum of Thessaloniki.

Stefanidou-Tiveriou's proposal of a Hadrianic rededication also challenges the original identification of the Ionic temple with the cult of Aphrodite Aineias, which is predicated essentially on the ideal propagandistic value of such a temple for Augustus. Schmidt-Dounas (2004), Karadedos (2006a), and Steimle (2008) have tended toward the proposal of Voutiras, that the temple was transported from Aineia to Roman Thessaloniki to serve the imperial cult. When new fieldwork at Karabournaki suggested that ancient Therme was in a suburb to the east of Thessaloniki, Tiverios (1990) amended Bakalakis's theory, identifying the Ionic temple as the cult Dionysos Thermaios and proposing that the temple had originally been extramural to Therme and formed a nucleus for the foundation of Thessalonikeia. This theory was bolstered by Tasia, Lola, and Peltekis (2000) in the preliminary publication of the rescue excavation, where it was argued that the temple was not moved far—a notion largely discredited by Steimle (2008). Boehm (2011, 2018), however, has advanced the proposal that the temple of Dionysos Thermaios was extramural to ancient Therme, suggesting that the regional gathering place "was a powerful symbolic center around which to build the core of the city."[109] The possible continuity of the temple of Dionysos Thermaios within the newly founded Thessalonikeia is a key case study for Boehm, who aims to reframe our impression of Hellenistic synoecisms by setting aside embellished tales, like the one of Cassander razing twenty-six cities in favor of understanding how new cities incentivized emigration. The itinerant temple of Ares in the Athenian Agora presents an essential caveat for overconfidence in identifying the origins of temples on patron alone. For close to a century, the Ares temple was thought to have originally been the temple of Ares from Acharnai. The discovery of the temple's foundations at Pallene, however, showed that the itinerant temple was originally the temple of Athena Pallenis, a structure that had never been considered as a candidate. The search for the identification of the itinerant temple in Thessaloniki may prove to be a wild goose chase until the building's original foundations are excavated. The many arguments about the temple's identification, however, seem to miss one of the key observations to be gleaned from a close inspection of the architectural elements of the temple, particularly the capitals: the Ionic temple had been destroyed before it was rebuilt in the Roman period.

Many of the elements of the itinerant temple exhibit signs of repair as part of the rebuilding—including repairs to substantial damage (fig. 4.21).[110] The extent of the damage and repairs to the architectural elements could be the subject of their own forensic study, but one particular example will serve to illustrate how the layering of breaks and recarving over each other reveals the history of each block. The left convex volute of KAMMΘ 4, for example, has layered cuttings and breaks that allow several historical phases to be distinguished (fig. 4.22). The volute in its current state (fig. 4.22, state) is now mangled to such an extent that it is difficult to picture the original geometrically determined design of the volute (fig. 4.22, reconstruction). A gouged channel on the top of the capital and the bottom of the volute, for example, served as sockets for the struts of the throne of the bishop of Thessaloniki in the Panagouda church (fig. 4.22; and see fig. 4.14). On the reverse of the volute is a set of three small, drilled holes with bronze residue that belonged to a dovetail clamp of a late Archaic or early Classical repair (fig. 4.22c) to earlier damage (fig. 4.22b), which in turn was almost completely cut away by later recarving (fig. 4.22f). Evidently, the perimeter of all of the volutes broke and were recarved within the remains of the broken area, producing the narrow first cycle of the volute. Damage to the volutes of this capital and its echinus, which were subsequently repaired (on the concave side the echinus was completely cut away to make way for a stone patch), indicates that the capital had likely tumbled to the ground. Recarving of the extremities of the volutes and echini appears on all three of the bilingual capitals (fig. 4.23) on both the convex and concave sides. On the convex sides a new helix could be carved into the convex canalis, but on the concave side, the new helix had to be cut back from the relief plane into the bolster of the capital. The carved volute eye patterns on the concave faces had attachments for metal ornaments, some of which were drilled out for replacements.

The inscribed letters on the capitals also reinforce the hypothesis that the capitals had tumbled to the ground before they were repurposed. The capital KAMMΘ 4 is inscribed "∇", which could easily be understood as a slightly off-kilter "Δ," the numeral 4. The capital KAMMΘ 2 is inscribed "I," the numeral 10. But capital KAMMΘ 3 is inscribed "ΘI," which does not form a conventional numeral.

Neapolis and Thessaloniki   135

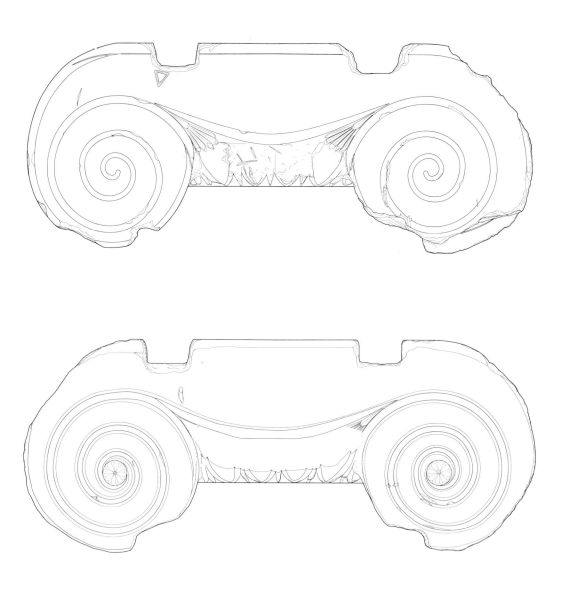

4.21. Thessaloniki, state and reconstruction of convex and concave faces of bilingual capital. Archaeological Museum of Thessaloniki [*KAMMΘ* 4].

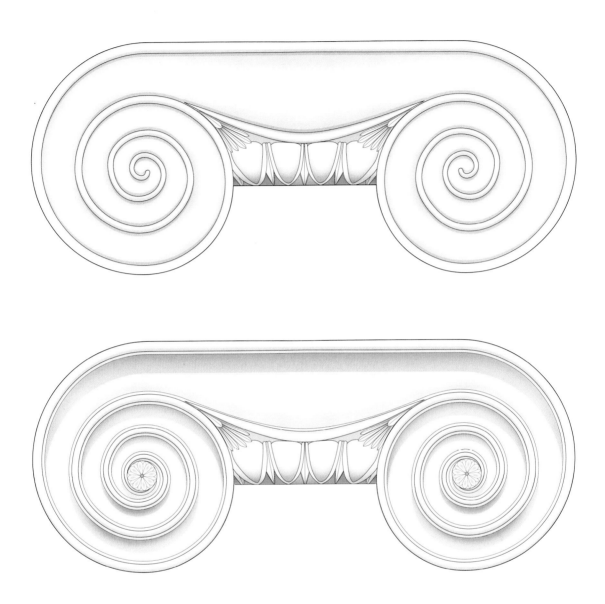

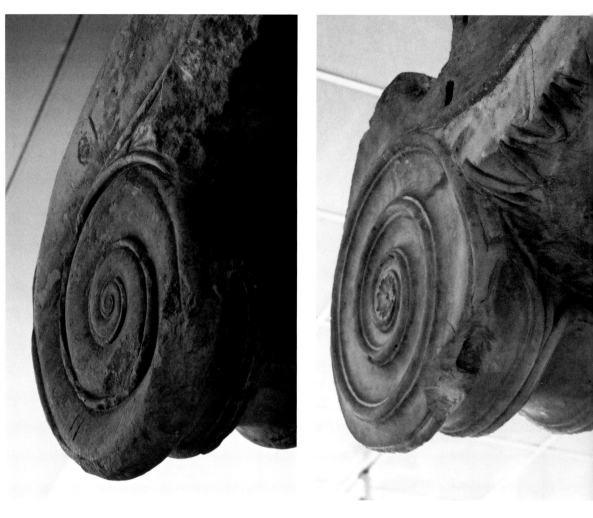

4.23. Thessaloniki, recarved convex and concave volutes. Archaeological Museum of Thessaloniki [*KAMMΘ* 3, 4].

This inscription must instead be read upside down on the right-side-up capital, and should be read as "IΘ," the numeral 19 (see fig. 4.23, left). Once this is observed, it becomes clear that the "∇" on KAMMΘ 4 is also upside-down, and must be read as "Δ," and that even the "I" on KAMMΘ 2 is an upside-down version of the right-side-up letter "I"—though one has no way of telling this (fig. 4.24). The Ionic capital discovered at Doubioti St. also certainly has its "KZ" ("26") inscribed upside down. Other itinerant temples bear disassembly marks that were cut on the blocks before or as they were being taken off the building to aid in disassembly, like the temple of Ares in the Athenian Agora where column drums were carefully labeled "AA, AB, AΓ, [etc.], BA, BB, BΓ, [etc.]," numbering the column and drum as they were taken off the building.[111] It must be recalled that Ionic column capitals, because they cannot be placed with their volutes on the ground without damage, are carved, stored, and transported upside down. Thus, it appears that the bilingual Ionic column capitals were already off the building and had been flipped upside down to rest on their top surfaces to minimize further damage to the volutes when they were numbered.[112]

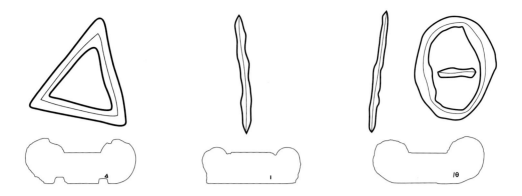

4.24. Numerals on capitals inscribed upside down. Archaeological Museum of Thessaloniki [*KAMMΘ* 2, 3, 4].

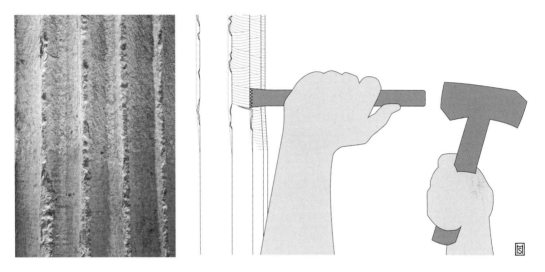

4.25. Thessaloniki, recarved column flutes. Archaeological Museum of Thessaloniki.

The numerals may not correspond to the exact placement of the capitals within the building, but may instead correspond to an accounting of salvageable elements of the building. The pattern of damage and repair to the capitals is also consistent with traces seen on the other members of the building.

There is further evidence of damage to the colonnade on many of the other elements. The spira drum from the column base found in situ has had its top half round completely cut away as if that part had been damaged and could not be repaired. One of the column drums has a cutaway for a patch to the flutes as well as distinct toolmarks within the flutes on the upper half of the drum (fig. 4.25). These indicate that chipped arrises were repaired by carving the flutes to a shallower profile.[113] A few blocks of the ovolo course of the temple are archaistic replicas, detectable by the mannered doughy outline of the eggs (fig. 4.26).[114] These may indicate that some of the original blocks of the entablature were deemed not salvageable. Only one lateral sima block with a lion head waterspout has been identified with the temple, but a number of Roman period lion head waterspouts in the depots of

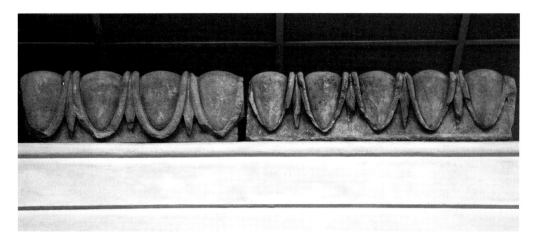

4.26. Thessaloniki, ovolo course, archaistic replacement (left) and late Archaic original (right). Archaeological Museum of Thessaloniki [ΚΑΜΜΘ 21, 12].

the Thessaloniki museum could also be replacement sima blocks that are simply unidentifiable because of their lack of stylistic similarity.[115] The pattern of damage escalates from minor chipping on the column bases and drums to major tumbling damage to all the extremities of the capitals and total damage to some elements of the entablature that left them unsalvageable. The complete replacement of the paving within the cella might also indicate that elements of the superstructure had crashed down and destroyed the original paving. There is little apparent damage to the doorframe, suggesting that the destruction of the temple may have been limited to the peristasis. Some modifications of the building are not repairs but stylistic updates. The tall krepis of six steps would be unusual for a late Archaic Ionic temple, which more often sat low to the ground. A similar update can be seen in other structures: the fourth-century temple of Artemis at Ephesos had a taller krepis than its Archaic predecessor, and the Greater Propylaia at Eleusis replicates the main building of the Propylaia on the Acropolis in most respects, but increases the number of its steps from four to six (see fig. 1.15).[116] The plinths below the column bases (absent in the closely related temples at Neapolis and Thasos) may also be additions. These alterations brought the temple more in line with Hellenistic and Roman tastes, by increasing the building's height, probably by about 10 percent (fig. 4.27). A rough estimate of the volume of the plinth and step blocks puts the minimum amount of new marble at around 400 cubic meters or about 1,000 metric tons. Frugality was hardly the main motivation.

The 2010–2012 rescue excavation at 27–29 Doubioti St. revealed that the columns of this temple were reused more than once. Does the collapse, lettering, and recarving of the columns belong to the Roman rebuilding of the temple or to the construction of the peristyle in late Antiquity? The recarving of the volutes is of a much rougher character than the careful repair work seen in the Augustan-era restoration of the Erechtheion after a fire, where masons inserted stone patches and carefully matched replacement pieces.[117] It is tempting, therefore, to attribute this coarse work to the late Antique phase, but the recarving also seems to coincide

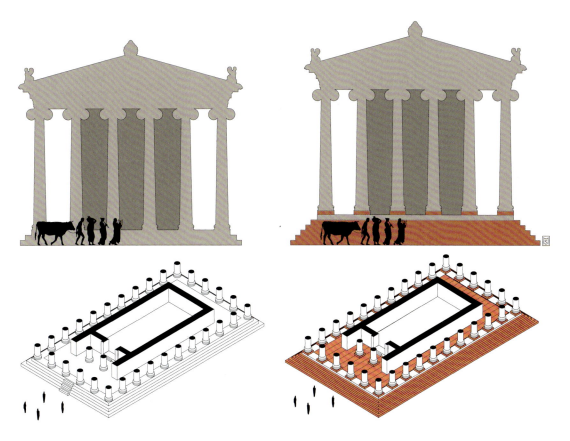

4.27. Schematic sketch of the likely elements of new marble (steps, plinths, paving) highlighted in red, compared to possible appearance ca. 500 BCE.

with the upside-down lettering of the capitals. The column base found still in situ at Antigonidon Plateia also has an inscribed number.[118] Therefore, it seems the blocks were lettered as part of the Roman rebuilding phase. This base also shows signs of recarving (the top bead molding was cut away). Although there are instances in Byzantine architecture of carving new moldings to match ancient spolia, the mannered archaistic style of the replacement piece of ovolo molding (see fig. 4.26) undoubtedly belongs to the Roman rebuilding phase.[119] Furthermore, the numbering of column elements may have been more useful in reassembling the temple colonnade in its original form rather than in the new shape of a peristyle. Bakalakis suggested that the letter forms on the architectural members could be dated to the first century BCE, but such chronological precision seems unlikely based on the rough carving of the letters.[120] Although it is likely that modifications were made in both phases, much of the evidence points to the major alterations to the colonnade belonging to the initial phase of Roman rebuilding.

Though there are many reasons why a temple might collapse, earthquakes or flooding seem likely culprits. Fire, which could knock over columns when roof timbers collapse, leaves obvious scars on marble, which do not appear on the elements of the itinerant temple. It is also difficult to ascertain when the temple collapsed. For Boehm, the itinerant temple in Thessalonikeia is a key example for his more balanced view of Hellenistic synoecism, "with a wider role for continuity, negotiation, and consensus."[121] The possibility that the continuity of a long-standing local religious site might have served as the glue uniting emigrants in a new urban environment is key to Boehm's argument that ancient claims of *ex novo* city foundations populated by razing dozens of neighboring cities should be critically reconsidered in order to return agency to urban populations in their own reorganization and centralization. Boehm is undoubtedly correct that more factors than coercion underlie urban consolidation in the Hellenistic period, but the signs that the colonnade of the Thessaloniki temple had collapsed raise the possibility that the temple may not have been standing at the time of the synoecism.

In its current state, the temple site in Thessaloniki is awkwardly bisected by the roundabout at Antigonidon Plateia and Karaoli-Dimitriou St.[122] It is essential to recall, however, that this square and street are the result of Ernést Hébrard's master plan for the redesigning of Thessaloniki after the fire of 1917, which introduced Beaux-Arts style diagonal boulevards bisecting the old grid (with Karaoli-Dimitriou St. connecting the old Golden Gate and the city hall).[123] Superimposing the location of the temple site on plans of the pre-fire street system shows a more harmonious position within a city block defined by the old street grid, including Antigonidon and Kristalli (fig. 4.28). Although much remains to be learned about the Hellenistic and Roman street grids of Thessalonikeia, it can be deduced that the temple was rebuilt within a one-half or one-third insula unit, positioned far enough to the west to accommodate an altar to the east.

Adding to the complexity of the Thessaloniki temple is the question of whether all the pieces belong to the same original building. Giorgos Karadedos, who oversaw the partial reconstruction of the architectural elements in the Thessaloniki Museum, suggested that the Roman period temple is built from pieces of two different Ionic temples, one from the late sixth century and the other from the early fifth century, that can be detected in the appearance of two different types of column bases in the rebuilt structure—one of the Ephesian type (with two *scotiae*), the other Samian (with one).[124] The variance in numbers of flutes among the attributed drums and the difference in design of the fourth, smaller capital (were it not also numbered like the others) could all contribute to the hypothesis of the recycling of more than one structure. This Samian base, however, has the same dimensions as the Ephesian base fragments and should thus not be used to hypothesize a second structure with exactly the same dimensions. As evident in the bilingual capitals, the designers of the original temple were eager to combine multiple models in juxtaposition. It is on the grounds of scale, however, that one piece attributed to the building does appear mismatched: the lateral sima block with the lion head waterspout.

The lateral sima block with the lion head waterspout can be confidently estimated to have had an original length of 64.4 centimeters (fig. 4.29).[125] The extant intercolumniation of the temple as rebuilt at Antigonidon Plateia is 2.42 meters. The resulting combinations do not align, with four sima blocks overshooting one bay of columns. As a result, water would have poured down from the gutter at irregular intervals in relation to the columns and the passageways between them. It was not uncommon for buildings with mass-produced terra-cotta roof tiles to have a misalignment between columns and gutter tiles, but buildings with bespoke marble roofs usually match.[126] The discrepancy may have arisen from a change in the

4.28. Thessaloniki, position of the temple site within (1) the modern street system, (2) the pre-1917 street system, and (3) the likely Hellenistic-Roman street grid.

interaxial spacing of the columns when the temple was rebuilt due to cracked architraves. The possibility that the sima block comes from a second structure should also be considered. The temple of Herakles on Thasos presents a notable correspondence. The main chamber of the temple was set up around 500 BCE as was a broad podium around the temple. The detached peripteral colonnade was added to the temple at a later date. It has been suggested that the colonnade was added as late as

Neapolis and Thessaloniki 147

the second century BCE, but neither stratified pottery nor the construction technique of the surviving stylobate (the cylindrical stylobate dowel is identical to the Parthenos temple) fix the date.[127] One stylobate block of the temple of Herakles on Thasos survives with dowel holes showing the spacing of the flank columns as 3.22 meters.[128] This corresponds exactly to five units of the sima block from Thessaloniki. This coincidence may simply indicate that the Herakles temple and the Thessaloniki temple were both produced by Thasian workshops relying on a common modular standard (32.2 centimeters, which is close to some ancient foot units).[129] It may, however, be a sign that the sima block in Thessaloniki originated on the Thasian Herakleion and was taken for the rebuilding effort, just as the construction of the temple of Ares in the Athenian Agora combined sima blocks from the temple of Poseidon at Sounion with the superstructure of the temple of Athena at Pallene.[130] Although the absence of major Roman Imperial finds at the sanctuary of Herakles on Thasos would allow for the disuse of the structure, the plundering of one of the island's major classical cults for spare parts would certainly be a humiliation for the island, and this hypothesis must be regarded as speculative until marble provenance of the piece can be conducted. A Thasian provenance, however, would impact the interpretation of the patron of the building project itself. While the Thessalonians alone had it in their power to remove and reconstruct a temple from Therme, commandeering the roof of a temple on Thasos would require overarching power at the scale of the Roman province of Macedonia.

The phenomenon of itinerant temples is best known from the Athenian Agora, where there are at least four buildings that are transported and rebuilt: the Temple of Ares, originally the temple of Athena at Pallene; the Southwest temple, originally the "Stoa" at Thorikos; the Southeast Temple, originally the temple of Athena at Sounion; and an unknown Ionic monument, possibly a propylon (see figs. 5.17–5.19).[131] This density has generated a range of localized explanations. Were the temples moved from the Attic countryside to the city center following changes in population density? Did the changing political nature of the Athenian Agora prompt the creation of an architectural museum through which Athenians promoted their fifth-century history for the cultural capital it brought them in the Roman empire? In a recent article, Elizabeth Baltes suggests that the plan of the Odeion of Agrippa is rotated slightly to respect an earlier monument base, one on which she reconstructs the statues of the Tyrannicides, a small courtesy that she says challenges "the persistent narrative of aggressive Romanization within the Agora."[132] There is a long history of moving and rebuilding older structures on new foundations. At Athens's Dipylon Gate, for example, is a small fountain house with foundations from the third quarter of the fourth century BCE, but with Ionic column bases, and presumably full columns now lost from an early fifth-century building.[133] Is the model of the Athenian Agora applicable in other areas of the Aegean?

The possible connection of a sima block used in the itinerant temple in Thessaloniki with the temple of Herakles on Thasos highlights the close interrelationship of a cluster of Ionic temples in the northern Aegean built in the decades around 500 BCE. It was in the North Aegean that the two largest bilingual Ionic buildings were constructed—largest both in terms of the scale of their capitals and in the number of

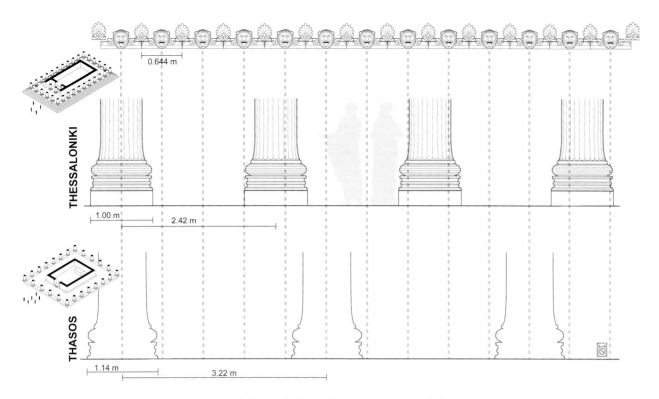

4.29. Thessaloniki, reconstruction of sima block, illustrating the nonalignment of the lion-head waterspouts with the column spacing of the Thessaloniki temple as built at Antigonidon Plateia and alignment with the column spacing of the temple of Herakles, Thasos.

columns used. The capitals of the temple of Parthenos at Neapolis and on the itinerant temple in Thessaloniki highlight the difference between the convex and concave faces by the use of the old east Ionian form of a helix terminating in a whorl for the convex face and a form with a volute eye common in Cycladic and Thasian architecture on the concave face. Both sets of capitals include rosettes and phialai in their relief carving. On the temple of Parthenos these elements mirror the attributes of the goddess specifically. In the case of Neapolis, the choice of one particularly archaistic face on the capitals may reference the antiquity of the goddess Parthenos—depicted in archaistic reliefs and coin types as a *xoanon*—and may have bolstered the nascent independence of the colony from Thasos. The itinerant temple in Thessaloniki is more difficult to identify, but its two candidate cults—Dionysos Thermaios or Aphrodite Aineias—both have syncretic elements that suggest the takeover of a Thracian god or Anatolian goddess, and the builders of this temple might have turned to a strategy akin to that of the Neapolitans. When the temple was moved and rebuilt in Thessaloniki around five centuries later, its bilingual Ionic capitals were preserved, with both sides roughly recarved in their own styles. Elements that had been broken in the apparent destruction of the first temple were replaced with elements in an archaistic style to match the originals, and new cult statues were added that borrowed types from the mid-fifth and fourth centuries BCE. These new elements added another dimension of historicizing pastiche to a building that was already a collage of old and new elements when it was built in the first quarter of the fifth century.

Chapter 5

Athens and Eretria
The Influence of Painting on Stone Carving

In fifth-century Athens, the Ionic order underwent several momentous transformations that are often diametrically opposed. First, the Ionic order was streamlined to a distinctly Attic style that prioritized flat surfaces for painted decoration. Then, there was a turn in the opposite direction, the most sculpturally elaborate relief carving possible. A drive for innovation that utilized the Ionic order in new ways and a retrograde tendency toward archaistic design were also at antipodes. A small Ionic building from the central Attic deme at ancient Pallene has bilingual Ionic capitals that mark an intersection of these trends. One side of each capital has a sculpturally rich, archaistic, convex volute referencing the Archaic east Ionian tradition, while the other side has a du jour plain and painted Attic Ionic type with a shallow concave canalis. A bilingual Ionic capital found at Athens's eastern neighbor Eretria also combines the Attic style with the convex forms of early Ionian architecture and preserves traces of the original painting. The self-contradictory monuments from Pallene and Eretria (fig. 5.1) show how the large-scale trends afoot in Athenian architecture of the Classical period played out in the daily work of marble carvers.

    The capitals from the building at ancient Pallene (represented by the Stavro and Jeraka capitals) have been dated to the Archaic period, but I argue that there are signs for a date in the middle of the fifth century. Polychromy was always a feature of the Ionic order, but in Athens the painting of architectural elements seems to have directly driven the development of forms on Attic Ionic capitals. Ionic polychromy poses a puzzle for bilingual Ionic capitals: did the addition of paint to capitals obscure the pairing of convex and concave carving or highlight the sculptural difference? Signs of painting on the bilingual Ionic capital from Eretria offer the opportunity to examine the impact of painting on the appearance of bilingual capitals that use the Attic style on one side. Although little can be said about the monument that the Eretria capital belonged to—the absence of dowels indicates an architectural

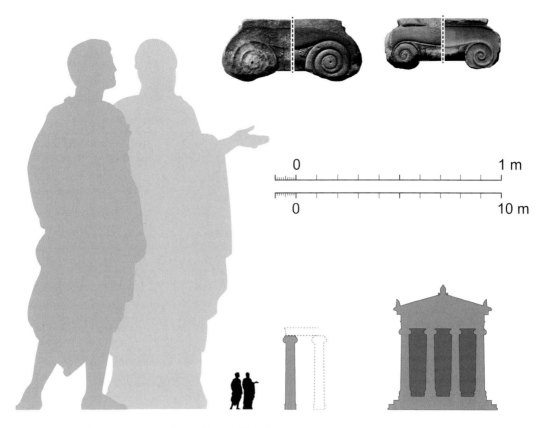

5.1. The bilingual Ionic monuments from Athens and Eretria.

rather than votive application—experimental reconstruction of its painted scheme shows that painting did not obscure the sculptural contrast of bilingual Ionic capitals, but instead highlighted them.

The Ionic Order in Athens

Athens adopted the Ionic order sparingly from the Cyclades and Ionia in the second half of the sixth century, but in the fifth century it made the order its own. Prior to the Persian sack of Athens in 480 BCE, Ionic columns appear primarily as freestanding monuments, either marking graves outside the city walls or supporting dedications on the Acropolis.[1] The most prominent Archaic-period Ionic column in Athens played both roles: a colossal freestanding column on the Acropolis that marked the tomb of Kekrops.[2] Richly carved Ionic moldings had also begun to emerge on grave stelai and altars, such as the Altar of Apollo Pythios dedicated by Peisistratos the Younger in commemoration of his archonship of 522 / 521 (see fig. 5.3).[3] After 480, the Athenians began wholeheartedly making Ionic temples, added Ionic porches to cult buildings, added Ionic friezes and moldings to Doric temples, and used Ionic columns as a second, subsidiary order in Doric buildings to create larger interior spaces with fewer columns and taller ceilings.[4] In short, public and religious buildings in fifth-century Athens that were untouched by the Ionic order are in the minority.

Athens and Eretria   151

5.2. Characteristics of Attic Ionic capitals.

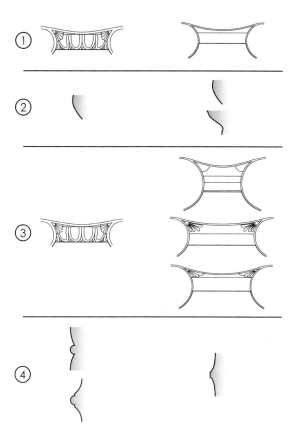

This fifth-century boom in Ionic construction in Athens both reshaped the Ionic order through the invention of enduring forms like the Attic column base and shifted the course of Greek and Roman architecture by showing that multiple orders could be combined to surmount spatial problems in order to create larger interior spaces (e.g., Stoa Poikile), cover sloping ground with multiple floor levels (e.g., the Propylaia), and have colonnades make L-shaped bends to envelop exterior space (e.g., the stoa at Brauron, which uses an Ionic geison to avoid the interior angle conflict).[5] It was no coincidence that Athens was the largest patron of Ionic architecture in the fifth century. The embrace of Ionic building signaled an ethnic affiliation underlying an empire that stretched across the Aegean islands and Ionia, while the extortionate tribute system that fed the Athenian Empire's building habit bankrupted Ionian cities that might otherwise have been building Ionic temples.[6]

Ionic architecture developed in Athens in the late Archaic and early Classical periods with special attention to the application of painted decoration. For example, four distinguishing features of the Athenian type of Ionic capital prioritize smooth surfaces for painted decoration rather than relief carving (fig. 5.2): (1) an echinus with a carved profile but not carved motifs (egg-and-dart or heart-and-dart patterns were painted but infrequently carved); (2) an echinus with a range of profiles, including cyma reversa as well as ovolo profiles; (3) the division of the echinus into two or three tiers to receive multiple stacked painted motifs or at least create a separate background for the corner palmettes; and (4) volute helices defined by a single flat fillet and a low-relief concave canalis rather than the standard half-round astragalus used on capitals with both convex and concave volutes.[7]

This trajectory of Athenian Ionic architecture in the first half of the fifth century toward smooth, planar surfaces for painted decoration rather than intricate carving might seem to come to a dead end in the last quarter of the fifth century with the Erechtheion (built 421–415, 409–404 BCE), representing a complete about-face. The Erechtheion's program of relief carving looks nothing like the flat surfaces of the Sounion Athena temple's marble elements built a few decades prior and seems to be a return to the rich sculptural tradition of late Archaic Ionia (e.g., with necking drums like those of the Samian Heraion) and the Cyclades. While the Erechtheion marked a renewed attention to elaborate relief carving, the Ionic order of the Erechtheion shows the transformations of Athens's century of painting-focused design. The capitals (which retain the two-tier echinus of painted capitals) add cavities for multi-color glass inlays and the building's frieze, composed of white marble appliqués on a background of Eleusinian gray stone, is an elaboration of the figure-ground color contrast pioneered in painting. Bilingual Ionic capitals from Attica and neighboring Eretria, which combine on opposite sides the Athenian early Classical flat-and-painted style and the sculpturally rich convex style of Archaic Ionia, are key examples of coexisting traditions of painting and relief design in architecture that sometimes worked with each other and sometimes worked against each other.

Ionic Polychromy

Color was an essential aspect of the perception of carved stone monuments in ancient Greece. An exceptional coincidence of survival illustrates ancient expectations. Thucydides (6.54) reports that "[an inscription] in the Pythian precinct can still be seen, *though in faded letters*, and is to the following effect:—Peisistratos, the son of Hippias, set up this record of his archonship in the precinct of Apollo Pythias."[8] In 1877, the remains of Peisistratos's altar were rediscovered on the banks of the Ilissos river, and the inscribed letters are as crisp as the day they were carved (fig. 5.3).[9] What Thucydides meant by "faded" (ἀμυδρός) was not the carving of the letters but the painted delineation of them, which had faded between the time the altar was set up and when Thucydides saw it—the better part of a century.[10] Recent experiments of restoring the paint to architectural sculpture have similarly shown that polychromy significantly improves the legibility of figural scenes for viewers.[11] Although the faded state of ancient stonework leaves the impression of its prevailing whiteness, an ancient viewer seeing inscriptions, sculpture, and architecture without painted elaboration would have found them to be incomplete.

The presence of painted decoration on Greek architecture has been noted since the early travelers, and it became a central matter of debate in the nineteenth century.[12] Astute architects documented traces of paint, now often faded, as blocks were uncovered for the first time. For example, the Danish architect, Christian Hansen, painted a color study of the Ionic capital that supported the Nike of Kallimachos (fig. 5.4), one of the votive monuments of the Acropolis destroyed in the Persian sack of 480, when it was newly excavated in 1836. Over time mineral pigments have oxidized, leading to their discoloration, and the organic binding agents have

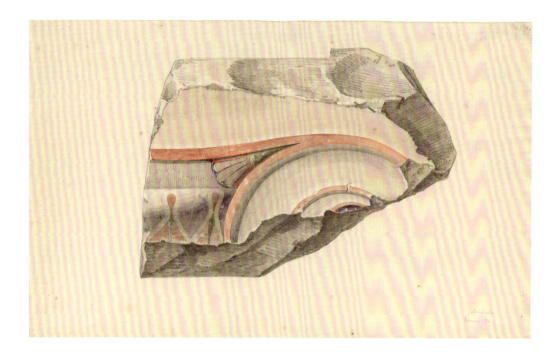

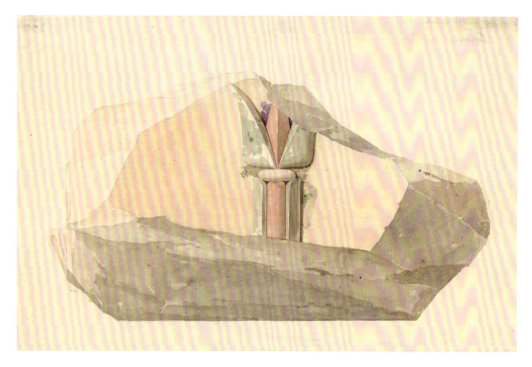

OPPOSITE

5.3. Athens, Altar of Apollo Pythios, dedicated by Peisistratos the younger.

5.4. Christian Hansen, color studies of the capital of the Kallimachos Nike, 1836. Danish National Art Library, Copenhagen.

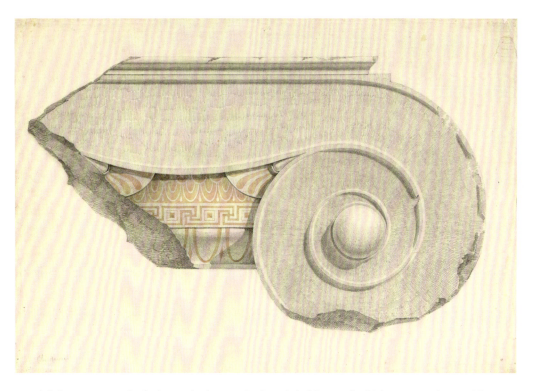

5.5. Christian Hansen, study of color weathering on an Ionic capital of the temple of Athena at Sounion. Danish National Art Library, Copenhagen.

deteriorated. The building accounts for the Erechtheion reference both encaustic painting and tempera painting in the elaboration of that temple, the former used for exterior ornament, the latter used within the colonnade.[13] In the last half century, new scientific techniques have begun to reveal the chemical components of pigments that are now no longer visible and have even detected particles of wax used in the encaustic medium.[14] Even in cases where paint itself does not survive, it is possible to observe the outline of painted patterns due to differences in the weathering of the surface of marble protected by paint, as Christian Hansen did on a capital from the temple of Athena at Sounion (fig. 5.5).

Painting stone architecture differed from painting sculpture and the two-dimensional art of panel painting because it required covering larger surface areas.[15] Therefore, the less expensive pigments of red ochre (extracted from iron oxides and clays) and Egyptian blue (synthesized from silica, copper, and lime) predominate, while more precious colors like green (made from rare green minerals like malachite) were used sparingly and then usually for small details.[16] Carbon black, though an inexpensive pigment, was also used less frequently—mostly as a substitute for dark blue or to outline color patterns. Unlike sculpture in the round, which could be painted completely from head to toe, columnar architecture was painted more sparingly to create contrast between color and exposed marble or white plaster. Some scholars have suggested that despite the range of colors used, the sharp contrast between color and exposed stone is more rightly "bichrome" or "oligochrome" rather than "polychrome."[17] Color was most often applied to crowning decoration

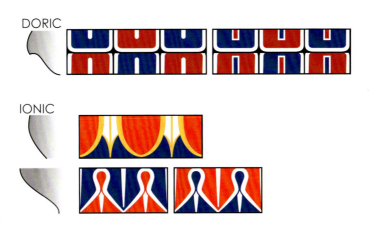

5.6. Figure ground contrast in the painting of Doric and Ionic moldings.

rather than supporting elements, with much paint applied to moldings, the frieze course, cornice, and ceiling coffers, while less or no paint was applied to column shafts, architraves, and steps.[18] This principle might be stretched to apply to the Ionic capital, where the abacus, which crowns the whole capital, and the echinus, which tops off the column shaft, rather than the volutes seem to be the focus of painted decoration.

A second guiding principle in the partial application of color to architecture was figure-ground contrast. The main motifs, carved or not, were left white or painted light colors to stand out against a dark or vividly colored background (as in red-figure vase painting). For example, it was standard in the Doric order to paint mutules and regulae blue as a background for the guttae, which stood out in white. Similarly the leaf motifs painted on moldings, like the Doric leaf pattern on hawksbeak or the egg-and-dart and heart-and-dart motifs added to the Ionic ovolo and cyma moldings, have dark colors like blue, black, and red added to the field and the body of the leaves, while the border of the leaves, central vein, and the darts are left unpainted or lightly colored (fig. 5.6).[19] While both the Doric and Ionic orders follow similar principles of which building elements and pattern motifs were painted, there seems to be a marked difference between Doric and Ionic in the standardization of colors and their application.

Early polychromy studies focused particularly on well preserved Doric temples, such as the Parthenon and the temple of Aphaia at Aigina.[20] Works such as Ludvig Peter Fenger's *Dorische Polychromie* (1886) outlined a painting system for the Doric order. This standardized "color code" consisted of painting the triglyphs, regulae, and mutules completely blue (sometimes black), set off by sharp red lines on the taenia and viae, while the guttae and metopes were left unpainted.[21] The main departures from this scheme occur when sculpted relief decoration was added, with figure-ground contrast trumping the conventional Doric color scheme. Thus, the sculpted metopes of temples such as the Parthenon and the temple of Zeus at Olympia were painted rather than left white. Marie-Christine Hellmann suggested that Doric color coding can be boiled down to an overarching principle,

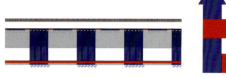

5.7. Hellmann's axial division of Doric polychromy, with dominant vertical blue lines and horizontal red lines.

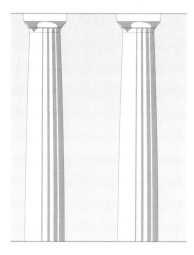

in which dominant vertical lines were blue or blue-black and horizontal lines were red (fig. 5.7).[22] So customary was it to paint triglyphs blue that Vitruvius includes the detail in his origin story for the Doric order (4.2.2), his only explicit reference to specific colors for elements of the columnar orders. Some elements of Doric architecture, especially anta capitals, had richly painted motifs, but color was sparse on columns. Ultimately, the Doric order's blue, red, and white coloring moved with the order when it was repurposed from temples to plastered tomb facades, public buildings, and peristyle houses.[23] There are notable departures from this fixed scheme, but they are better characterized as refinements of the established system than alternatives for the sake of variety.

On Aigina, the early Archaic and late Archaic phases of the temple of Aphaia each use two tones for the triglyphs depending on their position in the temples. The peripteral late Archaic temple of Aphaia has triglyphs on the exterior order frescoed blue-black with carbon black pigment, while the triglyphs over the cella were treated with lighter Egyptian blue pigment. Visualized three-dimensionally (fig. 5.8), it is evident that this tonal adjustment to the hue of architectural elements responds directly to the different lighting conditions of the exposed exterior and the shaded portico.[24] This same adjustment of blue-black outer triglyphs and light blue inner triglyphs had already been used in the early Archaic predecessor to the Aphaia temple.[25] In this structure, a Doric frieze of slightly reduced size ran around all sides of the interior of the prostyle porch. As a result, the entablature above the colonnade had blue-black triglyphs on the outside and lighter blue ones on the inside (fig. 5.9). Here a scheme for altering color to adjust for lighting conditions was under consideration in the first quarter of the sixth century BCE. Further modifications to the Doric color scheme with an eye for lighting effects occur in the fourth century BCE. Temple B at Selinous (ca. 300 BCE) had black pigment added to the cuttings of the

5.8. Aigina, late Archaic temple of Aphaia, reconstruction showing dark triglyphs (painted with carbon black) over the peristyle and lighter triglyphs (painted with Egyptian blue) over the cella. Digital rendering by Valentina Hinz and Stefan Franz according to the study of Hansgeorg Bankel.

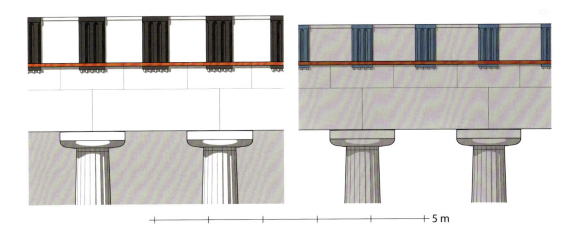

5.9. Aigina, early Archaic temple of Aphaia, reconstruction showing dark triglyphs (painted with carbon black) over the porch and lighter triglyphs (painted with Egyptian blue) within.

Athens and Eretria

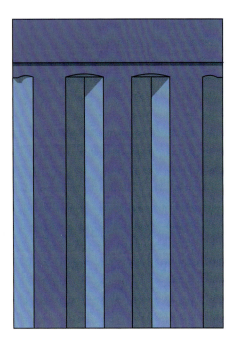 

5.10. Two-tone triglyph paint schemes from the tomb at Starosel, ca. 340 BCE, and Temple B, Selinous, ca. 300 BCE.

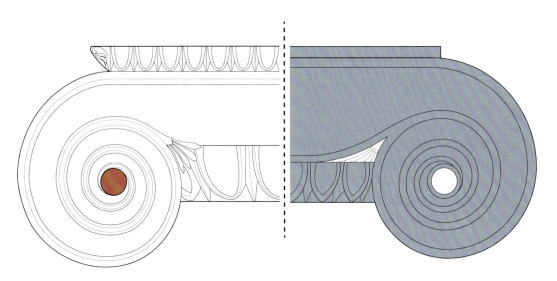

5.11. Stone inlays used to opposite coloristic effects on capitals from the temple at Messon, Lesbos (left) and the temple at Emporio, Chios (right).

triglyph to exaggerate the chiaroscuro modeling, while the triglyphs of the Starosel tomb in Thrace (ca. 340 BCE) have a lighter blue shade applied instead (fig. 5.10).[26] These nearly opposite applications of painted shadows and highlights are both attempts to counteract how the inherited tradition of painting the whole triglyph blue flattened its carving and frustrated perception (an effect explored for different ends by artists like Yves Klein and Anish Kapoor). Evidently, some ancient builders chafed at the limitations this Doric tradition imposed, but they sought out small improvements within the formalized system rather than alternatives to it. The evidence from the Ionic order is strikingly different.

Traces of paint on Ionic buildings show some similarities to painting in Doric architecture, particularly the predominance of red and blue pigments in sharp contrast to reserved areas, and the use of figure-ground contrast on moldings. General studies often present a homogenizing consensus view that "[Ionic polychromy] was not fundamentally different from Doric polychromy, despite the more complex Ionic ornamentation," or that "the same [Doric] principles hold sway in the Ionic order, even on the many zones with moldings."[27] Little in the Ionic order, however, comes close to the standardization of color coding seen in Doric architecture. It often appears that the Ionic evidence is more fragmentary because the wide variety makes it difficult to fill in the gaps based on other examples. Although the evidence is fragmentary, there are good reasons to conclude that color was sometimes used in a strikingly different way on Ionic temples than on Doric ones, and this elaboration begins with the capitals.

The adornment of Ionic column capitals includes embellishments more often seen in sculpture than on other architectural elements. Learning from the acrolithic and pseudoacrolithic sculpture that pieced statues together from multiple stone elements and other materials, some Ionic capitals combined different colored stones for chromatic effects. For example, the temple at Messon, Lesbos, had rosy volcanic stone inlays for the volute eyes on capitals of white limestone, while capitals from Chios have white marble inlays for the volute eyes and corner palmettes set into capitals of local blue-gray stone (fig. 5.11).[28] Innumerable columns have traces of metal pins for attachments to the volute eyes (including the bilingual capitals from Therme / Thessaloniki, Eretria, and Delphi), but the metal attachments never survive. One exceptional case of survival on one capital from the temple of Leto at Xanthos reveals traces of crumpled bronze petals around the volute eye (fig. 5.12).[29] This use of a thin metal gasket to embellish the volute eyes at Xanthos (fig. 5.13) borrows the technique for adding eyelashes to the eyes of statues, and this rare survival may explain the appearance of many capitals that have volute eyes formed from separately attached plugs with no difference in stone color (as is possible in some of the bilingual capitals from Ephesos). Ionic column capitals were also gilded: traces of gilding survive on the bolster of a capital from the Archaic temple of Artemis at Ephesos and the volute eyes of the tomb of Eurydice, and the Erechtheion building accounts attest that these capitals, too, had gilded eyes that are now lost.[30] The second dipteral temple of Artemis at Ephesos had such substantial attachments to the volute eyes that some were secured with a nested gasket coupling and pins (see fig. 0.1, upper right).[31] The most elaborate embellishments were to the capitals

Athens and Eretria

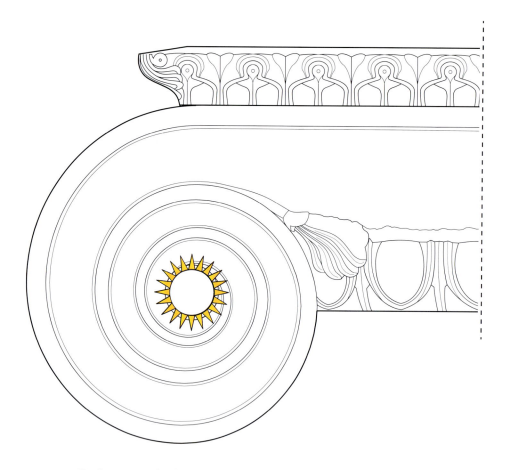

5.12. Xanthos, Letoon, sketch reconstruction of bronze attachments around the volute eye.

of the Erechtheion's north porch, where nineteenth-century travelers recorded that the guilloche band above the echinus (see fig. 1.19) had inlays of glass gems in a variety of alternating colors (fig. 5.14).[32] Although glass attachments are frequent for the volute eyes of *klinai* legs, Despina Ignatiadou has recently argued that glass was added in the first-century BCE restoration of the Erechtheion, replacing gilded metal attachments from the fifth century.[33] Doubled-up drill holes in the volute eyes of the bilingual Ionic capitals from Thessaloniki also attest to the replacement of fragile metal ornaments during ancient rebuilding projects. Added decoration of stone, gold, bronze, and glass had a chromatic aspect, but they also layered on value through the use of precious materials and painstaking work.

Pigments too were often precious materials, and their arrangement in bold, contrasting patterns on Ionic capitals evoked other precious objects.[34] The capitals of the Mausoleum at Halikarnassos, for example, have a bolster pattern of interlaced leaves colored red and blue in alternating rows (fig. 5.15).[35] This pattern is carved on other Ionic capitals without surviving paint traces, but a votive capital from the Athenian Acropolis that shows the same scheme of alternating red and blue leaves suggests it stretches back to the sixth century.[36] This dazzling harlequin pattern seems to evoke Near Eastern cloisonné jewelry, where a mosaic of lapis

162   Chapter 5

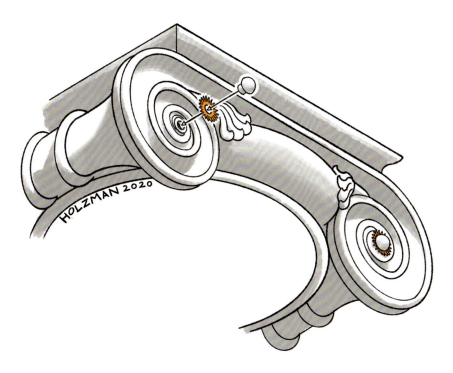

5.13. Xanthos, Letoon, Sketch of the possible assembly of the metal attachment to the volute eyes.

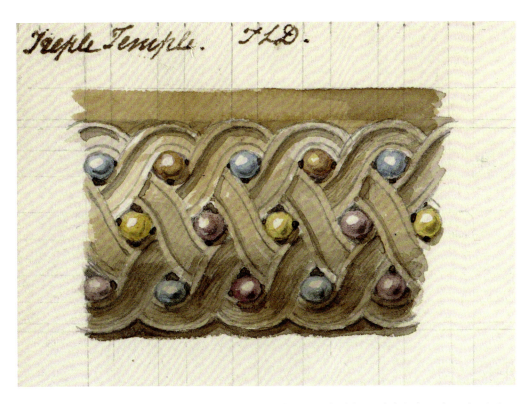

5.14. T. L. Donaldson, drawing of glass beads in the guilloche of the capitals of the Erechtheion's north porch, 1836. British Museum, London.

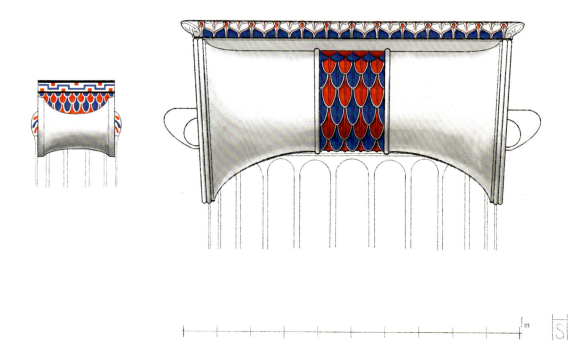

5.15. Paint schemes on Ionic capital bolsters reconstructed from documented color traces: Acropolis 4455, ca. 530 BCE; Mausoleum of Halikarnassos, ca. 350 BCE; temple of Artemis at Magnesia on the Maeander, ca. 200 BCE.

and carnelian tesserae was held together in a web of gold.[37] Polychromy on Ionic architecture changed over time. One change has recently been revealed by scientific analysis conducted on the remains of the temple of Artemis at Magnesia on the Maeander (built ca. 200 BCE) at the Pergamon Museum, Berlin.[38] The capitals have traces of multiple yellow pigments (including yellow ochre, goethite, and orpiment) mixed with red hematite, carbon black, and several white pigments (gypsum, marble powder, and possibly zinc white, lead white, and bone white). The pigments are mixed and layered in irregular strata that suggest a painterly, chiaroscuro application mimicking the appearance of gilding or polished bronze (see fig. 5.15).[39] Besides the spare palette of colors, two features are especially striking: a dark reddish brown contour line exaggerates the shadow contrast on the abacus molding, and a white splash along the ridge of the balteus bead molding lends a highlight to the illusion of yellow-orange metal. The painting scheme of the capitals from the Artemis temple marks a major departure from the typical color palette of vivid contrasting colors seen on the Mausoleum capitals. The faux metallic treatment might be a realization of a longstanding literary trope of architecture made of gold, silver, and bronze (e.g., Hom. *Od*. 7.88–90; Sappho frg. 1 l.8; Pind. Pae. 8, etc.). The spare white and gold palette of the Magnesia temple, however, seems more likely to evoke the ivory and gold of the chryselephantine medium, which not only appeared in sanctuaries

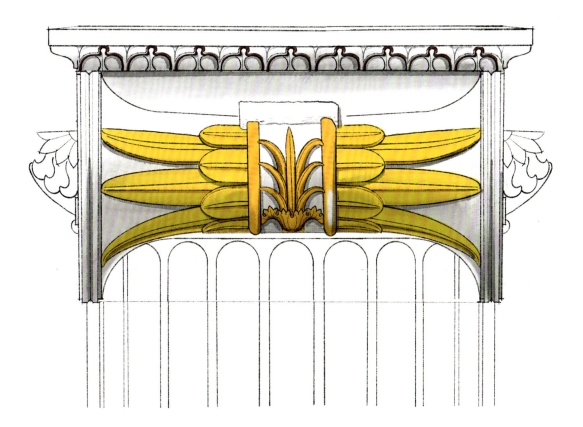

for cult statues and couches but was used for the doors of the most elaborate of temples.⁴⁰

A large corpus of whole paint schemes preserved for the Ionic order are to be found in the painted plaster facades of Macedonian tombs, especially the Tomb of Eurydice at Vergina, the Tomb of Palmettes at Lefkadia, and the Tomb of the Judgment at Mieza.⁴¹ Two painting features seem customary. Blue was frequently used as the ground color for Ionic friezes, which created a dark, vivid band wrapping around a building's superstructure—a feature that still stands out on the Erechtheion where grey Eleusinian stone was substituted. Like Doric guttae, dentils were left white against a background of color, but the vertical ground behind the dentils and the horizontal ground above the dentils were often painted in two different colors (almost inverse alternatives of the pairing of red and blue occur on the Tomb of Eurydice and the Tomb of Palmettes). What is particularly striking is that the same molding motifs, especially when used both for the abacus and echinus of Ionic capitals, were often painted differently with red and blue switched for ground and leaf. The Ionic order's freedom with color palette, color placement, and variation within the same building is nowhere more evident than in the sheer diversity of paint schemes applied to Ionic capitals from Athens.

Athens has produced the largest number of Ionic capitals with preserved paint and color weathering. Some of these capitals come from the Agora, but the majority were votive columns from the Archaic period that were buried with other debris from the Persian sack of the Acropolis in 480 BCE.[42] The good preservation of paint comes from intentional burial shortly after 479 BCE, although it seems the capitals were made over a long period with some being about fifty years old at the time of the sack. For example, Akr. 3776 (see fig. 5.4) belongs to a victory monument commissioned by Kallimachos of Aphidna to commemorate his athletic victory in the Panathenaic Festival of 490.[43] The Acropolis capitals, which belong to separate monuments, have a striking diversity of painted colors and patterns. The simple square abacus of Akr. 135 was enlivened with a three-color meander band, and the capital of Kallimachos's Nike makes liberal use of the color green, for the sheaths of the corner palmettes, the darts of the heart-and-dart molding on the echinus, and the lotus motif on the bolster. Elizabeth McGowan, however, has rightly cautioned that these dedicatory columns may have more elaborate painting than structural columns to match the painted statues they supported, which included korai in multicolor patterned garments.[44] Just as on this capital, the color green was liberally used on the Acropolis korai to highlight belts, crowns, and earrings, and the meander pattern, which occurs on several capitals (see fig. 5.15, left), was one of the most frequent patterns on the chitons of the Acropolis korai.[45] While these features fit well in the context of votive columns dedicated on the Acropolis, they also fit comfortably within the range of colors and patterns seen in the painting of other Ionic capitals used on Athenian buildings.

A summary of the range of colors and patterns observed on Ionic capitals can be seen in table 5.1, illustrating the color of each element on fifteen Ionic capitals with preserved paint that range between the sixth-century votive capitals from the Acropolis and the early third-century Macedonian tomb facades.[46] At the small-scale level of individual elements, there is almost no consistency in colors. The most consistent color use, for example, is blue for the leaves of the abacus molding, but yellow and reserved white are also attested. At the large-scale level there are some overarching trends for the painting of Ionic capitals. All the capitals on which at least two paint colors can be identified use red and blue—a standard pairing for most architecture and sculpture.[47] Red may be overrepresented because it was also used as a ground coat for gilding, as on one of the votive capitals from the Acropolis.[48] Another universal trend is that the canalis of Ionic capitals was left unpainted or plastered white. This is crucial to understanding bilingual capitals. The part of these capitals that was most varied was also the part of capitals that was never obscured by paint. Not only did painting not obscure carved differences on capitals, it may have added to their variety.

The Ionic order stood out from the Doric order by incorporating a greater diversity of painting, especially on capitals. Colors and painted patterns varied not just from building to building but even within the same building. This is most apparent on two fifth-century buildings from Athens. The capitals of the temple of Athena at Sounion have a smooth cyma reversa molding on the echinus that was painted with a heart-and-dart motif, but three of the surviving capitals have traces of color weathering that show that some of the capitals had an egg-and-dart motif on the

Table 5.1. Colors Observed on Fifteen Ionic Column Capitals

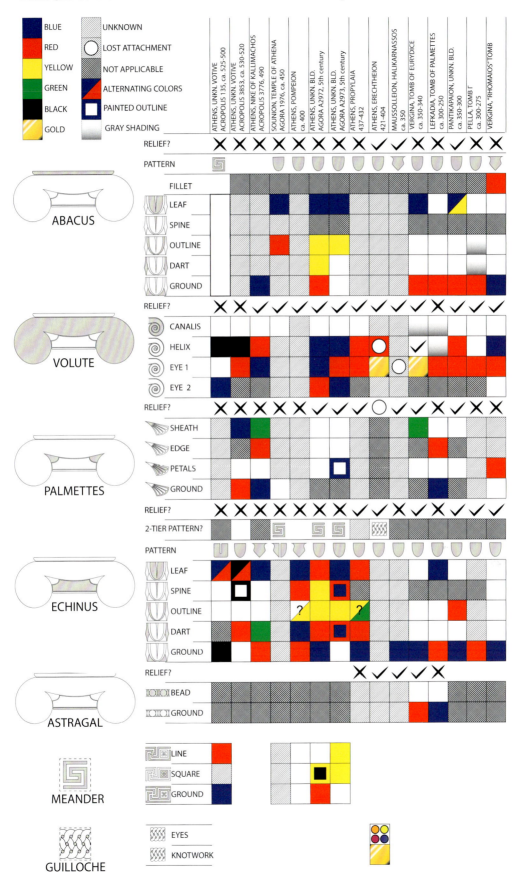

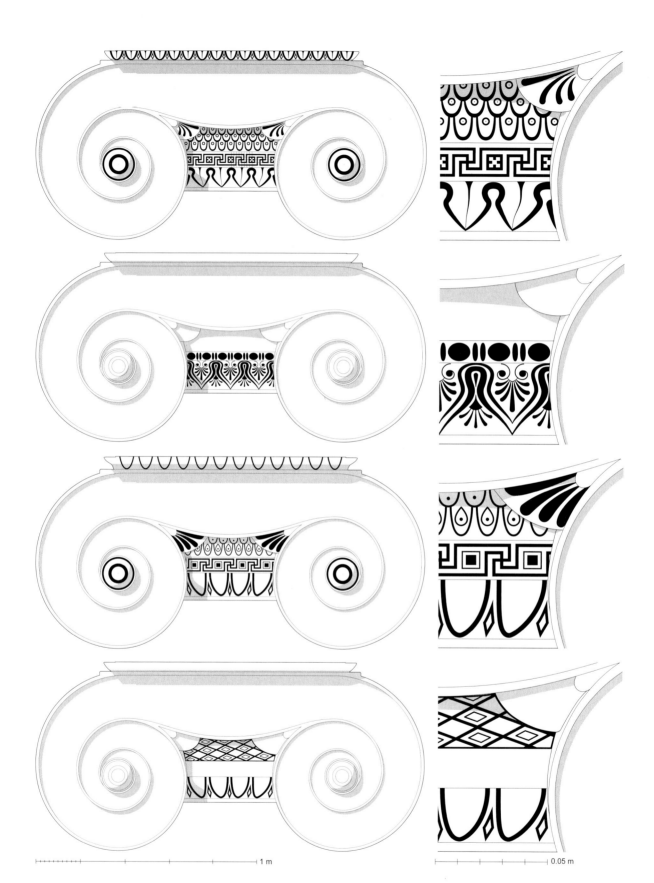

cyma reversa molding instead (fig. 5.16; and see fig. 5.5).[49] It was initially suggested that this substitution could be a miscommunication between an Athenian carver familiar with the local form of cyma-profiled echinus and a painter familiar with the Ionian tradition of the ovolo echinus.[50] But there was also variation among the heart-and-dart and egg-and-dart painted patterns, and the third tier of the capital echinus alternated lattice patterns and interlaced leaves. The Sounion temple had two columnar elevations and an interior colonnade, but there are more than three different schemes. Some adjacent columns, therefore, must have been different from one another in their patterns.

An incontrovertible instance of color variation occurs on two large Ionic capitals from an unknown Classical building (built around 450–430 BCE), which were discovered repurposed in the late Roman fortification wall in the Athenian Agora, A2972 and A2973.[51] Well-preserved traces of color were documented and reconstructed in watercolors by Piet de Jong soon after their discovery (fig. 5.17). The capitals belong to a monument that was disassembled and rebuilt in antiquity, with a consecutive sequence of letters inscribed on each element, allowing the two surviving capitals to be matched precisely with one surviving column base (belonging to the same column as capital A2973) and column drums belonging to three complete column shafts. The two capitals belonged to two shafts of the same height (5.18 meters tall), but the third set of drums belongs to a column taller by 80 centimeters, which had a corresponding twin implied by the sequence of inscribed letters (fig. 5.18).[52] The good preservation of the paint suggests the Ionic columns were sheltered in the interior of a building, and the two pairs of heights imply a structure with a change in floor level of three or four steps, possibly a propylon.[53] Had these two capitals survived without paint, it would be said that they are identical, except for a small variation in the abacus molding. The paint schemes of the two capitals, however, are substantially different, diverging in the patterns themselves (notably in the meander motifs of the two-tier echinus) and in the application of paint to the same egg-and-dart pattern on the echinus. New scientific analysis of the pigments on the two capitals undertaken by Vinzenz Brinkmann, Ulrike Koch-Brinkmann, and Heinrich Piening has greatly refined the initial impression of the capitals. The volute eyes of both capitals, illustrated as different by de Jong, were alike with a blue center and a red outer ring (fig. 5.19).[54] Yet, ultraviolet-visible absorption spectroscopy revealed an important difference not apparent to the naked eye. Visible traces of red, blue, and green color on the two capitals were each composed from different pigments or pigment blends (table 5.2).[55] Rich, dark blue azurite (A2973) and paler Egyptian blue (A2972) likely produced a noticeable tonal difference between the two capitals. Whether blending madder lake or cinnabar with red iron oxide produced an apparent contrast would depend on the quantities of each pigment and the binder, which are not yet known.[56] The pair of capitals offers crucial evidence that identically carved capitals could be painted with different motifs, different combinations of the same colors, and even different shades of the same colors.

5.16. Sounion, temple of Athena, examples of the different painted echinus patterns (drawn after Barletta 2017, capitals 43, 42, 72, and 56).

5.17. Piet de Jong, studies of the painted decoration of two mid-fifth-century Ionic capitals with different paint schemes, Agora of Athens, A2972 and A2973. Archives of the American School of Classical Studies, Athens.

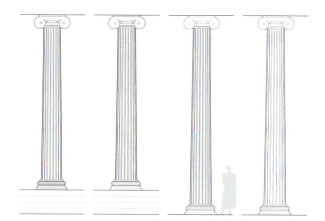

5.18. Schematic diagram of preserved Ionic elements corresponding to Agora A2972 and A2973.

    Seen individually, it is possible to attribute the painted differences among the sets of capitals from Sounion and the Agora to vagaries of the construction process. Together, however, the two varicolored Ionic buildings hint at a trend in Ionic architecture of capitals painted differently.[57] This trend is easily missed because of reliance on a Doric analogy and the tendency to homogenize reconstructions based on evidence of paint traces on individual surviving elements. Other evidence suggests that the variegation seen in the painted decoration of the capitals from Sounion and the Agora was a norm rather than an outlier. It is not uncommon to see Ionic capitals from the same building with bolsters sculpted with alternating motifs, both in the Classical period (Temple D at Metapontion) and especially in the Hellenistic period (the Stoa of Attalos in the Athenian Agora, the temple of Artemis at Magnesia, the Great Altar of Pergamon). In the temple at Messon, Lesbos, Robert

170   Chapter 5

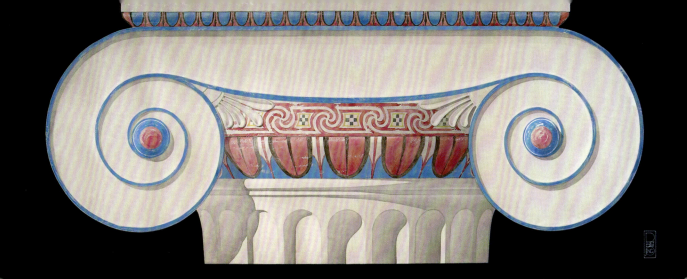

5.19. Painted reconstruction of capital A2972. Study and reconstruction by V. Brinkmann, U. Koch-Brinkmann, and H. Piening.

Table 5.2. Pigments Identified on Two Ionic Capitals from the Athenian Agora

Color	Capital A2972	Capital A2973
red	red iron oxide and red Madder lake	red iron oxide and cinnabar
blue	Egyptian blue	azurite
green	green earth	copper green (?)
yellow	yellow iron oxide ochre and lead yellow	n/a

Athens and Eretria 171

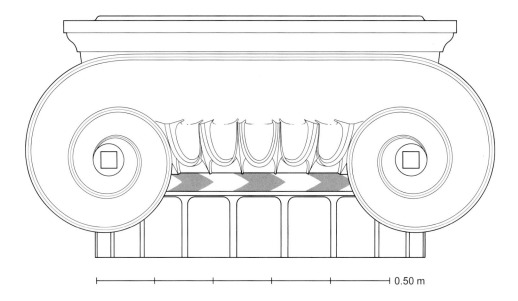

5.20. Corinth, South Stoa, painted pattern indicated in gray (color unknown) ca. 280 BCE (drawn after Broneer 1954, fig. 23).

Koldewey concluded that the balteus pattern on each one of the temple's forty-four Ionic capitals was different.[58] These carved differences were undoubtedly complemented by variations in the accompanying painted decoration. Some solitary paint traces suggest complementary alternation on other capitals. One capital from the South Stoa at Corinth preserves traces of a painted cord of chevrons (fig. 5.20).[59] The dominant directionality may have alternated with mirrored clockwise and counterclockwise versions in the same way as the guilloche pattern on the bases of the Erechtheion's north porch (see fig. 3.23). The alternating patterns of the bases corroborate the impression that Ionic columns set up side by side may have been ornamented differently.

To summarize, paint is an infrequently preserved but crucial component of Greek architecture. It was particularly essential to Ionic design in Athens in the fifth century. Nineteenth-century recording laid the groundwork for understanding the painting of ancient architecture, but new scientific techniques for recovering aspects of ancient painting are currently revolutionizing the study of polychromy. Doric polychromy is well understood because it is for the most part repetitive and predictable, but Ionic polychromy exhibits a greater range of painting, which in turn makes it difficult to fill in the blanks based on other preserved examples. Surprisingly, there is good evidence for color and pattern difference among Ionic capitals from the same building. Lack of certainty about specific colors, however, should not be confused with lack of certainty about which parts of a capital were often painted and which parts were left unpainted. For example, there is little doubt that the triglyphs of a Doric building were likely painted blue or blue-black. It is not possible to conjecture with certainty about the exact color of the helix of an Ionic capital because black, blue, and red are all attested, but one could speak confidently about the use of paint to create contrast between a painted helix and a reserved white volute channel. The use of paint, therefore, probably never masked bilingual carving by hiding convex and concave volutes behind a dark layer of blue or black paint on the volute channel. If anything, the tradition of variation in painting the Ionic order conditioned ancient observers to expect and look for variety in Ionic capitals. Paint may even have been used to accentuate differences between the opposite faces of bilingual Ionic capitals, especially when there were differences in carved ornament between the sides.

The Bilingual Capital from Eretria

A marble bilingual Ionic capital (fig. 5.21) was discovered at Eretria built into the foundations of a Christian-period house, a not uncommon fate for architectural elements at the site, including parts of the temple of Apollo Daphnephoros.[60] Vasilios Kallipolitis and Vasilios Petrakos, who first published the capital, proposed that it was originally a votive dedication of the Archaic period, though nothing of its archaeological context gives certain identification. The Persians sacked Eretria in 490 BCE and damaged the unfinished Temple of Apollo Daphnephoros. This Doric peripteral temple, built of poros limestone with marble pedimental sculpture, however, seems to have remained in use, and the Eretrians had sufficiently recovered from the Persian sack to muster a contingent of six hundred hoplites at the battle of Plataia in 479 (Hdt. 9.28).[61] While peculiarities of the Eretrian capital make it difficult to date with precision, it was likely carved in the decade or two prior to 490, during the energetic period of building and marble sculpting at Eretria. Perhaps it was

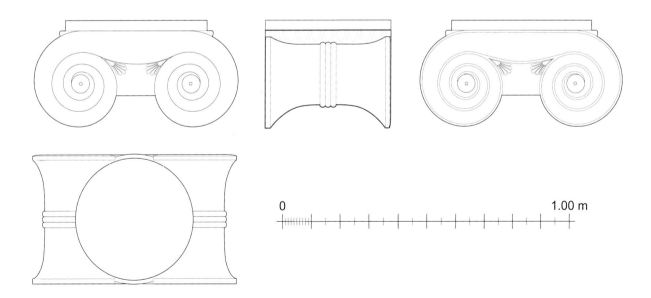

5.21. Eretria, bilingual Ionic capital (drawn after Kallipolitis and Petrakos 1965, figs. 6, 7). Archaeological Museum of Eretria.

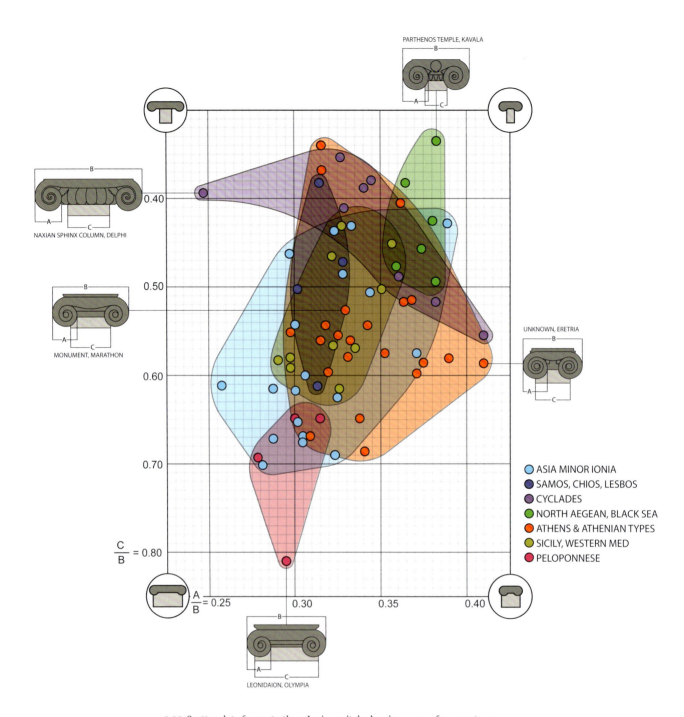

5.22. Scatter plot of seventy-three Ionic capitals showing range of compactness (x-axis, volute width / capital width) and size in relation to column diameter (y-axis: capital width / lower bed diameter) (drawn after the data set of Theodorescu 1980).

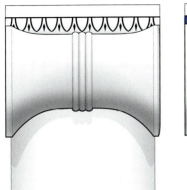

5.23. Eretria, capital bolster with speculative color reconstructions.

commissioned from one of the itinerant marble carvers who had come to Eretria to work on the pediment groups of the temple of Apollo Daphnephoros.

The capital is remarkable for its compact proportions. It has the most closely spaced volutes among Ionic capitals (fig. 5.22). Capitals destined to support votives were often stretched to proportions not seen for architectural supports (as with the elongated capital of the Naxian sphinx column at Delphi); thus, the unusual proportions of this singleton might suggest it was part of a freestanding dedication. Capitals used as pedestals for statues, however, have elaborate systems of doweling (as in the example from Oropos in chapter 3), and the complete absence here suggests an architectural use. Perhaps the capital belonged to a small Ionic portico with stone columns and a wooden superstructure similar to the Stoa of the Athenians at Delphi.[62]

On one of the sides of the capital, Kallipolitis and Petrakos illustrated visible traces of a painted egg-and-dart pattern on the ovolo molding under the abacus (fig. 5.23). Traces of this pattern can also be discerned in their published photograph.[63] In 2017, I scrutinized this area under different lighting conditions, but traces of paint were no longer observable; it seems that a half-century of outdoor display at the Eretria Museum degraded the paint traces that were once distinct to the naked eye. Kallipolitis and Petrakos, however, recorded enough of the pattern that it can be reconstructed in grisaille and form the basis for speculative visualizations with colors from other known capitals (fig. 5.23). It is unclear whether the discernable pattern outlines recorded in 1965 were the surviving traces of paint—in which case the pattern would have an outline style similar to the abacus of the Temple of Athena at Sounion—or color weathering of a more standard painted-ground arrangement. Kallipolitis and Petrakos indicate an ogival point to the egg-and-dart pattern, which is an Archaic feature. Given the evidence for lost painted patterns here, it is safe to assume that the echinus also had a painted pattern—whether egg-and-dart or heart-and-dart is hard to tell from the tall profile—and the flat faces of the plinth-like abacus may have carried a meander pattern known on Attic votive capitals (see, e.g., fig. 5.15, left). On the volute faces, the addition of paint would have increased the contrast between the carving styles.

Athens and Eretria   175

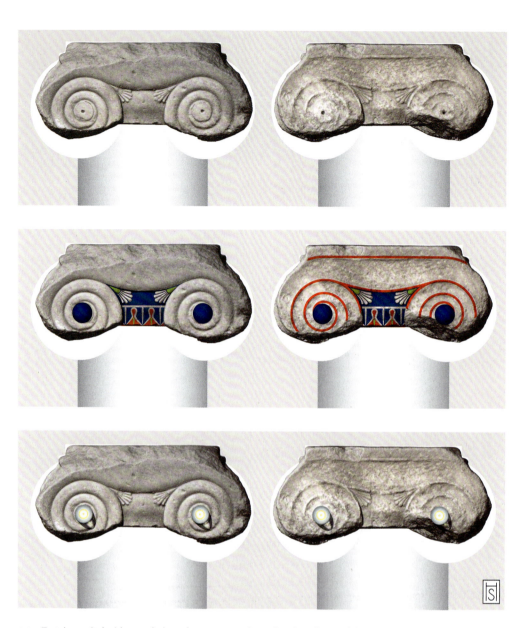

5.24. Eretria, capital with speculative color reconstruction using the scheme of the Kallimachos Nike Capital or glass volute eye attachments.

The convex face of the Eretria capital is unparalleled for its composition because it has no helix but is instead simply a single doughy coil wrapped around itself. The sculptural voluptuousness of the volutes resembles a pastry roll or the outside of a snail shell. This is the side that has garnered the most scholarly attention, in at least one model taking on the place of a missing link between purportedly lost early wooden prototypes of Ionic capitals and the preserved stone-carved iterations.[64] The concave side, however, takes the very recognizable form of the Attic type of Ionic capital from the late sixth and first half of the fifth century, where the helix is defined by a simple flat fillet and a low relief channel. This side of the capital has parallels to several capitals from the Athenian Agora, a votive capital from Delos that is possibly an Athenian dedication, and more generally the capitals of the temple of Athena at Sounion.[65] The simple balteus of three ropes is also typical of early Athenian capitals. The carver seems well versed in the Athenian tradition of Ionic capitals, and the concave side was likely the starting point for the design, though not necessarily the capital's primary face. From this model, the sculptor transposed the pattern to create the opposite convex side—likely inspired by the Archaic Ionian tradition—but the inversion of the Attic fillet-helix has become a single rounded-off v-cut. While the sculptor may have aimed at creating a contrast between the Athenian type and an east Ionian type, the result is something unique. One side of the capital has a flat fillet for a helix, which when painted would have created a distinct color line, while the other side completely lacks a helix element. When the faces of the capital were painted, the areas of paint must have been distributed differently because of the absent helix. Though the colors of each element are lost, applying the paint schemes of other capitals with preserved paint shows how painting created even greater contrast between the two faces (fig. 5.24).

The Eretria capital also has drilled connection points for attachments to the volute eyes on both sides of the capital, though it is not clear what the attachments were made of. As in the recorded case of glass beads inserted into the capitals of the Erechtheion (see fig 5.14), attachments to Ionic capitals could substantially change their appearance and complement polychromy and gilding (see fig. 5.23). The volute eyes of Attic capitals occasionally show sculpted designs (see, e.g., figs. 5.37 and 5.38) but are more often flat (e.g., Erechtheion) or with convex bosses, occasionally hemispherical (e.g., the temple of Athena at Sounion) but more often lentoid (e.g., the Athena Nike temple, Propylaia, and Agora A2972/A2973 capitals). It is possible that the eye attachments at Eretria were marble hemispheres that allowed the capital to be carved from a more compact block of marble. It is also possible that the attachment might be a gilded bronze ornament like a rosette or miniature phiale. The fastening points (ca. 2.8 centimeters deep and 0.9 centimeters in diameter) are deep enough for securing metal ornaments. But given the large circular bed prepared for each, it seems more likely that the attachments took the form of a solid boss just like those of capitals with carved eyes but made of a different material like glass. Boss volute eyes are often painted with concentric rings, a pattern that could easily be achieved in glass, either by hot-rolling opaque colored glass like core-formed vessels, or by adding rings of gilding to the back of semi-translucent glass, a form known from the inlaid volute eyes on klinai (see fig. 5.24). The traces of painted and added metal embellishments on the Eretria capital best illustrate that there were further layers of decoration than sculpting alone on bilingual Ionic capitals and that the textural effect of combining convex and concave surfaces worked in concert with the addition of colors and other precious materials.

Although it is not possible to identify the bilingual Ionic capital from Eretria with a specific building, a structural use seems more likely than a freestanding votive. Although the capital has no exact parallel, it shows a dominance of features of Athenian Ionic capitals of the first half of the fifth century in its stocky proportions, simple balteus decoration, painted rather than carved echinus and abacus molding, and the fillet helix on the concave side. The historical circumstances that

5.25. The Stavro capital, preserved state. National Archaeological Museum, Athens.

brought a sculptor familiar with the Athenian tradition to Eretria are not known, but it is not a surprise in a city whose political fortunes were often linked with those of Athens. The phenomenon of bilingual Ionic capitals began by juxtaposing the styles of East Ionian convex capitals and the concave capitals common to the Cyclades and on Thasos, but at Eretria this structure combines a different contemporary style, one that emerged from Athens. The pared down style of Athenian capitals, which favored painted rather than relief decoration, often seems at odds with the richly sculptural tradition of Ionic elsewhere, but that contrast has been juxtaposed on opposite sides of the Eretria capital. The carver, working backward from the Athenian style to recreate an east Ionian style of convex carving, has generated something completely original, a volute in the form of a single doughy coil with no helix. This mesmerizing sculptural treatment of the volute is an original, archaistic invention based on the eclectic recombination of historical, contemporary, and invented features. Archaistic design was also an undercurrent in the use of the Ionic order in Athens, appearing in three small Ionic buildings of the Classical period, each of which is represented by a pair of capitals: the bilingual Ionic building at ancient Pallene (the Stavro / Jeraka capitals), an Ionic building near the Acropolis (Akr. 13296 / Agora A616), and a fourth-century shrine near the Ilissos River (represented by the Inwood capital and Agora A3345).

In addition to archaistic design, the Eretria capital, which had traces of painted motifs, shows the importance of polychromy to bilingual Ionic capitals. An experiment of restoring paint to the Eretria capital based on the schemes of known contemporary Athenian Ionic votive capitals is informative. The absence of a helix on the convex face of the Eretria capitals produces a strong contrast between the richly sculptural convex face and the flat, painted fillet on the concave side, which is equally striking. This speculative visualization reinforces the impression given by surveying preserved Ionic polychromy, which shows the lack of paint applied to the canalis of Ionic capitals. It seems that paint never masked the contrast of bilingual carving by hiding the shaded modeling of convex and concave volutes with layers of dark paint. Instead, by painting details around the canalis, polychromy likely introduced additional contrast between the faces and preconditioned viewers to look for variation within the Ionic order.

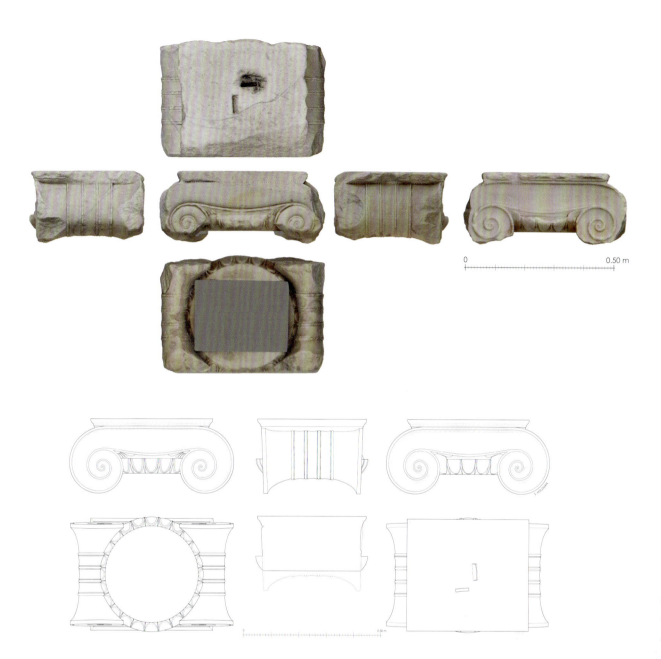

5.26. The Jeraka capital, preserved state and reconstruction. Archaeological Museum of Piraeus.

The Bilingual Building at Pallene

A group of bilingual Ionic capitals, including two complete capitals and a lost fragment of a third, were discovered in the area of the central Attic deme of Pallene to the north of Mt. Hymettos (fig. 5.25., fig. 5.26).[66] These capitals, their bonding system for stone epistyles, and a fragment of an Ionic base (fig. 5.27) are the remains of a jewel-box building, slightly smaller than the temple of Athena Nike on the Acropolis. Its colonnaded porch of Island marble blended contemporary Attic style of the fifth century and Archaic features best known from the coast of Asia Minor.

The capitals themselves have several features that show the methodical hand of an accomplished carver at work, including the scored compass lines for laying out

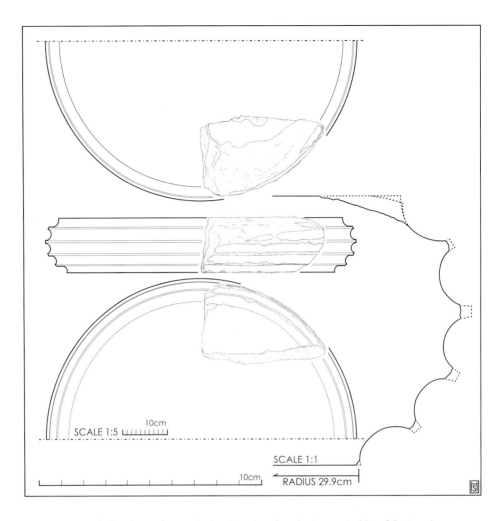

5.27. Fragment of a fluted torus from an Ionic column base found at Stavro. Archive of the American School of Classical Studies at Athens.

the volute with precise geometry and a slender dovetail patch repairing the molding of the abacus prior to construction assembly. Similarities between the capitals from ancient Pallene, along with a set of capitals from the city (Akr. 13296 / Agora A616 capitals) may all be the work of a single talented capital carver at work in Athens in the middle of the fifth century. The amalgam of contrasting features from different periods has made dating both sets of capitals difficult. Lucy Shoe Meritt emphasized the internal contradistinctions of their style before cautiously proposing an Archaic date.[67] Putting aside the convex volute as an indicator of a sixth-century date, the soft rounded forms of the egg-and-dart echinus molding are certainly Classical, and the bolster design and the treatment of the echinus below the bolster are direct predecessors of the capitals of the Propylaia and Athena Nike temple. I propose that the capitals are half-archaistic creations of the middle of the fifth century. Other Classical Ionic buildings in Athens, particularly the one represented by the "Inwood capital" and Agora A3345 (see fig. 5.38), which might belong to a shrine or tomb near

5.28. Map of the area of ancient Pallene showing the site of the Temple of Athena Pallenis, and the churches where the Ionic capitals and Archaic Doric triglyph were recovered.

the Ilissos River, reveal a trend for archaistic design that blended stylistic elements of Ionic capitals from different periods and regions. The building at Pallene stands out among Attic buildings for its distinctive archaism, but its attention to sculptural detail marks it as a predecessor to the more elaborate Ionic monuments of Athens's fifth-century heyday.

The two bilingual capitals were first reported in 1927 by Hans Möbius, who observed them in central Attica at the churches of Hagia Triada / Agios Ioannis Theologos at Stavro and of Agios Dimitrios at Yérakas (fig. 5.28, marked on the map).[68] (Confusingly, English-language scholarship on the capital has retained

Athens and Eretria 181

5.29. Graffiti on the bed surface of the Stavro capital. National Archaeological Museum, Athens.

Möbius's transliteration into German of the place name "Jeraka.")[69] Eight modern graffiti on the Stavro capital, including Greek names and initials as well as the dates "1906," "191[_]," and "1918" (fig. 5.29), all indicated the capital was exposed prior to Möbius's discovery and its transportation to the National Archaeological Museum in 1927.[70] One of Christian Hansen's Athens sketchbooks from 1834 includes a partial sketch of an Ionic capital (fig. 5.30) with profile lines drawn across the volute and the centerline of the capital to emphasize the convex profile of the canalis. The sketch clearly pictures the Stavro capital, which caught the eye of the astute architect as one of the only capitals with convex volutes to be seen in Greece in the 1830s. In the 1950s, Eugene Vanderpool observed Möbius's Jeraka capital again; it was subsequently removed to the Piraeus Museum.[71] Vanderpool also found a volute fragment from a third capital of the same series and a fragment of an Ionic column base that may belong to the same building (see fig. 5.29). This base fragment, like the capitals, is carved of Island marble—a rare material for columns in Attica and then largely for Archaic-period votives.[72] Vanderpool took the capital and base fragments from the ruin of the church at Stavro to the Archive Collection of the American School of Classical Studies at Athens; Manolis Korres has since identified two smaller fragments of a fourth possible capital.[73] Together the five architectural members testify to an Ionic monument with at least four columns, marking a formative experiment with Ionic sculptural styles in Attica.

These bilingual capitals have a composition familiar from Athens: a cyma reversa abacus, an ovolo echinus, and a narrow zone separating the echinus and the volute channel in which the corner palmettes are set apart. Like the Ionic capitals of the Propylaia and the Temple of Athena Nike, the egg-and-dart motif is outlined in an abbreviated fashion under the bolsters, but on the Stavro and Jeraka capitals the half-carved outlining is carried over onto one face, leaving only one side fully carved. There is no question that these capitals have a primary and a secondary face intended for the exterior and interior of a colonnade. The two volute faces are carved in different styles with a convex face drawing on the richly sculptural east Ionian style and a concave face in the Attic style of plain surfaces for painted decoration (fig. 5.31). In combining the two styles, the sculptor has transposed the design of the helix terminating in a whorl, common on convex capitals, onto the Attic style side. This is the only example of an Attic style fillet helix terminating in a whorl rather

5.30. Christian Hansen, sketch of an Ionic capital picturing the Stavro capital, 1834. Danish National Art Library, Copenhagen.

5.31. The Jeraka capital. Archaeological Museum of Piraeus.

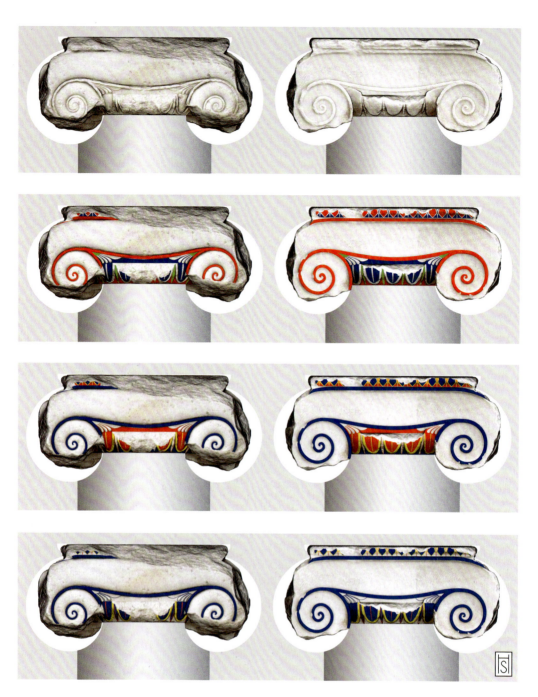

5.32. The Jeraka capital conjecturally restored with the paint schemes of the Kallimachos Nike capital, Agora A2972 and A2973.

than an eye, and it is a crucial piece of evidence for understanding the design process and combination of regional styles seen in Attica in the fifth century.

Because the carving of the echinus and corner palmettes were completed on the convex face, this seems the likely exterior side of the capital.[74] Although the traces of the original painting added to this capital do not survive, an experiment of restoring paint to the capitals (fig. 5.32) based on the schemes of Ionic capitals from

Athens from the first half of the fifth century reveals how paint complemented the two styles of carving. The detailed painting applied to the egg-and-dart motif and around the petals of the corner palmettes would obscure the difference between the fully modeled relief carving on one side and the half-carved silhouettes of each element on the reverse. As with the experimental reconstruction of paint on the Eretria capital, however, the sculptural difference between the volute faces shines through because paint was never applied to the volute channel, only the helix. The placement of the concave side within the building where there was not direct light to create shadow contrast seems counterintuitive, but this is also certainly the case of the Delian propylon (chapter 2). The marble from which the capitals are carved is also significant.

The capitals and base fragment are carved from a granular marble, now yellowed, that is not from Attica. It looks Cycladic; Möbius thought Naxian.[75] Shoe Meritt pointed out that the use of Island marble was an unusual feature of the capitals and proposed that it was a sure indicator of an Archaic date.[76] In the Classical period, marble from Mt. Pentele was almost universally used as the marble for state building projects because of its high quality, its local convenience, and the reduction in cost of material from state-owned quarries.[77] Fifth-century temple-building on the eastern coast of Attica offers exceptions that prove the rule: the temples of Athena and Poseidon at Sounion as well as the double stoa at Thorikos used lower-quality creamy-white marble from nearer quarries at Agrileza and Thorikos, and the temple of Nemesis at Rhamnous used marble from a quarry at Agia Marina two kilometers away.[78] Prior to consistent exploitation of the ancient quarries on Pentele in the Classical period, Island marble was imported for sculptural and roofline details added to limestone buildings as well as for individual votive columns. For example, two of the eight Ionic capitals from the Persian destruction deposits on the Acropolis are carved from Island marble rather than Pentelic. In the Classical period, Parian marble continued to be imported in large quantities, primarily for the roofs of temples, including the Asklepieion and the Parthenon (where the nearly ten thousand tiles and antefixes likely represent over five hundred tons of marble).[79] The use of Island marble for the bilingual Ionic building at ancient Pallene, however, is counterintuitive even if it dated to the late Archaic period when Pentelic marble was also available. Ancient Pallene, located in central Attica, is one of the closest demes to the Pentele quarry and the farthest away from any port. The walk from the ancient quarry to Pallene is eight kilometers, taking about an hour and three quarters, downhill all the way (the Acropolis, by comparison, is a twenty kilometer journey). The Island marble that was used at Pallene was brought overseas and unloaded at a port—the nearest one was fifteen kilometers away at Rafina (ancient Halai Araphenides) and transported uphill all the way over an elevation change of 200 meters. The small scale of the Ionic capitals, however, minimized any transportation challenge. Each capital originally weighed between 100 and 130 kilograms.[80] This can be compared with known shipwrecked marble shipments like the late-Hellenistic Kizilburun wreck, which contained eight drums and a Doric capital from one column of the temple of Apollo at Klaros weighing about fifty tons in total.[81] The small Ionic colonnade from the building at Pallene undoubtably fit on a single ship. The

5.33. Schematic diagram of the Jeraka capital's dowel hole and pry mark used during construction. Archaeological Museum of Piraeus.

appearance of Island marble at Pallene could also be an indication of stone carvers from the islands bringing their own materials, or a private patron for the project with connections in the Cyclades.

Considering that only the capitals and a fragment of a base have been associated with this building, it is uncertain whether Island marble was used for all the elements, or just these intricately carved pieces. The bottoms of the capitals have a square socket for doweling to the column shaft, and the Stavro capital has cuttings for laying stone architrave blocks. The top surface of the Stavro capital has a thin socket for an end-dowel and a shallow pry mark for positioning a stone epistyle block on top of the capital (fig. 5.33). Taking the convex side as the front, the pry mark is off-center to the left. This indicates that the first epistyle block was laid from the right and adjusted into place with a lever set against the pry mark. The workers would be standing on scaffolding and assured that the slender Ionic column was a stable base for using a metal lever. This first epistyle was then locked into place with a bronze or iron end-dowel secured with lead, which was off-center to the right, aligned with the centerline of the capital. The next epistyle block was placed against

5.34. Schematic diagram of the dovetail patch on the Stavro capital. National Archaeological Museum, Athens.

the one that had just been locked into place. These construction marks offer some information about the overall building. The Stavro capital cannot be at a corner (as in the fourth-century aedicular Ionic tomb monument of Nikeratos and Polyxenos from Kallithea now reassembled in the Piraeus Museum), but instead must be in the middle of a colonnade. It can be gleaned from the survival of three normal capitals that the structure was at its smallest either a stoa with at least three columns, a prostyle building with four normal capitals across the facade, or a tetrastyle amphi-prostyle building with corner capitals (like the temple on the Ilissos River and the Temple of Athena Nike). Importantly the cuttings indicate that the epistyle beams were also of finely fitted stone and not wood and thus could have supported a complete stone entablature. This system was the norm in Classical Athens.

The top of the Stavro capital looks considerably different than the top of the Jeraka capital because it was patched prior to assembly (see fig. 5.25). One side of the abacus has been cut away to form a dovetail setback. The horizontal surface is smoothed around the edges and lightly picked in the center to form delicate anathyrosis at a much smaller scale than is usually seen for joining whole blocks. Based on a symmetrical restoration of the top of the capital, it seems that this cutting was designed to receive a marble patch secured by dovetailing (fig. 5.34).[82] The delicate cyma reversa molding may have been damaged during carving, and so the whole section of the abacus was cut away to the line of the top of the volute and the top of the ovolo over the bolster. The dovetailing kept the patch from sliding out horizontally, as the weight of the epistyle block above prevented the patch from being lifted vertically. While one might get the impression from the abbreviated carving of the echinus on the concave side that the sculptor was cutting corners in carving, this repair shows a substantial investment of time in achieving a uniform appearance. The patch would have been a thin plaque only 2.6 centimeters thick that would need

Athens and Eretria   187

  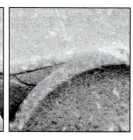 

5.35. The Jeraka capital, detail of compass marks from drawing the volutes prior to carving. Archaeological Museum of Piraeus.

to be tested multiple times to achieve a secure fit. Due to the delicacy of the patch, no dowel hole or pry mark was cut into the top of the capital during construction as with the Jeraka capital. This repair feature is remarkable because it shows the perfectionist tendencies of the capital carver that run contrary to the conspicuous half-finished state of the echinus on the concave side. A similar attention to detail may be seen in the carver's preparatory compass lines. On the concave side of both capitals, one can still detect the lightly scored compass lines from the initial drawing for carving the volutes (fig. 5.35). The whole face of the capital was smoothed to a flat plane before a compass was used to define the helix with geometric exactness. This line was carved away everywhere except at the points where the fillet of the helix bifurcates over the corner palmettes and at the junction with the abacus.

    The balteus pattern on the bolsters of the capitals is distinctive and a crucial hint toward their date. Attic Ionic capitals of the late Archaic and early Classical periods tend toward a simple cinched band at the center of the bolster, like the three half rounds on the Eretria capital, the two half rounds on the Stoa of the Athenians at Delphi, or the single half round elaborated into a lotus stem on the Kallimachos Nike capital (see fig. 5.4). The balteus of the Stavro and Jeraka capitals is an elaboration on the early Attic type with a wider central band formed of three ribbon-like channels separated by four half rounds. This pattern is the direct predecessor to the balteus design of the Ionic capitals within the Propylaia, built between 437 and 432 BCE (fig. 5.36). The Propylaia's design was then repeated on the capitals of the temple of Athena Nike, built ca. 420 BCE (fig. 5.36). These later monuments have refined the scheme by giving the whole bolster a more dramatic swooping curvature,

5.36. Scale comparison of the Jeraka capital, the capitals of the Propylaia, temple of Athena Nike, and temple on the Ilissos river.

while the bolster of the Stavro and Jeraka capitals suggests a stocky cylinder connecting the two volute faces. Although the capitals from ancient Pallene have long been assumed to be of an Archaic date because of their convex volutes, they are also direct predecessors of the Ionic buildings of the era of Perikles and the Peace of Nikias in the design of the sides of the capitals and the treatment of the egg-and-dart motif under the bolster through outline carving. The Stavro and Jeraka capitals have their closest parallels in a pair of capitals from the city center of Athens, which have also been given an unlikely Archaic date.

Two Ionic capitals discovered in Athens, one from the Acropolis (Akr. 13296; fig. 5.37), the other excavated in the Athenian Agora heavily recut for reuse (A616), have an uncanny similarity to the bilingual capitals from ancient Pallene. The two sets of capitals share many overarching features of construction (Island marble, bonding systems using pry marks and dowels) and design (the bolster design, abacus profile, the abbreviated concave side with half-carved egg-and-dart echinus). More startlingly, however, the capitals share some minute stylistic flourishes, particularly in the corner palmette design (a slightly concave pointed upper petal and convex, rounded lower petals). The Akr. 13296 / Agora A616 capitals are not strictly bilingual (both faces have concave volutes), but they do pair a plain Attic style of flat surfaces with a richly sculptural concave face featuring a half-round helix offset with fillets and elaborate rosette volute eyes. Just as the Stavro / Jeraka capitals pair the Attic style with an Archaic style of convex volutes most familiar from Ionia, the Akr. 13296 / Agora A616 capitals pair the Attic style with a style of concave volute familiar from the Late Archaic Cyclades and Thasos (exemplified in the rich carving of the concave faces of the bilingual capitals from Kavala and Thessaloniki). Hans Möbius initially compared the two pairs of capitals, though he identified those from ancient Pallene as Archaic and the capitals from the city as Classical.[83] The capitals are of different scales (the capitals from the city center are about 25 percent larger in total size), but they have similar proportions (including an identical height-to-width ratio). Looking past the compositional choice of a convex volute, volute eyes, and their different sizes, most aspects of the capitals are identical or a logical variant based on the difference in overall scale (the larger capitals have more petals on the corner palmettes). This spectrum of similarities leads to the conclusion that they are not simply contemporary building projects, but likely the work of a single talented capital carver. Based on the experiment of replicating the volute face of the Stavro and Jeraka capitals (presented in chapter 3), each of the capitals could be carved in one month. This would allow sufficient time for one carver to complete the capitals for a whole building project in a timely manner.

Möbius compared the two sets of capitals but divided their dates, identifying the Stavro and Jeraka capitals as Archaic and Akr. 13296 as Classical.[84] Shoe Meritt, in publishing Agora A616, was conflicted about the date to give it and its twin. Little about it implied an Archaic date, and the bolster design seemed to be Classical.[85] Shoe Meritt concluded, however, that these same Classical features could occur in the Archaic period because they were present on the Stavro and Jeraka capitals, which she—like Möbius—assumed were Archaic because of the presence of the convex volute. Shoe Meritt concluded that both sets of capitals marked a transition between the plain Attic style and a more richly sculptural tradition known especially in Ionia, but she was conflicted in choosing whether it marked the beginning of the plain Attic style in the third quarter of the sixth century or the movement away from it in the third quarter of the fifth century—cautiously settling on the former:

> What then of the group of half-painted, half-carved capitals? Do they represent a movement from a late 6th-century Ionian-influenced carved capital toward a revival of the earlier 6th-century Attic painted tradition to be seen in the many painted 5th-century forms? Or are they moving from the 6th-century painted (largely votive) toward the full carving of the Ilissos Temple, Propylaia, Nike Temple, and Erechtheion? … Perhaps we have in

5.37. Athens, Acropolis, Ionic capital from the Acropolis slope (Akr. 13296).

this pair of capitals not the renewal of Ionian influence in Attic architecture in the latter part of the 5th century but rather the work of an Ionian of that earlier period of Ionian ties a century earlier, an Ionian experimenting with details suggested by his association with Attic traditions and combining them with his own from Ionia.[86]

With this dose of caution, Shoe Meritt went further to speculate that the Akr. 13296 / Agora A616 capitals and three associated Ionic base fragments of Island marble from the Agora belonged to the three missing columns of the Southeast Fountain House in the Agora identified as the Enneakrounos fountain dedicated by

Athens and Eretria 191

Peisistratos (therefore prior to 527).[87] Jessica Paga has since shown that the Southeast Fountain House dates after Peisistratos, probably to the last decade of the sixth century, but the Ionic capitals are still an unlikely fit for this building.[88] Pry marks and dowel holes on top of the capitals indicate that they supported stone epistyle beams, but the ca. 2.40 meter span between columns on the Southeast Fountain House appears too great for stone epistyles of a proportional design small enough to match the capitals. While the development of the Ionic order in Athens has divergent trends, it is untenable that a monument that is on the cusp of Periclean style should be the creation of Peisistratos. Instead, it is the alternative option considered by Shoe Meritt that seems correct. The two Ionic buildings represented by the Stavro / Jeraka capitals and Akr. 13296 / Agora A616 capitals show "the renewal of Ionian influence in Attic architecture in the latter part of the 5th century" and a movement away from the flat and painted Ionic capital "toward the full carving of the Ilissos Temple, Propylaia, Nike Temple, and Erechtheion." Regarding the carving of the egg-and-dart molding on the echinus, Shoe Meritt pointed out two features as indicative of date: the rounded parabolic profile of the eggs indicates a date after the sixth century, and the lack of channels separating each "egg" from its "shell" suggests a date before the late fifth century. Oddly, however, Shoe Meritt cast these two dates as conflicting alternatives, when they seem to bookend a likely mid-fifth-century date with a sixth-century terminus post quem and late fifth-century terminus ante quem. This chronological conundrum is easily resolved if both the Stavro / Jeraka building and the Akr. 13296 / Agora A616 building are identified as creations of ca. 450s BCE as most of their features would suggest. The convex volutes of the bilingual building, long thought to be a sure anchor for an Archaic date, are an element of archaistic design, a phenomenon prominent on one other Attic Ionic building.

Another set of Ionic capitals from Athens, the "Inwood Capital" and Agora A3345 capital, have archaistic designs, in this case with convex volutes on both sides (fig. 5.38).[89] The English architect Henry William Inwood discovered the first capital in the Chapel of Hagia Marina on the left bank of the Ilissos River in 1819 (BM 1843.0531.23).[90] It was initially identified with the textually attested temple of Artemis Eukleia, but the evidence for this identification was slim. Möbius reported the second capital in 1927 among a pile of ancient marbles collected in the ruin of the Stoa of Attalos.[91] The pair of capitals have several Archaic features, including a simple plinth abacus, smooth bolsters, a convex canalis, large corner palmettes, and an Aeolic-like vertical blossom at the center of the capital (a lotus over volutes and palmettes). The central lotus, however, has a rigid, almost Egyptianizing combination of frontal and profile elements that suggests an affected archaism. The egg-and-dart molding of the echinus is certainly post-Archaic. Shoe Meritt identified the capitals as archaistic and described them as having an "unusually creative classicizing style combining island and Athenian and sixth- and fifth-century memories along with some contemporary form."[92] The small lower bed diameter of the columns (ca. 33 centimeters) suggests a diminutive scale. Shoe Meritt proposed that the capitals might belong to the period of Lykourgos, who promoted a nostalgic view of the Athenian past and oversaw several large building projects—including archaistic constructions like the cyclopean retaining wall of the Pnyx.[93] He initiated

5.38. The Inwood capital. British Museum, London.

the construction of the first stone phase of the Stadion on the left bank of the Ilissos River, and Shoe Meritt suggested that the Stadion construction project may have also led to the aggrandizement of one of the many small cults on the Ilissos in archaistic style.[94] Giuseppe Rignanese on the basis of proportions also proposes a date in the third quarter of the fourth century, but suggests that the construction could just as well form part of an elaborate funerary monument.[95] The Inwood / Agora A3345 capitals represent an extension of the tradition of producing archaistic Ionic capitals in Athens that originates in the middle of the fifth century.

Although the bilingual Ionic building at Pallene has not been identified, it must be understood within a fuller picture of monumental architecture in the area. In 1994, excavation for the construction of a house in Yérakas uncovered limestone ashlar foundations for a Doric peripteral temple, but with no trace of the building's superstructure or even steps. Manolis Korres showed that this was the original site for the Classical marble Doric temple excavated in the Athenian Agora with inscribed reassembly marks indicating that it had been moved during the early Roman Imperial period to be set up on a foundation with a concrete core.[96] It is now evident that this structure was the temple of Athena Pallenis at the ancient deme of Pallene. Möbius discovered an Archaic-period corner triglyph of poros limestone built into the Church of Agios Yiorgos at the Yérakas Cemetery, which he identified with the temple of Athena Pallenis, perhaps the Archaic predecessor of the Classical temple (fig. 5.39).[97] The asymmetrical treatment of the two sides indicates that the corner triglyph belongs to an in-antis Doric structure. The Ionic building with the bilingual capitals dates between the Archaic Doric building, which may have been

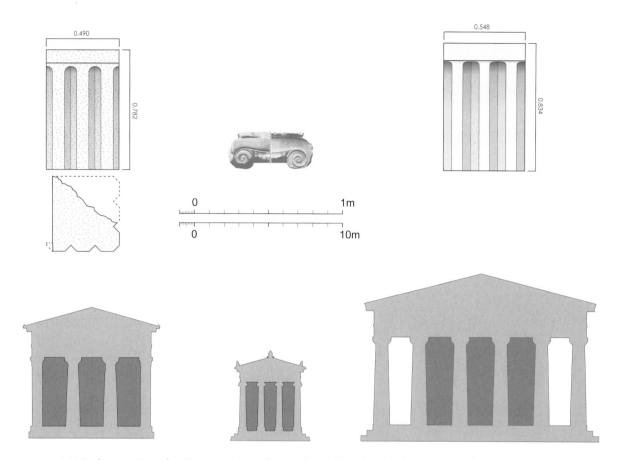

5.39. Scale comparison of architectural elements from ancient Pallene: the Archaic corner triglyph, the Jeraka capital, and one triglyph from the Classical temple of Athena Pallenis (temple of Ares in the Athenian Agora), as well as conjectural sketches of their elevations.

built ca. 550 and destroyed by the Persians in 480, and the beginning of construction of the Athena Pallenis / Ares Temple around the 430s. The small scale of the Ionic building seems to rule it out as an intermediate temple. Although the Ionic building may not relate to the cult of Athena Pallenis, this cult attests to the importance of Pallene as a major religious center for Attica, explaining how a sleepy deme attracted monumental, likely state-financed, temple constructions.

The modern suburbs at Stavro and Yérakas are unassuming and are passed through at high speed by most visitors on the highway between Athens and Eleftherios Venizelos Airport. In antiquity, this was the site of the ancient deme of Pallene (modern Pallini is not at the site of ancient Pallene for which it is named, nor does Yérakas correspond with ancient Gargettos, its namesake). This area remains the important pass on the north side of Mt. Hymettos connecting the central basin of Attica around the city of Athens to eastern Attica. Stavro marks the junction of the ancient road between Athens and Marathon (the route made famous by Pheidippides's legendary run) and the road south to Laurion. From the air (fig. 5.40), one can see how ancient Pallene, nestled at the northern foothills of Hymettos, controls much of the travel through Attica. When Peisistratos invaded Athens in

546 BCE to retake the tyranny, he embarked from Eretria with his allies, landed at Marathon, and then faced off with the city's defenders in a battle at the temple of Athena Pallenis (Hdt. 1.62). The distinction between this toponym and the deme's name ("Παλληνίς," "Παλλήνη") might be an indication of a more specific topographic feature, like a hill, where the temple was situated.[98] This pass was also the site of an important mythical battle; here Theseus—tipped off by a herald from the central Attic deme of Hagnous (modern Markopoulo)—surprised and defeated an ambush of the aristocratic faction of Pallantidai, who hoped to overthrow his kingship. According to Plutarch (*Vit. Thes.* 13), the mythical betrayal was so controversial that intermarriage was forbidden between people from Pallene and Hagnous. The special importance to the residents of Pallene of their local, mythical history, which maintained the ban on intermarriage, also emerges in the archaistic features seen in the Stavro / Jeraka capitals.

Critical evidence for understanding the reach of the cult of Athena Pallenis comes from its religious offices of *parasitoi*.[99] In 1943, Robert Schlaifer initially studied this aspect of the cult through quotations of ancient Athenian texts by Athenaeus (6.26) without knowing that an inscription from the 350s listing the *parasitoi* of Athena Pallenis had been uncovered in Athens the year prior (it would not be published until after the war).[100] Athenaeus quotes from inscribed dedications from Pallene naming the magistrates and "parasites"—representative participants who ate at public religious feasts—and from the "King's Law," which outlines that the Archon Basileus oversaw the selection of "parasites" from demes

5.40. Aerial view of central Attica showing the pass of ancient Pallene north of Mt. Hymettos.

Athens and Eretria   195

of Athens. Though the rituals associated with the *parasitoi* remain foggy, the demes of the named participants show a regional preference for central Attica. Schlaifer proposed convincingly that the cult of Athena Pallenis was the center of an early regional league that persisted through the unification of Attica and the institution of democracy. The Kleisthenic reforms splintered the cluster of neighbors that participated in this putative league of Athena Pallenis into the ten tribes (Pallene in Antiochis, Gargettos in Aigeis, Pithos in Kekropis, Acharnai in Oineis, etc.). The cult continued to be a point for regional assembly, but the selection of *parasitoi* was put under the supervision of the Archon Basileus, an officer of the state of Athens. Based on the recovered inscription, G. R. Stanton showed that the named *parasitoi* came from a wide number of demes, likely the entirety of Attica, while the *archontes* were from Pallene, Gargettos, Acharnai, and Paiania, which were likely the nucleus of the league of Athena Pallenis.[101] The case of the *parasitoi* shows the push and pull between local and state involvement in administering a cult and the balance between broad statewide participation and intensive regional interest that likely spurred building at Pallene. Attempts at centralizing Pallene's regional cult center may help explain the connection between the Ionic building represented by the Stavro / Jeraka capitals and the similar building represented by the Akr. 13296 / Agora A616 capitals in the city center.

Bilingual Ionic capitals emerge early on Delos, at Kavala, and Thessaloniki juxtaposing two sculptural styles of carving volutes, the old Ionian form of a convex whorl and the concave volute with a complex design for the sculpted volute eye that was growing in popularity in the late Archaic Cyclades and on Thasos. Athens in the late sixth century developed its own tradition of the Ionic order that replaced these modeled surfaces with flat ones that were embellished with paint. When bilingual Ionic capitals appear in Athens and neighboring Eretria, they contrast the Attic type of Ionic capital with a simple fillet helix with the richly sculptural convex volute familiar from Ionia. The surviving examples of painted Ionic capitals from Athens offer the opportunity to consider how Ionic polychromy may have complemented relief carving and impacted the perception of bilingual capitals. If anything, the tradition of painting different capitals from the same building with different colors and patterns likely enticed ancient viewers to look up and look closely at the differences in Ionic capitals, preconditioning viewers to observe the bilingual phenomenon.

While polychrome Ionic column capitals exhibit a wide array of colors, color combinations, and painted patterns, none has a painted volute channel, which indicates that dark paint likely never obscured the differences between the convex and concave volutes of bilingual Ionic capitals (see table 5.1). Experiments of applying color schemes from other known capitals to the bilingual Ionic capitals from Eretria (which survived with faint traces of paint above the bolster) and ancient Pallene exhibits this effect. The bilingual Ionic capitals from Stavro and Jeraka present a remarkable example for the experimentation with sculptural style in Attica in the fifth century. Close study has revealed more about their construction history, the form of the building to which they initially belonged, and their likely association with another Ionic building in the city. Most importantly, these capitals found near ancient Pallene can now be reliably dated for the first time to the middle of the Classical period. This building shows experimentation with Ionic sculptural styles, as Athenian architects and masons moved beyond the flat and painted style that had developed in Attica in the late Archaic and early Classical periods. The capitals also represent a foray into archaistic design, a phenomenon that would reappear in Attica in the archaistic building associated with the Inwood capital. But most importantly, they exhibit a movement toward experimenting with different modeled forms within the framework of Attic Ionic capitals. This in turn laid the groundwork for several of Athens's most important Ionic structures, including the Propylaia, the Temple of Athena Nike, and the Erechtheion.

Chapter 6

Ephesos, Selinous, and Delphi
Retrospective Design in Ionia and Abroad

A historical turning point for the Ionic order came in 356 BCE with the destruction of the temple of Artemis at Ephesos by Herostratos's infamous arson attack. The temple was the single most prominent reminder of the grand early age of Ionian building (the temple of Apollo at Didyma was sacked by the Persians at the end of the Ionian Revolt in 494, and on Samos, though spared, the temple of Hera remained permanently unfinished). Few new monuments were constructed in Ionia during the fifth century because of the overlap of the Persian Empire and the Athenian Empire, each of which demanded tribute that left few funds for building.[1] But this year was also the cusp of a resurgence of Ionic building, a phenomenon sometimes dubbed "the Ionian Renaissance," which was in part financed by the patronage of the Karian king, Maussollos, who in the next years would gather some of the period's most talented architects and sculptors to begin work on his elaborate Ionic tomb, the Mausoleum at Halikarnassos.[2] The late Classical and early Hellenistic resurgence in building in Ionia resuscitated Archaic east Ionian forms of the Ionic order, particularly the Ephesian-type column base and plinth, which has led to the criticism that the new movement was conservative and academic.[3] It is no surprise that bilingual Ionic capitals resurfaced in the late Classical and early Hellenistic periods as the Ionians rethought their own history of building and as individuals of other ethnic groups, like the Karian king Maussollos, appropriated venerable Greek architectural forms as an expression of newfound prominence in the politics of the Aegean.

The three bilingual Ionic monuments considered in this chapter (fig. 6.1) appeared at geographically distant centers: Ephesos on the western coast of Asia Minor, Delphi in central Greece on the western-facing Gulf of Corinth, and at Selinous at the western end of Sicily. The former was likely a peripteral temple dedicated to Athena on the legendary spot where the city of Ephesos was founded; the Delphic monument was an elaborate statue base commemorating a prominent

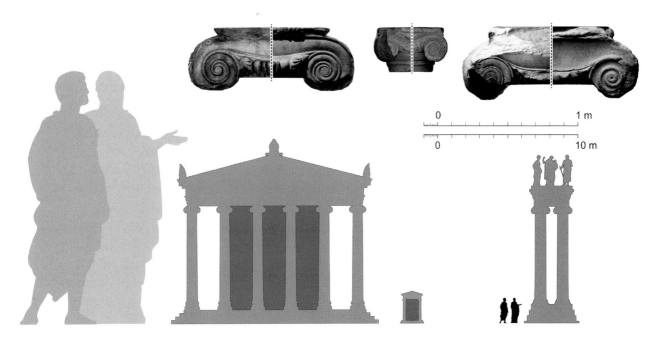

6.1. Bilingual Ionic capitals from Ephesos, Selinous, and Delphi.

Aetolian woman and her family; the Selinuntine capitals likely belong to a small extramural funerary monument. The monuments at Ephesos and Delphi take a deliberately retrospective approach at sites that had a deep history of building in the Ionic order, and where Ionic columns dating to the first half of the sixth century were still visible. At Ephesos the recreation of an Archaic form seems to reference the old dipteral temple of Artemis, the first temple built in the Ionic order according to Vitruvius, but recently destroyed. At Delphi the private dedication of Aristaineta was a bid to insert an elite Aetolian family into a Panhellenic site central to the history of Greek identity, from which the Aetolians had previously been excluded. Both sites had other major retrospective building projects underway in the fourth century: the temple of Artemis at Ephesos and the temple of Apollo at Delphi, which was destroyed by an earthquake in 373 BCE, were being rebuilt within the exact footprints of their Archaic predecessors.[4]

The Bilingual Temple at Ephesos

Ephesos was the preeminent Ionian city and a major center of commerce, politics, and the religious life of the Greeks living on the western coast of Asia Minor.[5] The Ephesia festival in the extramural sanctuary of Artemis took on pan-Ionian status and, reports Thucydides (3.104.3), became the main religious gathering place for the Ionians in the Classical period.[6] The colossal dipteral temple of Artemis was an architectural marvel, commented upon for its beauty, scale, and impressive engineering.[7] Vitruvius (4.1.7) reports that the Ephesians invented the Ionic order for Artemis's temple, and Pliny (*HN* 36.179) offers a similar, though more clinical claim: the temple of Artemis at Ephesos was the first with column capitals and bases carved of stone. Archaeological evidence shows that the Ionic order took form gradually across many sites, but the claim that reached Rome by the end of the first century BCE probably held great significance for the Ephesians, who may have played a part in propagating the story of their preeminence. The appearance of bilingual Ionic capitals at Ephesos, therefore, represents an important corollary for how the Ephesians shaped the impression of the early history of the Ionic order.

Seven associated capitals with archaistic features and one possible replacement capital of the Roman period attest to a bilingual Ionic monument at Ephesos in the form of a peripteral temple. While the convex canalis design recalls Ionic temples of the sixth century, the capitals seem to date to the second half of the fourth century or third century BCE. Anton Bammer published a catalog of the capitals (labeling them K1 through K7).[8] One of the capitals is displayed in the Ephesos Museum / Kunsthistorisches Museum, Vienna (K1, fig. 6.2); two are displayed in the courtyard of the Selçuk Museum (K2, inv. no. 1398; K3, inv. no. 1397).[9] The seven capitals can be associated because of their similarity in dimensions and close findspots in or near the theater, although there are design differences (fig. 6.3). Three of the capitals are bilingual, normal capitals with opposite convex and concave faces (K1, K2, K4); one is a corner capital of the bilingual type with concave volutes on the outside faces and convex half volutes at the inside corner (K7); one capital is fragmentary and only preserves one concave volute (K5); one is a normal capital with convex volutes on both faces (K3); and one capital is very fragmentary with both faces lost (K6). The volute eyes are hollowed out for inset ornaments—some traces of corrosion residue that may indicate bronze attachments—except for one capital (K1), in which this feature was never carved.[10] Notably, there are also two different bolster designs: one with four flutes separated by half rounds (K3, K4, K6, and K7), the other with an interlaced leaf motif (K1, K2, and K5). Both bolster patterns emerged in the Archaic period and are attested on the Archaic temple of Artemis (see fig. 1.7) and were revived in the second half of the fourth century.[11] An architrave block crowned with an egg-and-dart molding and a fragment of a pediment may also be associated with the structure.[12] The variations in the capitals, however, offer the best clue to the building's plan, which appears to have been peripteral.

Although the capitals seem at first glance to have a random mix of convex and concave faces and two different bolster designs, they may be arranged in a logical pattern on a plan for a peripteral temple. One of the capitals (K6) is a corner capital with concave volutes on the outer faces, convex volutes at the interior corner, and four flutes on the bolster. Therefore, at the corners of the building, concave faces belong to the exterior, while the convex volutes faced into the colonnade.[13] Another capital with the four-flute bolster (K3), however, has two convex faces. If it also belongs to the exterior colonnade, it creates a complex arrangement where all inward-facing volutes were convex, while the capitals of the facade alternated convex and concave.[14] In the slight variation in heights among the capitals, the fully convex

6.2. Bilingual Ionic capital from Ephesos (K1), convex and concave sides. Ephesos Museum, Vienna.

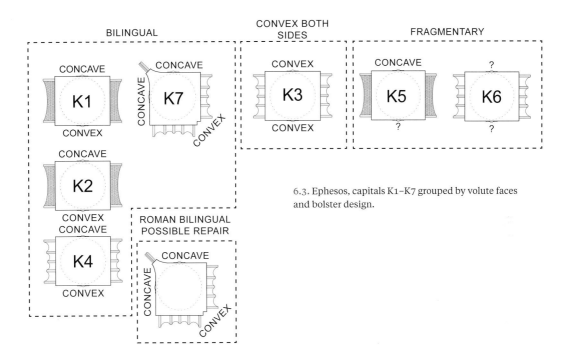

6.3. Ephesos, capitals K1–K7 grouped by volute faces and bolster design.

capital (K3) is the smallest of the set, though only by 1 centimeter. It would be most plausible to assign the capital with two convex faces to the columns of the pronaos or interior, allowing all outward-facing volutes to have concave carving, while all volute faces under the building's ceiling have convex carving. In this organization, the capitals of the colonnade alternate bolster designs between the interlaced leaf scheme and the scheme of four flutes, while the internal columns may feature only the latter (fig. 6.4).

Determining a narrower date for the building's construction would be possible if more architectural elements and the original site were discovered, but the capitals themselves offer much useful information about the period of construction. Wilhelm Alzinger, who first discussed the capitals, was particularly struck by the contrast of the bilingual capitals in embracing archaistic qualities while belonging to a later era because of proportions. Overall, the volutes are set closely around the echinus, while the Archaic capitals at Ephesos with convex volutes have more distinct

Ephesos, Selinous, and Delphi   201

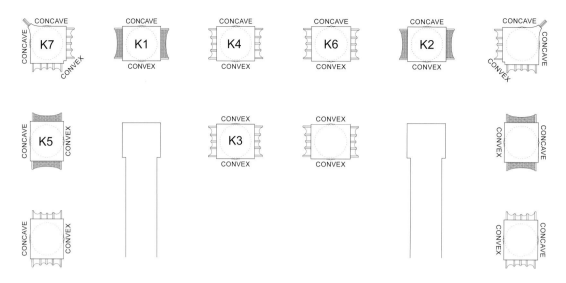

6.4. Ephesos, conjectural distribution of capitals K1–K7 on a hexastyle Ionic temple.

separation between the volute member and the echinus, a feature that suggests the capital developed from two separate superimposed elements, a wood bracket over a rounded column stop. Alzinger described this stylistic paradox exuberantly:

> [This capital type] still retains the traditional forms. The volute channel is convex and the bolster has four flutes. But what a difference there is from the capitals of the sixth century! While in the [Archaic] Artemision—despite all its progress—one still has the feeling of seeing [the capitals as] two heterogeneous elements, the round decorated column stop and the wood bracket; one hundred years later both forms have grown together into one unit, which can only be described—despite all archaism, despite all clumsiness—as Classical. There is nothing playful or frivolous here; the stonemason did not engage in any experimentation. Somehow we also sense here the majestic weightiness, which radiates from the cult statues of the same period.[15]

Although he identified the bilingual Ionic capitals as post-Archaic, Alzinger only downdated them to the fifth century BCE, a period in which there is not much other building at Ephesos for comparison. Bammer instead compared the bolster design with the late fourth-century Ionic capitals of the altar of the Artemision and pointed out unmistakable late Classical features, such as the large size of the corner palmettes, which cover much of the height of the echinus.[16] Bammer's comparisons are convincing, and the archaistic aspect of the capitals fits within the broader phenomenon of the Ionian Renaissance that revived other Archaic Ionian features such as the plinth below the column base. Late Classical and early Hellenistic Ephesos was a hive of building and a source of talent for the region: one of the new Artemision's architects, Paionios of Ephesos, was hired by the Milesians to help design the new temple of Apollo at Didyma (Vitr. 7.praef.16). The number and scale of new buildings

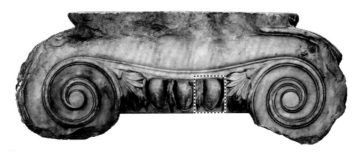

6.5. Marks from drilling on the echinus of K1. Ephesos Museum, Vienna.

at Ephesos, however, must have drawn upon workshops in the region, likely those at Miletos and Halikarnassos.

The capitals are very carefully carved. The echinus is in high relief with faint traces showing extensive use of the drill to block out the egg-and-dart molding so that the eggs could be carved in three-quarter relief (fig. 6.5). The carvers also carried over the alternation of convex and concave forms from the volutes to the corner palmettes. The petals of the corner palmettes have a convex profile on the side with convex volutes and concave petals on the side with concave volutes. A similar differentiation of corner palmettes is also seen on the bilingual Ionic capitals of the Aristaineta Monument (see fig. 6.16) and on the Propylon to the sanctuary of Apollo on Delos (see fig. 2.5).

An eighth capital came to light in 1965 on the Marble Street north of the theater.[17] This capital was carved in the Roman Imperial period to judge from the simplified, pointed eggs of the echinus molding and the notched helix that makes the volute look like a coiled rope. It is a corner capital with concave volutes on the outside faces, two convex volutes at the interior corner, and a bolster design with four flutes. Setting aside the stylistic differences that show the capital to be from a different period, it follows the scheme of the bilingual corner capital (K7) very closely. Alzinger noted the capital was of the same size as the others and might seem to belong to the same building if it were not for the difference in date; Bammer calls it a "Roman copy."[18] The capital may represent a Roman-period repair or expansion to the bilingual temple. It would signal the importance of this building and would fit with the phenomenon observed at Thessaloniki (chapter 4), where a bilingual temple was repaired with archaistic replacement parts.

Although the capitals were discovered in secondary contexts without other associated architectural elements, there are clues to the building's original site and identification. Five were found at the Theater, one (K3) on the Arcadian Street connecting the theater with the harbor, and the seventh capital is of unknown provenience.[19] The Roman copy was found nearby on the Marble Street north of the theater. The findspots in and near the theater are the result of spoliation for the construction of the early Byzantine wall, which transformed the scene building of the theater into the bridgehead of a fortification system for a more condensed city in the seventh century CE.[20] Alzinger proposed that the capitals had been taken from a temple that was near the theater, providing salvageable building materials close at hand.[21] Alzinger proposed that the bilingual Ionic capitals belonged to an important temple at Ephesos that has not yet been discovered, the temple of Athena at Trecheia.[22]

There are two major urban temples at Ephesos, attested in ancient texts, which have yet to be archaeologically identified: the temple of Apollo Pythios at the harbor and the temple of Athena at Trecheia. Athenaeus (8.62), paraphrasing Kreophylos's "Annals of the Ephesians," mentions these two temples as topographic markers connected to the city's legendary founding.[23] According to the story, the settlers of Ephesos received a Delphic oracle that a fish and a boar would guide them to the site for a new city. When the settlers arrived at the harbor, they witnessed fishermen cooking. A half-cooked fish leapt from the fire and set on fire a nearby thicket, in which a boar was sleeping. The settlers chased the startled boar up to a place called Trecheia, where Androklos, the founding hero of Ephesos, slew the boar. The Temple of Pythian Apollo at the Harbor commemorated the supposed spot of the fish sign predicted by the Pythia, and the temple of Athena at Trecheia marked the site where Androklos slew the boar. Strabo (14.1.4) offers the additional topographic clue that this Athenaion had once been the center of the original city, but that by his time the temple was outside the city's walls. The name itself implies a "rough" or "jagged" rocky topography, which has been tentatively identified with the heights on the north or northeast slope of Mt. Peion, modern Panayırdağ.[24] The Temple of Athena at Trecheia has been considered as a candidate for the Ionic capitals because it was an important civic cult that might justify so large a temple, and its likely position on Mt. Peion uphill from the theater would make it a ripe quarry for

6.6. Ephesian coin type of Antoninus Pius that may picture the temple of Athena at Trecheia on Mt. Peion (author's drawing after Karwiese 2012, cat. no. 250).

seventh-century CE builders searching for spolia. Since the work of Alzinger and Bammer, another structure, to which the Ionic capitals cannot have belonged, has been proposed as the temple of Athena Trecheia. On the cape to the northwest of the city that enclosed the ancient harbor are the remains of a prostyle temple, dubbed the *Felsspaltentempel*, with signs of intensive activity in the third and second centuries BCE and female figurines that suggest the veneration of a goddess.[25] Although an identification with the quayside Apollo temple was first considered, Peter Scherrer proposed that this temple might be the one for Athena Trecheia.[26] Recently, however, Sabine Ladstätter has dismissed this proposal and suggested that the temple, due to its proximity to the harbor, was a site for the veneration of Aphrodite as a patron of sailors.[27] Thus, the temple of Athena Trecheia is once more in contention as the structure to which these Ionic capitals belonged.

Two Ephesian coin types of Antoninus Pius depict a temple that may be the temple of Athena at Trecheia because they show it situated on Mt. Peion outside of the city walls of the Roman period (fig. 6.6).[28] The coins show an enthroned Zeus sprinkling rain onto Mt. Peion, which is represented by an allegorical recumbent figure labeled "Peion of the Ephesians." Zeus's throne sits on a rocky mountain with a cypress tree, three-story towers of the city's fortification wall, and a small gabled building. The building is rendered in very rudimentary three-quarter view with a distyle prostyle porch and a large four-panel door.[29] Bluma Trell identified the building as the Temple of Athena at Trecheia on Mt. Peion, and Stefan Karwiese follows more tentatively.[30] Given the simplified rendering of the building, it is impossible to infer much more about the building's plan. It seems possible, however, that the coins of Antoninus Pius may coincide with and even commemorate the major refurbishment indicated by the Roman-period replacement corner capital.

If the building with the bilingual Ionic capitals was the temple of Athena at Trecheia, the identification offers a compelling explanation for the archaistic design.

Ephesos, Selinous, and Delphi   205

The temple marked the mythical location for the city's foundation, the spot where Androklos planted the proverbial flag of Ephesos. Given the reorganization of the city in the late Classical and early Hellenistic period that left the temple outside the city walls, it is understandable that the building may have been completely rebuilt in this period. Although it was a new temple, the design evokes the antiquity of the spot by partially recreating an aspect of early Ionic capitals at Ephesos. The application of convex volutes to the inner faces of the capitals—as well as both faces of the capitals in the pronaos—created the effect of stepping back in time as one moved inside and closer to the mythical epicenter of Ephesos's founding. A similar effect was on display in the Ionic temple at Messon on Lesbos, also built in the second half of the fourth century BCE (see figs. 1.9, 1.10).

The recreation of the Archaic volutes on the bilingual Ionic building must be seen within the historical context of Ephesos in the late Classical and early Hellenistic period, and particularly the aftermath of the destruction of the Temple of Artemis. The arson attack on the city's famous temple was a cultural trauma for the Ephesians, which was compounded when the arsonist, Herostratos, revealed under torture that he had destroyed the temple simply for the fame of it (Str. 14.1.22; Val. Max. 8.14). The sheer senselessness of the attack was a psychological wound to the Ephesians' belief in Artemis's protection. If doubt arose that Artemis protected the city and her temple, it was assuaged later by synchronizing the date of the destruction with the birth date of Alexander. The salving interpretation posited that Artemis, who protected childbirth, was too occupied with attending to the birth of so consequential a historical figure to notice that her temple was on fire (Plut. *Vit. Alex.* 1.3.5).[31] Plutarch additionally reports that diviners at Ephesos ran about the city beating their faces, crying, and prophesying that the day of the temple's destruction marked the birth of an even greater calamity for Asia—in other words, the defeat of the Achaemenid Empire. The propagation of the synchronism, prophecy, and legends that tied the temple's destruction with the Alexander mythos were narratives that brought rational stability to the randomness of Ephesos's misfortune. The Ephesians also sought to combat Herostratos's desire for fame by supposedly sentencing to death all those who spoke the arsonist's name, and they recreated the temple with the same plan and within the same footprint.[32]

Cultural responses to historical disasters in the premodern world—particularly environmental disasters—have attracted considerable scholarly attention of late.[33] Recent developments in the field of disaster studies and the development of a social theory of trauma offer valuable perspectives on the disaster at Ephesos and bolster the notion that buildings may be social responses to disaster.[34] These approaches suggest that the trauma of disasters should be studied beyond individual psychology as group experiences, with recognizable trends in collective social responses to trauma, including the development of competing and discordant narratives, rationalizations, and tendencies to universalize traumatic events. The varied responses of the Ephesian community, including rebuilding the temple of Artemis and the *damnatio memoriae* of Herostratos, correspond to several of these trends. The narratives that linked the temple's destruction with the birth of Alexander and the downfall of the Achaemenid Empire correspond to Jeffrey Alexander's paradigm of disaster narratives that give community injuries "*Weltgeschichte* [world-historical] relevance" as a source of hope and resilience.[35] Researchers in the field of psychotherapy have shown that the process of "making meaning" out of disaster as a coping strategy begins early: interviews with the survivors of deadly earthquakes show that some offer positive-value meanings (i.e., "silver linings") of events within weeks.[36] Given the many and varied responses of the Ephesians to this defining event, it is useful to consider how the bilingual Ionic building may combine the drive to replace the lost monument through new building and to weave rationalizing stories that make sense out of trauma.

The Archaic temple of Artemis was central to the civic identity of the Ephesians long before the temple's facade became a standard design for the city's Roman period coins. The singular pride that the Ephesians took in the temple of Artemis is embedded in an anecdote that Alexander the Great offered to pay to rebuild the temple, an offer refused by the Ephesians, who preferred to take all the credit themselves (Str. 14.1.22). The anecdote falls among a class of likely apocryphal accounts of famous almost-patrons, including the story related by Plutarch that Perikles goaded the Athenian assembly into paying for the Parthenon by threatening to pay for it himself and take the credit that was due Athens (*Vit. Per.* 14.2).[37] The Lydian king, Kroisos, however, had paid for many of the older Artemision's columns, which bore dedicatory inscriptions (*IEphesos* 1518; Hdt. 1.92). The story inflating the extent of Alexander's actual patronage of Artemis Ephesia reflects the trend of aggrandizement and mythmaking surrounding the temple.[38] But if there is a kernel of truth to the story, it illustrates the way Ephesians' thinking about the temple had changed between Kroisos's patronage (ca. 550 BCE) and Alexander's (ca. 330). The temple and its reputation had become such a cornerstone of Ephesian identity that credit for the reconstruction effort could not be given to someone else. The project was instead financed privately, Strabo (14.1.22) reports, through donations by the citizens of Ephesos and especially gifts of jewelry by Ephesian women.[39]

Artemis was the civic patron of the Ephesians, but as the fame of Artemis's temple grew, the building itself became a part of the Ephesians' sense of self.[40] Some pride likely stemmed from the claim that the building was the first temple built in the Ionic order (Vitr. 4.1.7; Plin. *HN* 36.179), and thus marked the city as a leader among the other Ionian cities. The partial recreation of the archaic form of convex volutes on the structure with bilingual Ionic capitals in the aftermath of the destruction of the temple of Artemis preserved the vanishing evidence of Ephesos's early history of building. If the bilingual temple—which dates to the late fourth or third century—is correctly associated with the Temple of Athena at Trecheia, its archaism gives a sense of the legendary spot related to the city's foundation. In both cases the application of historicism represents attempts through architecture to create a contemporary visual landscape at Ephesos that correlated to storytelling about the mythic past and the early history of the city. Social memory studies emphasize the importance of place to collective memory, and the pronaos of this temple would have been an ideal location for remembering a history whose physical traces were no longer visible elsewhere.[41]

A Bilingual Ionic Monument at Selinunte, Sicily

While catastrophe at Ephesos spurred the city to revisit its earlier architectural heritage to bolster its claims to primacy in Ionia, bilingual Ionic capitals were also produced well outside the Ionian sphere. These monuments are distinctly of a private character and seem to mark the work of elite families seeking to distinguish themselves rather than knitting themselves within community identities. One of these monuments appears in western Sicily at Selinunte, the Dorian polis of Selinous: a pair of bilingual capitals belonging to a small monument set up in the area of the city's north gate (fig. 6.7).[42]

Unlike the other bilingual Ionic capitals, the pair from Selinous are carved not from white marble, but from a yellowish brown, local limestone. The capitals stand out for many other features as well, both in their construction and style. For example, these capitals are carved together with the top of the column shaft itself—a feature of economy of carving that emerged in the west in the Temple of Athena at Paestum (ca. 510–500) but in the Aegean only after the fifth century. The design of the capitals has many local forms not widely seen outside the Greek west.[43] The volute channel droops in the center on many of the Ionic capitals from Selinunte, but on the bilingual monument, it is pinched into an especially pronounced V-shape. The corner palmettes too have been completely schematized and pushed into an intermediary zone above the echinus. The echinus itself has a simple profile and does not project beyond the face of the volutes. The bolsters, often carved with a pattern of interlaced leaves on other Sicilian capitals, are unadorned and almost cylindrical in outline. All in all, the choice to carve one face with concave volutes and the other with convex volutes is one of the few features of the capitals that links the monument with the wider Aegean rather than a local school of carving. Dinu Theodorescu, who first published the capitals, questioned whether there was even an intermediary model for the bilingual design, which seemed too far removed from developments in the Aegean to take inspiration from other bilingual capitals, positing mediation either by another more prominent bilingual monument in Sicily that is now lost or precious metal objects with architectonic motifs.[44]

The capitals are part of a series of smaller Ionic monuments at Selinunte, attested by ten different capitals, an Ionic base, and an entablature fragment.[45] Most of these Ionic columns were freestanding monuments. Three of the capitals, for example, have cuttings for the plinths of marble statues.[46] One of these plinth cuttings includes the advanced left foot of a striding or contrapposto human figure around one-third life-size scale.[47] A circular impression on another capital suggests it may have supported a vessel such as a loutrophoros or lekythos.[48] While some may be votive dedications associated with the city's many sanctuaries, at least one certainly belonged to a funerary monument.[49] The bilingual Ionic capitals stand out from the rest because a pair survives, signaling an architectonic rather than freestanding arrangement. Theodorescu suggested that the pair of columns framed a naiskos or small portico. The findspot of one of the capitals near the north gate rather than in the vicinity of one of the city's many sanctuaries, however, raises the possibility that these capitals too were funerary, belonging to an extramural, aedicular tomb monument. An aedicular grave monument from Gela, executed in

6.7. Selinous, bilingual capital. Museo Archeologico Salinas, Palermo.

the Doric order, but with a miniature Ionic column depicted in the pediment, offers some precedent for this form in the west.[50]

The chronology of the capitals has been challenging to pin down because of their local peculiarity. For example, the convex volute lingered in Magna Graecia into the second half of the fourth century BCE, well after it died out in the rest of Greece in the first quarter of the fifth.[51] Theodorescu reframed this feature, arguing that the "conservative spirit" sensed in the persistence of the convex volutes was "less a sign of backwardness than a proof of the personality of the Sicilian architectural school."[52] In fact, the presence of concave volutes on one side of the capitals from Selinous puts them in the minority of local capitals. In the sequence of the Ionic monuments, Theodorescu proposed that the bilingual capitals belonged to the end of the fifth or beginning of the fourth century but could not determine whether they belonged before or after the Carthaginian sack of Selinunte in 409.[53] The disastrous result of the siege brought an end to the city's prosperity, and when Hermokrates of Syracuse resettled survivors, it was within the shell of the former city, with a much-reduced circuit of walls. The new wall made extensive use of spolia from earlier structures, and the new north gate became a focal point in the city's new defensive circuit, reaching an exceptional phase of defensive elaboration in the Hellenistic period.[54] If the inference is correct that the capitals belonged to an aedicular funerary monument just outside the north gate, then it would certainly date to after the contraction of the city's urban footprint.

One feature, as yet unobserved, offers chronological parameters for the fabrication of the monument. Both capitals have oblong cuttings on their top surfaces, which were interpreted as dowels by Theodorescu. The cutting in the top of the capital in the Palermo Museum, however, was still filled with earth (as it was in earlier published photos). When the conservation team at the Palermo Museum cleaned it out in spring 2017, it revealed that cutting has a trapezoidal profile for inserting a lewis iron, used to lift the capitals with block and tackle. The use of the lewis seems

6.9. Delphi, schematic east elevation of the Temple Terrace with the fourth-century temple, the Aristaineta Monument, and the Pillar of Prusias II.

a pair of Ionic columns, where bilingual capitals blended a new form of dedication into a crowded architectural landscape (fig. 6.9).

The precedent for columnar monuments in the Sanctuary of Apollo was set early on by the column of the Naxians, built ca. 575 BCE (fig. 6.10). This imposing column with a megalithic sphinx, totaling ca. 12.5 meters in height, showed that verticality could provide visual prominence in a sanctuary where inclined topography and the clutter of previous dedications prevented expansive building. Many different types of pillar monuments were set up on the Temple Terrace, including the triangular pillar of the Naupaktians and Messenians that mirrors their pillar at Olympia topped by the Nike of Paionios, Aemilius Paullus's rectangular pedestal commemorating his victory in the battle of Pydna, and a freestanding column (Ionic or Corinthian) topped with an honorific portrait of Drusilla, the sister of the emperor Caligula.[61] Pillar monuments erected directly in front of the fourth-century temple of Apollo, notably the pillar of Aemilius Paullus, added new columns to the view of the temple's facade and elevated honorees to the level of the east pediment sculptures, subtly inserting them among the screen figures of Apollo, Artemis, Leto, and the Muses.[62]

Jean Replat collected together the toppled elements of the Aristaineta Monument excavated on the Temple Terrace and identified the form of the bicolumnar monuments characteristic at Delphi.[63] While Ionic columnar monuments supporting statues were a popular form of dedication at several sanctuaries in the Hellenistic and Roman periods, at each site they follow a different scheme (see fig. 6.10), such as single columns on orthostate bases at the Sanctuary of Apollo at Klaros.[64] The bicolumnar monuments are a distinctive phenomenon of Delphi, which has four examples that can be confidently reconstructed, but as many as eight possible examples. They take the form of a statue group elevated on top of a pair of Ionic columns spanned by a segment of entablature, in what appeared to be "a 'slice' of an Ionic colonnade" in the words of Courby, who first published Aristaineta's monument.[65] Even the later unitary column honoring Drusilla was topped with a section of entablature in keeping with the tradition of bicolumnar monuments (by comparison, at Klaros the gilded bronze statues of Roman officials were doweled directly into the tops of Ionic capitals).[66] Delphic bicolumnar monuments may have captured the imagination of painters, as Third Style and Fourth Style Roman wall painting features similar pairs of columns in sacro-idyllic landscapes.[67] The bicolumnar form may owe something to the monument of Ptolemy II and Arsinoe II at Olympia dedicated by their general Kallikrates of Samos, which pictured the couple separately on freestanding columns united by a long exedra base (see fig. 6.10).[68] Most of the pieces of the Aristaineta Monument have now been moved to the Delphi Museum, where the capitals and the entablature are partially reconstructed on a terrace before the museum's entrance (fig. 6.11).[69]

The Aristaineta Monument was erected on a simple stepped base of gray Profitis Elias limestone surmounted by two columns and an entablature of white Parian marble. The top step bore a short dedicatory inscription beginning with Aristaineta's name and patronymic, which has been reconstructed to include an ethnonym like other bicolumnar monuments:

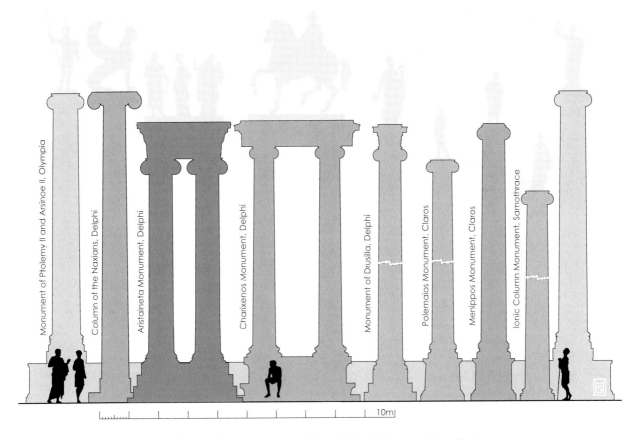

6.10. Scale comparison of Ionic column monuments at Olympia, Delphi, Klaros, and Samothrace.

6.11. Delphi, elements of the Aristaineta Monument. Archaeological Museum of Delphi.

Ἀρισ]ται[ν]έτα Τιμολάο[υ Αἰτωλὶς Ἀπόλλωνι Πυθίωι[70]
Aris]tai[n]eta, daughter of Timolao[s, (dedicated) to Apollo Pythios

The two Ionic columns are particularly close together: the lower diameter of the columns is ca. 85 centimeters and the intercolumniation ca. 73 centimeters. It was unusual for buildings to have an intercolumnar space less than the diameter of the columns, let alone a space barely wide enough to pass through. Yet for an architectonic statue base the spacing prioritizes stability over standard considerations for buildings (fig. 6.12). The two Ionic columns had capitals with alternate convex and concave volute faces (fig. 6.13). The columns supported a segment of an Ionic entablature with a second, longer inscription on the architrave:

[Ἀρισταινέτα Αἰτωλὶς τὸμ πατέρ]α Τιμόλαον
[καὶ τὰμ] ματέρα [_ _ ca.8 _ _] καὶ αὐτὰν
[καὶ τὸν υ]ἱ[ὸ]ν Τιμ[όλαον Ἀπ]όλλωνι.[71]
[Aristaineta, an Aetolian, (dedicated figures of) her fath]er Timolaos,
[her] mother [...], herself,
and her son Timolaos for Apollo.

6.13. Delphi, Aristaineta Monument, opposite convex and concave sides of the bilingual capitals.

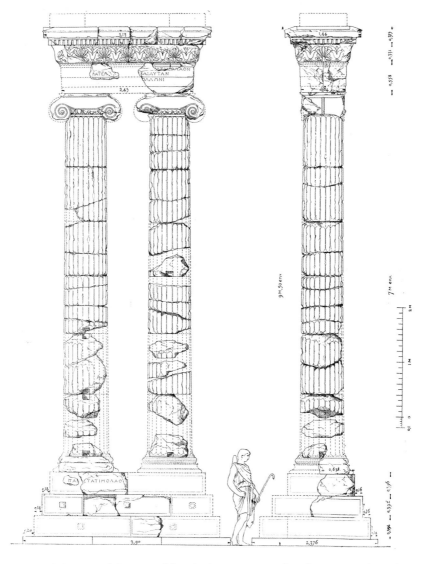

6.12. Delphi, restored elevations of the Aristaineta Monument (Courby 1927, 258, fig. 202).

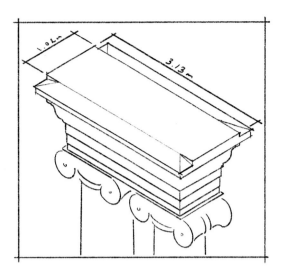
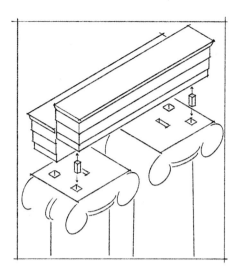

6.14. Schematic diagram of base for plinth of statue group on the Aristaineta Monument.

6.15. Schematic diagram of capital doweling on the Aristaineta Monument.

The epistyle inscription indicates that the monument was topped off with statues depicting three generations of Aristaineta's family. Above the epistyle are a frieze course and a coping course with a miniature Ionic cornice of dentils and geison. The frieze course has a large relief palmette-and-lotus pattern carved over a cyma reversa profile, a form that is previously known in sima courses but is applied to friezes in the fourth and third centuries (as in the Tholos at Epidauros and the naiskos at Didyma).[72] Usefully, the cyma reversa frieze course cantilevers outward to create a larger platform for the statue group on top. Anne Jacquemin and Elena Partida compare the lotus-and-palmette chain decorating the frieze to the richly carved anthemion pattern on the Siphnian treasury (see fig. 3.14), but Didier Laroche dismisses the comparison.[73] Relief anthemion patterns are not unusual in the third century, but at Delphi they were prominent on the sixth-century Ionic treasuries and occasionally feature the play of convex and concave elements.

There are no signs of how the statues were affixed to the top of the monument. Either there was an additional stone course for securing bronze statues that has not survived, or stone figures rested freely above the cornice. The cornice of the Aristaineta Monument has a sloped edge at front and back but not at the sides, which creates a long base for statues (3.13 × 1.02 m). Courby reconstructs a lost level of a stone plinth for socketing bronze statues (ca. 3.00 × 0.94 m) that was positioned on top of the cornice level (fig. 6.14). The inscription attests that the figures in the statue group were Aristaineta's father Timolaos I, her mother, whose name was about eight characters long, Aristaineta herself, and her son Timolaos II. Partida proposed that there were only three freestanding figures, with Aristaineta holding an infant Timolaos II in her arms.[74] Three figures would fit well on the roughly 3:1 proportions of the base. But a snapshot of three generations of a family at their relative ages should not necessarily be expected. Other dynastic monuments depict non-contemporaneous generations, such as the nearby Daochos Monument, which included a depiction of the dedicator's great-grand-uncle as a teenage athlete.[75]

6.16. Comparison of the corner palmettes on opposite faces of the Aristaineta Monument capitals. Archaeological Museum of Delphi.

Sheila Dillon, in a photomontage reconstruction of Aristaineta's monument, restores four freestanding figures, which could also be squeezed onto the footprint of the monument more closely together.[76] The three-column monument of the Aetolians Lykos and Diokles supported a group of six or seven figures.[77] Given Aristaineta's emphasis on enumerating family members and the generational parallelism between Timolaos I and Timolaos II, it seems likely that grandfather and grandson were freestanding figures at opposite ends of the architrave.

To add stability to the bicolumnar shape, the epistyle was doweled to the capitals at their outside edges rather than at their centers (fig. 6.15). The dowel holes in turn secure the relationship between the capitals and the inscription on the epistyle: the concave volutes were paired with the inscription and faced southeast over the Temple Terrace. The convex volutes were oriented northwest away from the terrace. This is one of the few monuments with bilingual Ionic capitals where the orientation and direction of the capitals is fixed with certainty by internal construction features.

The Aristaineta Monument applies the familiar pairing of opposite convex and concave faces on bilingual Ionic capitals to a monument with distinctly Hellenistic proportioning. The volutes are smaller and more widely spaced, and the echinus is exceptionally low.[78] Although the echinus is shortened on the front, the egg-and-dart molding is carefully executed all the way around the capital below the bolsters, and the molding is tilted downward considerably, showing a concern for the low angle of viewers looking up at the monument on the Temple Terrace (see fig. 6.18).[79] The concave face has a half round helix set off from the shallow concavity by thin fillets. The convex face has a smoothed, bulging canalis separated from the helix by an inscribed line. On both sides the volute eye is a flat disk with a drilled hole for attaching a metal ornament. Pointing to the plain ovolo molding of the abacus, Courby described the capitals as "of a very simplified type," and concluded that the convex volutes, which were on the northern side of the monument facing away from the terrace, were a simplification to save time.[80] The difference between the two sides, however, extends also to the corner palmettes, which have different forms on opposite sides (fig. 6.16). The concave side has a standard six-petal palmette

Ephesos, Selinous, and Delphi   217

6.17. Delphi, bolsters of the capitals of the Aristaineta Monument and Stoa of the Athenians. Archaeological Museum of Delphi.

springing from a leaf-shaped sheath, while the convex face has a rounded bell-shaped flower springing from a bifurcated sheath and stem node. It is understandable that this feature has escaped notice since the capitals are very badly damaged and only one such bell-shaped flower survives sufficiently to be differentiated.

Another feature of the capital that could be taken for a simplification is the bolster design. The sides of the Ionic capitals of the Aristaineta Monument have a plain bolster with only a narrow balteus of two half rounds (fig. 6.17). The design, however, is taken directly from the capitals of the nearby Stoa of the Athenians (fig. 6.18), replicating one of the distinguishing features of the early Classical Attic style of the Ionic order. The Atticizing bolster and convex canalis of the capitals suggest that the monument should be interpreted within the broader historical context and the close-knit architectural landscape of the Sanctuary of Apollo, where a woman from a prominent third-century Aetolian family and a relative late comer to Delphi sought to embed herself within a tradition of architectural dedications and perhaps capture a bit of their prestige.[81]

6.18. Photomontage of the Aristaineta Monument (view from below).

Courby, working with Replat, restored the Aristaineta Monument to a foundation in a conspicuous spot on the Temple Terrace, on axis with the flank colonnade of the temple of Apollo and surrounded by commemoratives of famous historical events. Just to the west of Aristaineta's monument was the Eurymedon Palm, a gilded bronze date palm topped off with a gold statue of Athena that celebrated the decisive victory of the Delian League over the Persians in 465.[82] When the Athenians were preparing their expedition to Sicily in 415, crows supposedly swarmed this dedication and pecked off the gilding and gold fruit in a portent of defeat—although to the eyes of Pausanias the damage looked more like the work of vandals than birds (Paus. 10.15.4–5). Nearby to the east was the stone base for a gold tripod erected by Gelon, the tyrant of Syracuse, to commemorate his victory at the battle of Himera in 480 BCE. Gelon may have intended his gold tripod at Delphi to mirror the gold tripod of the Plataea victory monument and to invite comparison between the contemporary victories over Persians and Carthaginians.[83] Both gold tripods caught the eye of the Phokian army, who melted them down during the Third Sacred War (355–346), though their inscribed bases remained. The Phokians, in turn, were punished with an indemnity for looting the sanctuary, part of which—Pausanias reports—paid for a colossal 15.5-meter-tall statue of Apollo Sitalkas that Courby restored to the large square base between Gelon's empty tripod base and the Aristaineta Monument (Paus. 10.15.2).[84] When Aristaineta secured this prime location for her dedication, she must have appreciated that it would be seen in comparison with other towering monuments and that more tall dedications would follow.

Courby's reconstruction of the position of the Aristaineta Monument seemed secured by the Pillar of Prusias II, which was erected later, slightly overlapping the step blocks of the adjacent monument (now that the Pillar of Prusias II has been reerected on site, one can see the void at its base with the impression of the missing steps).[85] The Aetolian League erected this statue and pedestal to honor Prusias II after he became the king of Bithynia in 188 BCE. Aristaineta's monument was certainly earlier, and is often identified as the first in the series of bicolumnar dedications, probably dating to the second quarter of the third century BCE.[86] A small orthostate base was later erected just in front of the Aristaineta Monument and probably obscured the inscription on its steps. Courby criticized the reconstructed design of the bicolumnar monument for appearing top-heavy: the large entablature and closely spaced columns seem too large for the truncated base with steps of impractically shallow treads.[87] These departures from the aesthetics of architectural orders are the result of making the most of a limited ground plan and exploiting height for visual prominence in an already crowded area.

The reconstructed position of the monument has been disputed, first by Pierre Amandry, who thought that it was incompatible with the foundation.[88] Anne Jacquemin and Didier Laroche have recently attributed a block from a different monument to this foundation: a marble step block with recessed rebates so similar to the steps of the fourth-century Apollo temple that the block was initially restored as part of the temple, perhaps for a statue base within.[89] Jacquemin and Laroche suggest that this step block may instead be the base for the statue of Apollo made by the Amphictyony from the war indemnity against the Phokians, which Pausanias (10.15.7) mentions in this area. This new identification would unmoor the Aristaineta Monument, which Laroche has elsewhere suggested may belong a bit farther to the west.[90] Courby's original preference for placing the Apollo Sitalkas figure on the adjacent base was based on the assumption that the large square base had the footprint required for so colossal a statue, and it is difficult to envision how a figure might fit on the elongated base that so well fit the bicolumnar monument of Aristaineta.

At first glance, the bilingual Ionic capitals on the Aristaineta Monument might seem to be a simplification on columns that were surrounded on both sides by other monuments and backed up against a terrace wall. But adding different types of corner palmettes to each side drew attention to the difference as a design feature, which may have been further differentiated by the painting and metal ornaments added to both sides. A three-dimensional analysis of the sanctuary shows that not only were the convex faces of the capitals visible, but that a visitor walking to the theater would have stood almost at eye level with the convex faces of the capitals. The monument must be viewed in context, both in terms of the historical setting of a dedication by an elite Aetolian woman at Delphi and its architectural setting within a forest of other, older Ionic orders at Delphi. Seen in this setting, Aristaineta created a retrospective monument that combined features of earlier Ionic monuments to situate it among other Delphic votives and to lend an aspect of historicism to a family portrait emphasizing matrilineal genealogy.

The Aristaineta Monument is one part of a wave of third-century Aetolian dedications at Delphi. The Aetolians, despite their geographic proximity to Delphi, were peripheral to the Sanctuary of Apollo in the Archaic and Classical periods—congregating instead at their ancestral sanctuary at Thermon.[91] The confederation of the Aetolians into a league (*koinon*) in the fourth century BCE expanded their regional power rapidly. When the Aetolian League helped resist Macedonian control of Delphi in the 330s, they were rewarded with the privilege of promanteia, the right of first consultation of Apollo's oracle.[92] But when the Aetolians then installed a governor and garrison at Delphi and sought to control the Delphic Amphyctyony, the international council that administered the sanctuary, Sparta, and allied states led an expedition to liberate Delphi from the Aetolians in 280.[93] The next year, the Aetolians repulsed the invasion of the Gauls into central Greece before they could sack Delphi. The victory was commemorated at the sanctuary with the regular celebration of a new festival, the *Soteria*, and a slew of monuments, including the arms of the Gauls dedicated in the West Stoa, a statue of an allegorical figure of Aetolia seated on a pile of spoils, and a statue of the general Eurydamos, who had led the Aetolians to victory.[94] Anne Jacquemin has pointed out that the Aetolian commemorations of their Gallic victory did not appear overnight but were built over the next four decades as the Aetolians began to exploit the ideological significance of their defense of Delphi.[95] Like the Macedonians, the Aetolians had occupied a gray area of Greekness in the Classical period, but the defeat of the Gauls offered them a pivot to change how they were perceived and reframe their relationship to Delphi. Michael C. Scott emphasizes that the Aetolian defense of Delphi "confirmed their right to occupy the sanctuary, and more importantly, confirmed them once and for all as defenders of Greece, and thus Greek."[96] Through state dedications and private benefactions by elite families, the Aetolians inserted themselves into the landscape and history of the sanctuary to affirm their place within a Greek identity from which they had long been excluded.

Aetolian dedications of this period include the new form of bicolumnar monuments. The dedicator of one of the monuments—Charixenos, son of Kydrion— has a well-documented historical career at the highest level of Aetolian society.

Charixenos was the annual *strategos* of the Aetolian League for four annual terms between 255 / 254 and 235 / 234, including in 241 / 240 when the Aetolian League began a campaign against Sparta.[97] The initial reconstruction of the bicolumnar monument of Charixenos by S. da Fonseca topped the tall pedestal with an equestrian statue of Charixenos in his role as a general (see fig. 6.10).[98] Jacquemin, however, emphasized Charixenos's religious involvement at Delphi—marked by his reorganization of the *Soteria* in 242—and proposed that the bicolumnar monument should instead be topped with a figural group including Charixenos, Apollo, and the "White Virgins" of the *Soteria*.[99] Another bicolumnar monument was set up by Pleistainos, who was the son of Eurydamos, the Aetolian *strategos* in the war against the Gauls.[100] Pleistainos's bicolumnar monument featured statues of himself and his daughter Lacedaimonia, whose name likely attests to her father's involvement in the Aetolian campaign against Sparta in 240.[101] Although the historical careers of Aristaineta and her family members are not documented, the Aristaineta Monument appears to have been a similar monument of elite Aetolian representation at Delphi.

Timolaos is not attested among the known names of the Aetolian *strategoi*, but Pausanias may have this monument in mind when he glosses over the Aetolian dedications: "The Aetolians have statues of most of their generals" (10.15.2).[102] A viewer might have been struck by the absence of the father of Aristaineta's son. It is not simply that he is not among the family portraits or named in the inscription, but the choice to repeat the maternal grandfather's name seems to cut the child's father out of the picture. Reading between the lines, it seems that Aristaineta may have had an unconventional family group, and this may have been the impetus for creating a monumental family portrait that emphasized the matrilineal genealogy of Timolaos II.

Sheila Dillon has raised the question of visibility in this monument: portrait statues were more often set on low bases that presented a subject with individualized facial details near the viewer, but columnar monuments like Aristaineta's elevated the figures to a level where most of their identity was visible through formulaic body types and postures.[103] For Dillon, "the emphasis was on the monument itself, which was massive in relation to the scale of the figures."[104] While the architectonic pedestal set the figures distant from the viewer, it also gave them a conspicuously privileged position overlooking the heart of the sanctuary. The figures of Aristaineta and her family stood as lofty spectators permanently watching rituals take place before the altar and the temple. The two Ionic columns also elevated the portraits near the level of the pediment figures of Apollo, Artemis, and Leto. This was a bold juxtaposition; when the proud mother Niobe made a comparison of her family to Leto's, it ended badly. The degree of visibility should also be considered for the monument's bilingual Ionic capitals. This is the rare instance where bilingual Ionic capitals can be repositioned exactly—in this case with the convex faces on the northwest side, out of direct sunlight for most of the day. The arrangement represents the design principle of positioning high-relief elements in direct light for greater shadow contrast. But it is also worth questioning the visibility of the convex faces of the capitals since the standpoints from which the monument could be seen

6.19. Photomontage of the Aristaineta Monument (view ascending the path to the east).

were limited to the Temple Terrace and the path up to the theater (see figs. 6.18–20).

When viewed in plan, it seems that the rear of the Aristaineta Monument was largely obstructed since it was built near a terrace wall for the path leading up to the Daochos Monument and the theater. An investigation of the levels in this area, however, shows that the Aristaineta Monument extended to a greater height than the terrace. Figures 6.18–6.20 represent reconstructed views of the Aristaineta Monument from below in the court before the temple (see fig. 6.18) and following the itinerary of

6.20. Photomontages of the Aristaineta Monument (view from the terrace to the north).

a visitor walking past the altar up to the terrace of the Daochos Monument (fig. 6.19) and continuing toward the theater (fig. 6.20). Following this path, a visitor encountered the northwest side of the monument at a higher level, passing directly behind the pair of columns at nearly eye level with the convex faces of the capitals.

Although the southeast side of the Aristaineta Monument presented the primary intended viewpoint with the inscriptions and frontal figures, one received a new impression of it while walking around the monument and seeing it from an elevated angle. A visitor walking up the path to the theater could glimpse the court of the temple and altar between the Ionic columns and appreciate the special vantage point enjoyed by Aristaineta's family. Looking up at the monument from below (see fig. 6.18), the figures were silhouetted alone against the sky, but seen from behind (see fig. 6.20), the anonymous backs of the figures blended into an elevated zone of other statues such as the neighboring figure of Athena standing on the Eurymedon Palm to create the impression of an above-ground habitat like the tree canopy of a forest. It is also from this angle, where the monument blends more completely into a landscape crammed with dedications, that one saw the convex volutes with their archaistic aspect.

The Aristaineta Monument has several archaistic features creating an eclectic mix of Archaic, Classical, and contemporary styles. The convex volutes of the capitals must have called to mind Archaic Ionic capitals since there was at least one early votive Ionic column at Delphi with convex volutes.[105] It might seem that the addition of bell-shaped flowers—a design that only became popular in Greek relief carving in the fifth and fourth centuries—negated an archaistic appearance to this side of the capitals, but bell-shaped flowers occur in other archaistic monuments (like the reliefs of the Gate of Zeus and Hera, Thasos), and a Greek viewer might not have viewed this flower shape as obviously modern.[106]

The combination of convex and concave volutes may have also called to mind another neighboring monument, the Chian Altar, to which Didier Laroche has restored a fragment of a volute with convex and concave sides.[107] Elena Partida proposes that the bilingual Ionic capitals were explicitly a Cycladic tradition (given their presence at Delos and Neapolis), and in conjunction with the identification of the Aristaineta Monument's marble as Parian, she proposes that the whole structure is the design of a Parian Architect.[108] Is it possible that the bilingual Ionic capitals called to mind the Propylon to the Sanctuary of Apollo on Delos, which had not yet been replaced? The adjacent monument of the Eurymedon Palm replicates an element of the Delian landscape, the palm tree under which Apollo was born, and it is possible that Aristaineta meant to reference the gateway to Apollo's other most important sanctuary. The bolster design also mirrors the capitals of the nearby Stoa of the Athenians (see fig. 6.18). The Stoa of the Athenians commemorated a major military victory, which was expressed in the large inscription on the monument's steps: "the Athenians dedicated this stoa and the weapons and ship-finials they took from their enemies."[109] The vague wording leaves open which of the "enemies" that the Athenians defeated at land and sea are meant, the Persians (in 480–479) or the Peloponnesians (459–450).[110] Pausanias reports seeing spoils from an Athenian victory over the Peloponnesians, which he thought came from a battle in 429, though the building and inscription are surely earlier (Paus. 10.11.6). Comparison to either Athens's victories against Persian or Spartan enemies was ideologically significant for an Aetolian because the defense of Delphi against the Gauls mirrored the similar salvation of Delphi from the Persians, and the Aetolian League was frequently in conflict with Sparta.

Aristaineta's bicolumnar monument was not alone in having archaizing and Atticizing attributes; two other bicolumnar monuments show the same traits. One monument is represented by a pair of Pentelic marble Ionic capitals that were first identified as belonging to an interior Ionic order for the fourth-century temple of Apollo.[111] Replat argued convincingly that, although no epistyle for the columns survived, the dowel cuttings on the tops of the capitals indicated that they belonged to a bicolumnar monument.[112] This bicolumnar monument duplicates closely the design of the columns of the north porch of the Erechtheion on the Athenian Acropolis in the design of the capitals, necking drums, and bases. The monument of Lykos and Diokles also imitates the design of the Erechtheion capitals, but only on the bolster with bead-and-reel chains. In effect, the historicizing bicolumnar monuments at Delphi recreated "slices" of historical Ionic orders, both internally replicating older monuments at Delphi—as with the Aristaineta Monument—and replicating the central cult structure on the Athenian Acropolis.

Aristaineta produced the last instances of bilingual Ionic capitals in a monument that was fitting of the early Hellenistic period. As a personal dedication presenting a family portrait, the replication of historical forms may have emphasized a respect for tradition in a monument that framed matrilineal genealogy. In some small way, the two versions of Ionic capitals, one in contemporary concave style and the other in an archaistic convex style, may have mirrored the figures of two men named Timolaos a generation removed. The Aetolians had won their control of Delphi through the defeat of the Spartans in 280 and by repulsing the Gauls in 279, so the partial replication of an Athenian victory monument over Peloponnesians or Persians was fitting. Although a member of an elite family like Aristaineta could secure a prime spot for a dedication within the sanctuary, it was through an architectonic monument that mirrored the sanctuary's long history of dedications that she successfully inserted herself into the Delphic landscape. The phenomenon of bilingual capitals comes to an end with this monument, but it does not mark an end to interests in archaism and eclecticism in design in the early Hellenistic period. While this specific form was not repeated further, architects and patrons developed the impetus behind this phenomenon in larger and more elaborate ways.

The sites of Ephesos, Selinous, and Delphi, though widely dispersed in the Greek world show new responses to older Ionic monuments. Ephesos and Delphi had a long history of building in the Ionic order stretching back to the first half of the sixth century BCE. Architects, stone carvers, and patrons active at these sites in the fourth and third centuries could not help but engage with the built landscape or, in the case of Ephesos, a landscape of ruins. The Ephesians addressed the trauma of the arson attack on the Temple of Artemis at Ephesos through building and mythmaking—two impulses that may be felt at work in the Ionic building with bilingual Ionic capitals. By recreating the convex volutes from the Archaic temple of Artemis, Ephesian builders restored to the city's visual landscape the early form of Ionic capital, which they must have taken pride in inventing. At Delphi in the third century, the Aetolians took on a new role as the defenders of the Panhellenic sanctuary of Apollo, from which they had previously been excluded. Aristaineta, a prominent Aetolian woman, borrowed from a range of Ionic monuments at Delphi, including the Stoa of the Athenians and the sixth-century Ionic treasuries, to make a statue base that inserted her own family into the collage of famous Greek monuments and asserted the inheritance of her son. At Selinous too, private patrons turned to the Ionic order to distinguish themselves, setting their constructions apart from the Doric backdrop of the city's major public buildings.

The examples from Ephesos and Delphi show a developed system for placing high-relief carving in direct sunlight for maximum contrast. At Delphi, the convex sides of the capitals are oriented to the northwest and out of sunlight for most of the day. At Ephesos, the capitals were oriented with the convex forms within the building's colonnade. This is a change from the sixth and fifth centuries, when bilingual

Ionic capitals at Delos and Pallene in Attica had the convex sides of the bilingual Ionic capitals oriented outward and southward (on Delos). This is not to say that the convex sides were completely subordinated and out of view in the late Classical and Hellenistic periods. At Delphi, the convex faces of the capitals could be seen almost on eye level from the path up to the theater, where a viewer might picture the archaistic monument within the landscape of important historical dedications. At Ephesos, secondary interior columns with convex faces on both sides created an effect of stepping back in time by entering the portico, which might have been particularly meaningful if the capitals belonged to the temple of Athena at Trecheia that marked the spot of Ephesos's foundation. Both monuments carried their retrospective program to the design of the bolsters: Aristaineta copied directly from the Stoa of the Athenians, while the Ephesians drew from the older Temple of Artemis. Both teams of marble carvers delighted in commissions to use different sculptural approaches to opposite faces and created different designs for the corner palmettes on opposite sides of the capitals for each monument.

Chapter 7

Conclusion

This book assembles the full corpus of Ionic column capitals with one convex face and one concave face, arguing that they represent a distinctive and informative phenomenon in Greek architecture. This type depended on the skills of stone carvers, who easily switched between convex and concave surface modeling and often combined the two for dazzling textural effects in moldings and floral ornament. More so than Doric, the Ionic architectural tradition embraced variegation— in ornamental patterns, the use of color, and textural modulation. These capitals form a striking counterpart to bilingual Attic vases, which combine older and newer painting techniques, initially at a period of transition but motivated by an aesthetic interest in variety or *poikilia*. Bilingual Ionic capitals represent an epitome of the delight in variation (*Variationsfreude*) evident in so many works of Ionic architecture. The corpus of these monuments also has a wide scope, spanning much of the Greek world, from western Asia Minor to Sicily and the Thracian coastline, including major Panhellenic sanctuaries at Delos and Delphi, continuing from the second half of the sixth through the first half of the third centuries BCE, and including temples, a sanctuary propylon, votive dedications, and one possible funerary monument.

The seemingly marginal place of bilingual capitals in the story of Ionic architecture comes from three unavoidable factors. None survive in situ, and the ruined state of the monuments to which they belonged makes them difficult to picture. Those well-preserved examples displayed in museums are often backed up against walls with the contrast between their faces hidden from view. Therefore, this study presents bilingual Ionic capitals so that they can be compared one to another and in their revisualized settings. It considers the tools and techniques of stone carvers shaping their final visual appearance, the effect of light, shadow, and angle of view, the orientation of the capitals as part of an observer's movement through and around a building, and principally the retrospective reflection of early Ionian building styles in changing social and religious settings. This concluding chapter summarizes the overarching connections that emerge from viewing all these structures synoptically.

Previously bilingual Ionic capitals have been linked to other possible origins— most often to half-carved Ionic capitals where one blank or unfinished side was presumably out of sight in a building. Were marble carvers taking a shortcut on less visible parts of columns by reverting to the older convex style? To test this notion, I performed a marble carving test, replicating part of a convex and concave volute from the Pallene building. Although the concave volute required scooping out six times as much material as the carving of the convex volute, it took in total only three minutes more per hour of work (see fig. 3.9). Time saved was negligible. Viewed in aggregate bilingual capitals demonstrate that the differences in carving techniques were deployed to heighten visual contrast rather than as a timesaving measure. Only one monument shows signs of unfinished carving on one side (Pallene, chapter 5) and there it is on the concave side, contrary to expectations. When the capitals have drilled holes for affixing metal, stone, or glass attachments to the volute eyes, it appears on both sides (Eretria, chapter 5; Ephesos, Delphi, chapter 6), unless the scheme for the capital has the convex volute terminating in a whorl (Neapolis, Thessaloniki, chapter 4). Not only were the faces given the same attention in carving and embellishment, but several of the capitals also have other sculptural differentiation that draws attention to the contrast between the two sides. These variations include different corner palmette designs (Delos, chapter 2; Ephesos, Delphi, chapter 6), different designs in the volute eyes (Delos, chapter 2), contrasting volute eyes with whorls (Thessaloniki and Kavala, chapter 4), differences in the molding of the echinus (Delos, chapter 2), or the addition of relief embellishment to the canalis (Neapolis, chapter 4). Two buildings have varied bolster designs among multiple capitals (Delos, chapter 2; Ephesos, chapter 6), and two temples have secondary, smaller capitals with either two concave faces (Thessaloniki, chapter 4) or two convex faces (Ephesos, chapter 6) that represent a uniform treatment of the columns of the interior or pronaos of those buildings.

Many examples exist of alternating convex and concave elements in Ionic architectural moldings, particularly on column bases (see, e.g., figs. 1.6, 2.18, 2.19) and in anthemion patterns (see, e.g., figs. 3.16, 3.19). These cases show how effortlessly marble carvers switched between convex and concave surface modeling, deploying it for textural variety and coloristic effect. In some instances, carvers inverted surface modeling when there were kinks in patterns, where moldings were interrupted, or turned corners (see figs. 3.14, 3.15). Over time, builders fine-tuned the relief carving of Ionic capitals and Doric column flutes to exaggerate shading and make buildings "more painterly" (Vitr. 4.4.4), but they also delighted in the mixture of convex and concave forms as a type of ornament.

Bilingual capitals suggest a consciousness among builders about the different visibility conditions outside and inside colonnades. This awareness is also attested by trends in polychromy presented in chapter 5. On Aigina, both the early Archaic and late Archaic phases of the temple of Aphaia used a scheme of tonal adjustments to balance the appearance of the sunlit exterior triglyphs and the shaded triglyphs within the colonnade (see figs. 5.8, 5.10). Ancient builders often tried to rescue rather than abandon columns in suboptimal viewing conditions. This echoes patterns in architectural sculpture, where parts of figures not visible to pedestrian viewers were still carved in an effort to make perfect dedications for the gods. A legacy of this concern for balancing exterior and interior views of column surfaces in the work of Vitruvius (4.4.2), who recommended slimming inner columns and adding more flutes to harmonize with the outer peristyle columns. One fundamental observation of this survey of bilingual capitals is that all the examples did not have a consistent orientation in relation to exterior or interior and exposure to sunlight. Yet, builders grappling with the same problem at different sites should not be expected to always hit upon the same answer. When builders of the fourth century began to add painted shadows and highlights to triglyphs to offset the flattening effect of the traditional blue coating, they produced completely opposite solutions at Selinous and Starosel (see fig. 5.10). The double-sided variation of bilingual capitals combined two established forms that could counterbalance different lighting and visibility conditions, but the underlying rationale seems to shift over time. The high-relief sides of capitals at late sixth-century Delos and mid fifth-century Pallene faced inward to lend distinction to areas in shadow; at late fourth-century Ephesos and early third-century Delphi, the high-relief sides were oriented outward or toward direct sunlight.

Only one capital (Eretria, chapter 4) had certain traces of paint when it was discovered, but all were assuredly painted. A survey of painted traces on other Ionic capitals (see table 5.1) shows a great range of hues and patterns. One constant, however, was the volute channel, which was never obscured with dark paint. In all cases, the canalis of Ionic capitals appears to have been reserved unpainted or plastered white. There is little reason, therefore, to suspect that the sculpted forms of convex and concave volutes were obscured by polychrome decoration. Not only did paint not mask the sculpting of bilingual Ionic capitals, but the addition of paint to the helix and volute eyes likely heightened the divergence of the two faces. Most noteworthy of all are two fifth-century Athenian buildings with Ionic capitals that are carved the same but were painted differently from one another, including different patterns, different colors, and even different palettes of pigments (see figs. 5.16, 5.17). Although few examples of color variegation still survive, it must have been more widespread, given the frequency with which Ionic buildings include multiple bolster designs, which sometimes alternate, or—as in the temple at Messon on Lesbos— have subtle variations on every capital. These more widespread practices of crafting Ionic capitals on the same building with different sculpted patterns and painted designs must have preconditioned the ancient viewers of bilingual capitals to look for differences rather than ignore them.

One late sixth-century building (Delos, chapter 2) and one fifth century building (Pallene, chapter 5) had capitals oriented with the convex volutes on the exterior, while one building of the late fourth century (Ephesos, chapter 6) had concave faces on the exterior and two others of the first quarter of the fifth century (Thessaloniki and Neapolis, chapter 4) likely did as well. Only two capitals can be restored in relation to their cardinal direction. The late sixth-century Propylon to the Sanctuary of Apollo on Delos (chapter 2) had the convex faces of the capitals oriented southward and in direct sunlight, while the third-century Aristaineta Monument at Delphi had the concave faces of the capitals oriented southeast in direct light for most of the day. The change in orientation of bilingual Ionic capitals over time corresponds to the development of a design principal that put higher relief carving in direct sunlight to maximize shadow contrast. This principle may often be detected (e.g., the Parthenon has high-relief metopes on the exterior and a low-relief Ionic frieze over the cella), but it was rarely applied with consistency, and sometimes an opposite principle seems to be at work (e.g., Temple E at Selinous and the temple of Zeus at

Olympia both have high-relief metopes within their colonnades over the cella and no exterior metope sculpture). The taste for shadow definition underlies the development of high-relief Ionic capitals with a concave volute and their eventual uniform acceptance. However, the two earlier bilingual Ionic monuments with capitals oriented with the convex faces on the facade (at Delos and Pallene) show that this principle was not accepted immediately. Early architects were evidently not of one mind when it came to relief carving and visual contrast, and the designers of these two monuments perhaps rationalized that high-relief design helped add definition to elements in shadow.

The design choices that underlie bilingual Ionic column capitals must be understood through a model of distributed agency, combining the input of stone carvers, architects, and patrons—a model sketched out in chapter 1. This meeting of minds is amply attested by an inscription from Delos (*IG* II^2 1678, ll. 10–13) that alludes to a process of contracting a master carver to produce a full-scale, functional prototype, approved by the architect and building committee, and then replicated on site by the team of builders. Stone carvers held in reserve the techniques for swapping convex and concave surface modeling so often seen in Ionic moldings and anthemion patterns. Yet bilingual capitals implement this trade secret at a much larger scale and in a more prominent position, deployed by architects to meet the goals of their patrons. This book argues that the staying power of bilingual Ionic capitals lies in their retrospective aspect. Patrons harnessed variegation at large scale to draw connections between their own buildings and the grand temples of sixth-century Ionia. The three Ionian dipteral temples at Ephesos, Samos, and Didyma were all somewhat eclectic, with columns varying from one to the next and revealing to visitors their long and often piecemeal construction history but that nevertheless impressed through a scale and ambition attesting to the prosperity of Ionia's sixth-century heyday. The popularity of the bilingual design owes much to the embrace of the motley elevations of the dipteral temples in a new, calculated design by patrons who sought to assert their connections to the cults of Ionian mother cities. As with the Massalians and Xenophon, who crafted likenesses of the cult statue of Artemis Ephesia and her temple at Ephesos, visual fidelity sounded a note of piety, but it also proclaimed an identity based on ties of kinship and personal history spanning the Mediterranean.

Bilingual Ionic capitals first occur on Delos, at the interface between the Cycladic and east Ionian architectural traditions. Capitals from Delos, which can possibly be restored to the Propylon to the Sanctuary of Apollo, unite two regional styles in an expression of the sanctuary's aspirations to serve as a center of pan-Ionian religion. It is certain that the convex volutes faced outward on the facade of the structure with the more deeply carved concave sides of the capitals facing into the building. In the context of a propylon, the orientation aligned along the paths of visitors entering the sanctuary and exiting back into the city, rather than as a simple aesthetic optimization of shadow contrast.

At the city of Neapolis in Thrace, the temple of Parthenos had capitals combining a form then common on Thasos and the Cyclades on one side and the older Ionian form on the other. Here, the convex volute may look less to Asia Minor and more to the form's perceived antiquity, which served as an expression of the age of the Greco-Thracian goddess Parthenos, who was worshiped in the form of a *xoanon*. The addition of phiale and flower relief ornaments to the capitals further embodied those attributes that distinguished the cult statue of the goddess. The capitals from Neapolis hint at the janiform nature of a syncretic deity. A similar effect may have been at play in the temple of Dionysos Thermaios, which has the largest capitals of this type. It is difficult to consider this building in its original condition and context because it was transported and rebuilt in Roman Thessaloniki.

In the ancient deme of Pallene in northeast Attica, a building with bilingual Ionic capitals, long identified as Archaic, is redated here to the Classical period (ca. 460–450). The capitals merge the Archaic Ionian sculptural style and the plain and painted style of early Attic Ionic capitals. They mark the beginning of a turn toward a more sculptural style of Athenian Ionic architecture in the mid-fifth century, notably on the monuments of the Acropolis. The appropriation of a sculptural style from the other end of the Aegean is one part of a wider embrace of the Ionic order as Athens justified its empire through an underlying ethnic affiliation with Ionians.

The phenomenon continues into the late Classical and early Hellenistic period at Ephesos, Selinous, and Delphi. At Ephesos, bilingual Ionic capitals suggest an act of preservation, keeping alive an anecdotal history of the city as the birthplace of the Ionic order. In the aftermath of the destruction of the temple of Artemis, these columns served as a visual link with a fading past. The new temple of Athena Trecheia marked the location of the city's foundation. The positioning of the retrospective faces of the capitals on the interior imparts the sense that moving into the building's colonnade marked a step backward toward the founding of the city. After a period of depression and a momentous calamity, the city of Ephesos as an architectural patron sought to reassert its own long history of Ionic building in the fourth century. Bilingual Ionic design, however, was by this time no longer the sole prerogative of patrons asserting Ionian heritage, as is evidenced by two private undertakings outside the Ionian sphere. At Delphi, an Aetolian named Aristaineta adopted the form to borrow historical grandeur from earlier Ionic monuments to aggrandize her own. Aetolians were relative latecomers at Delphi and were often held at the margins of Greek identity. Her collagist bicolumnar monument, which supported portraits of her family members, borrows not only from the wider history of Ionic architecture but also from the nearby Stoa of the Athenians. One can almost picture Aristaineta walking through the sanctuary with the sculptor she commissioned pointing out preferred features of previous dedications. Similarly, at Dorian Selinous, where Doric was the de facto scheme for all temple edifices, Ionic was the preference of elite dedicators who sought to distinguish their votives and tomb monuments.

Textual accounts, like Xenophon's description of his temple of Artemis Ephesia at Skillous or Strabo's description of the cult of Artemis Ephesia among the Massalians, offer paradigms for the intentions of ancient patrons (both individuals and cities) in propagating replicas of an Archaic Ionian prototype when they settled overseas. Yet bilingual Ionic capitals engage only partly in replication. They also reflect the charm of those large old temples that were heterogeneous by circumstance, rather than the propagation of a single authoritative design. Beginning in the fourth century BCE more pronounced architectural quotations emerge (see fig. 1.17), and ultimately in the era of the Roman empire there are full-scale replicas relying upon careful surveys and templates drawn from the monuments of the Athenian Acropolis (see fig. 1.18). The inventive design of the Ionic capitals of the Erechtheion's north porch inspired many imitations, which begin in the fourth century BCE, including a bicolumn monument at Delphi that likely stood not far from Aristaineta's monument. The project of the Forum of Augustus carried the concept of copying to its greatest extent of fidelity by producing exact scale replicas of the capitals, likely transmitted from Athens to Rome by plaster casts (see fig. 1.19). These projects employed new techniques of replication to achieve a degree of faithfulness that was never in the minds of the makers of bilingual capitals, yet they represent a continuation of the same architectural impetus. Fifth-century Athens also supplanted sixth-century Ionia as a subject of nostalgia. Bilingual Ionic capitals represent a prelude to notions of fidelity to historical models that took shape at the same time as the restoration of major temples, the veneration of ruins, and the symbolic reuse of older architectural members as spolia. The practice of carving bilingual Ionic capitals came to an end in the late fourth and early third century BCE, but not because builders lost interest in retrospective columns. Instead, they embraced retrospection wholeheartedly and explored increasingly elaborate and total forms of recreating architectural archetypes from the past.

Appendix

The text of this book relies on specialized terminology to refer to elements of the Doric and Ionic orders (fig. A.1), Ionic capitals in particular (fig. A.2), and the distinctive moldings of Ionic architecture, with their profiles and patterns (fig. A.3). This visual glossary offers a reference for the position and appearance of these elements.

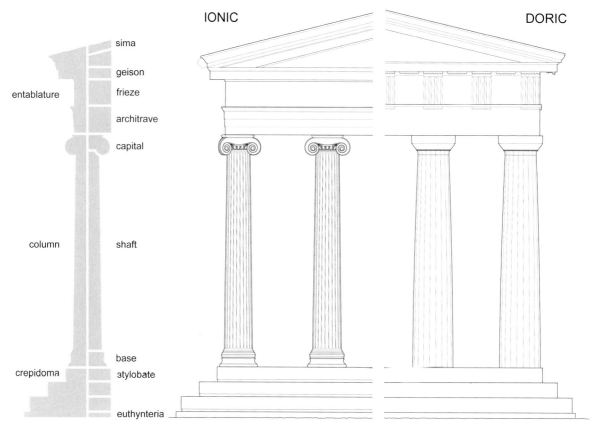

A.1. Elements of a colonnade.

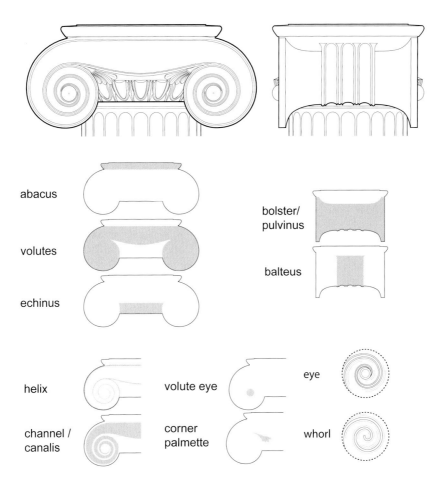

A.2. Elements of an Ionic capital and volute.

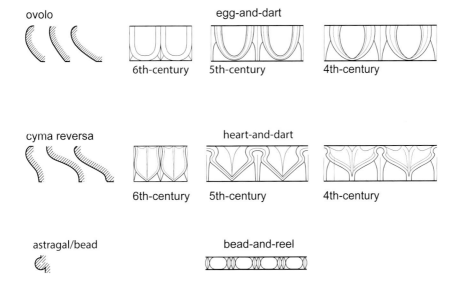

A.3. Ionic moldings, profiles, and patterns.

Acknowledgments

The present book has its origin in my PhD dissertation at the University of Pennsylvania. Lothar Haselberger, Brian Rose, Jeremy McInerney, and Bonna Wescoat, the mentors who encouraged me as a committee and have guided me since, receive my heartfelt thanks. It was only possible to bring together archaeological remains scattered across five different countries through the support of a Williams Fellowship from the University of Pennsylvania, the Greenewalt Extraordinary Fieldwork Grant of the Kolb Society of Fellows, a Fulbright Fellowship in Greece, and the Gorham Phillips Stevens Fellowship of the American School of Classical Studies at Athens. I put the final touches on the text while a fellow at the Center for Hellenic Studies in Washington, DC.

In 2017 and 2019, I had the uncommon opportunity to participate in the Parthenon Restoration Project on the Athenian Acropolis as a draftsperson assisting with the documentation of the west tympanum orthostates and west geison. Vasileia Manidaki, Vasiliki Eleftheriou, and Rosalia Christodoulopoulou of the Acropolis Restoration Service (Υ.Σ.Μ.Α.) made this collaboration possible. In turn, what I learned about marble carving from Petros Georgopoulos, Yorgos Desypris, and the many other marble carvers of the Parthenon Restoration Project transformed my understanding of ancient stone working.

I am grateful to the two anonymous peer reviewers of the book manuscript for their insights, as well as to Aenne Ohnesorg, Jean-Charles Moretti, Jacques des Courtils, Nathan Arrington, and Carolyn Yerkes for reading the text. This project benefited from discussions with archaeologists and architectural historians, often on late nights at Athenian tavernas after the lectures of Κύκλος / The Circle: Dialogues on Greek and Roman Architecture. Advice at early stages from Tasos Tanoulas, David Scahill, Nils Hellner, Vasileia Manidaki, Christoph Baier, Jan-Henrik Hartung, and Georg Herdt shaped my thinking on this subject. William Aylward, Basile Baudez, Lee Brice, John Camp, Laurence Cavalier, Caroline Cheung, Jim Coulton, Kevin Daly, Sheila Dillon, Sylvian Fachard, Panagiotis Faklaris, Jasper Gaunt, Cam Grey, Matthias Grawehr, Donald Haggis, Alexander Herda, John Hinchman, Frank Hulek, Chrysanthos Kanellopoulos, Manolis Korres, Tony Kozelj, Stephanie Larson, Carolina Mangone, Clementi Marconi, Margie Miles, Bridget Murnaghan, Jenifer Neils, Robert Ousterhout, Jessica Paga, Alessandro Pierattini, Molly Richardson, Julia Shear, Elisavet Sioumpara, Vassiliki Stamatopoulou, Philip Stinson, Daniela Stoyanova, Jim Wright, Manuela Wurch-Kozelj, and Mantha Zarmakoupi also offered guiding advice on this project.

Permission and assistance in studying architectural remains were generously offered by the Sculpture Collection of the National Archaeological Museum, Athens, the Ephorate of Antiquities of Western Attica, Piraeus, and Islands and the Archaeological Museum of Piraeus, the Ephorate of Antiquities of Euboea and the Archaeological Museum of Eretria, the Ephorate of Antiquities of Ilia and the Archaeological Museum of Olympia, the Ephorate of Antiquities of Phokis and the Archaeological Museum of Delphi, the Ephorate of Antiquities of Thessaloniki and the Archaeological Museum of Thessaloniki, the Ephorate of Antiquities of Kavala-Thasos and the Archaeological Museum of Kavala, the Blegen Library Archive and Natalia Vogeikoff-Brogan, the German Archaeological Institute, Athens, the French School at Athens, the Archaeological Museum of Palermo and Sandra Ruvituso, the National Museum of Warsaw and Alfred Twardecki, and the Kunsthistorisches Museum, Vienna, and Georg Plattner, and the Greece and Rome Department of the British Museum, London, and Alexandra Villing. I am also grateful to the Archive of the École des Beaux-Arts and Emmanuelle Brugerolles for the opportunity to study the drawings of Henri-Paul Nénot in person. Clémence Fort located and transcribed Nénot's report. The American School of Classical Studies at Athens and Ioanna Damanaki, Elena Kourakou, Dimitra Minaoglou, Eleni Pantazi, Martha Polyzoidi, and Julia Gearhart facilitated my studies at archaeological sites and museums as well as securing image permissions.

My editors at Princeton University Press, Michelle Komie and Annie Miller, were inspiring collaborators in this project. I thank the whole design, production, and marketing team that had a hand in shaping this book, including Jeff Wincapaw, Steven Sears, Sara Lerner, Lachlan Brooks, Jerry Danzig, Elise Hess, and William Pagdatoon. This book's production was supported by a grant from the Barr Ferree Publication Fund of the Department of Art and Archaeology.

Warm thanks go to friends and colleagues who contributed to the development of the ideas presented here as well as to the physical documentation behind it, including holding the other end of the measuring tape: Vincent Baillet, Bill Beck, Jeanne Capelle, Juan Carmona Zabala, Alice Clinch, Chiara De Gregorio, Bela Dimova, Eric Driscoll, Sofia Economou, Ashleigh Fata, Madeline Glennon, Constanze Graml, Aineias Kapouranis, Constantine Karathanasis, Philip J. Katz, MaryAnn Kontonicolas, Giovanni Lovisetto, Denitsa Nenova, Carissa Nicholson, Alice Ognier, Hüseyin Öztürk, Alaya Palamidis, Maria Papaioannou, Christopher Parmenter, Manolis Petrakis, Hannah Rich, Nazim Can Serbest, Anna Sitz, Abigail Teller, Chavdar Tzochev, Michiel Van Veldhuizen, Konstantina Venieri, Andrew Ward, and Louis Zweig.

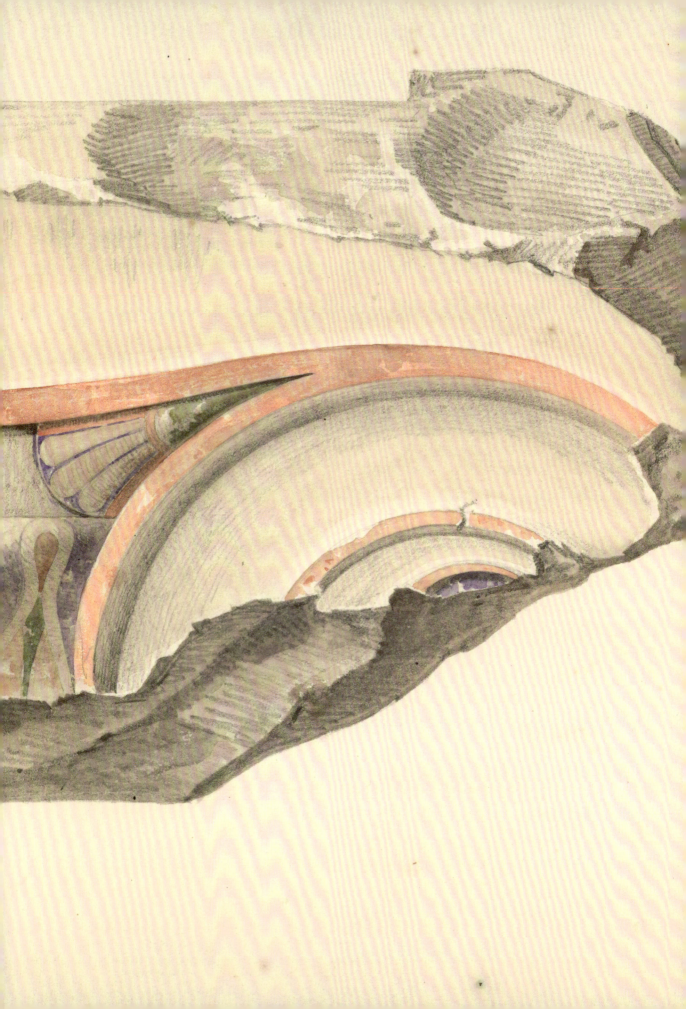

Notes

Introduction

1. "Konvex-Konkave Kapitelle": Gruben 1963, 174–75n16; Ohnesorg 1993a, 116n36; Schmidt-Dounas 2004. "Kapitelle mit hohlen und vollen Voluten": Bammer 1968–1971, 13.
2. For accounts of the early development of the Ionic order, see Gruben 1996; Barletta 2001, 84–124; Wilson Jones 2014, 119–35, 214–15.
3. Gruben 1965, 207–8; Kirchhoff 1988, 135–90; Ohnesorg 1996; Barletta 2001, 100–106; Herdt 2013, 1–8, passim; Wilson Jones 2014, 170–74.
4. Betancourt 1977; Wilson Jones 2014, 100–106, 124–25.
5. For a review of *Rundkapitelle*, see Hulek 2018, 97–103. At Ephesos: Ohnesorg 2007, 70. At Didyma: Dirschedl 2012, 61–63; Dirschedl 2018, 14. At Samos: Hendrich 2007, 19–20, 28–38. In the Cyclades: Ohnesorg 2017, 59–62; Schmidt-Dounas 2019, 16–17.
6. Barletta 2001, 5–7, 124–31; Wilson Jones 2002, 353–55.
7. For an overview of archaism and the archaistic style in sculpture, see Pollitt 1986, 175–84; Fullerton 1990, 1–13; Hölscher 2010. For the significance of the frieze on Samothrace, see Pollitt 1986, 183; Lehmann and Spittle 1982; Fullerton 1990, 3–4; Marconi 2010.
8. For early archaism in fifth century Athens, including Parthenon metopes North 25 and South 21, see Palagia 2009, 25–26, passim.
9. For a survey of architectural repairs and rebuilding in ancient Greece and Rome, see Broeck-Parant and Ismaelli 2021; Ismaelli 2021; Ng and Swetnam-Burland 2018. While some scholars (e.g., Buchert 2000) have been keen to ascribe these acts of rebuilding to "historic preservation" and "architectural restoration," others (Ohnesorg 2012, 38) have critiqued this as an anachronism. Korres 1997, 204–5 argues that only a few ancient rebuilding projects, notably the first-century rebuilding of the Erechtheion, rise to the quality of work in matching ancient styles to be comparable to modern restoration projects.
10. For Greek architectural spolia, particularly in Athens after the Persian sack, see Miles 2014, 123–26; Barletta 2017, 235–49; Rous 2019; Rous 2020. Not all reused material had symbolic meaning, and Sioumpara 2020 has set out a clear case for seeing frugality and efficiency motivating most cases of reuse of architectural blocks, even on the post-Persian Acropolis.
11. For an overview of archaistic sculpture, see Fullerton 1990, 1–13. For the turn toward the "archaeology of the past" or "archaeology of nostalgia," see Antonaccio 1995, Alcock 2002, Boardman 2002, Holtorf 2005, Rojas 2019. For the impact of this scholarly turn in archaeology on the study of ancient literature, see Grethlein 2008.
12. Mace 1978, 137; Shoe Meritt 1996, 128; Schmidt-Dounas 2004, 140–41.
13. For a catalog of half-carved capitals, see Schmidt-Dounas 2004, 140–41; Ohnesorg and Büyükkolancı 2007.
14. Elena Partida 2013, 488, highlights the likely importance of chiaroscuro design.
15. Alzinger 1967, 36; Bammer 1968–1971, 13. For other "bilingual" buildings, see Wescoat 2012b, 97.
16. For self-critique of this method, see Gruben 2000, 158.
17. Madzharov 2016, 143–47, figs. 32.1–34.4.

Chapter 1. Bilingual Ionic Capitals in Context: How Buildings Tell Stories about the Past

1. For recent discussion of the Tuscan order's roots in ancient adaptations of Doric, see Kosmopoulos 2022.
2. Armstrong 2012, 89–92.
3. Miles 2015, 162–65; Armstrong 2012, 102.
4. For Le Roy's impact, see Middleton 2004, 12; Armstrong 2012, 156–78; Armstrong 2016, 493–96.
5. For Robert Sayer's alterations to Le Roy's work, see Middleton 2004, 15, 16; Armstrong 2012, 6–7.
6. Armstrong 2012, 170–71.
7. Le Roy 1758a, part II, 1. For Le Roy's debt to Vitruvius, see Middleton 2004, 86.
8. Vitr. 4.1.8: "posteri vero elegantia subtilitateque iudiciorum progressi et gracilioribus modulis delectati."
9. Translated by Schiefsky 2015, 626: "τοὺς γὰρ τῶν οἰκοδομικῶν ἔργων ῥυθμοὺς οὐ δυνατὸν ἦν ἐξ ἀρχῆς συστήσασθαι μὴ πρότερον πείρας προσαχθείσης, καθ' ὅτι καὶ δῆλόν ἐστιν ἐκ τῶν ἀρχαίων καθ' ὑπερβολὴν ἀτεχνῶν οὐ μόνον κατὰ τὴν οἰκοδομίαν, ἀλλὰ καὶ ἐν ταῖς κατὰ μέρος εἰδοποιίαις."
10. Schiefsky 2015, 619–29, passim.
11. " ... τῷ παλαιῷ τῆς Ἑλλάδος τρόπῳ ... "
12. "οὗτοι ἀπ᾽ ἀρχῆς πάντα θεοὶ θνητοῖς ὑπέδειξαν, / ἀλλὰ χρόνῳ ζητοῦντες ἐφευρίσκουσιν ἄμεινον." Xenophanes frg. 18; translated by Burnet 1920, 119.
13. The exception may be Pindar's account (*Pae.* 8; also in Paus. 10.5.9) of the phases of the temple of Apollo at Delphi, which mirrors Hesiod's account of the ages of man (*Op.* 109–201); Sourvinou-Inwood 1979, 251. For sculpture, notably Porphyr. *Abst.* 2.18, discussed by Hölscher 2010.
14. Martin 1973, 372: "Mais on reconnaît de plus en plus que le décor est loin d'être l'élément essentiel

permettant de définir les caractères spécifiques d'un groupe; il se plaque, souvent comme un apport extérieur, à des structures très différentes et seules celles-ci peuvent fournir les critères indispensables au classement des chapiteaux." See also, Martin 1944–1945, 360; Theodorescu 1968, 273. For a complete articulation of the challenges of using convex and concave volutes and volute eyes and whorls as dating criteria, see Gruben 1963, 174–75n168. Theodorescu (1974, 33) draws a regional distinction, noting that convex volutes lingered in Magna Graecia long after they disappeared elsewhere by the second quarter of the fifth century.

15 For proportional studies in this vein, see Theodorescu 1968; Theodorescu 1980; Collombier 1983; Mărgineanu-Cârstoiu 2002–2003.
16 Boardman 1959, 209–11; Mace 1978, 137; Schmidt-Dounas 2004, 140.
17 Bammer 1968–1971, 13.
18 Ridgway 1970, 14–15; Stewart 2008, 593; Stewart 2013, 136–39. There has been considerable disagreement on chronology: Dieter Ohly (1971) put work on the pediment in the last decade of the sixth century, but the pottery from the terraces around the temple militated against work beginning before 490 (Gill 1993), and Stewart 2008 has argued that the temple's predecessor was destroyed by the Persians in 480 BCE. For a review of the varying chronologies of the Aphaia Temple, see recently Fendt 2019, 197–200. The chronological debate has hinged on pottery and sculptural style, but Bankel and Stewart 2022 have offered architectural evidence bolstering the post-480 date.
19 For the metopes of Temple E, see Marconi 1994.
20 Dörpfeld 1884, 148. For a review of Dörpfeld's theory of petrification and the dating of the temple of Hera at Olympia, see Sapirstein 2016, 565–75.
21 Sapirstein 2016.
22 For Temple G, see Luni and Mei 2016; Mertens 2006, 231–36. For the capital design, see Coulton 1977, 27; Wilson Jones 1991, 126–27.
23 Luni and Mei 2016, 125–26; Mertens 2006, 231–36.
24 Pliny, HN 36.95: "CXX annis factum a tota Asia." Translated by Eichholz 1962, 75. Pollitt 1965, 37, casts doubt on the length of construction, though Muss 1994 proposes at least a century worth of work on the building's sculpture.
25 Ohnesorg 2007, 132.
26 Muss 1994.
27 Krischen 1938, pl. 33; Ohnesorg 2007, pl. 180. For the importance of Krischen's work at Ephesos, see Ohnesorg 2007, 9; for Krischen's importance in the study of architecture and archaeological illustration more generally, see Bernhardt 2015, 96–100, 125–29; Marinatos 2015, 107–10.
28 Ohnesorg 2007, 60–68; for a similar "limitless variability" on the Archaic Didymaion, see Gruben 1963, 105.
29 Ohnesorg 2007, 45–52.
30 Ohnesorg 2007, 89. The fragments with interlaced leaf have a smaller diameter as the capital bolsters and may belong elsewhere in the temple or sanctuary.
31 Ohnesorg 2001, 185–87; Ohnesorg 2007, pl. 40. The reidentification derives from the discovery of a more complete, smaller capital of the same type: Mărgineanu-Cârstoiu and Büyükkolancı 1996/1998.
32 "Cetera eius operis ornamenta plurium librorum instar optinent." Translated by Eichholz 1962, 77.
33 Hellmann 1999, 91–92, with previous bibliography.
34 Yegül 2014, 214–17. The temple of Zeus at Euromos is the most remarkable case, but its one dozen inscribed columns attest only three donors: Errington 1993, 15–31; Yegül 2014, 216. Olympia: Williams 1984, 69; Sapirstein 2016, 572–73n45.
35 Achilara et al. 2004, 34.
36 Achilara et al. 2004, 16.
37 Even Neer 2012, 211, while challenging the transitional status of bilingual vases, uses them as paradigmatic examples to introduce red-figure painting.
38 Neer 2002, 27–42. For bilingual vases, see Cohen 1978; Cohen 2006. Rotroff 2009, 256, notes that downdating the Andokides Painter by a decade impacts the dating of bilingual vases but refrains from proposing a new chronology (presumably pushed down from ca. 530–525 to ca. 520–515).
39 Pollitt 1986, 180–82.
40 Palermo V650: Schneider 1889, pl. 4; Cohen 1978, 247; Cohen 2006, 22–23.
41 Beazley 1928, 25, implies that he picked the term up from contemporary parlance; Cohen 1978, 9.
42 Cohen 1978, 26–27. For connoisseurship, see Arrington 2017.
43 Cohen 1978, 26–27; Hurwit 1985, 282.
44 Neer 2002, 32.
45 Neer 2002, 32–33.
46 For *poikilia* broadly as an aesthetic criterion, see Grand-Clément 2015; Berardi, Lisi, and Micalella 2009; in sculpture, Neer 2010, 113; in music, LeVen 2013; Wallace 2009. Ancient texts applying the term to architecture typically use it as a name for public buildings with painted decoration, including "painted" stoas at Athens, Olympia, and Sparta: Hellmann 1992, 344.
47 "Mit künstlerischer Freiheit": Gruben 1997, 369.
48 Korres 1996, 96, similarly appeals to *Variationsfreude* to explain differences in Ionic capitals. On *Variationsfreude* and German postmodernism, see Krier 2015, 280–81.
49 Wescoat 1987; Wescoat 2012a, 49–55. Even major Roman building projects like the Colosseum appear to have eschewed the use of templates for moldings: Lancaster 2005, 71–72.
50 Below the abacus, the capitals of the Assos temple were subdivided at the one-third mark to divide the necking and the echinus, in a general principle of Archaic Doric design noted by Coulton 1979, 97–98. Wescoat 1987 deduced that, on the earlier capitals of the temple's short ends the annulets are set above this one-third mark, and on the capitals of the flanks the annulets are set below.
51 Palagia 2003, 56; *IG* IV² 1 102.
52 Partida 2013, 488–90. McGowan 1993, 191, attributes the Oropos capital to a Parian workshop.
53 Shoe Meritt 1996, 86–87.
54 Pitt 2016, 194–95.
55 Gruben 2014, 184–99; Mertens 2006, 245–47.
56 For the breakdown of the status of the Erechtheion workmen, see Randall 1955.
57 Stissi 2002, 120.
58 Coulton 1977, 26.
59 For the Throne of Apollo at Amyklai, see Fiechter

60 Paus. 3.18.9–3.19.2; Pollitt 1965, 39–40.
61 For a recent proposed identification of the Skias, see Greco and Voza 2016.
62 The architect as a client-duping trickster was an ancient literary trope (e.g., Hdt. 2.121). The architect Sostratos of Knidos has a well-attested historical career and loyal patronage relationship (Meeus 2015) that was humorously twisted to fit the trickster-architect trope (Lucian, *Hist. conscr.* 62).
63 *IG* I³ 35, ll. 11–12: "νεὸν δὲ οἰκοδομέσαι κατ' ὅ τι / ἂν Καλλικράτες χσυγγράφσει..."
64 Hodge 1960, 66.
65 Pitt 2016, 382; Hansen 2016.
66 The so-called "Stele of the Punishments," lines 51–55 (Kritzas and Prignitz 2020). The salary of architects at Epidauros was 1 dr. per day, also what it was for the architects of the Erechtheion in fifth-century Athens (Burford 1969, 106). The fourth-century architect Athenodoros working at Eleusis received about twice as much (*IG* II² 1672 and 1673; Hellmann 1999, 45).
67 Kritzas and Prignitz 2020, 38.
68 *IG* II² 1678; Hellmann 1999, 39–44; Lattermann 1908, 64–80; the temple is reconstructed in Fraisse and Llinas 1995, 491.
69 *IG* II² 1678, ll. 10–13: "τοῦ δὲ παραδείγματος τοῦ πεποιημένου [τ]οῦ ἐ[π]ικράνου [ἔσ]ται μίσ[θω]σις [κατὰ λόγο]ν τοῦ [ἀρ]γυρίο/υ, ὅσου ἂμ μισθωθῆι τὸ ἔργο[ν] ὅ [τ]ι ἂν τάξει ὁ ἀρχιτέκτων· κομιεῖ δὲ καὶ τὸ παράδ[ειγμα τ]οῦ ἐπικράνου / εἰς Δῆλ[ον] ὁ μισθωσάμενος τὸ ἔργον τέ[λ].εσι τοῖς αὐτοῦ ὑγιὲ{ι}ς καὶ θήσει καθάπερ περὶ τῶν ἄλλων γέ/γραπται, παραλαβὼν ὑγιὲ{ι}ς Ἀθήνησι ... "
70 Burford 1969, 103.
71 Miles 2017 directly critiques the application of vase-painting connoisseurship in attributing different temple designs to the same architects, especially given the central role of collaboration.
72 For incuse coins, see Sheedy et al. 2021; Gorini 1975. For the challenges in carving incuse dies in relief, see Sutherland 1948, 16. For new evidence of annealing, see Sheedy et al. 2021; Salvemini et al. 2018.
73 De Luynes 1836, 388; for arguments for and against the Pythagorean attribution, see Seaford 2004, 268; Gorini 1975, 43–51; Demand 1976, 1–2; Seltman 1949.
74 Sheedy et al. 2021, 254–55; Demand 1976, 2; Burkert 1972, 110.
75 For recent discussion of the Pythagorean Table of Opposites, see Goldin 2015.
76 For Alkmaion's theories of opposites in relationship to Pythagoras's, see Zhmud 2012, 358–61.
77 For Philolaos and the Counter-Earth, see Burch 1954; Montelle 2011, 105.
78 Demand 1976 proposes a direct connection between incuse coins and intaglio seals and sealings.
79 Sheedy et al. 2021, 1; Demand 1976, 3n1; Sutherland 1948, 17. For cases of colonies sharing the same *parasemon* (city insignia) connected to shared foundation stories, see Killen 2017, 76; Panait-Bîrzescu 2020.
80 Shaya 2005, 423.
81 For the full list, see Shaya 2005, 437–39. For the Lindian Chronicle, local history and memory, see Price 2012, 18–19; Boardman 2002, 27–9, 115–17; Kirk 2021, 217–22; McInerney 2023. The sanctuary of Athena at Ilion similarly displayed relics of the Trojan War that were key to the later city's status (Rose 2013, 62–63, 158, 191–92).
82 Shaya 2005, 424.
83 For the pillar of Oinomaos, see Brulotte 1994; Boardman 2002, 112; Yeğül 2014, 214; Ismaelli 2021, 19–20, 31.
84 Cook and Nicholls 1998, 100–101, 137n1.
85 Paus. 5.20.7: "καὶ γὰρ ἐγὼ κεινῶν εἴμ᾽, ὦ ξένε λείψανον οἴκων, / στυλὶς ἐν Οἰνομάου πρίν ποτ᾽ ἐοῦσα δόμοις· / νῦν δὲ παρὰ Κρονίδῃν κεῖμαι τάδ᾽ ἔχουσα τὰ δεσμὰ / τίμιος· οὐδ᾽ ὀλοὴ δαίσατο φλόξ με πυρός." Translation by Brulotte 1994, 53.
86 For ancient restoration of sculpture, see Harrison 1990; Leka 2021.
87 "Ἀρχίλοχος Πάριος Τελεσικλέος ἐνθάδε κεῖται / τὸ Δόκιμος μνημήιον ὁ Νεοκρέωντος τόδ᾽ ἔθηκεν." Translated by McGowan 1993, 182. Paros Museum 733: Kontoleon 1964; Ohnesorg 1993a, 114n23 with previous bibliography; McGowan 1997, 181–88; Bakker 1999, 28; Herdt 2013, 206.
88 *Anth. Pal.* 7.441. Friedländer and Hoffleit, 1948, 67; McGowan 1995, 617; Yeğül 2014, 215–16n45–46.
89 Ca. 550: Ohnesorg 1993a, 114; Haselberger 1986, 213, places just after the middle of the sixth; Kirchhoff 1988, 26, just before.
90 Kontoleon 1964, 44–46.
91 Riegl 1903, 72–73, 74.
92 Krautheimer 1942, 7–9; Carpo 2001a, 37.
93 Carpo 2001a; Carpo 2001b.
94 Waters 2012; Yerkes 2017, 21.
95 Pliny, *NH* 25.4–5; Galen, *Simpl. Med.* 4.1; Ptolemy, *Geog.* 1.18; Carpo 2001a, 147–49n18–19; Carpo 2001b, 225.
96 Borchhardt 1976, 27–37; Şare 2013, 56, passim; Shear 2016, 385.
97 Townsend 2004, 307–9, fig. 16.1.
98 Giraud 1989; Miles 2012, 128.
99 Richter 1970; Landwehr 1985; Landwehr 2010; Frederiksen 2010, 18–22.
100 Landwehr 2010, 37.
101 Kockel 1991. For recent work on copies of the capitals of the Erechtheion, see Petrakis 2021; Mazzilli 2021. For the copying of the Erechtheion's caryatids in the Forum of Augustus, Hadrian's Villa, and Emerita Augusta (Mérida, Spain), see Lesk 2007.
102 Lucian makes light of the task for a moment of absurd humor in *Iuppiter tragoedus* (33), where a statue of Hermes in the Agora of Athens narrates the personal indignity of being covered with pitch by sculptors making a mold.
103 Stevens et al. 1927, 178–80, 223–24, 478–79; Korres 1997, 199–202; Papanikolaou 2012, 470–501.
104 For Xenophon's shrine and Artemis Ephesia, see Tuplin 2004; Malkin 2011, 182–83. For the relevance of Xenophon's account to ancient copying practices, see Gaifman 2006, 272–74.
105 Other Greek historians engage in geographic comparisons (Hdt. 4.99.5; Thuk. 4.36.3), but Xenophon's comparison of the precincts at Skillous and Ephesos is by far the most elaborate.
106 "ὁ δὲ ναὸς ὡς μικρὸς μεγάλῳ τῷ ἐν Ἐφέσῳ εἴκασται, καὶ τὸ

ξόανον ἔοικεν ὡς κυπαρίττινον χρυσῷ ὄντι τῷ ἐν Ἐφέσῳ." Xenophon's perfect passive form of εἰκάζω ("to make a likeness of," "imitate") simply means "resembles" and is added for variety in a repetitive sentence, but there is an emphasis on the act of imitation in a verb Xenophon elsewhere uses for portrait painting (*Oec.* 10.1) and battlefield feints (*Hell.* 7.5.22).
107 Pl. *Leg.* 955e–956a.
108 For a complete catalog of copies of the Artemis Ephesia cult statue, see Fleischer 1973. LiDonnici 1992 emphasizes that copies of the cult statue must also be understood within changing Hellenistic and Roman contexts.
109 Strabo 4.1.4: "ἔν τε ταῖς ἀποίκοις πόλεσι πανταχοῦ τιμῶν ἐν τοῖς πρώτοις ταύτην τὴν θεὸν καὶ τοῦ ξοάνου τὴν διάθεσιν τὴν αὐτὴν καὶ τἆλλα νόμιμα φυλάττειν τὰ αὐτὰ ἅπερ ἐν τῇ μητροπόλει νενόμισται." Malkin 2011, 199–200.
110 Witcombe 2018, 65–88.
111 Theodorescu and Tréziny 2000.
112 Mertens 2006, 245.
113 For the Artemis Aristoboule temple, see Threpsiades and Vanderpool 1965; Garland 1992, 64–81. Tuplin 2004, 260, suggests more similarities between Themistocles's and Xenophon's Artemis temples.
114 "Die Vorstellung von … Entwicklung bestimmt weitgehend das Bild von griechischer Architektur. Für Fragen nach hiervon abweichenden Phänomenen blieb bislang kaum Raum." Knell 1993, 7. For the origins of the master narrative of development in architecture, rooted in the writing of Julien-David Le Roy, see Armstrong 2012; Kisacky 2001.
115 Knell 1993, 7–9, 14–16. For further aspects of the retention of the plan of the Ephesos temple, see Ohnesorg 2012. Boardman 2002, 178–79, summarizes the challenges of seeing continuity in the megaron plan between Bronze Age palaces and Archaic temples.
116 For Lykourgos and the creation of the tragic canon, see Hanink 2014; Marx 2022; Lardinois 2022. For the creation of canons in antiquity more generally, see Papadopoulos 2022.
117 For the date of Lykourgos's decree, see Hanink 2014, 11; Lardinois 2022, 155.
118 For archaistic architecture under Lykourgos, see Shoe Meritt 1996, 139; Rignanese 2021. For the fountain house, see Gruben 1969, 39; Gruben 1986. For the dating of the bases, see Dirschedl 2013, cat no. W2.
119 Broeck-Parant 2021.

Chapter 2. Delos: Synthesis at the End of the Archaic Period

1 "ἦν δέ ποτε καὶ τὸ πάλαι μεγάλη ξύνοδος ἐς τὴν Δῆλον τῶν Ἰώνων τε καὶ περικτιόνων νησιωτῶν· ξύν τε γὰρ γυναιξὶ καὶ παισὶν ἐθεώρουν, ὥσπερ νῦν ἐς τὰ Ἐφέσια Ἴωνες, καὶ ἀγὼν ἐποιεῖτο αὐτόθι καὶ γυμνικὸς καὶ μουσικός, χορούς τε ἀνῆγον αἱ πόλεις. δηλοῖ δὲ μάλιστα Ὅμηρος ὅτι τοιαῦτα ἦν ἐν τοῖς ἔπεσι τοῖσδε, ἅ ἐστιν ἐκ προοιμίου Ἀπόλλωνος· ἄλλοτε Δήλῳ, Φοῖβε, μάλιστά γε θυμὸν ἐτέρφθης, ἔνθα τοι ἑλκεχίτωνες Ἰάονες ἠγερέθονται σὺν σφοῖσιν τεκέεσσι γυναιξί τε σὴν ἐς ἄγυιαν· ἔνθα σε πυγμαχίῃ καὶ ὀρχηστυῖ καὶ ἀοιδῇ μνησάμενοι τέρπουσιν, ὅταν καθέσωσιν ἀγῶνα."
2 For overviews of the distinction, see Ohnesorg 2017; Gruben 1993. For volute designs between the two styles, see Gruben 1963, 174–75.
3 For the corner capital, see Étienne 2011; Gruben 1997, n254 for the previous publication history of the corner capital.
4 Straub 2019, 208 (cat no. III.54), 34, 36–37.
5 Hellmann and Fraisse 1982, 263, figs. 5 and 6; Pourchet 1897, pl. 63.
6 Gruben 1997, 360.
7 Richens and Herdt 2009, 813, present a 3D laser-scan of the capital with a revised illustration of the interior angle.
8 Confronted with this challenge for the Archaic temple of Apollo at Didyma, Gruben 1963, 163–64, fig. 42, produced a physical model that showed the corner capital had its center of gravity within the capital.
9 Bakker 1999, 32–33.
10 Archives of the École des Beaux-Arts, Paris, MS 283, Env 72–06 and 72–05. Pourchet 1897, pl. 63. For Nénot's involvement on Delos, see Mulliez 2007, 96–97; Hellmann and Fraisse 1982, 258–59. For Nénot's career at the École des Beaux-Arts, see Drexler 1977, 254.
11 Écoles des Beaux-Arts MS 283, 5: "J'ai relevé plus de dix chapiteaux ioniques différents sans pouvoir indiquer à quel monument au juste ils appartenaient; j'en donne deux, très intéressants à mon sens à cause de l'époque reculée à laquelle ils doivent appartenir. Délos recevait les hommages non seulement de la Grèce mais aussi de l'Asie et de l'Égypte, ce qui explique la différence des types qu'on y retrouve."
12 Vallois 1966, 163–65; Wilson Jones 2014, 102n3 with previous bibliography.
13 A 583 and A 584: Amandry 1953, 19–26; Vallois 1966, 170–75, Martin 1973, 387–88, McGowan 1993, 166–75, cat. nos. 2, 3; Donos 2008 465–66, cat. nos. 10–11; Moretti, Fraisse, and Llinas 2022, 38 with previous bibliography.
14 Moretti, Fraisse, and Llinas 2022, 38; Vallois 1966, 203n3; Coulton 1977, 231; Bruneau and Ducat 2005, 101.
15 Vallois 1966, 194–98; Étienne 2018, 82.
16 For Le Roy's drawing, see Armstrong 2012, 156–78.
17 Concerning his approach to the restitution of polychromy in general, Nénot n.d., 7 writes, "Une plus large part de supposition est faite à la décoration peinte en général; les métopes ne portent aucune trace de sculpture, il est admis que comme à Sélinonte elles portaient souvent des motifs peints et au lieu d'ornements j'ai supposé qu'on y avait des figures."
18 Hellmann and Fraisse 1982, 259.
19 For the history of Arkadia, the Nieborów Palace, and its collection, see Mikocki and Piwkowski 2001.
20 Mikocki and Piwkowski 2001, 94–97.
21 Mikocki 1986, 137 (NB / NMW 2570).
22 Sadurska 1983, 328, initially suggested that the capital might have come from south Italy through a dealer in Rome for the collection of King Stanisław II August (1732–1798).
23 Mikocki 1986, 143.
24 Sadurska 1983, 327–28.
25 For the Rheneian Grave stele, see Sadurska 1979; Sadurska 1983.

26 Michaud, 1974, 618–19, pl. 96; Mallwitz 1980, 108ff., pl. 6; Schmidt-Dounas 2004, 140; Gruben 1997, 370.
27 Mallwitz 1980, 364–65; Partida 2013, 489.
28 Gruben 1997, 370.
29 Couilloud 1974, 43–44. For another case of ballast, see the "Pesaro Capital," in Ohnesorg 1999, 228, fig. 8.
30 Gruben 1997, 371.
31 Wölfflin 1896 first evangelized for photographing marble sculpture with studio lighting, which was quickly applied to the study of Ionic capitals being brought to the Pergamon Museum (Humann 1904, Haselberger and Holzman 2015, 373n6). Mallwitz 1980, working with photographer Gösta Hellner, has so far been the only one to photograph a bilingual capital with identical, ideal studio lighting on both faces (cf. Alzinger 1967, 37).
32 Gruben 1997, 369.
33 The Nieborów capital has four leaves, with a dart in the center, while the Pheia and Delos capitals have the canonical form of three.
34 The Nieborów capital has no astragal, but it may have been included at the top of the column shaft. The Pheia capital includes the astragal below the echinus, and the carver has taken advantage of the change to extend the leaves and darts of the echinus molding to overlap the lower members slightly. The Delos corner capital does not have an astragal, but Ohnesorg draws a reconstruction of an unlikely pendant astragalus in profile that does not appear in the elevation or bed surface drawings (Gruben 1997, 358, fig. 49).
35 An eight-petal flower on the Nieborów capital, a whorl with six crescent-shaped tendrils on the Pheia capital, and a plain disk with a small knob in the center on the Delos corner capital that may be an omphalos phiale.
36 The Nieborów capital and Delos corner capital have four large channels. The Pheia capital has six.
37 The Nieborów capital and Delos corner capital have flutes that terminate in tongues with small darts interspersed. They intersect the top of the abacus in a straight line. The Pheia capital has channels that intersect the abacus abruptly in an arc with no decorative terminations. The Nieborów capital and Delos corner capital terminate the bolster decoration just short of the bed surface, allowing the inclusion of an abbreviated egg-and-dart pattern to continue. On the Pheia capital, the echinus modeling does not continue under the bolster.
38 Walls: e.g., *IG* XI, 2 161B, ll. 8–9. Ceiling: *IDelos* 441, face B, l. 212.
39 The date of the first phase of the Propylon is debated: ca. 600–575 according to Courbin, ca. 575 according to Gruben, and ca. 550-540 according to Vallois.
40 Gruben 1997, n254.
41 Bruneau and Ducat 2005, 169.
42 Étienne 2011, 220; Étienne and Braun 2018, 93.
43 Gruben 1997, 374, fig. 56.
44 Bruneau and Ducat 2005, 175.
45 Gruben 1997, 372–77; Étienne 2011, 222–23.
46 Étienne 2011; Étienne 2018; Étienne and Braun 2018.
47 Gruben 1997, 377 fig. 56.
48 Étienne and Braun 2018, 97; *IG* XI, 2, 161 A, l. 51-55, 73–75.
49 *IG* XI, 2 161 B, ll. 8–9, 94–95.
50 Courby 1931, 208, 213; Vallois 1978, 538; Étienne and Braun 2018, 97; Prost 2018, 187.
51 Étienne and Braun 2018, 97; Prost 2018, 197–208.
52 Byzes's son, the sculptor Euergus, promoted his father's innovation in an epigram recorded by Pausanias (5.10.3). For the Oikos of the Naxians and its innovative Ionic order, see Ohnesorg 2017, 55–59; Bruneau and Ducat 2005, 171–76; Barletta 2001, 85–91; Gruben 1997, 301–50; Courbin 1980.
53 Ohnesorg 1996, 40, fig. 1; Barletta 2001, 101.
54 For a summary of opposing opinions, see Bruneau and Ducat 2005, 171, 176; Mazarakis Ainian 2016, 27.
55 "... τὴν στοὰν ἣν ἀνέθ<ε>σαν Νάξιοι ... " *IG* XI, 2 287, A, l.89. For the Naxian Stoa, see Bruneau and Ducat 2005, 199–200; Hellmann and Fraisse 1979, 85–124.
56 *IG* I³ 1464; *SIG* 29; *SEG* 39.473; Meiggs and Lewis 1969, no. 25. For the dating of the Stoa of the Athenians, see Walsh 1986. For the dating of the Treasury of the Athenians and the Marathon base, thought by some to be connected, see Neer 1992, 63–67.
57 Hellmann and Fraisse 1979, 103–4.
58 All capitals have four flutes on the bolster except C, which has six, and the flutes on the bolsters are divided by one or two astragali, except on B where a third astragalus is added at the center of the bolster.
59 This capital may have been placed in an area of the stoa where it was known the capital's interior face would not be seen; stylobate cuttings show that stelai set up piecemeal between the columns completely walled up the second and third intercolumniations, and the end of the stoa adjacent to the Propylon may well have been completely inaccessible. Hellmann and Fraisse (1979, 104) observe that each of the other capitals appears to have one face that is more deeply carved (*plus gras*) and one face that is flatter (*plus plane*) perhaps corresponding to placement on the building's exterior and interior. Perhaps the capital's apparently flatter "interior" face may well be the exterior face of the capital that was subjected to centuries of weathering.
60 Hellmann and Fraisse 1979, 104, pl. 15.
61 Hellmann and Fraisse 1979, 104; Bruneau and Ducat 2005, 199.
62 Johannes 1937, 13. For overview, see Kienast 2012.
63 Johannes 1937, 14–15, concluded that the interior columns were rough for the utilitarian reason that they were erected rapidly to shelter the cella for immediate use while the rest of the building was under construction, but he entertained the hypothesis that the columns were given an antiquated appearance to match the earlier cult statue housed within.
64 " ... quarum in officina turbines ita librati pependerunt ut puero circumagente tornarentur." Translation from Pollitt 2001, 181. Theodoros is also credited with inventing the lathe (Plin. *HN* 7.198). For a full commentary on Pliny's anecdote and its interpretation, see Svenson-Evers 1996, 9–11. For a summary of the use of the lathe in antiquity and the earliest clear use of the wood lathe

on bowls from Tumulus W at Gordion (ca. 850 BCE), see Simpson 1999.

65 Johannes 1937, 16–17: "Man glaubt, in den mannigfaltigen zarten Schattierungen der Rundstäbe, Rillen, Kanneluren, Prismen und Wülste der in den Gruppen 2, 3 und 5–7 zusammengefaßten Basen noch die erste Freude an der in ihrer Anwendung auf die Architektur neuartigen Erfindung des Drehens zu spüren, welche die Phantasie der Werkleute zu immer neuen Variationen anregte. … Dann gelangte man von dem flimmernden Reichtum der Gestaltung zu einer Vereinheitlichung der Zierformen, zu einer tektonisch strafferen Norm einfacher Schattenbänder von 6–8 Kanneluren."
66 Hendrich 2007, 19–20, 28–38.
67 Ohnesorg 2007, 70; Dirschedl 2012, 61–63; Dirschedl 2018, 14. For discussion of the larger phenomenon, see Hulek 2018, 97–103.
68 Didyma: Tuchelt 1991, fig. 58, 1–2; Tuchelt 1994, 20; Ohnesorg 1996, 45, fig. 5; Bakker 1999, 40. Delphi: Frotier de la Coste-Messelière 1957, 27, 310, fig. 17; Buschor 1957, 8; Hahland 1964, 194; Kirchhoff 1988, 100; Bakker 1999, 40.
69 Lohmann 2007, 162–63, fig. 43–45; Lohmann 2012, 40–41, fig. 4.3; Hulek 2018, 82–88.
70 Hulek 2018, 94.
71 Hulek 2018, 13–15.
72 Gruben 1963, 175n168; Mace 1978; Schmidt-Dounas 2004.
73 A recent edited volume on this subject (Neer 2019) has illustrated that modern assumptions about visibility are challenging to map onto ancient art across cultures.
74 Wescoat and Levitan 2017; Marconi 2009; Barletta 2009; Stillwell 1969. See Marconi 2009, n3 for prior bibliography.
75 Marconi 2009, 160–61.
76 Hölscher 2018, 301–2, passim; Veyne 1988.
77 Gehl 1980, 65.
78 Gehl 1980, 65.
79 Marconi 2004, 214. For a summary of early temple decoration, see Pierattini 2022, 156–67.
80 For votive columns, see McGowan 1993; Herdt 2013.
81 Marconi 2007, 119, 178–79.
82 Mylonopoulos 2013, 136–37; Mylonopoulos 2019, 233n7.
83 Mylonopoulos 2013.
84 IMylasa 869, ll. 11–13; Mylonopoulos 2013, 137.
85 Wescoat 2012a, 56, 50, fig. 26b, pl. 44a–b.
86 Based on the capital's profile, Wescoat 2012a, 56, attributes it to one of the flank colonnades and suggests the spot for greatest visibility would be near the corners, where a viewer could see that capital across the porch. Alternatively, it is possible that the capital was replaced during a phase of repairs and inscribed once it was off the building (Wescoat 2012a, 56n56).
87 For examples of capitals inscribed on the exterior, one need only look to Delphi, where the two Doric capitals of the treasury of the Athenians and one Ionic capital from the Stoa of the Athenians carry a series of formulaic inscriptions honoring individual Athenians as Delphians. Colin 1909–1913, 116–17 (cat. nos. 110 and 111); Jacquemin and Laroche 2019, 189n24.
88 For the Propylon to the Sanctuary of the Great Gods, see Frazer 1990; Lehmann 1998, 53–54, 94–96. For the Propylon as a "bilingual" building, see Wescoat 2012b, 97.
89 Frazer 1990, 14; Wescoat 2012b, 95–99. For Samothracian initiation rituals that may have occurred in the vicinity of the Propylon, see Wescoat 2018, 60–61.
90 Burkert 1988, 34.
91 Burkert 1988, 35. Zuchtriegel 2023, 122–24 has recently gone much further in asserting the power of temple architecture in delimiting sacred space, not simply for religious but social and political ends.

Chapter 3. Oropos: Stone Carving and an Eye for Shadows

1 Athens, National Museum 4797: Betancourt 1977, 106, 137, 141, pl. 67; Kirchhoff 1988, 215; Ohnesorg 1993a, 116, pl. 21.8; Shoe Meritt 1996, 122–24, pls. 34–35; McGowan 1993, 189–92; McGowan 1997, 222n67; Bakker 1999, 41; Richens and Herdt 2009, fig. 8; Herdt 2013, 204; Wilson Jones 2014, 100, 102; Korres 2021.
2 Ionic columns supporting sphinxes as votives are widespread, with exceptionally large examples at Delphi (Amandry 1953), Aigina (Gruben 1965), Delos (Martin 1973, 387–89), and Kyrene (White 1971). For Archaic Ionic votive columns, see McGowan 1997; Herdt 2013; Wilson Jones 2014, 170–74.
3 McGowan 1997, 215–16. Of the ten archaic Ionic capitals found on the Acropolis that served as statue bases, one supported a bronze (Athens, Acropolis 4455), while the other nine supported statues secured with this same system of a dowel, connected to a lower tenon through a drilled pour channel (Akr. 124, 135, 3776, 7797, 3850, 3851, 3852, 3853, 4455, NM 85).
4 Ohnesorg 1993a, 116, thinks Parian marble.
5 51 percent of sixth- and fifth-century statues in Attica are of Island marble, but only 13 percent of their bases were: Hochscheid 2015, 106–7. Among Archaic votive Ionic and Aeolic capitals on the Acropolis, Island marble was common: McGowan 1997, 21n10.
6 For a concise illustrated comparison of the early Cycladic capital form, see Richens and Herdt 2009.
7 Korres 2021, 335–36, fig. 17.
8 For the capital from Paros (Paroikia Museum, inv. 793) found built into the wall of a house below the Asklepieion, see Fastje 2012 / 2013. It is the most clearly related to the Oropos capital, but about two-thirds the size and with only five central petals and twelve total eggs (the Oropos capital has twenty-two). Its compact dimensions place it nearer to the proportioning of Attic capitals, and the use of central eyes in the form of flat disks is certainly a later feature. Its small size suggests that it too was for a freestanding monument, but it lacks any cuttings on top (Fastje 2012 / 2013, 163).
9 Barletta 2001, 99; Ohnesorg 1993a.

10   For reviews of Cycladic Ionic style and their capitals, see Ohnesorg 2005a; Ohnesorg 2017.
11   For ca. 550, Shoe Meritt 1996, 122–23; Betancourt 1977, 106; McGowan 1993, 192, places it in the decade before the middle of the century, while Kirchhoff 1988, 216, places it in the decade after.
12   Petrakos 1968. Petropoulou 1981, 57–58, proposes a convincing date for the foundation of the Amphiareion around 421 BCE that fits within the window fixed by the archaeological and epigraphic evidence and the ancient political context (a renewal of Athenian building outside Athens with the pause in the Peloponnesian War). However, her main argument based on the absence of Oropos in a joke of Aristophanes (*Vesp.* 121–23) is tenuous.
13   This illustration contains the following conjectures: I assume that the column shaft was about 2.5 meters tall to judge from its upper diameter: 34 centimeters. The Cycladic style of the capital was probably paired with a shaft with sharp arrises and a simple cylindrical base.
14   Radt 1970, 238–42, pl. 39–40; Betancourt 1977, 137, pls. 29–31, figs. 17. For recent studies and 3D visualization of this building, see des Courtils 2011; Cavalier and Mora 2011.
15   This method is specific to hard stones like marble; medium and soft limestones are approached differently. Miller 1948, 44–47 (particularly figs. 14 and 19) usefully illustrates the methods for lettering stones of different hardness.
16   For half-carved capitals, Schmidt-Dounas 2004, 140–41.
17   Purchase 1904, 149.
18   Petros Georgopoulos and Giorgos Desypris, personal communication with the author, May 10, 2017.
19   The opportunity to participate as a volunteer draftsperson in the Parthenon Restoration Project was made possible by Rosalia Eleftheriou, Rosalia Christodoulopoulou, and Vasileia Manidaki of the Acropolis Restoration Service (Υ.Σ.Μ.Α.). Allyson Vieira has recently published interviews with Desypris and Georgopoulos (Vieira 2019, 142–63) and other marble workers of the Acropolis Restoration Service that give a sense of their deep knowledge about craft and history and dedication to archaeological preservation at a moment of economic crisis.
20   For stone grain, see Korres 1990, 1787–90; Korres 1994, 74–75.
21   The twelve-hour project took me over three days to complete because I did not have the stamina to carve marble for more than four hours daily; practiced stone carvers can work more consecutive hours.
22   Casson 1933, 192–94. For stone working chisels, see Rockwell 1993, 39–40.
23   The punch was essential for stone masonry, but it is difficult to trace because the rough marks it leaves behind are erased by subsequent finer tools, and its visually uninteresting shape absents it from iconography (Adam 1966, 11–16).
24   Sobak 2015, 676.
25   Adam 1966, 26, treats bullnose chisels as equivalent to flat chisels, suggesting they were often made from worn-down chisels with straight blades. My own chisels were made this way. Yet simplifying the taxonomy of tools misses the point that essential forms of stone architecture and sculpture—like column flutes and drapery folds—require bullnose chisels, for which flat chisels cannot be substituted.
26   Architectural energetics analysis is an archaeological method using mathematical modeling of volumes and work rates to estimate labor required to create ancient buildings: Abrams 1994; DeLaine 1997; Pickett et al. 2016.
27   Sozopol Archaeological Museum, no. 3594, 2: Panayotova et al. 2014, 597, fig. 2.1; Stoyanova and Damyanov 2021, 24n5, fig. 6.6; Stoyanova 2022, 48, 53–54, fig. 21.6. Part of a cutting for a dovetail clamp shows that this is an ovolo course with pendant palmettes.
28   Gruben 2014, pl. 16, pl. 30 (frag. 19).
29   The extent to which Greek moldings are derived from the observation of plant forms was debated in the late nineteenth century, with Riegl 1893 envisioning a continuous process of artistic development independent from the imitation of nature and Meurer 1897 arguing for elements of close botanical observation.
30   Koenigs 2007, cat. no. 31, 335–36, pl. 22–23.
31   Kyrieleis 1986, 203–4, fig. 16; Buschor 1933.
32   Balandat 2023, 81.
33   "Die Wirkung des Hohlen und Vollen gegeneinander auszuspielen": Bammer 1968-1971, 13.
34   Gruben 2014, pl. 16–17: volute frag. 55, pl. 34: volute frag. 65a, pl. 42: volute frag. B 66.
35   Ohnesorg 2007, 87–88; cat. no. B40 pl. 74.4.
36   For the importance of this image and previous bibliography, see Lyons 2005, 47–48, fig. 11, n36.
37   Ruskin 1851, 305.
38   Mayeux's 1885 manual was reprinted, translated into English (Mayeux 1889), and reprinted serially in the New York monthly *The Decorator and the Furnisher*.
39   Michaelsen 1975, 52–53, traces the early exploration of solid-void equivalence in cubist sculpture first to Umberto Boccioni's *Abstract Solids and Voids of a Head* (1912), followed by Archipenko's *Geometric Statuette* (1914). For the early sequence of Archipenko's convex-concave substitution effects, see Gray 1953, 92–93. For Archipenko, see Calhoun 2016, passim, particularly 126–27, 134–35. Michaelsen 1975, passim, especially 57–58, 65–67.
40   Calhoun 2016, 124.
41   For Pre-Socratics, see Montelle 2011, 103–7.
42   For the challenge of seeing the Moon with volume and Warren De La Rue's landmark stereoscopic presentations of the Moon, see Salvesen 2018, 26–27; Hankins and Silverman 1995, 170–72.
43   Montelle 2011, 105; Diels 1929, 354 (Aet. ii.24 3).
44   For a summary of issues concerning what ancient architects' technical drawings may have looked like, see Coulton 1977, 51–73.
45   "Item circum coagmenta et cubilia eminentes expressiones graphicoteran efficient in aspectu delectationem." Translation after Rowland and Howe 1999, 59.
46   Wilson Jones 2014, 8.
47   For theories of depth cues and binocular vision, see Vishwanath 2014, 151–52.
48   Vtr. 4.4.3. Translated by Rowland and Howe 1999, 59.
49   Rowland and Howe 1999, 229.
50   Wilson Jones 2014, 8.

51 Vishwanath 2006, 60–61.
52 Barker 1918, 23, fig. 11. For more recent attempts to place Greek architecture in relation to contemporary biomimetic design, see Mazzoleni 2013, 6–7.
53 Barker 1918, 22.
54 Using a computer model, I tallied up the total visible surface area of a Doric column from the Parthenon and found that it is just over 90 percent concave surfaces, 6 percent flat surfaces (the abacus), and less than 4 percent convex surfaces (the echinus).
55 Zambas 2002, 154–68.
56 Zambas 2002, 171–82.
57 Hennemeyer 2011, 106–9; Haselberger 2020, 213–14.
58 Hennemeyer 2011, 104.
59 Rowland and Howe 1999, xvi.
60 For Vitruvius's discussion of column flutes in relationship to theories of vision (4.4.2–3), see Rowland and Howe 1999, 221–29.
61 For Apollodoros, *skiagraphia*, and chiaroscuro painting in ancient Greece, see Keuls 1975; Rouveret 2006. Pliny (*HN* 35.29) offers a description of a three-tone system of painting (mid tones, highlights, and shadow) that is still extensively used (Baxandall 1995, 148). For the importance of Greek painting in the broader history of the depiction of shadows in the visual arts, see Gombrich 1995.
62 "Umbraeque corpus ex ipsa dedit." Pausias's painting, transported to the Portico of Pompey in Rome, is lost, but some sense of the effect may be gained from Peter Paul Rubens's attempt to recreate Pliny's description of Pausias's feat in the *Decius Mus Cycle* (1616–1618 CE); Baumstark 1985, 6–7.
63 Lazaridis 1997, 50–51.
64 For the importance of metaphors of vision in Greek philosophy, see Nightingale 2004, 14, for the critique of ocularcentrism.
65 Cf. Pl. *Phdr.* 260c; Soph. *Phil.* 946. For a broad consideration of the semiotics of shadows with special attention to the ancient Mediterranean world, see Sharpe 2017.
66 Montelle 2011, 105–6.
67 Sharpe 2017, 11.
68 Plin. *HN* 35. 43; Quint. 10.2.7; Sharpe 2017, 102–10.
69 For a lucid summary of Aristarchos's astronomic achievements, see Montelle 2011, 108–11; Carman and Buzón 2023.
70 Montelle 2011, 105, identifies Herakleitos as the first Greek thinker whose "conceptions of the heavenly bodies were very much inspired from earthly everyday objects." The notion is reminiscent of Ovid's praise of astronomers (*Fast.* 1.305): "They brought close the distant stars to the eyes of our mind."
71 Baxandall 1995, 120–21. For a more recent study of the interplay of shadows in art and science, see Sharpe 2017.
72 Baxandall 1995, 146–55.
73 For Vitruvius's Ionian sources, see Gros 1975, 1001–3. Pytheos's characterization of the architect as polymath has had a long history of rephrasing, notably including the opening lines of Laugier's 1753 (1997) *Essai sur l'Architecture*.
74 "Quam multa vident pictores in umbris et in eminentia quae nos non videmus!" Translated by Rackham 1933, 493.

Chapter 4. Neapolis and Thessaloniki: Stylistic Pluralism in *Apoikiai*

1 For *apoikiai* as sites of identity building, see Antonaccio 2003; Demetriou 2012. Osborne 1998 argues against the use of the term "colonization" as obscuring the ancient phenomenon through modern associations. For the larger subject, see notably Graham 1983; Graham 2001a; Boardman 2001; Purcell 2005; Malkin 2011; Zuchtriegel 2017.
2 The capitals from Thessaloniki are larger and wider than the capitals from Kavala, and thus their designs have four eggs on the echinus and four channels on the bolster, while the Kavala capitals have only three of each.
3 For the Thasian connection, see Schmidt-Dounas 2004, 117; des Courtils 1997, 515–17.
4 Their fully developed high-relief egg-and-dart echinus, retaining the Archaic pointed forms, has particularly close connections to a group of Ionic capitals from Thasos (compare to Martin 1972).
5 For the interpretation of the pits, see Prokova 2014, 38; Prokova 2017; Lazaridis 1962, 237. For the dating of the terracing, which hinges largely on the absence of red-figure pottery, see Bakalakis 1937, 6; Bakalakis 1938, 77–78; Lazaridis 1960, 219; Lazaridis 1962, 237–38; Prokova 2014, 51.
6 Bakalakis 1936, 22–24, figs. 30–31. The finely worked circle for the bedding of the base shows that the column was set up without a plinth.
7 Heuzey and Daumet 1876, 22–24. Heuzey assumed that the cult at Neapolis was the cult of Athena Parthenos that was brought from Athens in the Classical period, but Daumet pointed out that the large capital belonged to an age before the Classical monuments of the Athenian Acropolis.
8 Prokova 2014, 51–52; Avramidou 2021. For the peribolos wall, see Bakalakis 1936, 30–32, figs. 43–46; Lazaridis 1960, 219.
9 Bakalakis 1936, 22–24, figs. 30–31. The finely worked circle for the bedding of the base shows that the column was set up without a plinth.
10 Schmidt-Dounas 2004, pl. 17.2.
11 Bakalakis 1936, 24 figs. 32–33.
12 Bakalakis 1936, 7–19, figs. 10–23, fig. 27.
13 Bakalakis 1936, 24–25, figs. 34–5. The ovolo moldings come in four sizes, three with carved egg-and-dart motifs (h. 21.0, h. 15.7, h. 11.7 centimeters) and one without carving (h. 17.0 centimeters). They are similar in style and scale to the treatment of the echinus of the capitals (cf. h. ca. 13 centimeters). Some of these courses could come from a separate construction such as the temple's altar, but all could conceivably belong to the Ionic temple, which would need different molding courses to crown the epistyle at front and back, a crowning molding over the frieze or dentil course, and crowning moldings for the doorframe and wall.
14 Bakalakis 1936, 26–27, fig. 36.
15 Compare this to the 19.5 centimeter maximum riser height of American building codes, and Vitruvius's recommended range of 22.2–24.7 centimeters

16. (3.4.4). For monumental step sizes, see Hollinshead 2015, 19–21.
17. For the Ionic capitals of Thasos, see Martin 1972. Theodorescu 1980 showed that the capitals from Thasos, Neapolis, and Thessaloniki fit within a proportional grouping of particularly compact designs that appear in the late Archaic northern Aegean (see fig. 5.19).
17. Schmidt-Dounas 2004, 127. Fisher 2015 cautions that peripteral temples are given outsize weight in the history of Greek architecture.
18. For the temple of Athena on Thasos, see des Courtils 2020.
19. Prokova 2014, 31n16; Bakalakis 1936, 44; Collart 1937, 103–4.
20. The sherds from these sites are dated 650–625; Isaac 1986, 10.
21. For Archilochos and the colonization of Thasos, see Owen 2003; Graham 2001b; Graham 1978; as well as Prokova 2014, 32; Isaac 1986, 8; Koukouli-Chrysanthaki 1980, 310; Bakalakis 1936, 43.
22. Prokova 2014, 34; Lazaridis 1969, 43.
23. The best case for the continuity of religion in the Thasian peraia occurs at the cave of the Nymphs near ancient Oisyme, where pottery extends back to prehistory (Isaac 1986, 9–10).
24. For sherds in the Parthenos sanctuary dating to the seventh century and the likely continuity of the cult from the foundation of the city, see Prokova 2014, 50.
25. Prokova 2014, 35; Lazaridis 1971, 54. For the harbor of Neapolis, see Malamidou 2022.
26. Hdt. 6.46. Meiggs 1972, 570–71.
27. *IG* I³ 101, 27–28. Translation by Isaac 1986, 67. For *IG* I³ 101 (*IG* I² 108; *ML* no. 89; *OR* 187). The money referenced appears to have been a loan from Neapolis to the Athenian general Thrasyboulos to sustain the siege of Thasos in 407 (Prokova 2014, 14; Lazaridis 1969, 23; Poulios 1998, 235).
28. Prokova 2014, 39.
29. Thuk. 1.100–101.
30. Meiggs 1972, 266; de Ste. Croix 1972, 42–43.
31. Meiggs 1972, 365.
32. The possible peace treaty of ca. 390 is attested in the fragmentary inscription *IG* XII 5, 109, which is not without problems of interpretation (Isaac 1986, 68; Pouilloux 1954, 178–92; Moretti 1987; Prokova 2014, 43n108–9). The Thasian grant of citizenship appears in *IG* XII 8, 264 (Pouilloux 1954, 204–12; Lazaridis 1969, 23–24; Picard 1990, 545; Prokova 2014, 43).
33. A late fifth-century Thasian inscription attests that Thasos had selected state officials "who are entrusted with the peraia," though by this time Neapolis was completely autonomous (Lazaridis 1971, 55).
34. Prokova 2014, 36.
35. For the problem of correlating coinage and city autonomy, see Thonemann 2016, 48–49.
36. Prokova 2014, 36; Koukouli-Chrysanthaki 1990, 502.
37. Prokova 2014, 38; Giouri and Koukouli 1987, 373.
38. Prokova 2014, 48–49, compares the position of the temple of Parthenos to the position of the Artemision on Thasos. This connection is also pertinent because the sanctuaries have a similar array of terra-cotta figurines (Prokova 2014, 107–9).
39. Collart 1937, 109n1; Prokova 2014, 52.
40. For the possibility of Persian destruction, see Giouri and Koukouli 1987, 373.
41. The generic nature of the fifth-century heads led to the initial identification of the figure as Nike, and Picard 1990, 544n4, proposes that she is a local nymph.
42. Isaac 1986, 68; Friedländer and von Sallet 1889, 103, no. 36. Coins of Neapolis also picture the portrait of Parthenos with a locust and ivy-leaf (*SNG Macedonia* no. 231–32).
43. NM 1480. For description of the relief and her attributes, see Prokova 2014, 90–91.
44. Friedländer and von Sallet 1889, 103–4; Bakalakis 1936, 36. Strabo (7.4.2) mentions the worship of the goddess Parthenos in the form of a *xoanon* in Crimea. Prokova 2014, 90–92, pushes back, pointing out that the Athenian carver of the fourth-century relief likely had never seen the cult statue of Parthenos and may have cribbed the iconography from contemporary depictions of Hekate.
45. For the inscription dedicating a "κρεοφυλάκιον" for Parthenos, Heuzey and Daumet 1876, 21–22, no. 5; Bakalakis 1936, 32–33; Prokova 2014, 52–53.
46. Theophrastus, *Char.* 9.2. For distribution of meat at sacrifices, see McInerney 2010, 173–77, 183–86. Provisions were often made for allotting the hides of sacrificial animals to the officiating priests or priestesses as a sort of remuneration (McInerney 2010, 185–86).
47. Worship of Parthenos is attested at Sparta, Halicarnassus, Patmos, Lemnos, Chersonesus, and in the vicinity of Neapolis, at Thasos, Oisyme, and Amphipolis. For cults of Parthenos in the Greek world, see Bakalakis 1936, 36n2; Koukouli-Chrysanthaki 1997, 944–45; Bilde 2003; Bilde 2009; Prokova 2014, 87; McInerney 2015, 298–301.
48. For a list of identifications of Parthenos with Athena, see Prokova 2014, 88n375.
49. Collart 1937, 112; Bakalakis 1936, 36, hinted at the connection with Artemis Tauropolos previously. Cf. Prokova 2014, 88; Avramidou 2021, 13.
50. For the Black Sea connections of the cult of Parthenos, see Bilde 2003; Bilde 2009; McInerney 2015, 298–301.
51. A similar phenomenon might be seen in the late Classical rebranding of idiosyncratic local gods at Samothrace and Histria as "Great Gods."
52. Owen 2000; Grandjean and Salviat 2000, 117–19.
53. Editio princeps: Velkov and Domaradzka 1994. For a review of interpretations of the Vetren / Pistiros inscription, see Demetriou 2012, 158–87.
54. For a review of the dating of the inscription, see Demetriou 2012, 162–65; Velkov and Domaradzka 1994.
55. Velkov and Domaradzka 1994, ll. 7–10. For a review of the provision about debt cancellation, see Demetriou 2012, 173–74.
56. Diod. Sic. 4.4.1. For the syncretism of Sabazios and Dionysos, see Demetriou 2012, 170.
57. Demetriou 2012, 156n9. Hdt. 7.111 further elaborates the worship of Dionysos in Thrace.
58. Demetriou 2012, 171.
59. Bakalakis 1963, 31.
60. With the rescue excavation began the slow process of expropriating the land on which a high-rise

61. Karadedos 2006a, 319–20, 322.
62. Hatzioannidis et al. 2014.
63. Hatzioannidis et al. 2014, 386–88.
64. Members from this building have been cataloged with different systems; all are referred to here using the references of Grammenos and Knithakis's *Catalog of Architectural Members of the Museum of Thessaloniki* (*KAMMΘ*). Base: *KAMMΘ* 5.
65. Hatzioannidis et al. 2014, 386–88.
66. Cat. nos. 5, 6, 92, 94, 95.
67. Ohnesorg 2007, 60–68; Dirschedl 2018, 17–20, pl. 3; Hulek 2018, 71–74.
68. The three bilinguals are *KAMMΘ* 1, 3, 4; the fourth capital, concave on both sides, is *KAMMΘ* 2.
69. Hatzioannidis et al. 2014, 387–88, fig. 7.
70. *KAMMΘ* 7.
71. *KAMMΘ* 23.
72. *KAMMΘ* 8–26.
73. This feature is most apparent in the Doric order, where it is possible to tell the orientation of the flutes because they leave an impression on the stylobate and are included in the block of the capital. The temple of Athena at Assos has both (Wescoat 2012a, 41).
74. The maximum depth of carving on the convex faces of the capitals is 0.9 centimeters, and the maximum depth of carving on the concave faces of the capitals is 3.0 centimeters.
75. Bakalakis 1963, 33; *KAMMΘ*, p. 21.
76. Bakalakis 1963, 33. Numbering a pronaos column "10," can be fit somewhat logically into a plan of counting a hexastyle peristyle building, if one first counts the columns of the facade (1–6), then the first pair of columns of the flanks (7 and 8), and then the pronaos columns (9 and 10).
77. Schmidt-Dounas 2004, 117.
78. For the Thasian doorframe, see Launey 1944, 73–75, figs. 42–45; des Courtils 1997, 512–17.
79. Des Courtils 1997, 516.
80. Boehm 2011, 12, 16.
81. F.Gr.Hist. 1F 146. Boehm 2011, 17n37.
82. E.g., Athens conquered and quickly lost Therme in 432 BCE (Thuc. 1.61.2).
83. Strabo 7.fr.24.
84. See Boehm 2011, 17–18 for the continued existence of several of these cities.
85. Translated by Vince 1930, 239. Hypereides (frag. 80) puts the number of displaced cities at forty (Boehm 2011, 13).
86. Boehm 2018, 165. There was an oracle of Dionysos in the mountains among the Thracian Satrai, at Mt. Pangaion (Hdt. 7.111). The cult of Dionysos was particularly important on Thasos, and Samothrace had a Dionysia (Dimitrova 2008, 72–74).
87. Bakalakis 1983. Laurent 1964, 287.
88. Boehm 2018, 91. The phalloi in the Thessaloniki Museum (*KΓMΘ I*, no. 7) comes from Amphipolis and not Thessaloniki (Bakalakis 1963, 33). For phallic processions, see Hdt. 2.48–49. Inscribed accounts mention a large wood phallus for processions of Dionysos on Delos (Nilsson 1906, 280–82), and phalloi were regularly sent from the colonies of the Athenian Empire to the Dionysia in Athens (*IG* I³ 46, ll. 43–46). Otto 1965, 164–65. Phalloi might even be sung to (Heraclitus, fr. 15).
89. Lambrinoudakis and Gruben 1987, 604–14, abb. 47–49.
90. Voutiras 1999.
91. *IG* X 2.1, 31, l. 4.
92. Dio. Ha. 1.44.1–4. Given that the two named authors of this opinion (Hegesianax of Alexandria Troas and Hegesippus of Mekyberna) were both Greeks born in the North Aegean in the early Hellenistic period, Aeneas's death in the area must be a particularly local tradition, and the cult of Aeneas at Aineia may have been centered around a tomb heroon.
93. Liv. 40.4.9. Steimle 2008, 36.
94. Galinsky 1969, 65–70.
95. Malten 1931, 46; Galinsky 1969, 72.
96. Galinsky 1969, 66; Gardner 1883, 179–80, nos. 78–103, pl. 28.15–16.
97. Bakalakis 1963, 31–34.
98. Steimle 2008, 49–54. Stefanidou-Tiveriou 2012, 278.
99. Tasia, Lola, and Peltekis 2000, 229.
100. Tasia, Lola, and Peltekis 2000, 240, 246, fig. 20. For the implications of this argument, see also Palamidis 2017, 89–90.
101. Stefanidou-Tiveriou 2012, 281n46. Steimle 2008, 34–36.
102. Sismanidis 2021; Sismanidis 2012.
103. Sismanidis 2021.
104. The large 19.5–20.0 centimeter ovolo molding: Grammenos and Knithakis 1994, cat. nos. 10, 12, 14 22. The small 15.5–16.0 centimeter ovolo molding: Grammenos and Knithakis 1994, cat. nos. 11, 13; Sismanidis 2021, 500, figs. 12–13.
105. Grammenos and Knithakis 1994, cat. no. 26; Sismanidis 2021, 500, 512, figs. 10–11.
106. Roma: inv. no. 1526, *KΓMΘ II*, n. 212 (pl. 358–60). Hadrian with a captive (inv. no. 1527+1529, *KΓMΘ II*, no. 261).
107. Stefanidou-Tiveriou 2012, 285–82.
108. Richter 1933, 76.
109. Boehm 2018, 165.
110. One Ionic capital from the Temple of Athena at Sounion shows two different methods of repair to broken volutes with metal pins (Barletta 2017, 111). This capital was abandoned at Sounion when other capitals were taken to the Athenian Agora in the Roman period.
111. Dinsmoor 1940, 15–18.
112. Vokotopoulou 1993, 91 argued that the inscribed letters represented a repair rather than displacement of the temple.
113. A similar treatment is reported on rebuilding projects in Athens, including the temple of Ares in the Agora, and the Ionic building at Ambelokepoi (Korres 1997, 204).
114. The most remarkable occurrence of Roman-period archaistic replacements for moldings appears in the altar of Hera on Samos (Kienast 2016).
115. The surviving lion head sima block (inv. no. 11.449; *KAMMΘ* 7; *KΓMΘ I* 2) is 27.5 centimeters tall. A Roman period lion head waterspout (inv. no. 1252;

KAMMΘ, no. 607) 24 centimeters tall and not yet identified with a monument could be a replacement.
116 Ohnesorg 2012, 30, fig. 6; Giraud 1989, pl. 14.
117 Stevens et al. 1927, 178–80, 223–24, 478–79; Korres 1997, 199–202; Papanikolaou 2012, 470–501.
118 Tasia, Lola, and Peltekis 2000, 232.
119 Ohnesorg 2018, 273–74.
120 Bakalakis 1963, 34; Palamidis 2017, 89.
121 Boehm 2011, 12.
122 Karadedos 2006b offered an intriguing proposal to redesign the roundabout to expose more of the temple and make the site accessible to visitors.
123 For the ancient city plan of Thessaloniki, see Vickers 1972; Vitti 1996. For Hébrard's plan in context, see Lagopoulos 2005.
124 Karadedos 2006a, 322–23.
125 Ohnesorg 1993b, 97–99, pl. 26, 64.1–5. A fragmentary marble stroter may also belong to the roof (Ohnesorg 1993b, 98, pl. 64.6).
126 For the axial alignment of waterspouts with columns (*Jochbindung*), see Ohnesorg 1993b, 120–22. There are some early cases of misalignment of marble waterspouts, but the alignment may begin as early as the first dipteral temples at Ephesos and Didyma.
127 Launey 1944, 76; Blondé et al. 1985, 882–84; Grandjean and Salviat 2000, 143–44.
128 Launey 1944, 69–71, fig. 36.
129 Martin 1959, 93–96 calculates the Thasian foot at 35 centimeters.
130 Dinsmoor 1974, 233–34.
131 Dinsmoor 1943; Dinsmoor 1982; Korres 1992–1998.
132 Baltes 2020, 339. For the Romanization of the Agora, see Alcock 2002; Vera 2018. For the Thessaloniki temple as an example of this practice, see Vera 2018, 158–59; Miles 2014, 137–39; Allamani-Souri 2003, 80–82; Spawforth 2012, 65–66.
133 Gruben 1969, 39; Gruben 1986. For the dating of the bases, see Dirschedl 2013, cat. no. W2.

Chapter 5. Athens and Eretria: The Influence of Painting on Stone Carving

1 The first Ionic temple in Attica, the Temple of Apollo at Cape Zoster (ancient Halai Aixonides) from ca. 500, seems to be purely an import; it is made of Island marble and is in Cycladic style (Kourouniotis 1927–1928).
2 Korres 1997; the height of the column is not known, but the volute capital was about 2 meters long (McGowan 1997, 213). For a scale comparison to other early Ionic monuments, see Wilson Jones 2014, 132–33, fig. 5.22.
3 *IG* I^3 948; *IG* I^2 761. Welter 1939; Arnush 1995; Ohnesorg 2005b, 246.
4 Temples: the temple of Athena at Sounion, the Erechtheion and Temple of Athena Nike on the Acropolis, the temple on the Areopagus, the temple on the Ilissos River. Ionic porches added to cult buildings: the Pompeion in the Kerameikos, the Telesterion at Eleusis. Ionic friezes added to Doric temples: the Parthenon on the Acropolis, the Hephaisteion in the Agora, the temple of Poseidon at Sounion. Ionic as a second interior order: the Stoa Poikile and the Stoa of Zeus Eleutherios in the Agora, the Parthenon and the Propylaia on the Acropolis.
5 Bouras 1967, 61–71. For Attic influence on Ionic architecture of later centuries, see Schädler 1991.
6 For the contested notion of a Classical gap in Ionia caused by Athenian taxation, see Cook 1962; Osborne 1999, 320.
7 For the features of the Athenian Ionic capital, see McGowan 1997 (I have subdivided her two categories into four, but they are the same points); Shoe Meritt 1982; Shoe Meritt 1993; Shoe Meritt 1996.
8 Translation adapted from Crawley 1910, 391.
9 EM. 6787: *IG* I^3 948; Arnush 1995, 144–50.
10 Dinsmoor 1942, 197–98; Arnush 1995, 137n86; Duggan 2016, 272.
11 Wescoat and Levitan 2017.
12 For a summary of eighteenth- and nineteenth-century responses to architectural polychromy, see Armstrong 2012, 500–50; Hellmann 2014, 227; Brinkmann 2004b; Jenkins and Middleton 1988.
13 Stevens et al. 1927, 368.
14 For the detection of wax from encaustic painting on the Parthenon, see Aggelakopoulou, Sotiropoulou, and Karagiannis 2022, 782–83, passim.
15 Polychromy in architecture technically also includes architectural terra-cottas, wall paintings, floor mosaics, etc. For overview, see Neils 2016; Zink 2019.
16 Hellmann 2014, 231–33.
17 For "bichrome," Hellmann 2014, 231. For "oligochrome," see Fenger 1886, 5.
18 The blue krepis of the temple near Asea in Arcadia and the yellow krepis of Temple B at Selinunte are noteworthy exceptions (Hellmann 2014, 235n15).
19 Only in later periods were the leaves of Ionic moldings left unpainted (Fenger 1886, 28–29).
20 For the history of research on the Polychromy of the Aphaia temple, see Bankel 2004; for the Parthenon, Jenkins and Middleton 1988; Brinkmann 2004a.
21 Hellmann 2014, 233.
22 Hellmann 2002, 234; for similar conclusions concerning the Aphaia temple, see Bankel 1993, 112–13; Bankel 2004, 100.
23 Hellmann 2014, 235.
24 Bankel 1993, 112–13; Bankel 2004, 103; Zink 2019.
25 Schwandner 1985, 130.
26 For new scientific analysis of the paint traces on Temple B, see Lazzarini and Marconi 2017. For an image of the triglyph, see Brinkmann 2004b, 33, fig. 24. For Starosel, see Tzochev 2021, 142–43.
27 Zink 2019; Hellmann 2002, 234: "Les mêmes principes règnent dans l'ordre ionique, jusque sur les nombreuses zones moulurées."
28 Achilara et al. 2004, 16. For polychromy in Chian Ionic architecture, see Boardman 1959, 187.
29 Des Courtils and Laroche 2002, 327–29; Hansen and Le Roy 2012, 167; Hellmann 2014, 231.
30 Ephesos: Jenkins 2006, 38, fig. 19; Ohnesorg 2007, 71. Tomb of Eurydice: Drougou and Saatsoglou-Paliadeli 2006, 185; Ignatiadou 2020, 121, fig. 5. Erechtheion: *IG* I^3 476, ll. 299–303, 355–56; Stevens

et al. 1927, 22–23. For discussion of metal attachments, see Ignatiadou 2020, 120–22.
31. Bammer 1972, pl. 5. a, c, e.
32. For a review of previous scholarship on the glass inlays of the Erechtheion capitals, see Ignatiadou 2020.
33. Ignatiadou 2020. For glass on klinai, see Baughan 2013, 268–89, passim.
34. The materiality of color has become an important strand of recent studies of polychromy: Stager 2022, 34–37, 60–70, passim; Nagel 2023, 196–99.
35. Koenigs 2016, 221, fig. 6, 7. The abacus molding paint scheme is here reconstructed based on other moldings from the Mausoleum: Newton 1862–1863, 185, pl. 29; Jenkins, Gratziu, and Middleton 1997. Similar color schemes appear on contemporary buildings at Labraunda (Blid 2017). For the interlaced leaf pattern on Ionic capitals, see Barletta 2017, 194–96. For interlaced leaf on Archaic sculpture, see Brinkmann 2004c.
36. Acropolis Museum 4455: Kawerau 1907, 197–207, figs. 1–3, pl. 4; McGowan 1993, 94–95; McGowan 1997, 216n31.
37. Herzfeld 1941, 255, pl. 64; Tilia 1978, 38–39, pl. B, C; Nagel 2010, 22, 114; Nagel 2023, 27, 108.
38. Zink et al. 2019.
39. Zink et al. 2019, 21–25.
40. For chryselephantine doors attested on temples at Athens, Delos, Delphi, Didyma, Epidauros, and Syracuse, see Pope and Schultz 2014, 22–25.
41. For an overview of Macedonian painted tombs, see Palagia 2016, 383–86; Rhomiopoulou and Schmidt-Dounas 2010; Avlonitou 2016, as well as Rhomiopoulou and Schmidt-Dounas 2010, offer scientific analysis of the pigments used in the painting of these tomb facades.
42. For early attempts to restore the paint schemes of the Acropolis capitals, see Fenger 1886, 30.
43. For the Nike of Kallimachos, see Raubitschek 1940, 53–55; Korres 1994, 174, 178.
44. McGowan 1997, 215.
45. For the breakdown of the use of color on the Acropolis korai and other archaic statues, see Manzelli 1994. Green appears on belts (Akr. Korai 593, 592, 678, 679), crowns (Akr. Korai 592, 669, 673, 675, 616, 666, 641, 687, Akr. Head 652, 61, 63, 662, 650, 71, 78), and earrings (korai Kore 666, 670, 661, 641, 662, 650). Meander pattern appears on chitons (673, Kore 670, 675, 674, 600, 337; Akr. frg. α1, Akr. frg. A6), Athena's helmet (Akr. 648, 305), and the mantle of a kouros (Akr. 633).
46. Akr. 135: Borrmann 1888; McGowan 1997, 215. Acropolis 3853: Borrmann 1887; McGowan 1997, 215. Acropolis 3776: recorded in drawing by Christian Hansen (Danish National Art Library 14697a); McGowan 1997, 211. Agora 1976: Barletta 2017, fig. 129. Athens, Pompeion: Hoepfner 1976, 59, figs. 80–81. Agora A2972 and Agora A2973: Thompson 1960, 351–56, pl. 76–7; Shoe Meritt 1993, 314, 317–18; Barletta 2017, 229–30, 232–33; Brinkmann, Koch-Brinkmann, and Piening 2024. Athens, Propylaia: recorded in drawing by Christian Hansen (Danish National Art Library 14950 d). Athens, Erechtheion: Stevens et al. 1927, 220–22, 227; Ignatiadou 2020. Mausoleum, Halikarnassos: Newton 1862–1863, 185, pl. 29; Jenkins, Gratziu, and Middleton 1997; Koenigs 2016, 221. Vergina, Tomb of Eurydice: Drougou and Saatsoglou-Paliadeli 2006, 96, 184–85. Lefkadia, Tomb of the Palmettes: Rhomiopoulou and Schmidt-Dounas 2010, 35–7, pl. 3–5, color plates 6, 8. Pantikapaion: Bujskich 2010, 29, pl. 21, color pl. 1. Vergina, Rhomaios Tomb: Rhomaios 1951; Drougou and Saatsoglou-Paliadeli 2006, 188, 278.
47. Ohnesorg 1993b, 129–33.
48. Borrmann 1888, 8, notes that the use of red paint on the roughened surface of the volute eyes of Akr. 3853, rather than the smoothed surfaces elsewhere on the capital, suggests this painting marks the preparation for gilding.
49. On the variety of painted motifs on the Sounion capitals, see Barletta 2017, 114–18, 194.
50. Shoe Meritt 1993, 320–21. One might also suggest that the alteration was a late change to differentiate the four interior Ionic columns from the columns of the exterior.
51. Thompson 1960, 351–56, pl. 76–7; Shoe Meritt 1993, 314, 317–18; Barletta 2017, 229–30, 232–33; Brinkmann, Koch-Brinkmann, and Piening 2024.
52. Thompson 1960, 351–53; Brinkmann, Koch-Brinkmann, and Piening 2024, 78.
53. Thompson 1960, 354; Shoe Meritt 1993, 314; Brinkmann, Koch-Brinkmann, and Piening 2024, 78.
54. Brinkmann, Koch-Brinkmann, and Piening 2024, 80.
55. Brinkmann, Koch-Brinkmann, and Piening 2024, 83–84.
56. Brinkmann, Koch-Brinkmann, and Piening 2024, 89–90.
57. For a similar sentiment, see Brinkmann, Koch-Brinkmann, and Piening 2024, 90–92.
58. Koldewey 1890, 55, pl. 25.
59. Broneer 1954, 46, pl. 9.8.
60. Kallipolitis and Petrakos 1965, 127, fig. 6, 7, pl. 162b.
61. For the temple of Apollo Daphnephoros, see Auberson 1968. Recent scientific analysis (Lazzarini, Persano, and Maniatis 2019) confirmed that the marble used for the pediment sculpture originated on Paros.
62. For the wooden superstructure of the Stoa of the Athenians at Delphi, see Jacquemin and Laroche 2019, 186–87.
63. Kallipolitis and Petrakos 1965, 162b.
64. The convex face of the Eretria capital figures prominently as a missing link in Theodorescu's summarizing diagram (Theodorescu 1980, pl. 3).
65. Shoe Meritt 1996, 145–47, fig. 9.
66. For the capitals, see Möbius 1927; Shoe Meritt 1996; Goette 1992–1998, 112n19; Paga 2021, 234–35.
67. Shoe Meritt 1996, 137. Bammer 1968–1971, 13, identified the Stavro / Jeraka capitals as Classical, but his observation has not garnered attention. For a recent discussion, see Paga 2021, 234–35.
68. Möbius 1927, 167.
69. Möbius transliterated the Greek place name "Γέρακα" into German as "Jeraka," which persists in English language scholarship even though it is an uncommon transliteration.
70. NM 1570 (previously Δ972). The bed surface of the capital bears the graffiti initials "ΔKM," "KΔM," "IΔM," "AΔM," "ΣAM," "KΠI," and "ΣΣMΓΓ." The

last may be related to the longest inscription, "ΣΣΜΗΤΡΟV," surely the name "Σ. Σ. Μήτρου" as well as the three dates.
71. IIM 3773: Shoe Meritt 1996, 137n46.
72. Möbius 1927, 168.
73. American School of Classical Studies at Athens, Archives, Antiquities Collection 24 and 25 (ASA 24 and 25). Dimensions of the capital were recorded but not whether the volute belonged to the convex or concave side. Korres 1996, 113n73.
74. Contra Mace 1978, 137.
75. Möbius 1927, 168.
76. Shoe Meritt 1982, 83.
77. For marble extraction on Pentele, see Korres 2001.
78. Marble at Sounion: Barletta 2017, 86–88; Goette 1991. Marble at Thorikos, which might be from Agrileza or more locally sourced at Thorikos: Miles 2015, 170, 178n29; Vanhove 1994, 44; Goette 1991, 213. Rhamnous: Miles 1989, 145–46, 203.
79. Stanier 1953, 72; Orlandos 1949. I calculate the figures from rough volume estimates based on the dimensions of the roof elements and an assumed volumetric mass density of marble (2.71 tons per cubic meter).
80. When I studied the fragmentary Stavro capital at the National Archaeological Museum, Athens, two people were easily able to lift it together.
81. Carlson and Aylward 2010.
82. For Archaic patching and repairs, see Klein 2015. The builders of the Erechtheion made extensive use of inserted marble patches in almost every level of the building from the stylobate to the cornice, particular in moldings. Stevens et al. 1927, 207–14, describe 106 marble patches and mention unnumbered others—ranging from small replacement reels to the whole left arm of the caryatid second from east. Dovetailing was used to secure some of the patches, while others are held with metal pins and clamps, and in some cases, cement.
83. Möbius 1927, 167–71.
84. Möbius 1927, 167–71.
85. Möbius 1927, 170; Shoe Meritt 1982, 86.
86. Shoe Meritt 1982, 86–87.
87. Shoe Meritt 1982, 91–92.
88. Paga 2015; Paga 2021, 108–11.
89. Adding to the complexity of this monument, Korres 1997, 204–5 has suggested that the capital from the Agora (Agora A3345) is a Roman-period replica of the Inwood capital.
90. Shoe Meritt 1996, 138–39; Rignanese 2021.
91. Möbius 1927, 170. Shoe Meritt 1996, 165–67.
92. Shoe Meritt 1996, 139.
93. Shoe Meritt 1996, 139.
94. Thucydides's offhand addition of "and other temples in this area" (2.15) gives the impression that the river hosted many small shrines.
95. Rignanese 2021, 291–93.
96. Korres 1992–1998; McAllister 1959. Summarized by Hellmann 2009, 281–82. The Agora's Ares Temple had previously been identified as an itinerant temple, though it was initially proposed to have come from the deme of Acharnai, which had one of the rare Classical cults to Ares (Kellogg 2013, 163–65). Alcock 2002, 55.
97. Möbius 1927, 162–63, pl. 18.1. The asymmetry of the triglyph's sides, with one overlapping a metope plaque and one flush with an adjacent metope block, suggests that the triglyph belongs to the right corner of the facade of an in-antis, not peripteral, structure. For the difficulty in identifying the Ionic structure as the predecessor to the temple of Athena, see Paga 2021, 234–35.
98. Schlaifer 1943, 39n7.
99. For the most recent study of the parasitoi at Pallene, see March 2008.
100. Schlaifer 1943. SEG 34, 157.
101. Stanton 1984, 292–98; Jones 1999, 239; March 2008, 134–38.

Chapter 6. Ephesos, Selinous, and Delphi: Retrospective Design in Ionia and Abroad

1. Cook 1961; Cook 1962, put forward the theory that the "Classical Gap" in temple building in Ionia may result from double taxation of the Persian and Athenian Empires. Osborne 1999, 320, questions Cook's "decline-of-Ionia thesis." While Osborne is correct in insisting that temple construction should not be the only metric of assessing the economic health of Ionia, the phenomenon remains.
2. For the Ionian Renaissance, see Isager 1994; Pedersen 1994; Pedersen 2001; Pedersen 2004; Henry 2013.
3. For criticisms, see Pollitt 1986, 242–44.
4. For the earthquake at Delphi, see Scott 2014, 145–46. For the archaism of the new temple plans, see Knell 1993, 14–16; Ohnesorg 2012.
5. For architecture in the rhetoric of "civic beauty" and civic pride, see Saliou 2015, 133–34. In the Roman period, inscriptions from Ephesos, Pergamon, and Smyrna show a jockeying to claim to be the "first," "first and largest," and "first in terms of beauty and size" (Saliou 2015, 135).
6. Malkin 2011, 171–89.
7. For enthusiastic ancient descriptions of the temple: Pausanias 4.31.8, Pliny, HN 36.97, Strabo 14.1.21.
8. Bammer 1968–1971.
9. Bammer K1: Ephesos Museum / Kunsthistorisches Museum, Vienna, inv. no. I1631.
10. Alzinger 1967, 37.
11. The pattern of a fluted bolster appears on both the older and younger Artemision. The interlaced leaf motif occurs early at Metapontion and again in the early Hellenistic period on the Ptolemaion at Samothrace.
12. Alzinger 1967, 37.
13. Bammer 1968–1971, 16.
14. If the building was a regular six by thirteen peristyle, the surviving capitals represent one of four bilingual corner capitals, four of sixteen bilingual capitals, and one of eighteen capitals with two convex faces.
15. Alzinger 1967, 35–36: "Eines von diesen hat noch ganz die traditionellen Formen bewahrt. Der Kanal ist konvex und das Polster vierfach eingeschnürt. Aber welch ein Unterschied besteht zu den Kapitellen des sechsten Jahrhunderts! Während man beim Artemision noch immer—trotz allem

Fortschritt—das Gefühl hat, zwei heterogene Elemente, das runde verzierte Säulenende und das horizontale Sattelholz, zu sehen, sind hundert Jahre später beide Formen zu einer Einheit zusammengewachsen, die man—trotz allem Archaismus, trotz aller Schwerfälligkeit—nur als klassisch bezeichnen kann. Hier ist nichts verspielt oder vertändelt; der Steinmetz ließ sich auf keine Experimente ein. Wir empfinden irgendwie auch hier die majestätische Schwere, die von den Götterbildern der gleichen Zeit ausstrahlt." Author's translation.

16. Bammer 1968–1971, 12–16.
17. Alzinger 1967, 37–38. Bammer 1968–1971, 12, 19, fig. 15.
18. Bammer 1968–1971. Korres 1997, 204–5 identifies three Ionic monuments in Athens that have at least one capital that was a Roman-period replacement.
19. Bammer, 1968–1971, 2.
20. Bammer, 1968–1971, 2.
21. Alzinger 1967, 38n1.
22. Alzinger 1967, 37–38. Bammer 1968–1971, 1, also weighed the identification but was more cautious.
23. For close analysis of the account, see Fowler 2013, 580–83.
24. For the location of Trecheia, see Engelmann 1991, 277, 289–90.
25. Scherrer 1999, 381–83; Ladstätter 2016, 257–60.
26. Keil 1929, 48–50; Scherrer 1999, 381–83.
27. Ladstätter 2016, 257–59.
28. Karwiese 2012, cat. nos. 250–251.
29. Trell 1942, 66, identifies the four-panel door as the "building blocks" of the side wall.
30. Trell 1942, 66; Karwiese 2012, cat. no. 250. On another coin type, the temple of Athena may be indicated by a small prostyle building next to which strides a boar pierced by a spear (Oster 1990, 1671n66).
31. Plutarch attributes this new myth to the early third-century philosopher Hegesias of Cyrene.
32. Knell 1993, 14–16; Ohnesorg 2012.
33. For an introduction to cultural responses to historical disasters, see Schenk 2017. See also Oliver-Smith 1986; Oliver-Smith and Hoffmann 1999; Toner 2013.
34. For social theory of trauma and how group response to trauma structures identity, see Alexander 2012, 6–30; Alexander et al. 2004; Kalayjian and Eugene 2010.
35. Alexander 2012, 94–96.
36. Kalayjian, Shigemoto, and Patel 2010; Kalayjian and Di Liberto 2010.
37. Umholtz 2002, 287. Botermann 1994, 182.
38. Alexander did make a gift of real estate to Artemis by expanding the territory of the sanctuary by a stade in all directions (Str. 14.1.23), which was further enlarged again by Mithridates and then Antony.
39. Strabo (14.1.22) also reports that the new construction was financed by selling the pillars of the old temple, which seems dubious—especially given that excavations at the Artemision have recovered pieces of the Archaic columns.
40. A point of civic pride must lie behind the minority opinion of the Ephesians that the temple site marked Artemis's true birthplace rather than Delos (Strabo 14.1.20).
41. For the application of social memory to the ancient Greek world, see Alcock 2002; Shaya 2005; Steinbock 2012; Price 2012.
42. Theodorescu 1974, 19–20, figs. 17, 18 ("capital V"); Palermo Museum no. 338; Barletta 1993, 58.
43. Theodorescu 1974, 19–20.
44. Theodorescu 1974, 34, 48.
45. For the series, see Theodorescu 1974; Barletta 1993.
46. Palermo Museum no. 348, 339, 340: Theodorescu 1974, pl. 4, figs. 20, 19; pl. 5, fig. 9.
47. Palermo Museum no. 339; Theodorescu 1974, pl. 4, fig. 19.
48. Theodorescu, 1974, 22.
49. Theodorescu, 1974, 23; no. 11, fig. 22.
50. Mertens 2006, 249.
51. Theodorescu 1974, 33.
52. Theodorescu 1974, 51: " ... cet esprit conservateur nous paraît moins un signe de retardement du'une preuve de la personalité de l'école architecturale sicilienne."
53. Theodorescu 1974, 41–42.
54. Mertens 2006, 421–23.
55. Koldewey and Puchstein 1899, 115, fig. 92.
56. Costabile 1997; Mertens 2006, 249–50; Marconi 2007, 52–53; Marconi 2016, 82, 86, 88; Lippolis, Livadiotti, and Rocco 2007, 811.
57. For the marble analysis of the Ludovisi and Boston Thrones, see Young and Ashmole 1968.
58. For possible Ionian influences at Selinous in the Archaic period, see Barletta 1983, 182–222. Barletta's identification of features, such as the widely dispersed volute acroteria, as distinctly Ionian connection is doubted by Billot 1989, 380.
59. For the bicolumnar monument of Aristaineta, see Laroche 2015, 25–26; Partida 2013, 486–89; Courby 1927, 257–62.
60. For a treasury as a "frame," see Neer 2001, 281–87.
61. For the triangular pillar of the Naupaktians and the Messenians commemorating their victory over Kalydon, see Partida 2009, 281.
62. Jacquemin and Laroche 1986, fig. 1, fig. 10, have vividly reconstructed the spatial correspondence between the chariot of Helios of the Rhodian pillar dedication and the figure of Apollo in the pediment of the fourth-century temple.
63. Courby 1927, 257. Amandry 1940, 67–71. Amandry and Martin 1944–1945, 435–40. Jacquemin 1999, 135–36.
64. For the Ionic column monuments of Menippos and Polemaios, and the Corinthian column monument of Appuleius at Klaros, see Étienne and Varène 2004.
65. Courby 1927, 257.
66. For the monument of Drusilla, see Courby 1927, 269–72. The inscription on the base of the column of Polemaios mentions that the statue was gilded (Étienne and Varène 2004, 137).
67. Jacquemin 1999, 136; Dall'Olio 1989. Nilsson 1925 saw the impact of Delphic bicolumnar monuments on Roman triumphal arches, though Laroche 2015, 26, dismisses this.
68. Jacquemin 1999, 135. For the monument at Olympia, see Hoepfner 1971; Hoepfner 1984.
69. Partida 2009.
70. *FD* 3.4.130 (Courby 1927, 257).
71. *FD* 3.4.131 (Courby 1927, 259).
72. Winter 2006, 293n108.

73 Jacquemin 1999, 136; Partida 2013, 489; Laroche 2015, 26.
74 Partida 2009, 285.
75 For the Daochos Monument, see Ridgway 2003, 46–50.
76 Dillon 2010, 37, fig. 23. For the problem of the number of the figures, see Grzesik 2021, 163n117; Grzesik 2018, 34–35.
77 Jacquemin 1999, 136; Laroche 2015, 25.
78 The capitals differ in height by 1.8 centimeters, or about 5 percent of their total height. The difference is mostly hidden in the abacus: the left capital has a 5 centimeter tall abacus and right capital has a 7.1 centimeter tall abacus. The taller capital is rougher on top, with point chisel marks. Evidently, the capitals were hoisted into place with a rough upper surface that was then cut down to level the heights of the two columns before setting the epistyle—a procedure alluded to by Vitruvius (3.5.8).
79 Partida 2013, 489.
80 Courby 1927, 258: "type très simplifié."
81 For the significance of Aristaineta among female patrons at Delphi, see Martínez López et al. 2019, 56–57.
82 Bommelaer and Laroche 1991, 186.
83 Scott 2014, 168n92.
84 Bommelaer and Laroche 1991, 187–89. Scott 2014, 126.
85 For the Pillar of Prusias II, see Courby 1927, 262–65. For the observation that this cavity did not seem to fit the steps of the Aristaineta Monument when it was reconstructed, see Amandry and François 1947, 451.
86 Jacquemin 1999, 136; Scott 2014, 176.
87 Courby 1927, 259. Laroche 2015, 25, points out that the bicolumnar monuments are all relatively the same height, but with considerably different spacing between the columns.
88 The position of the monument has been disputed. Amandry and François 1947, 451, suggested that it is incompatible with the crepis in this location, and Laroche pushes it toward the west.
89 Jacquemin and Laroche 2020.
90 Laroche 2015.
91 For the Aetolians at Delphi, see Jacquemin 1999, 63–64; Scott 2014, 175–78.
92 Scott 2014, 169.
93 Scott 2014, 169.
94 For the establishment of the Soteria, see Scott 2014, 348n41.
95 Jacquemin 1999, 63–64.
96 Scott 2014, 171.
97 Flacelière 1937, 349–52; Marcadé 1953, 73; Partida 2013, 283. *IG* II³ 1 1007. For Charixenos's magistracies, see Granger 1999, 555–56; Scholten 2000, 45n54.
98 Bourguet 1914, 167, fig. 56.
99 Jacquemin 1985, 34. *IG* II² 680; FD 3.3.215.
100 Paus. 10.1.6.4.
101 Scholten 2000, 128n134.
102 Translated from Jones 1918, 449.
103 Dillon 2010, 48–49.
104 Dillon 2010, 49. See also Grzesik 2021, 166.
105 Frotier de la Coste-Messelière 1943, 27, fig. 17.
106 Grandjean and Salviat 2000, 134. For an early instance of bell-shaped flowers in Ionic decoration, see a mid-fifth-century altar parapet from Paros (Ohnesorg 2005b, 34–36, pl. 13).
107 Partida 2013, 489.
108 Partida 2013, 488–90.
109 "Ἀθεναῖοι ἀνέθεσαν τὲν στοὰν καὶ τὰ hόπλ[α κ]αὶ τἀκροτέρια hελόντες τὀν πολε[μίο]ν." Amandry 1953, 39; *SEG* 39, 473; Meiggs and Lewis 1969, no. 25.
110 For the possible dates of the Stoa of the Athenians, see Walsh 1986.
111 Jacquemin 1999, cat. no. 637. Replat 1922; Amandry and Martin 1944–1945, 439.
112 Replat 1922.

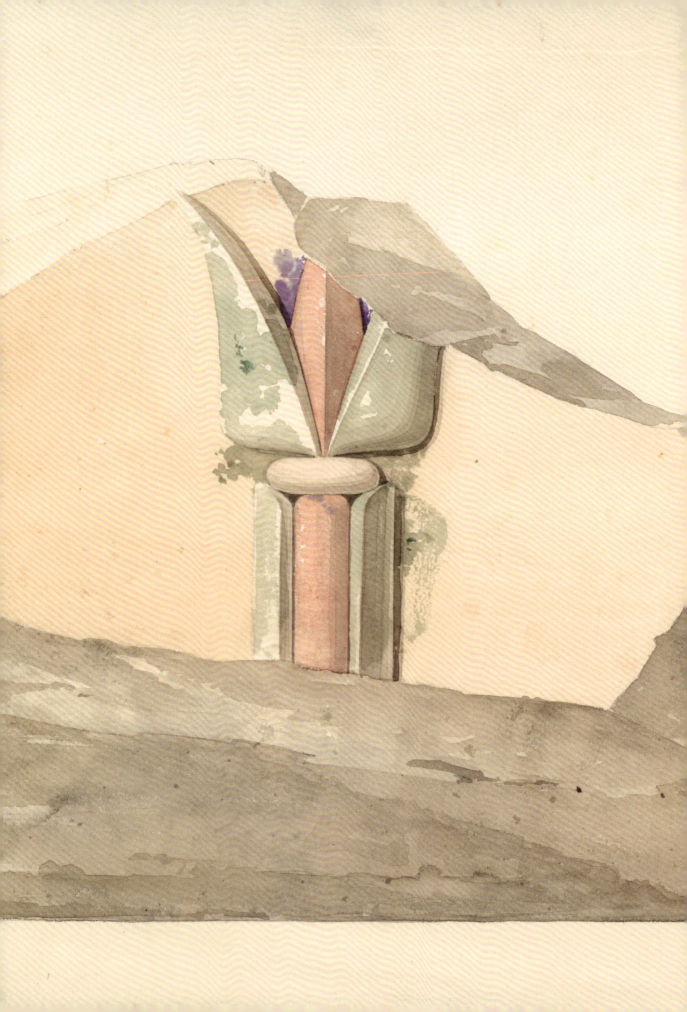

Bibliography

Abrams, E. M. 1994. *How the Maya Built Their World: Energetics and Ancient Architecture*. Austin: University of Texas Press.

Achilara, L., J. Kourtzellis, N. Nemitsas, and D. Pitsiou. 2004. *ἐν τῶ ἴρω τῶ ἐμ Μέσσω: Rehabilitation Works*. Mytilene: Ministry of Culture, K' Ephorate of Prehistoric and Classical Antiquities.

Adam, S. 1966. *The Technique of Greek Sculpture in the Archaic and Classical Periods*. Oxford: Thames and Hudson.

Aggelakopoulou, E., S. Sotiropoulou, and G. Karagiannis. 2022. "Architectural Polychromy on the Athenian Acropolis: An In Situ Non-Invasive Analytical Investigation of the Colour Remains." *Heritage* 5: 756–87.

Alcock, S. E. 2002. *Archaeologies of the Greek Past: Landscape, Monuments, and Memories*. Cambridge: Cambridge University Press.

Alexander, J. C. 2012. *Trauma: A Social Theory*. Cambridge: Polity Press.

Alexander, J. C., R. Eyerman, B. Giesen, N. J. Smelser, and P. Sztompka. 2004. *Cultural Trauma and Collective Identity*. Berkeley: University of California Press.

Allamani-Souri, V. 2003. "Brief History of Imperial Thessaloniki as Derived from Epigraphic and Archaeological Evidence." In *Roman Thessaloniki*, edited by D. V. Grammenos, 80–91. Thessaloniki: Thessaloniki Archaeological Museum Publications.

Alzinger, W. 1967. "Alt-Ephesos: Topographie und Architektur." *Das Altertum* 13, no. 1: 20–44.

Amandry, P. 1940. "Dédicaces delphiques." *Bulletin de Correspondance Hellénique [BCH]* 64/65: 60–75.

———. 1953. *Fouilles de Delphes II: La Colonne des Naxiens et le Portique des Athéniens*. Paris: E. de Boccard.

Amandry, P., and C. François. 1947. "Delphes." *BCH* 71/72: 445–54.

Amandry, P., and R. Martin. 1944–1945. "Chronique des fouilles et découvertes archéologiques en Grèce de 1943 à 1945." *BCH* 68/69: 422–45.

Antonaccio, A. 1995. *An Archaeology of Ancestors: Tomb Cult and Hero Cult in Early Greece*. Lanham, MD: Rowman and Littlefield.

———. 2003. "Hybridity and the Cultures within Greek Culture." In *The Cultures within Ancient Greek Culture: Contact, Conflict, Collaboration*, edited by C.Dougherty and L. Kurke, 57–74. Cambridge: Cambridge University Press.

Armstrong, C. D. 2012. *Julien-David Le Roy and the Making of Architectural History*. Abingdon: Routledge.

———. 2016. "French Architectural Thought and the Idea of Greece." In *A Companion to Greek Architecture*, edited by M. M. Miles, 487–508. Chichester, West Sussex: John Wiley & Sons.

Arnush, M. F. 1995. "The Career of Peisistratos Son of Hippias." *Hesperia* 64, no. 2: 135–62.

Arrington, N. T. 2017. "Connoisseurship, Vases, and Greek Art and Archaeology." In *The Berlin Painter and His World: Athenian Vase-Painting in the Early Fifth Century B.C.*, edited by J. M. Padgett, 21–39. Princeton, NJ: Princeton University Press.

Auberson, P. 1968. *Temple d'Apollon Daphnéphoros: Architecture*. Eretria 1. Bern: Éditions Francke.

Avlonitou, L. 2016. "Pigments and Colours: An Inside Look at the Painted Decoration of the Macedonian Funerary Monuments." *Journal of Archaeological Science: Reports* 7: 668–78.

Avramidou, A. 2021. "Inscribed Pottery from the Sanctuary of Parthenos at Ancient Neapolis (Kavala)." In *Studi miscellanei di ceramografia greca, vol. 7*, edited by E. Giudice and G. Giudice, 13–30. Catania: Ediarch.

Bakalakis, G. 1936. "Νεάπολις, Χριστούπολις, Καβάλα" *AEphem* 75: 1–48.

———. 1937. "Ανασκαφή εν Καβάλα και Καλαμίτσα." *Praktika* 1937: 59–67.

———. 1938. "Ανασκαφή εν Καβάλα και τοις πέριξ." *Praktika* 1938: 75–102.

———. 1963. "Therme—Thessaloniki." Supplement, *AntK* 1: 30–34.

———. 1983. "Ιερό Διονύσου και φαλλικά δρώμενα στη Θεσσαλονίκη." *Αρχαία Μακεδονία / Ancient Macedonia III*: 30–43.

Bakker, K. A. 1999. "A Corpus of Early Ionic Capitals." PhD diss., University of Pretoria.

Balandat, L. 2023. *Eine "Trübung des attischen Geistes"? Ursprung, Entwicklung und Bedeutung archaischer Grabreliefs außerhalb Attikas*. Rahden: Marie Leidorf.

Baltes, E. 2020. "A Monumental Stepped Statue Base in the Athenian Agora." *Hesperia* 89: 339–77.

Bammer, A. 1968–1971. "Beiträge zur ephesischen Architektur." *Jahreshefte des Österreichischen Archäologischen Instituts* 49: 1–22.

———. 1972. *Die Architektur des jüngeren Artemision von Ephesos*. Wiesbaden: F. Steiner.

Bankel, H. 1993. *Der spätarchaische Tempel der Aphaia auf Aegina*. Berlin: De Gruyter.

———. 2004. "Modelli policromi del tempio tardo-arcaico di Aphaia a Egina." In *I Colori del Bianco: Policromia nella scultura antica*, edited by H. Bankel and P. Liverani, 91–106. Rome: De Luca Editori d'Arte.

Bankel, H., and A. Stewart. 2022. "New Observations on the Pediments of the Early Classical Temple of Aphaia on Aegina and on Other Works by the 'Aphaia Architect.'" *Journal of Greek Archaeology* 7: 173–212.

Barker, A. W. 1918. "The Subjective Factor in Greek Architectural Design." *American Journal of Archaeology [AJA]* 22, no. 1: 1–24.

Barletta, B. A. 1983. *Ionic Influence in Archaic Sicily: The Monumental Art*. Gothenburg: Åström.

———. 1993. "Some Ionic Architectural Elements from Selinus in the Getty Museum." In *Studia Varia from *the J. Paul Getty Museum*, vol. 1, edited by M. True and K. Hamma, 55–62. Malibu: Getty Museum.

———. 2001. *The Origins of the Greek Architectural Orders*. Cambridge: Cambridge University Press.

———. 2009. "In Defense of the Ionic Frieze of the Parthenon." *American Journal of Archaeology* 113, no. 4: 547–68.

———. 2017. *The Sanctuary of Athena at Sounion*. Ancient Art in Context 4. Princeton, NJ: American School of Classical Studies at Athens.

Baughan, E. P. 2013. *Couched in Death: Klinai and Identity in Anatolia and Beyond*. London: University of Wisconsin Press.

Baumstark, R. 1985. *Peter Paul Rubens: The Decius Mus Cycle*. New York: Metropolitan Museum of Art.

Baxandall, M. 1995. *Shadows and Enlightenment*. New Haven, CT: Yale University Press.

Beazley, J. D. 1928. *Attic Black-Figure: A Sketch*. London: Humphrey Milford.

———. 1956. *Attic Black-Figure Vase-Painters*. London: Oxford University Press.

Berardi, E., F. L. Lisi, and D. Micalella. 2009. *Poikilia: Variazioni sul tema*. Acireale: Bonanno.

Bernhardt, K. 2015. *Stil—Raum—Ordnung: Architekturlehre in Danzig 1904–1945*. Berlin: Gebr. Mann.

Betancourt, P. P. 1977. *The Aeolic Style in Architecture: A Survey of Its Development in Palestine, the Halikarnassos Peninsula, and Greece, 1000–500 B.C.* Princeton, NJ: Princeton University Press.

Bilde, P. G. 2003. "Wandering Images: From Taurian (and Chersonesean) Parthenos to (Artemis) Tauropolos and (Artemis) Persike." In *The Cauldron of Ariantas, Studies Presented to A. N. Ščeglov on the Occasion of his 70th Birthday*, edited by P. G. Bilde, J. M. Højte, and V. F. Stolba, 165–83. Black Sea Studies 1. Aarhus: Aarhus University Press.

———. 2009. "Quantifying Black Sea Artemis: Some Methodological Reflections." In *From Artemis to Diana: The Goddess of Man and Beast*, edited by T. Fischer-Hansen and B. Poulsen, 303–32. Copenhagen: Museum Tusculanum.

Billot, M. F. 1989. Review of *Ionic Influence in Archaic Sicily: The Monumental Art*, by B. Barletta. *Revue Archéologique*: 378–81.

Blid, J. 2017. "Architectural Polychromy at Hekatomnid Labraunda." In *Restituer les couleurs: Le rôle de la restitution dans les recherches sur la polychromie en sculpture, architecture et peinture mural*, edited by M. Mulliez, 113–22. Bordeaux: Open Editions.

Blondé, F., A. Muller, D. Mulliez, J. Des Courtils, A. Pariente, and Y. Garlan. 1985. "Thasos." *BCH* 109, no. 2: 874–85.

Boardman, J. 1959. "Chian and Early Ionic Architecture." *Antiquaries Journal* 39: 170–218.

———. 2001. "Aspects of 'Colonization.'" *Bulletin of the American Schools of Oriental Research* 322: 33–42.

———. 2002. *The Archaeology of Nostalgia: How the Greeks Re-created Their Mythical Past*. London: Thames and Hudson.

Boehm, R. 2011. "Synoikismos, Urbanization, and Empire in the Early Hellenistic Period." PhD diss., University of California, Berkeley.

———. 2018. *City and Empire in the Age of the Successors: Urbanization and Social Response in the Making of the Hellenistic Kingdoms*. Berkeley: University of California Press.

Bommelaer, J.-F., and D. Laroche. 1991. *Guide de Delphes: Le Site*. Paris: Éditions E. de Boccard.

Borchhardt, J. 1976. *Die Bauskulptur des Heroons von Limyra: Das Grabmal des lykischen Königs Perikles*. Berlin: Gebr. Mann.

Borrmann, R. 1887. "Altionische Kapitelle aus Athen." *Antike Denkmäler* 1: pl. 18.

———. 1888. "Altattische Kapitelle." *Antike Denkmäler* 1: 15, pl. 29.

Botermann, H. 1994. "Wer baute das neue Priene?: Zur Interpretation der Inschriften von Priene Nr. 1 und 156." *Hermes* 122: 162–87.

Bourguet, É. 1914. *Les Ruines de Delphes*. Paris: Écoles françaises d'Athènes et de Rome.

Bouras, C. 1967. *Η αναστήλωσις της στοάς της Βραυρώνος: Τα αρχιτεκτονικά της προβλήματα*. Athens: Publications of Archaiologikon Deltion.

Brinkmann, V. 2004a. "Die nüchterne farbigkeit der Parthenonskulpturen." In *Bunte Götter: Die Farbigkeit antiker Skulptur*, edited by V. Brinkmann and R. Wünsche, 120–25. Munich: Mediahaus Biering.

———. 2004b. "La ricerca sulla policromia della scultura antica." In *I Colori del Bianco: Policromia nella scultura antica*, edited by A. Grammiccia, 27–40. Rome: De Luca Editori d'Arte.

———. 2004c. "Il principe e la divinità: La riscoperta della policromia sulle sculture del Tempio di Egina." In *I Colori del Bianco: Policromia nella scultura antica*, edited by A. Grammiccia, 107–32. Rome: De Luca Editori d'Arte.

Brinkmann, V., U. Koch-Brinkmann, and H. Piening. 2024. "Two Polychrome Ionic Capitals from the Athenian Agora: Documentation and Experimental Reconstruction." In *Archaeology of Colour: Technical Art History Studies in Greek and Roman Painting and Polychromy*, edited by H. Brecoulaki, 76–92. Athens: Brepols.

Broeck-Parant, J. V. 2021. "The Episkeuastai and the Administration of Finance in Athens in the 4th Century BC." In *Ancient Architectural Restoration in the Greek World: Proceedings of the International Workshop Held at Wolfson College, Oxford*, edited by J. V. Broeck-Parant and T. Ismaelli, 67–80. Rome: Quasar.

Broeck-Parant, J. V., and T. Ismaelli, eds. 2021. *Ancient Architectural Restoration in the Greek World: Proceedings of the International Workshop Held at Wolfson College, Oxford*. Rome: Quasar.

Broneer, O. T. 1954. *The South Stoa and Its Roman Successors*. Corinth 1, part 4. Princeton, NJ: American School of Classical Studies at Athens.

Brulotte, E. L. 1994. "The 'Pillar of Oinomaos' and the Location of Stadium I at Olympia." *AJA* 98: 53–64.

Bruneau, P., and J. Ducat. 2005. *Guide de Délos*. Athens: l'École française d'Athènes.

Buchert, U. 2000. *Denkmalpflege im antiken Griechenland Massnahmen zur Bewahrung antiker Bausubstanz*. Frankfurt: P. Lang.

Bujskich, A. 2010. *Die antiken Architekturformen im nördlichen Schwarzmeergebiet: Herkunft und Entwicklung*. Wiesbaden: Reichert.

Burch, G. B. 1954. "The Counter-Earth." *Osiris* 11: 267–94.

Burford, A. 1969. *The Greek Temple Builders at Epidauros*. Toronto: University of Toronto Press.

Burkert, W. 1972. *Lore and Science in Ancient Pythagore-*

anism. Translated by E. L. Minar, Jr. Cambridge, MA: Harvard University Press.

———. 1988. "The Meaning and Function of the Temple in Classical Greece." In *Temple in Society*, edited by M. V. Fox, 27–47. Winona Lake: Eisenbrauns.

Burnet, J. 1920. *Early Greek Philosophy*. London: A. & C. Black.

Buschor, E. 1933. "Heraion von Samos: Porosfriese; Altsamische Grabstelen." *Mitteilungen des Deutschen Archäologischen Instituts, Athenische Abteilung* 58: 1–46.

———. 1957. "Altsamischer Bauschmuck." *Mitteilungen des Deutschen Archäologischen Instituts, Athenische Abteilung* 72: 1–34.

Buschor, E., and W. von Massow. 1927. "Vom Amyklaion." *Mitteilungen des Deutschen Archäologischen Instituts, Athenische Abteilung* 52: 51–79.

Calhoun, R. D. 2016. "Dynamism, Creativeness, and Evolutionary Progress in the Work of Alexander Archipenko." PhD diss., The Ohio State University.

Carlson, D. N., and W. Aylward. 2010. "The Kızılburun Shipwreck and the Temple of Apollo at Claros." *AJA* 114, no. 1: 145–59.

Carman, C. C., and R. P. Buzón. 2023. *Aristarchus of Samos: On the Sizes and Distances of the Sun and Moon; Greek Text, Translation, Analysis, and Relevant Scholia*. London: Routledge.

Carpo, M. 2001a. *Architecture in the Age of Printing: Orality, Writing, Typography, and Printed Images in the History of Architectural Theory*. Translated by S. Benson. Cambridge, MA: MIT Press.

———. 2001b. "How Do You Imitate a Building That You Have Never Seen? Printed Images, Ancient Models, and Handmade Drawings in Renaissance Architectural Theory." *Zeitschrift für Kunstgeschichte*, 64, no. 2: 223–33.

Casson, S. 1933. *The Technique of Early Greek Sculpture*. Oxford: Clarendon Press.

Cavalier, L., and P. Mora. 2011. "Présentation du modèle 3D d'Alâzeytin." *Anatolia Antiqua* 19: 377–84.

Cohen, B. 1978. *Attic Bilingual Vases and Their Painters*. New York: Garland.

———. 2006. "Bilingual Vases and Vase Painters." In *The Colors of Clay: Special Techniques in Athenian Vases*, edited by B. Cohen, 17–42. Los Angeles: J. Paul Getty Museum.

Colin, M. G. 1909–1913. *Fouilles de Delphes III*, part 2, *Inscriptions du Trésor des Athéniens*. Paris: De Boccard.

Collart, P. P. 1937. *Ville de Macédoine depuis ses origines jusqu'à la fin de l'époque romaine*. Paris: École française d'Athènes.

Collombier, A.-M. 1983. "L'examen de l'évolution du chapiteau Ionique Grec par analyse factorielle." *Revue Archéologique*, n.s., 1: 79–96.

Conze, A., A. Hauser, and O. Benndorf. 1880. *Neue archaeologische Untersuchungen auf Samothrake*. Vienna: Gerold's Sohn.

Cook, J. M. 1961. *The Greeks in Ionia and the East*. Ancient Peoples and Places 31. London: Thames and Hudson.

———. 1962. "The Problem of Classical Ionia." *PCPhS* 7: 9–18.

Cook, J. M., and R. V. Nicholls. 1998. *Old Smyrna Excavations: The Temples of Athena*. London: British School at Athens.

Costabile, F. 1997. *L'Architettura Samia di Occidente dalla cava al Tempio: Siracusa, Locri, Caulonia*. Catanzaro: Rubbettino.

Couilloud, M.-T. 1974. *Exploration Archéologique de Délos faite par l'École française d'Athènes 30: Les Monuments Funéraires de Rhénée*. Paris: Diffusion de Boccard.

Coulton, J. J. 1977. *Ancient Greek Architects at Work: Problems of Structure and Design*. Ithaca, NY: Cornell University Press.

———. 1979. "Doric Capitals: A Proportional Analysis." In *Annual of the British School at Athens* 74: 81–153.

Courbin, P. 1980. *L'Oikos des Naxiens*. Exploration archéologique de Délos faite par l'École française d'Athènes 34. Paris: Boccard.

Courby, F. 1927. *Fouilles de Delphes*. Vol. 2: *La terrasse du temple*. Paris: Boccard.

———. 1931. *Les temples d'Apollon*. Exploration archéologique de Délos faite par l'École française d'Athènes 12. Paris: Boccard.

Crawley, R. 1910. *History of the Peloponnesian War Done into English*. London: Dent.

Curtius, E., and F. Adler, eds. 1892. *Olympia: die Ergebnisse der von dem Deutschen Reich veranstalteten Ausgrabung*. Vol. 1, *Die Baudenkmäler*. Berlin: Asher.

Dall'Olio, L. 1989. "Il motivo della 'porta sacra' nella pittura romana di paesaggio." *Latomus: Revue d'études latines* 48: 513–31.

DeLaine, J. 1997. *The Baths of Caracalla: A Study in the Design, Construction, and Economics of Large-Scale Building Projects in Imperial Rome*. Portsmouth, RI: Journal of Roman Archaeology.

Delivorrias, A. 2009. "The Throne of Apollo at the Amyklaion: Old Proposals, New Perspectives." In *Sparta and Laconia: From Prehistory to Pre-Modern*, edited by W. G. Cavanagh, C. Gallou, and M. Georgiadis, 133–35. Athens: British School at Athens.

de Luynes, H. T. d'A. 1836. "Monnaies incuses de la Grande Grèce." *Les Annales de l'Institut archéologique* 1: 372–91.

Demand, N. 1976. "The Incuse Coins: A Modern Pythagorean Tradition Re-Examined." *Apeiron* 10, no. 1: 1–5.

Demetriou, D. 2012. *Negotiating Identity in the Ancient Mediterranean: The Archaic and Classical Greek Multiethnic Emporia*. Cambridge: Cambridge University Press.

de Ste. Croix, G.E.M. 1972. *The Origins of the Peloponnesian War*. London: Duckworth.

des Courtils, J. 1997. "Moulures architecturales en marbre de l'île de Thasos." *BCH* 121, no. 2: 489–552.

———. 2011. "Alazeytin Kalesi et l'architecture éolique." *Anatolia Antiqua* 19: 385–92.

———. 2020. "Le temple inachevé d'Athéna à Thasos." *BCH* 144, no. 2: https://doi.org/10.4000/bch.1145.

des Courtils, J., and D. Laroche. 2002. "Xanthos et le Létôon: Rapport sur la campagne de 2001." *Anatolia Antiqua* 10: 297–333.

Diels, H. 1929. *Doxographi graeci*. 2nd ed. Berlin: De Gruyter.

Dillon, S. 2010. *The Female Portrait Statue in the Greek World*. Cambridge: Cambridge University Press.

Dimitrova, N. M. 2008. *Theoroi and Initiates in Samothrace: The Epigraphical Evidence*. Princeton, NJ: American School of Classical Studies at Athens.

Dinsmoor, W. B. 1940. "The Temple of Ares at Athens." *Hesperia* 9, no. 1: 1–52.

———. 1942. "The Correlation of Greek Archaeology with History." In *Studies in the History of Culture: The Disciplines of the Humanities; Essays in Honor of Waldo Gifford Leland*, 87–92, 185–216. Menasha, WI: Banta.

Dinsmoor, W. B., Jr. 1974. "The Temple of Poseidon: A Missing Sima and Other Matters." *AJA* 78, no. 3: 211–38.

———. 1982. "Anchoring Two Floating Temples." *Hesperia* 51, no. 4: 410–52.

Dirschedl, U. 2012. "Der archaische Apollontempel ('Tempel II') in Didyma—Erste Ergebnisse der Aufarbeitungskampagnen 2003–2009." In *Dipteros und Pseudodipteros: Bauhistorische und archäologische Forschungen; Internationale Tagung 13.11-15.11.2009 an der Hochschule Regensburg*, edited by T. Schulz, 41–68. Byzas 12. Istanbul: Ege Yayinlari.

———. 2013. *Die griechischen Säulenbasen*. Wiesbaden: Reichert.

———. 2018. "Das archaische Didymeion: Zur Rekonstruktion der Säulen und *columnae caelatae*." In *Ad summum templum architecturae: Forschungen zur antiken Architektur im Spannungsfeld der Fragestellungen und Methoden*, edited by H. Frielinghaus and T. Schattner, 9–34. Möhnesee: Bibliopolis.

Donos, D. 2008. *Studien zu Säulen- und Pfeilermonumenten der archaischen Zeit*. Hamburg: Kovač.

Dörpfeld, W. 1884. "Der antike Ziegelbau und sein Einfluss auf den dorischen Stil." In *Historische und philologische Aufsätze: Ernst Curtius zu seinem siebenzigsten Geburtstage am zweiten September 1884 gewidmet*, edited by E. Curtius, 137–50. Berlin: Asher.

Drexler, A. 1977. *The Architecture of the École des Beaux-Arts*. Cambridge, MA: MIT Press.

Drougou, S., and C. Saatsoglou-Paliadeli. 2006. *Vergina: The Land and Its history*. Athens: Militos.

Duggan, T.M.P. 2016. "Not Just the Shadows on the Stone: The Greek, Lycian and Roman Craft of Encaustica (ἔγκαυσις) and the Polishing (γάνωσις) of Coloured Inscriptions, That Is, of Graphō (γράφω) and Its Study—Epigraphy." *Phaselis* 2: 269–83.

Eichholz, D. E. 1962. *Pliny: Natural History Books 36–37*. Loeb Classical Library 419. Cambridge, MA: Harvard University Press.

Engelmann, H. 1991. "Beiträge zur ephesischen Topographie." *Zeitschrift für Papyrologie und Epigraphik* 89: 275–95.

Errington, M. 1993. "Inschriften von Euromos." *Epigraphica Anatolica* 21: 15–32.

Étienne, R. 2011. "Le chapiteau d'angle ionique de Délos." In *Arqueologia do Mediterrâneo antigo: Estudos em homenagem a Haiganuch Sarian*, 219–28. Campo Grande: Life Editora.

———. 2018. "Les Propylées et autres entrées." In *Le Sanctuaire d'Apollon a Delos*, vol. 1, *Architecture, topographie, histoire*, edited by R. Étienne, 61–82. Athens: École française d'Athènes.

Étienne, R., and J.-P. Braun. 2018. "Le Pôrinos naos." In *Le Sanctuaire d'Apollon a Delos*, vol. 1, *Architecture, topographie, histoire*, edited by R. Étienne, 91–98. Athens: École française d'Athènes.

Étienne, R., and P. Varène. 2004. *Sanctuaire de Claros: L'Architecture; Les Propylées et les monuments de la Voie Sacrée*. Paris: Etudes et Recherche sur les Civilisations.

Fastje, H. 2012 / 2013. "Ein archaisches Kapitell aus Paros." *Mitteilungen des deutschen Archäologischen Instituts, Athenische Abteilung* 127 / 128: 159–67.

Faustoferri, A. 1996. *Il trono de Amyklai e Sparta: Bathykles al servizio del potere*. Naples: Edizioni scientifiche italiane.

Fendt, A. 2019. "The Sculptures of the Temple of Aphaia on Aigina in Their Contemporary Context." In *From Hippias to Kallias: Greek Art in Athens and beyond: 527–449 BC; Proceedings of an International Conference Held at the Acropolis Museum, Athens, May 19–20, 2017*, edited by O. Palagia and E. P. Sioumpara, 192–205. Athens: Acropolis Museum Editions.

Fenger, L. P. 1886. *Dorische Polychromie: Untersuchungen über die Anwendung der Farbe auf dem dorischen Tempel*. Berlin: Asher.

Fiechter, E. 1918. "Amyklae: Der Thron des Aopollon." *Jahrbuch des Deutschen Archäologischen Instituts*, 33: 107–245, pl. 4–20.

Fisher, M. 2015. "How to Look at a Non-Peripteral Temple." In *Autopsy in Athens: Recent Archaeological Research on Athens and Attica*, edited by M. M. Miles, 154–62. Oxford: Oxbow Books.

Flacelière, R. 1937. *Les Aitoliens à Delphes, contribution à l'histoire de la Grèce centrale au IIIe siècle av. J.-C.* Paris: Écoles françaises d'Athènes.

Fleischer, R. 1973. *Artemis von Ephesos und verwandte Kultstatuen aus Anatolien und Syrien*. Leiden: Brill.

Fowler, R. L. 2013. *Early Greek Mythography*, vol. 1, *Commentary*. Oxford: Oxford University Press.

Fraisse, P., and C. Llinas. 1995. *Documents d'architecture hellénique et hellénistique*. Paris: De Boccard.

Frazer, A. 1982. "Macedonia and Samothrace: Two Architectural Late Bloomers." In *Studies in the History of Art 10, Symposium Series I: Macedonia and Greece in Late Classical and Early Hellenistic Times*, 190–203. Washington, DC: National Gallery of Art.

———. 1990. *Samothrace: Excavations Conducted by the Institute of Fine Arts of New York University*, vol. 10, *The Propylon of Ptolemy II*. Princeton, NJ: Princeton University Press.

Frederiksen, R. 2010. "Plaster Casts in Antiquity." In *Plaster Casts: Making, Collecting and Displaying from Classical Antiquity to the Present*, edited by R. Frederiksen and E. Marchand, 13–33. Berlin: De Gruyter.

Friedländer, J., and A. von Sallet. 1889. *Beschreibung der antiken Münzen*, vol. 2, *Paeonien, Macedonien, die macedonischen Könige bis Perdiccas III*. Berlin: W. Spemann.

Friedländer, P., and H. B. Hoffleit. 1948. *Epigrammata, Greek Inscriptions in Verse from the Beginnings to the Persian War*. Berkeley: University of California Press.

Frotier de la Coste-Messelière, P. 1943. *Delphi*. Paris: Editions du Chêne.

———. 1957. *Sculptures du Trésor des Athéniens*. Paris: E. de Boccard.

Fullerton, M. D. 1990. *The Archaistic Style in Roman Statuary*. Leiden: E. J. Brill.

Gaifman, M. 2006. "Statue, Cult and Reproduction." *Art History* 29, no. 2: 258–79.

———. 2018. *The Art of Libation in Classical Athens*. New Haven, CT: Yale University Press.

Galinsky, G. K. 1969. *Aeneas, Sicily, and Rome*. Princeton, NJ: Princeton University Press.

Gardner, P. 1883. *A Catalogue of the Greek Coins in the British Museum: Thessaly to Aetolia*. [= BMC Coins of Thessaly] London: Longmans.

Garland, R. 1992. *Introducing New Gods: The Politics of Athenian Religion*. Ithaca, NY: Cornell University Press.

Gehl, J. 1980. *Life Between Buildings: Using Public Spaces*. New York: Van Nostrand Reinhold.

Gill, D.W.J. 1993. "The Temple of Aphaia on Aegina: Further Thoughts on the Date of the Reconstruction." *Annual of the British School at Athens* 88: 173–81.

Giouri, E., and C. Koukouli. 1987. "Ἀνασκαφή στην αρχαία Οισύμη." *ΑΕΜΘ* 1: 363–88.

Giraud, D. 1989. "The Greater Propylaia at Eleusis, a Copy of Mnesikles' Propylaia." In *The Greek Renaissance in the Roman Empire: Papers from the Tenth British Museum Classical Colloquium*, edited by S. Walker and A. Cameron, 69–75. London: Institute of Classical Studies.

Goette, H. R. 1991. "Die Steinbrüche von Sounion im Agrileza-Tal." *Mitteilungen des Deutschen Archäologischen Instituts, Athenische Abteilung* 106: 201–22.

———. 1992–1998. "Ὁ δῆμος τῆς Παλλήνης. Ἐπιγραφές από την περιοχή του ναού της Ἀθηνᾶς Παλληνίδος." *Horos* 10/12: 105–18.

Goldin, O. 2015. "The Pythagorean Table of Opposites, Symbolic Classification, and Aristotle." *Science in Context* 28, no. 2: 171–93.

Gombrich, E. H. 1995. *Shadows: The Depiction of Cast Shadows in Western Art*. New Haven, CT: Yale University Press.

Gorini, G. 1975. *La monetazione incusa della Magna Grecia*. Milan: Arte e Moneta.

Graham, A. J. 1978. "The Foundation of Thasos." *Annual of the British School at Athens* 73: 61–98.

———. 1983. *Colony and Mother City in Ancient Greece*. 2nd ed. Chicago: Ares.

———. 2001a. *Collected Papers on Greek Colonization*. Mnemosyne Supplements 214. Leiden: Brill.

———. 2001b. "Thasian Controversies." In *Collected Papers on Greek Colonization: Mnemosyne Supplements 214*, by A. J. Graham, 365–402. Leiden: Brill.

Grammenos, D. B., and G. Knithakis. 1994. *Κατάλογος των Ἀρχιτεκτονικῶν Μελῶν του Μουσείου τῆς Θεσσαλονίκης*. Thessaloniki: Library of the University of Macedonia.

Grand-Clément, A. 2015. "Poikilia." In *A Companion to Ancient Aesthetics*, edited by P. Destrée and P. Murray, 406–21. Malden, MA: Wiley Blackwell.

Grandjean, Y., and Fr. Salviat. 2000. *Guide de Thasos*. 2nd ed. Athens: École française d'Athènes.

Granger, J. D. 1999. *The League of the Aitolians*. Leiden: Brill.

Gray, C. 1953. *Cubist Aesthetic Theories*. Baltimore: Johns Hopkins Press.

Greco, E., and O. Voza, 2016. "For a Reconstruction of the 'Round Building' at Sparta as the Skias." In *Ἀρχιτέκτων: τιμητικός τόμος για τον καθηγητή Μανόλη Κορρέ*, edited by K. Zambas, V. K. Lambrinoudakis, E. Simantoni-Bournia, and A. Ohnesorg, 343–50. Athens: Melissa.

Grethlein, J. 2008. "Memory and Material Objects in the Iliad and the Odyssey." In *The Journal of Hellenic Studies* 128: 27–51.

Gros, P. 1975. "Structures et limites de la compilation vitruvienne dans les livres III et IV du De Architectura." *Latomus* 34: 986–1009.

Gruben, G. 1963. "Das archaische Didymaion." *Jahrbuch des Deutschen Archäologischen Instituts* 78: 78–182.

———. 1965. "Die Sphinx-Säule von Aigina." *Mitteilungen des deutschen Archäologischen Instituts, Athenische Abteilung* 80: 170–208.

———. 1969. "Untersuchungen am Dipylon 1964–1966." *Archäologischer Anzeiger* 84: 31–40.

———. 1986. "Das Brunnenhaus beim Dipylon in Athen." In *Carl Haller von Hallerstein in Griechenland*, edited by H. Bankel, 218–19. Berlin: Reimer.

———. 1993. "Die inselionische Ordnung." In *Les Grandes Ateliers d'architecture dans le monde égéen du VI siècle av. J.-C. Actes du colloque d'Istanbul, 23–25 mai 1991*, edited by J. des Courtils and J.-C. Moretti, 97–109. Istanbul: Institut français d'études anatoliennes-Georges-Dumézil.

———. 1996. "Griechische Un-Ordnung." In *Säule und Gebälk*, edited by E.-L. Schwandner, 61–77. Mainz am Rhein: P. von Zabern.

———. 1997. "Naxos und Delos: Studien zur archaischen Architektur der Kykladen." *Jahrbuch des Deutschen Archäologischen Instituts* 112: 261–416.

———. 2000. "Klassische Bauforschung." In *Klassische Archäologie*, edited by A. H. Borbein, T. Hölscher, and P. Zanker, 251–79. Berlin: Reimer.

———. 2014. *Der polykratische Tempel im Heraion von Samos*. Samos 27. Wiesbaden: Reichert.

Grzesik, D. 2018. "The Power of Space and Memory: The Honorific Statuescape of Delphi." *Antichthon* 52: 23–42.

———. 2021. *Honorific Culture at Delphi in the Hellenistic and Roman Periods*. Leiden: Brill.

Hahland, W. 1964. "Didyma im 5. Jahrhundert v. Chr." *Jahrbuch des Deutschen Archäologischen Instituts* 79: 142–240.

Hanink, J. 2014. *Lycurgan Athens and the Making of Classical Tragedy*. Cambridge: Cambridge University Press.

Hankins, T. L., and R. J. Silverman. 1995. *Instruments and the Imagination*. Princeton, NJ: Princeton University Press.

Hansen, E. 2016. "Ein Marmorfragment vom Vorparthenon und der Baukontrakt vom Zeustempel in Lebadeia." In *Ἀρχιτέκτων: τιμητικός τόμος για τον καθηγητή Μανόλη Κορρέ*, edited by K. Zambas, V. K. Lambrinoudakis, E. Simantoni-Bournia, and A. Ohnesorg, 59–64. Athens: Melissa.

Hansen, E., and C. Le Roy. 2012. *Le Temple de Léeto au Létoon de Xanthos*. Fouilles de Xanthos 11. Copenhagen: Aarhus University Press.

Harrison. E. B. 1990. "Repair, Reuse and Reworking of Ancient Greek Sculpture." *Marble: Art Historical and Scientific Perspectives on Ancient Sculpture; Papers Delivered at a Symposium Organized by the Departments of Antiquities and Antiquities Conservation and Held at the J. Paul Getty Museum April 28–30, 1988*, edited by M. True and J. Podany, 163–84. Malibu: J. Paul Getty Museum, 1990.

Haselberger, L. 1986. "Das 'Archilochoskapitell' von Paros." In *Carl Haller von Hallerstein in Griechenland*, edited by H. Bankel, 213. Berlin: Reimer.

———. 2020. *Pergamonaltar und der Architekt Hermogenes: Schatten, Raum und Wahrnehmung*. Berlin: Reimer.

Haselberger, L., and S. Holzman. 2015. "Visualizing *Asperitas*: Vitruvius (3.3.9) and the 'Asperity' of Hermogenes' Pseudodipteros." *Journal of Roman Archaeology* 28: 371–91.

Hatzioannidis, A. X., H. Koutsoyiannis, M. T. Arvanitaki, C. E. Gouidis. 2014. "Σωτική ανασκαφή οικοπέδου στην οδό Δουμπιώτη 27–29: αποκαλύπτοντας ένα παλαιοχριστιανικό συγκρότημα." *ΑΕΜΘ* 28: 381–96.

Hellmann, M.-C. 1992. *Recherches sur le Vocabulaire de l'Architecture Grecque, d'après les Inscriptions de Délos*. Paris: De Boccard.

———. 1999. *Choix d'inscriptions architecturales grecques, traduites et commentées*. Lyon: Maison de l'Orient et de la Méditerranée Jean Pouilloux.

———. 2002. *L'Architecture Grecque*, vol. 1, *Les principes de la construction*. Paris: Éditions A. et J. Picard.

———. 2009. "Chronique d'architecture grecque (2007–2008)." *Revue archéologique* 48: 265–82.

———. 2014. "Polychromy in Greek Architecture." In *Transformations: Classical Sculpture in Colour*, edited by J. S. Østergaard and A. M. Nielsen, 224–35. Copenhagen: Ny Carlsberg Glyptotek.

Hellmann, M.-C., and P. Fraisse. 1979. *Le Monument aux hexagones et le Portique des Naxiens*. EAD 32. Paris: Fontemoing.

———. 1982. *Paris-Rome-Athens: Travels in Greece by French Architects in the Nineteenth and Twentieth Centuries*. Houston: Museum of Fine Arts.

Hendrich, C. 2007. *Die Säulenordnung des ersten Dipteros von Samos*. Samos 25. Bonn: Habelt.

Hennemeyer, A. 2011. "Zur Lichtwirkung am Zeustempel von Olympia." In *Licht—Konzepte in der vormodernen Architektur: Internationales Kolloquium in Berlin vom 26. Februar–1. März 2009 veranstaltet vom Architekturreferat des DAI*, edited by P. I. Schneider and U. Wulf-Rheidt, 101–10. Regensburg: Schnell and Steiner.

Henry, O. 2013. "A Tribute to the Ionian Renaissance." In *4th Century Karia: Defining a Karian Identity under the Hekatomnids*, edited by O. Henry, 81–90. Paris: De Boccard.

Herdt, G. 2013. "Votive Columns in Greek Sanctuaries of the Archaic Period." PhD diss., University of Bath, UK.

Herzfeld, E. E. 1941. *Iran in the ancient East*. London: Oxford University Press.

Heuzey, L. A., and H. Daumet. 1876. *Mission archéologique de Macédoine*. Paris: Librairie de Firmin-Didot et Cie.

Hochscheid, H. 2015. *Networks of Stone: Sculpture and Society in Archaic and Classical Athens*. Oxford: Peter Lang.

Hodge, A. T. 1960. *The Woodwork of Greek Roofs*. Cambridge: Cambridge University Press.

Hoepfner, W. 1971. *Zwei Ptolemaierbauten: das Ptolemaierweihgeschenk in Olympia und ein Bauvorhaben in Alexandria*. Mitteilungen des Deutschen Archäologischen Instituts, Athenische Abteilung 1. Berlin: Gebr. Mann.

———. 1976. *Kerameikos X: Das Pompeion und seine Nachfolgerbauten*. Berlin: De Gruyter.

———. 1984. "Φιλαδέλφεια: Ein Beitrag zur frühen hellenistischen Architektur." *Athener Mitteilungen* 99: 353–64.

Hollinshead, M. B. 2015. *Shaping Ceremony: Monumental Steps and Greek Architecture*. Madison: University of Wisconsin Press.

Hölscher, F. 2010. "Gods and Statues—An Approach to Archaistic Images in the Fifth Century BCE." In *Divine Images and Human Imaginations in Ancient Greece and Rome*, edited by J. Mylonopoulos, 105–20. Leiden and Boston: Brill.

Hölscher, T. 2018. *Visual Power in Ancient Greece and Rome: Between Art and Social Reality*. Oakland: University of California Press.

Holtorf, C. 2005. "Geschichtskultur in ur- und frühgeschichtlichen Kulturen Europas." In *Der Ursprung der Geschichte: Archaische Kulturen, das Alte Ägypten und das Frühe Griechenland*, edited by J. Assmann and K.E. Müller, 87–111. Stuttgart: Klett Cotta.

Hulek, F. 2018. *Forschungen in der Mykale*, vol. 3, *Der hocharchaische Tempel am Çatallar Tepe: Architektur und Rekonstruktion*. Bonn: Habelt.

Humann, C. 1904. *Magnesia am Maeander*. Berlin: Georg Reimer.

Hurwit, J. M. 1985. *The Art and Culture of Early Greece, 1100–480 B.C.* Ithaca, NY: Cornell University Press.

Ignatiadou, D. 2020. "The Erechtheion Glass Gems: Classical Innovation or Roman Addition?" In *Wonders Lost and Found: A Celebration of the Archaeological Work of Professor Michael Vickers*, edited by N. Sekunda, 117–24. Oxford: Archaeopress.

Isaac, B. H. 1986. *The Greek Settlements in Thrace until the Macedonian Conquest*. Leiden: Brill.

Isager, J. 1994. *Hekatomnid Caria and the Ionian Renaissance*. Halicarnassian Studies 1. Odense: Odense University Press.

Ismaelli, T. 2021. "Ancient Architectural Restoration: Approaches and Scenarios." In *Ancient Architectural Restoration in the Greek World: Proceedings of the International Workshop Held at Wolfson College, Oxford*, edited by J. V. Broeck-Parant and T. Ismaelli, 19–43. Rome: Edizioni Quasar.

Jacquemin, A. 1985. "Aitolia et Aristaineta—offrandes monumentales à Delphes au IIIe s. av. J.-C." *Ktèma* 10: 27–35.

———. 1999. *Offrandes monumentales à Delphes*. Athens: École française d'Athènes.

Jacquemin, A., and D. Laroche. 1986. "Le char d'or consacré par le peuple rhodien." *BCH* 110: 285–307.

———. 2019. "La Portique des Athéniens Revisité." In *From Hippias to Kallias: Greek Art in Athens and Beyond, 527–449 BC*, edited by O. Palagia, and E. P Sioumpara, 182–91. Athens: Acropolis Museum Additions.

———. 2020. "Apollon à Delphes au IVe siècle." *BCH* 144, no. 1: 107–54.

Jenkins, I. 2006. *Greek Architecture and Its Sculpture in the British Museum*. London: British Museum Press.

Jenkins, I., and A. P. Middleton. 1988. "Paint on the Parthenon Sculptures." *Annual of the British School at Athens* 83: 183–207.

Jenkins, I., C. Gratziu, and A. Middleton. 1997. "The Polychromy of the Mausoleum." In *Sculptors and Sculpture of Caria and the Dodecanese*, edited by I. Jenkins and G. B. Waywell, 35–41. London: British Museum Press.

Johannes, H. 1937. "Die Säulenbasen vom Heratempel des Rhoikos." In *Mitteilungen des deutschen*

Archäologischen Instituts, Athenische Abteilung 62: 13–37.
Jones, N. F. 1999. *The Associations of Classical Athens: The Response to Democracy*. New York: Oxford University Press.
Jones, W. H. S. 1918. *Pausanias. Descriptions of Greece Books VIII:22-X*. Loeb Classical Library 297. Cambridge, MA: Harvard University Press.
ΚΑΜΜΘ = Grammenos, D. B., and G. Knithakis. 1994. *Κατάλογος των Αρχιτεκτονικών Μελών του Μουσείου της Θεσσαλονίκης*. Thessaloniki: Library of the University of Macedonia.
ΚΓΜΘ I = Despinis, G., T. Stefanidou Tiveriou, and E. Voutiras. 1997. *Κατάλογος γλυπτών του Αρχαιολογικού Μουσείου Θεσσαλονίκης I* Thessaloniki: National Bank Education Foundation.
ΚΓΜΘ II = Despinis, G., T. Stefanidou Tiveriou, and E. Voutiras. 2003. *Κατάλογος γλυπτών του Αρχαιολογικού Μουσείου Θεσσαλονίκης II*. Thessaloniki: National Bank of Greece Educational Foundation.
Kalayjian, A., and C. Di Liberto. 2010. "Northridge Earthquake in Southern California: Lessons Learned and Meanings Discovered." In *Mass Trauma and Emotional Healing around the World: Rituals and Practices for Resilience and Meaning Making*, vol. 1, *Natural Disasters*, edited by A. Kalayjian, D. Eugene, 23–36. Santa Barbara: ABC-CLIO.
Kalayjian, A., and D. Eugene. 2010. *Mass Trauma and Emotional Healing around the World: Rituals and Practices for Resilience and Meaning Making*, vol. 1, *Natural Disasters*. Santa Barbara: ABC-CLIO.
Kalayjian, A., Y. Shigemoto, and B. Patel. 2010. "Earthquake in Soviet Armenia: Coping, Integration, and Meaning-Making." In *Mass Trauma and Emotional Healing around the World: Rituals and Practices for Resilience and Meaning Making*, vol. 1, *Natural Disasters*, edited by A. Kalayjian, D. Eugene, 1–21. Santa Barbara: ABC-CLIO.
Kallipolitis, V., and V. Petrakos. 1965. "Εύβοια." *Archaiologikon Deltion* 18: 121–27.
Karadedos, G. 2006a. "Ο περιπλανώμενος υστεροαρχαϊκός ναός της Θεσσαλονίκης. Πρώτες εκτιμήσεις για την αρχιτεκτονική του." *ΑΕΜΘ* 20: 319–31.
———. 2006b. "Ο περιπλανώμενος υστεροαρχαϊκός ναός της Θεσσαλονίκης. Μουσειολογική παρουσίαση των αρχιτεκτονικών μελών—Προοπτικές." *ΑΕΜΘ* 20: 334–39.
Karwiese, S. 2012. *Die Münzprägung von Ephesos*, vol. 5, *Katalog und Aufbau der römerzeitlichen Stadtprägung mit allen erfassbaren Stempelnachweisen*. Vienna: Österreichische Forschungsgesellschaft für Numismatik.
Kawerau, G. 1907. "Eine ionische Säule von der Akropolis zu Athen." *Jahrbuch des Deutschen Archäologischen Instituts* 22: 197–207.
Keil, J. 1929. "Vorläufiger Bericht über Ausgrabungen in Ephesos." *Jahreshefte des Österreichischen Archäologischen Instituts* 24: 7–68.
Kellogg, D. L. 2013. *Marathon Fighters and Men of Maple: Ancient Acharnai*. Oxford: Oxford University Press.
Keuls, E. C. 1975. "Skiagraphia Once Again." *AJA* 79, no. 1: 1–16.
Kienast, H. J. 2012. "Die Dipteroi im Heraion von Samos." In *Dipteros und Pseudodipteros: bauhistorische und archäologische Forschungen: Internationale Tagung 13.11.-15.11.2009 an der Hochschule Regensburg*, edited by T. Schulz, 5–18. Byzas 12. Istanbul: Ege Yayınları.
———. 2016. "Die römische Erneuerung des grossen Altares der Hera von Samos." In *Αρχιτέκτων: τιμητικός τόμος για τον καθηγητή Μανόλη Κορρέ*, edited by K. Zambas, V. K. Lambrinoudakis, E. Simantoni-Bournia, and A. Ohnesorg, 423–28. Athens: Melissa.
Killen, S. 2017. *Parasema: Offizielle Symbole griechischer Poleis und Bundesstaaten*. Wiesbaden: Reichert.
Kirchhoff, W. 1988. *Die Entwicklung des ionischen Volutenkapitells im 6. und 5. Jhd. und seine Entstehung*. Bonn: Rudolf Habelt.
Kirk, A. 2021. *Ancient Greek Lists: Catalogue and Inventory across Genres*. Cambridge: Cambridge University Press.
Kisacky, J. 2001. "History and Science: Julien-David Leroy's 'Dualistic Method of Architectural History.'" *Journal of the Society of Architectural Historians* 60, no. 3: 260–89.
Klein, N. L. 2015. "Architectural Repairs of the Small Limestone Buildings on the Athenian Acropolis in the Archaic Period." In *Autopsy in Athens: Recent Archaeological Research on Athens and Attica*, edited by M. M. Miles, 1–8. Oxford: Oxbow Books.
Knell, H. 1993. *Die Anfänge des Archaismus in der griechischen Architektur*. Xenia 33. Konstanz: Universitätverlag Konstanz.
Kockel, V. 1991. "Überlegungen zu einer Kopie der ionischen Kapitelle der Erechtheion-Nord-Halle." *Archäologischer Anzeiger* 106: 281–85.
Koenigs, W. 2007. "Die archaischen griechischen Bauteile aus Naukratis." In *Archäologische Studien zu Naukratis*, vol. 2, part 1, *Zyprisch-griechische Kleinplastik: Kouroi, andere Figuren und plastisch verzierte Gefässe*, part 2, *Archaische griechische Bauteile*, edited by Ursula Höckmann, 309–52. Worms: Wernersche Verlagsgesellschaft.
———. 2016. "Die Maussolleionkapitelle in London." In *Death and Burial in Karia*, edited by E. Mortensen and B. Poulesn, 171–225. Odense: University Press of Southern Denmark.
Koldewey, R. 1890. *Die antiken Baureste der Insel Lesbos*. Berlin: Reimer.
Koldewey, R., and O. Puchstein. 1899. *Die griechischen Tempel in Unteritalien und Sicilien*. Berlin: Asher.
Kontes, I. D. 1978. *Λέσβος καί ή μικρασιατική της περιοχή*. Ancient Greek Cities 24. Athens: Athens Center of Ekistics.
———. 1996. "The Architecture of the Parthenon." In *The Parthenon and Its Impact in Modern Times*, edited by P. Tournikiotis, 54–97. Athens: Melissa.
Kontoleon, N. M. 1964. "Archilochos und Paros." In *Archiloque: Sept exposés et discussions*, edited by J. Pouilloux, 37–86. Vandœuvres: Foundation Hardt.
Korres, M. 1990. "The Geological Factor in Ancient Greek Architecture." *The Engineering Geology of Ancient Works, Monuments and Historical Sites, Proceedings of an International Symposium, Athens 19–23 Sept. 1988*, edited by P. G. Marinos and G. C. Koukis, 1779–93. Rotterdam: Brookfield.
———. 1992–1998. "Από τον Σταυρό στην αρχαία Αγορά." *HOROS* 10–12: 83–104.
———. 1994. "Recent Discoveries on the Acropolis." In *Acropolis Restoration: The CCAM Interventions*, edited by R. Economakis, 174–79. London: Academy Editions.

———. 1996. "Ein Beitrag zur Kenntnis der attisch-ionischen Architektur." In *Säule und Gebälk: Zu Struktur und Wandlungsprozess griechisch-römischer Architektur. Bauforschungskolloquium in Berlin vom 16. bis 18. Juni 1994*, edited by E.-L. Schwandner, 90–113. Mainz: Philipp von Zabern.

———. 1997. "Restoration and Reconstruction Work on Monuments in Antiquity." In *La reintegrazione nel restauro dell'antico: La protezione del patrimonio dal rischio sismico. Atti del seminario di studi, Paestum 11-12 aprile 1997*, edited by M. M. Segarra Lagunes, 197–208. Rome: Gangemi.

———. 2001. *From Pentelicon to the Parthenon: The Ancient Quarries and the Story of a Half-Worked Column Capital of the First Marble Parthenon*. Athens: Melissa.

———. 2021. "Das Volutenkapitell aus Sykaminos." In *Sidelights on Greek Antiquity: Archaeological and Epigraphical Essays in Honour of Vasileios Petrakos*, edited by K. Kalogeropoulos, D. Vassilikou, M. Tiverios, 321–57. Berlin: De Gruyter.

Kosmopoulos, L. 2022. *Tuscanicae dispositiones sive opera dorica: Architetture doricizzanti in Italia centro-meridionale*. Rome: L'Erma di Bretschneider.

Koukouli-Chrysanthaki. C. 1980. "Οι αποικίες της Θάσου στο Β. Αιγαίο. Νεώτερα ευρήματα." In *Α΄ Τοπικό Συνέδριο. Η Καβάλα και η περιοχή της, Καβάλα 18–20 Απριλίου 1977*, 309–25. Thessaloniki: Institute of Balkan Studies.

———. 1990. "Τα «μέταλλα» της θασιακής περαίας" In *Μνήμη Λαζαρίδη. Πόλις και χώρα στην αρχαία Μακεδονία και Θράκη*, edited by C. Koukouli-Chrysanthaki and O. Picard, 493–533. Thessaloniki: Ministry of Culture and Sports.

———. 1997. "Parthenos." In *Lexicon Iconographicum Mythologiae Classicae* [LIMC] VIII 1B, 944–48. Zürich and Düsseldorf: Artemis and Winkler.

Kourouniotis, K. 1927-1928. "Το ιερόν του Απόλλωνος του Ζωστήρος." *Archaiologikon Deltion* 11: 9–53.

Krautheimer, R. 1942. "Introduction to an Iconography of Mediaeval Architecture." *Journal of the Warburg and Courtauld Institutes* 5: 1–33.

Krier, R. 2015. *Architectural Journal / Architektonisches Tagbuch: 1960–1975*. Berlin: De Gruyter.

Krischen, F. 1938. *Die griechische Stadt: Wiederherstellungen*. Berlin: Gebr. Mann.

Kritzas, C., and S. Prignitz. 2020. "The 'Stele of the Punishments': A New Inscription from Epidauros." *Archaiologike Ephemeris* 159: 1–61.

Kyrieleis, H. 1986. "Chios and Samos in the Archaic Period." In *Chios: A Conference at the Homereion in Chios 1984*, edited by J. Boardman and C. E. Vaphopoulou-Richardson, 187–204. Oxford: Clarendon Press.

Ladstätter, S. 2016. "Hafen und Stadt von Ephesos in hellenistischer Zeit." *Jahreshefte des Österreichischen Archäologischen Instituts* 85: 233–72.

Lambrinoudakis, V., and G. Gruben. 1987. "Das neuentdeckte Heiligtum von Iria auf Naxos: Zur Baugeschichte des 2. Tempels." *Archäologischer Anzeiger*: 569–621.

Lancaster, L. C. 2005. "The Process of Building the Colosseum: The Site, Materials, and Construction Techniques." *Journal of Roman Archaeology* 18: 57–82.

Landwehr, C. 1985. *Die antiken Gipsabgüsse aus Baiae: Griechische Bronzestatuen in Abgüssen römischer Zeit*. Archäologische Forschungen 14. Berlin: Gebr. Mann.

———. 2010. "The Baiae Casts and the Uniqueness of Roman Copies." In *Plaster Casts: Making, Collecting and Displaying from Classical Antiquity to the Present*, edited by R. Frederiksen and E. Marchand, 35–46. Berlin: De Gruyter.

Lagopoulos, A. P. 2005. "Monumental Urban Space and National Identity: The Early Twentieth Century New Plan of Thessaloniki." *Journal of Historical Geography* 31, no. 1: 61–77.

Lardinois, A. 2022. "Creation or Confirmation of the Canon? The Measures of Lycurgus and the Selection of Athenian Tragedy in Antiquity." In *Canonisation as Innovation: Anchoring Cultural Formation in the First Millennium BCE*, edited by Damien Agut-Labordère and Miguel John Versluys, 152–64. Leiden: Brill.

Laroche, D. 1991. "L'Autel d'Apollon à Delphes: Éléments nouveaux." In *L'Espace Sacrificiel dans les civilisations méditerranéennes de l'Antiquité (actes du colloque tenu à la Maison de l'Orient, Lyon 4-7 juin 1988)*, edited by R. Étienne and M.-T. Le Dinahet, 103–7. Paris: Boccard.

———. 2015. "L'architecture à Delphes au IIIe s. a.C." In *L'architecture monumentale grecque au IIIe siècle a.C.*, edited by J. des Courtils, 21–28. Bordeaux: Ausonius.

Lattermann, H. 1908. *Griechische Bauinschriften*. Strasbourg: Trübner.

Laugier, M.-A. 1997. "An Essay on Architecture." Translated by Wolfgang Herrmann and Anni Herrmann. Los Angeles: Hennessey and Ingalls, Inc.

Launey, M. 1944. *Le sanctuaire et le culte d'Héraclès à Thasos*. Études Thasiennes 1. Paris: E. de Boccard.

Laurent, V. 1964. "Une Homélie inédite de l'archevêque de Thessalonique Léon le Philosophe sur l'Annonciation (25 mars 842)." In *Mélanges Eugène Tisserant. II, Orient chrétien, première partie*, 281–302. Studi e Testi 232. Vatican City: Biblioteca Apostolica Vaticana.

Lazaridis, D. 1960. "Νεάπολις (Καβάλα)." *Archaiologikon Deltion* 16, Chronika: 219–20.

———. 1962. "Νεάπολις (Καβάλα)." *Archaiologikon Deltion* 17, Chronika B: 235–38.

———. 1969. *Νεάπολις, Χριστούπολις, Καβάλα, Οδηγός του Μουσείου Καβάλας*. Athens: P. Konstantinidis and K. Michalas.

———. 1971. *Thasos and Its Peraia*. Ancient Cities 5. Athens: Athens Center of Ekistics.

———. 1997. *Amphipolis*. Athens: Ministry of Culture, Archaeological Receipts Fund.

Lazzarini, L. P., and C. Marconi. 2017. "A Scientific Analysis of the Polychromy of Temple B at Selinunte." In *"Sicile Ancienne": Hittorff and the Architecture of Classical Sicily*, edited by M. Kiene, L. Lazzarini, and C. Marconi, 193–203. Cologne: USB Köln.

Lazzarini, L., P. Persano, and Y. Maniatis. 2019. "Provenance Identification of the Daphnephoros Apollo Temple Marbles in the Eretria Museum (Euboea, Greece)." *Marmora* 15: 15–38.

Lehmann, K. 1998. *Samothrace: A Guide to the Excavations and the Museum*. Thessaloniki: Institute of Fine Arts, New York University.

Lehmann, P. W., and D. Spittle. 1982. *The Temenos*.

Samothrace 5. Princeton, NJ: Princeton University Press.

Leka, E. 2021. "Maintenance and Repair of Marble Sculpture in Antiquity: the case of an Archaic Nike from the Athenian Acropolis." In *Ancient Architectural Restoration in the Greek World: Proceedings of the International Workshop Held at Wolfson College, Oxford*, edited by J. V. Broeck-Parant and T. Ismaelli, 127–42. Rome: Quasar.

Le Roy, J.-D. 1758a. *Les ruines des plus beaux monuments de la Grèce*. Paris: Guerin and Delatour.

———. 1758b. *Ruins of Athens, with Remains and Other Valuable Antiquities in Greece*. London: Robert Sayer.

Lesk, A. L. 2005. "A Diachronic Examination of the Erechtheion and Its Reception." PhD diss., University of Cincinnati.

———. 2007. " 'Caryatides probantur inter pauca operum': Pliny, Vitruvius, and the Semiotics of the Erechtheion Maidens at Rome." *Arethusa* 40, no. 1: 25–42.

LeVen, P. A. 2013. "The Colors of Sound: Poikilia and Its Aesthetic Contexts." *Greek and Roman Musical Studies* 1: 229–42.

LiDonnici, L. R. 1992. "The Images of Artemis Ephesia and Greco-Roman Worship: A Reconsideration." *Harvard Theological Review* 85, no. 4: 389–415.

Lippolis, E., M. Livadiotti, and G. Rocco. 2007. *Architettura greca: Storia e monumenti del mondo della polis dalle origini al V secolo a.C.* Milan: Bruno Mondadori.

Lohmann, H. 2007. "Forschungen und Ausgrabungen in der Mykale 2001–2006." *Istanbuler Mitteilungen* 57: 59–178.

———. 2012. "Ionians and Carians in the Mycale: The Discovery of Carian Melia and the Archaic Panionion." In *Landscape, Ethnicity and Identity in the Archaic Mediterranean Area*, edited by G. Cifani and S. Stoddart, 32–50. Oxford: Oxbow.

Luni, M., and O. Mei. 2016. "Il tempio G di Selinunte." In *Selinunte: Restauri dell'antico*, edited by C. F. Greco and V. Nicolucci, 123–38. Roma: De Luca Editore.

Lyons, C. L. 2005. "The Art and Science of Antiquity in Nineteenth-Century Photography." In *Antiquity & Photography: Early Views of Ancient Mediterranean Sites*, 22–65. Los Angeles: J. Paul Getty Museum.

Mace, H. L. 1978. "The Archaic Ionic Capital: Studies in Formal and Stylistic Development." PhD diss., University of North Carolina.

Madzharov, M. 2016. "Светилище и храм от v в. пр. Хр. При с. Кръстевич, Община Хисаря (предварително съобщение)." *Kazanlak Problems and Studies of Thracian Culture* 8: 105–58.

Malamidou, D. 2022. "The Harbours of Thasos and Neapolis on the Ancient Northern Aegean Sea Routes." In *Mare Thracium: Archaeology and History of Coastal Landscapes and Islands of the Thracian Sea during Antiquity and the Byzantine Era*, edited by T. Schmidts and I. Triantafillidis, 77–95. Mainz: Verlag des Römisch-Germanischen Zentralmuseums.

Malkin, I. 2011. *A Small Greek World: Networks in the Ancient Mediterranean*. Greeks Overseas. Oxford: Oxford University Press.

Mallwitz, A. 1980. "Kykladen und Olympia." *Στήλη: Τόμος εις μνήμην Νικολάου Κοντολέοντος*, edited by G. Kanellopoulou, 361–79. Athens: Association of Friends of Nikolaos Kontoleon.

Malten, L. 1931. "Aineias." *Archiv für Religionswissenschaft* 29: 33–59.

Manzelli, V. 1994. *La Policromia Nella Statuaria Greca Arcaica*. Rome: "L'Erma" di Bretschneider.

Marcadé, J. 1953. *Recueil des signatures de sculpteurs grecs*. Vol. 1. Paris: de Boccard.

March, D. A. 2008. "Kleisthenes and the League of Athena Pallenis." *Zeitschrift für Papyrologie und Epigraphik* 57, no. 2: 134–41.

Marconi, C. 1994. *Selinunte: Le metope dell'Heraion*. Modena: Panini.

———. 2004. "Kosmos: The Imagery of the Archaic Greek Temple." *RES: Anthropology and Aesthetics* 45: 211–24.

———. 2007. *Temple Decoration and Cultural Identity in the Archaic Greek World*. Cambridge: Cambridge University Press.

———. 2009. "The Parthenon Frieze: Degrees of Visibility." *RES: Anthropology and Aesthetics* 55/56: 156–73.

———. 2010. "Choroi, Theōriai and International Ambitions: The Hall of Choral Dancers and Its Frieze." In *Samothracian Connections: Essays in Honor of James R. McCredie*, edited by O. Palagia and B. D. Wescoat, 106–35. Oxford: Oxbow Books.

———. 2016. "The Greek West: Temples and Their Decoration." In *A Companion to Greek Architecture*, edited by M. M. Miles, 75–91. Malden, MA: Wiley Blackwell.

Mărgineanu-Cârstoiu, M. 2002–2003. "The Evolution of the Ionic Capitals from the Hellenistic Age to the Roman Age: A Standstill in Geometry?" *Dacia*, n.s., 46–47: 53–112.

Mărgineanu-Cârstoiu, M., and M. Büyükkolancı. 1996/1998. "Neue ionische Kapitelle von Ephesos und Bemerkungen zu ihrer geometrischen Komposition." *Dacia* 40–42: 103–39.

———. 2011. "Un chapiteau ionique de Callatis: Observations sur la composition des chapiteaux hellénistiques avec le canal décoré." *Dacia* 55: 57–83.

Marinatos, N. 2015. *Sir Arthur Evans and Minoan Crete: Creating the Vision of Knossos*. London: I. B. Tauris.

Martin, R. R. 1944–1945. "Chapiteaux ioniques de l'Asclépiéion d'Athènes." *BCH* 68/69: 340–74.

———. 1959. *L'Agora*. Études Thasiennes 6. Paris: E. de Boccard.

———. 1972. "Chapiteaux Ioniques de Thasos." *BCH* 96, no. 1: 303–25.

———. 1973. "Compléments à l'étude des chapiteaux ioniques de Délos." In "Études Déliennes," supplement 1, *BCH*: 371–98.

———. 1987. *Architecture et urbanisme*. Athens: École française d'Athènes.

Martínez López, C., H. Gallego Franco, M. D. Mirón Pérez, and M. Oria Segura. 2019. *Constructoras de Ciudad: Mujeres y Arquitectura en el Occidente Romano*. Albolote: Comares.

Marx, W. 2022. "How Canonization Transformed Greek Tragedy." In *Canonisation as Innovation: Anchoring Cultural Formation in the First Millennium BCE*, edited by Damien Agut-Labordère & Miguel John Versluys, 164–77. Leiden: Brill.

Mayeux, H. 1885. *La Composition Décorative: Texte et Dessins*. Paris: A. Quantin.

———. 1889. *A Manual of Decorative Composition for Designers, Decorators, Architects, and Industrial Artists*. London: Virtue.

Mazarakis Ainian, A. 2016. "Early Greek Temples." In *A Companion to Greek Architecture*, edited by M. M. Miles, 15–30. Malden, MA: Wiley Blackwell.

Mazzilli, G. 2021. "Da Atene a Berlino e viceversa: su un capitello ionico del tipo 'Eretteo' presso l'Antikensammlung." *Annuario della Scuola Archeologica di Atene* 99, no. 1: 344–70.

Mazzoleni, I. 2013. *Architecture Follows Nature. Biomimetic Principles for Innovative Design*. Boca Raton, FL: CRC Press.

McAllister, M. H. 1959. "The Temple of Ares at Athens: A Review of the Evidence." *Hesperia* 28, no. 1: 1–64.

McGowan, E. P. 1993. "Votive Columns of the Aegean Islands and the Athenian Acropolis in the Archaic Period." PhD diss., Institute of Fine Arts, New York University.

———. 1995. "Tomb Marker and Turning Post: Funerary Columns in the Archaic Period." *AJA* 99, no. 4: 615–32.

———. 1997. "The Origins of the Athenian Ionic Capital." *Hesperia* 66, no. 2: 209–33.

McInerney, J. 2010. *Cattle of the Sun: Herding and Sanctuaries in Ancient Greece*. Princeton, NJ: Princeton University Press.

———. 2015. "'There Will Be Blood …': The Cult of Artemis Tauropolos at Halai Araphenides." In *Cities Called Athens: Studies Honoring John McK; Camp II*, edited by K. F. Daly and L. A. Riccardi, 289–320. Lewisburg: Bucknell University Press.

———. 2023. "The Lindian Chronicle and Local Identity." In *The Local Horizon of Ancient Greek Religion*, edited by H. Beck and J. Kindt, 232–61. Cambridge: Cambridge University Press.

Meeus, A. 2015. "The Career of Sostratos of Knidos: Politics, Diplomacy and the Alexandrian Building Programme in the Early Hellenistic Period." In *Greece, Macedon and Persia: Studies in Social, Political and Military History in Honour of Waldemar Heckel*, edited by E. E. Garvin, W. Heckel, T. Howe, and G. Wrightson, 143–71. Philadelphia: Oxbow Books.

Meiggs, R. 1972. *The Athenian Empire*. Oxford: Clarendon Press.

Meiggs, R., and D. M. Lewis. 1969. *A Selection of Greek Historical Inscriptions to the End of the Fifth Century B.C.* Oxford: Clarendon Press.

Mertens, D. 2006. *Städte und Bauten der Westgriechen: Von der Kolonisationszeit bis zur Krise um 400 vor Christus*. Munich: Hirmer.

Meurer, M. 1897. "Das griechische Akanthusornament und seine natürlichen Vorbilder." *Jahrbuch des Deutschen Archäologischen Instituts* 11: 117–59.

Michaelsen, K. J. 1975. "Archipenko: A Study of the Early Works, 1908–1920." PhD diss., Columbia University.

Michaud, J.-P. 1974. "Chronique des fouilles en 1973." *BCH* 98: 579–722.

Middleton, R. 2004. "Introduction." In *Julien-David Le Roy: The Ruins of the Most Beautiful Monuments of Greece*, translated by David Britt, 1–199. Los Angeles: Getty Research Institute.

Mikocki, T. 1986. "Un Chapiteau Grec Ionique en Pologne." *BCH* 110/111: 137–43.

Mikocki, T., and W. Piwkowski. 2001. *Et in Arcadia Ego; Muzeum Księżny Heleny Radziwiłłowej: Katalog wystawy w Świątyni Diany w Arkadii, maj-wrzesień 2001*. Warsaw: Muzeum Narodowe w Warszawie.

Miles, M. M. 1989. "A Reconstruction of the Temple of Nemesis at Rhamnous." *Hesperia* 58: 131–249.

———. 2012. "Entering Demeter's Gateway: The Roman Propylon in the City Eleusinion." In *Architecture of the Sacred: Space, Ritual, and Experience from Classical Greece to Byzantium*, edited by B. D. Wescoat and R. G. Ousterhout, 114–51. Cambridge: Cambridge University Press.

———. 2014. "Burnt Temples in the Landscape of the Past." In *Valuing the Past in the Greco-Roman World: Proceedings from the Penn–Leiden Colloquia on Ancient Values VII*, edited by J. Ker and C. Pieper, 111–45. Leiden: Koninklijke Brill.

———. 2015. "The Vanishing Double Stoa at Thorikos and its Afterlives." In *Autopsy in Athens: Recent Archaeological Research on Athens and Attica*, edited by M. M. Miles, 165–80. Oxford: Oxbow Books.

———. 2017. "Constructing Architects: The So-Called 'Theseum Architect.'" In *Artists and Artistic Production in Ancient Greece*, edited by K. Seaman and P. Schultz, 101–23. Cambridge: Cambridge University Press.

Miller, A. 1948. *Stone and Marble Carving: A Manual for the Student Sculptor*. Berkeley: University of California Press.

Möbius, H. 1927. "Attische Architekturstudien." *Mitteilungen des deutschen Archäologischen Instituts, Athenische Abteilung* 52: 163–65.

Montelle, C. 2011. *Chasing Shadows. Mathematics, Astronomy, and the Early History of Eclipse Reckoning*. Baltimore: Johns Hopkins University Press.

Moretti, J.-C. 1987. "Une vignette de traité à Delphes." *BCH* 111, no. 1: 157–66.

Moretti, J.-C., P. Fraisse, and C. Llinas. 2022. *L'Artémision*, vol. 1, *L'histoire des fouilles et le temple hellénistique*. Exploration archéologique de Délos faite par l'École française d'Athènes 46. Athens: École française d'Athènes.

Mulliez, D. 2007. "Delos: The Excavation of the Sacred Island of Apollo." In *Great Moments in Greek Archaeology*, edited by P. Valavanis and A. Delivorrias, 78–99. Los Angeles: J. Paul Getty Museum.

Muss, U. 1994. *Die Bauplastik des archaischen Artemisions von Ephesos*. Vienna: Eigenverlag des Österreichischen Archäologischen Instituts.

Mylonopoulos, I. 2013. "Commemorating Pious Service: Images in Honour of Male and Female Priestly Officers in Asia Minor and the Eastern Aegean in Hellenistic and Roman Times." In *Cities and Priests: Cult Personnel in Asia Minor and the Aegean Islands from the Hellenistic to the Imperial Period*, edited by M. Horster and A. Klöckner, 121–53. Berlin: De Gruyter.

———. 2019. "The Power of the Absent Text: Dedicatory Inscriptions on Greek Sacred Architecture and Altars." In *The Materiality of Text—Placement, Perception, and Presence of Inscribed Texts in Classical Antiquity*, edited by A Petrovic, I. Petrovic, and E. Thomas, 231–74. Leiden: Brill.

Nagel, A. 2010. "Colors, Gilding and Painted Motifs at Persepolis: Approaching the Polychromy of Achaemenid Persian Architectural Sculpture, ca. 520–330 BCE." PhD diss., University of Michigan.

———. 2023. *Color and Meaning in the Art of Achaemenid Persia*. Cambridge: Cambridge University Press.

Neer, R. T. 1992. "The Athenian Treasury at Delphi and

the Material of Politics." *Classical Antiquity* 23, no. 1: 63–93.

———. 2001. "Framing the Gift: The Politics of the Siphnian Treasury at Delphi." *Classical Antiquity* 20: 273–344.

———. 2002. *Style and Politics in Athenian Vase-Painting: The Craft of Democracy, ca. 530–460 B.C.E.* Cambridge: Cambridge University Press.

———. 2010. *The Emergence of the Classical Style in Greek Sculpture.* Chicago: University of Chicago Press.

———. 2012. *Greek Art and Archaeology: A New History, C. 2500–c. 150 BCE.* New York: Thames and Hudson.

———. 2019. *Conditions of Visibility.* Oxford: Oxford University Press.

Neils, J. 2016. "Color and Carving: Architectural Decoration in Mainland Greece." In *A Companion to Greek Architecture*, edited by M. M. Miles, 164–77. Malden, MA: Wiley Blackwell.

Nénot, H. P. n.d. *Rapport de Monsieur H. P. Nénot, architecte Pensionnaire de l'Académie de France à Rome.* Unpublished report in the archive of the École des Beaux Arts, Paris. Env. 72, MS 283.

Newton, C. T. 1862–1863. *A History of Discoveries at Halicarnassus, Cnidus & Branchidae.* London: Day and Son.

Ng, D. Y., and M. Swetnam-Burland. 2018. "Introduction: Reuse, Renovation, Reiteration." In *Reuse and Renovation in Roman Material Culture: Functions, Aesthetics, Interpretations*, edited by D. Y. Ng and M. Swetnam-Burland, 1–23. Cambridge: Cambridge University Press.

Nightingale, A. W. 2004. *Spectacles of Truth in Classical Greek Philosophy: Theoria in Its Cultural Context.* Cambridge: Cambridge University Press.

Nilsson, M. P. 1906. *Griechische Feste von religiöser Bedeutung mit Ausschluss der Attischen.* Leipzig: De Gruyter.

———. 1925. "Les bases votives à double colonne et l'arc de triomphe." *BCH* 49: 143–57.

Ohly, D. 1971. *Tempel und Heiligtum der Aphaia auf Ägina.* Munich: Beck.

Ohnesorg, A. 1993a. "Parische Kapitelle." In *Les Grands Ateliers d'architecture dans le monde égéen du VIe siècle av. J.-C. Actes du colloque d'Istanbul, 23–25 mai 1991*, edited by J. des Courtils and J.-C. Moretti, 111–18. Istanbul: Institut Français d'Études Anatoliennes.

———. 1993b. *Inselionische Marmordächer.* Berlin: De Gruyter.

———. 1996. "Votiv- oder Architektursäulen." In *Säule und Gebälk*, edited by E.-L. Schwandener, 39–47. Mainz: P. von Zabern.

———. 1999. "Das 'Zapheiropoulos-Kapitell' in Paros. Eine Votivsäule ohne Bildwerk?" In *Φως Κυκλαδικόν. Τιμητικός τόμος στη μνήμη του Νίκου Ζαφειρόπουλου*, ed. N. C. Satampolidis, 220–231. Athens: Museum of Cycladic Art.

———. 2001. "Ephesische Rosettenkapitelle." In *Der Kosmos der Artemis von Ephesos*, edited by U. Muss, 185–98. Vienna: Österreichisches Archäologisches Institut.

———. 2005a. "Naxian and Parian Architecture. General Features and New Discoveries." In *Architecture and Archaeology in the Cyclades. Papers in Honour of J. J. Coulton*, edited by M. Yeroulanou and M. Stamatopoulou, 135–52. Oxford: Archaeopress.

———. 2005b. *Ionische Altäre: Formen und Varianten einer Architekturgattung aus Insel- und Ostionien.* Berling: Gebr. Mann.

———. 2007. *Der Kroisos-Tempel Neue Forschungen zum archaischen Dipteros der Artemis von Ephesos.* Vienna: Verlag der Österreichischen Akademie der Wissenschaften.

———. 2012. "Die beiden Dipteroi der Artemis von Ephesos—Tradition, Archaismus, Denkmalpflege?" In *Dipteros und Pseudodipteros: Bauhistorische und archäologische Forschungen; Internationale Tagung 13.11.–15.11. 2009 an der Hochschule Regensburg*, edited by T. Schulz, 19–40. Byzas 12. Istanbul: Ege Yayınları.

———. 2017. "Island-Ionic and Island-Doric Architecture on the Cyclades: An Overview." In *Les sanctuaires archaïques des Cyclades*, edited by A. Mazarakis Ainian, 55–72. Rennes: Presses Universitaires de Rennes.

———. 2018. "'Byzantinischer Archaismus' auf Paros und Naxos." In *Ήρως κτίστης: μνήμη Χαράλαμπου Μπούρα*, vol. 2, edited by M. Korres, F. Mallouchou-Tufano, S. V. Mamaloukos, and K. Zambas, 273–86. Athens: Melissa.

Ohnesorg, A., and M. Büyükkolancı. 2007. "Ein ionisches Kapitell mit glatten Voluten in Ephesos." *Istanbuler Mitteilungen* 57: 209–33.

Oliver-Smith, A. 1986. *Natural Disasters and Cultural Responses.* Williamsburg, VA: Department of Anthropology, College of William and Mary.

Oliver-Smith, A., and S. Hoffman. 1999. *The Angry Earth: Disaster in Anthropological Perspective.* New York: Routledge.

Orlandos, A. K. 1949. "Notes on the Roof Tiles of the Parthenon." In "Commemorative Studies in Honor of Theodore Leslie Shear," supplement 8, *Hesperia*: 259–67.

Osborne, R. 1998. "Early Greek Colonization? The Nature of Greek Settlement in the West." In *Archaic Greece: New Approaches and New Evidence*, edited by N. Fisher and H. van Wees, 251–69. London: Duckworth.

———. 1999. "Archaeology and the Athenian Empire." *Transactions of the American Philological Association* 129: 319–32.

Oster, R. 1990. *Ephesus as a Religious Center Under the Principate I: Paganism before Constantine.* New York: De Gruyter.

Otto, W. F. 1965. *Dionysus: Myth and Cult.* Bloomington: Indiana University Press.

Owen, S. 2000. "New Light on Thracian Thasos: A Reinterpretation of the 'Cave of Pan.'" *Journal of Hellenic Studies* 120: 139–43.

———. 2003. "Of Dogs and Men: Archilochos, Archaeology and the Greek Settlement of Thasos." *Cambridge Classical Journal* 49: 1–18.

Paga, J. 2015. "The Southeast Fountain House in the Athenian Agora: A Reappraisal of Its Date and Historical Context." *Hesperia* 84, no. 2: 355–87.

———. 2021. *Building Democracy in Late Archaic Athens.* New York: Oxford University Press.

Palagia, O. 2003. "Did the Greeks Use a Pointing Machine?" *Bulletin Archéologique* 30: 55–64.

———. 2009. "Archaism and the Quest for Immortality in Attic Sculpture during the Peloponnesian War." In *Art in Athens during the Peloponnesian War*, edited by O. Palagia, 24–51. Cambridge: Cambridge University Press.

———. 2016. "Commemorating the Dead: Grave Markers, Tombs, and Tomb Paintings, 400–30 BCE." In *A Companion to Greek Architecture*, edited by M. M. Miles, 374–89. Malden, MA: Wiley-Blackwell.

Palamidis, A. 2017. "L'abandon de sanctuaires et le transfert de cultes en Grèce antique." PhD diss., Université de Liège.

Panait-Bîrzescu, F. 2020. "The Eagle on Dolphin on the Coins of Olbia, Histria and Sinope: Its Origin and Meaning." *Dacia*, n.s., 64, 144–62.

Panayotova, K., M. Damyanov, D. Stoyanova, and T. Bogdanova. 2014. "Apollonia Pontica: The Archaic Temenos and Settlement on the Island of St. Kirik." In *Centre and Periphery in the Ancient World: Proceedings of the XVIIIth International Congress of Classical Archaeology*, vol. 1, edited by J. M. Alvarez, T. Nogales, and I. Roda, 595–98. Mérida: Museo Nacional de Arte Romano.

Papadopoulos, J. K. 2022. "Canon Creation / Destruction and Cultural Formation: Authority, Reception, Canonicity, Marginality." In *Canonisation as Innovation: Anchoring Cultural Formation in the First Millennium BCE*, edited by D. Agut-Labordère and M. J. Versluys, 3–33. Leiden: Brill.

Papanikolaou, A. 2012. *Η αποκατάσταση του Ερεχθείου (1979–1987)*. Vol. 2. Athens: Committee for the Conservation of the Acropolis Monuments, Hellenic Ministry of Culture and Tourism.

Partida, E. C. 2009. "From Hypaethral Depots to Hypaethral Exhibitions, Casting Light on Architecture and Society in 4th-3rd Century BC Delphi." *Athenische Mitteilungen* 124: 273–324.

———. 2013. "Parian Creators of the Age of Skopas at Delphi." In *Paros III: Skopas of Paros and His World; Proceedings of the Third International Conference on the Archaeology of Paros and the Cyclades. Paroikia, Paros, 11–14 June 2010*, edited by D. Katsonopoulou and A. Stewart, 477–97. Athens: The Paros and Cyclades Institute of Archaeology.

Pedersen, P. 1994. "Ionian Renaissance and Some Aspects of Its Origin within the Field of Architecture and Planning." In *Hekatomnid Karia and the Ionian Renaissance*, edited by J. Isager, 11–35. Halicarnassian Studies 1. Odense: Odense University Press.

———. 2001. "Reflections on the Ionian Renaissance in Greek Architecture and Its Historical Background." *Hephaistos* 19/20: 97–130.

———. 2004. "Pergamon and the Ionian Renaissance." *Istanbuler Mitteilungen* 54: 409–34.

Petrakis, M. 2021. "More Erechtheion Echoes and the Temple of Apollo *Patroos*." *Annuario della Scuola Archeologica di Atene* 99, no. 1: 404–19.

Petrakos, V. C. 1968. *Ο Ωρωπός και το ιερόν του Αμφιαράου*. Athens: Archaeological Society of Athens.

Petropoulou, A. B. 1981. "The Eparche Documents and the Early Oracle at Oropus." *GRBS* 22: 39–63.

Picard, O. 1990. "Thasos et Néapolis." In *Μνήμη Δ. Λαζαρίδη: Πόλις και χώρα στην αρχαία Μακεδονία και Θράκη*, edited by C. Koukouli-Chrysanthaki and O. Picard, 541–48. Thessaloniki: Hypourgeio Politismou, École Française d'Athènes.

Pickett, J., J. Schreck, R. Holod, Y. Rassamakin, O. Halenko, and W. Woodfin. 2016. "Architectural Energetics for Tumuli Construction: The Case of the Medieval Chungul Kurgan on the Eurasian Steppe." *Journal of Archaeological Science* 75: 101–14.

Pierattini, A. 2022. *The Origins of Greek Temple Architecture*. Cambridge: Cambridge University Press.

Pitt, R. K. 2016. "Inscribing Construction: The Financing and Administration of Public Building in Greek Sanctuaries." In *A Companion to Greek architecture*, edited by M. M. Miles, 194–205. Malden, MA: Wiley-Blackwell.

Pollitt, J. J. 1965. *The Art of Greece, 1400–31 B.C.: Sources & Documents*. Englewood Cliffs, NJ: Prentice-Hall.

———. 1986. *Art in the Hellenistic Age*. Cambridge: Cambridge University Press.

———. 2001. *The Art of Ancient Greece: Sources and Documents*. Cambridge: Cambridge University Press.

Pope, S., and P. Schultz. 2014. "The Chryselephantine Doors of the Parthenon." *AJA* 118, no. 1: 19–31.

Pouilloux, J. 1954. *Recherches sur l'histoire et les cultes de Thasos I: De la fondation de la cité à 196 avant J.-C*. Études Thasiennes 3. Athens: De Boccard.

Poulios, V. 1998. "Θησαυρός αργυρών νομισμάτων Φιλίππου Β΄, Θάσου και Νεάπολης από τους Ποταμούς Δράμας." *Archaiologikon Deltion* 53: 187–256.

Pourchet, E. 1897. *Les Envois de Rome: Restaurations des monuments anciens reproduits d'après les dessins originaux de messieurs les architectes pensionnaires de l'Académie de France à Rome, première partie, architecture grecque*. Paris: Aron.

Price, S. 2012. "Memory and Ancient Greece." In *Historical and Religious Memory in the Ancient World*, edited by B. Dignas and R.R.R. Smith, 15–36. Oxford: Oxford University Press.

Prokova, A. 2014 "Die figürlichen Tonvotive aus dem Heiligtum der Parthenos in der antiken Stadt Neapolis: Zu Kult und materieller Kultur einer griechischen Stadt an der nordägäischen thrakischen Küste." PhD diss., University of Cologne.

———. 2017. "Aspekte kollektiver Identität im antiken Neapolis—zwischen Abgrenzung und Zugehörigkeit." In *Urbanitas—urbane Qualitäten: Die antike Stadt als kulturelle Selbstverwirklichung*, edited by A. W. Busch, J. Griesbach, and J. Lipps, 273–86. Heidelberg: Propylaeum.

Prost, F. 2018. " Le Sanctuaire d'Apollon aux VIIe et VIe siècles." In *Le Sanctuaire d'Apollon a Delos*, vol. 1, *Architecture, topographie, histoire*, edited by R. Étienne, 155–74. Athens: École française d'Athènes.

Purcell, N. 2005. "Colonization and Mediterranean History." In *Ancient Colonization: Analogy, Similarity and Difference*, edited by H. Hurst and S. Owens, 115–139. London: Duckworth.

Purchase, W. R. 1904. *Practical Masonry: A Guide to the Art of Stone Cutting*. London: Crosby Lockwood and Son.

Rackham, H. 1933. *Cicero: On the Nature of the Gods, Academics*. Loeb Classical Library 268. Cambridge, MA: Harvard University Press.

Radt, W. 1970. *Siedlungen und Bauten auf der Halbinsel von Halikarnassos: Unter besonderer Berücksichtigung der archaischen Epoche*. Tübingen: Ernst Wasmuth.

Randall, R. H., Jr. 1955. "The Erechtheum Workmen." *AJA* 57, no. 3: 199–210.

Raubitschek, A. E. 1940. "Two Monuments Erected after the Victory of Marathon." *AJA* 44: 53–59.

Replat, J. 1922. "Questions d'architecture delphique: Remarques sur un chapiteau ionique attribué à l'ordre intérieur du temple d'Apollon à Delphes." *BCH* 46: 435–38.

Rhomaios, K. A. 1951. *Ο Μακεδονικός Τάφος της Βεργίνας*. Athens: Society for Macedonian Studies.

Rhomiopoulou, A., and B. Schmidt-Dounas. 2010. *Das Palmettengrab in Lefkadia*. Mainz: Von Zabern.

Richens, P., and G. Herdt. 2009. "Modeling the Ionic Capital." In *Computation: The New Realm of Architectural Design; Proceedings of the 27th Conference on Education and Research in Computer Aided Architectural Design in Europe, September 16–19, 2009, Istanbul Technical University and Yildiz Technical University, Istanbul: eCAADe, Istanbul*, 809–16. Istanbul: ITU / YTU.

Richter, G. 1933. "A Statuette of an Amazon." *Metropolitan Museum of Art Bulletin* 28, no. 4, part 1: 76–78.

———. 1970. "An Aristogeiton from Baiae." *AJA* 74: 296–97.

Ridgway, B. S. 1970. *The Severe Style in Greek Sculpture*. Princeton, NJ: Princeton University Press.

———. 2003. *Hellenistic Sculpture*. Vol. 1. Madison: University of Wisconsin Press.

Riegl, A. 1893. *Stilfragen: Grundlegungen zu einer Geschichte der Ornamentik*. Berlin: Siemens.

———. 1903. *Moderne Denkmalkultus: Sein Wesen und seine Entstehung*. Vienna: Braumüller.

Rignanese, G. 2021. "Un Capitello Ionico nel British Museum: Modelli, Forma e Contesto." *Annuario della Scuola Archeologica di Atene* 99, no. 1: 284–308.

Rockwell, P. 1993. *The Art of Stoneworking: A Reference Guide*. New York: Cambridge University Press.

Rojas, P. 2019. *The Pasts of Roman Anatolia: Interpreters, Traces, Horizons*. Cambridge: Cambridge University Press.

Rose, C. B. 2013. *The Archaeology of Greek and Roman Troy*. New York: Cambridge University Press.

Rotroff, S. I. 2009. "Early Red-Figure in Context." In *Athenian Potters and Painters*, vol. 2, edited by J. H. Oakley and O. Palagia, 250–60. Oxford: Oxbow.

Rous, S. A. 2019. *Reset in Stone: Memory and Reuse in Ancient Athens*. Madison: University of Wisconsin Press.

———. 2020. "Upcycling as a New Methodological Approach to Reuse in Greek Architecture." In *New Directions and Paradigms for the Study of Greek Architecture: Interdisciplinary Dialogues in the Field*, edited by D. Scahill and P. Sapirstein, 215–28. Leiden: Brill.

Rouveret, A. 2006. "Skiagraphia/scaenographia: Quelques remarques." *Pallas* 71: 71–80.

Rowland, I. D., and T. N. Howe. 1999. *Vitruvius: Ten Books on Architecture*. Cambridge: Cambridge University Press.

Ruskin, J. 1851. *The Stones of Venice*, vol. 1, *The Foundations*. New York: Merrill and Baker.

Sadurska, A. 1979. "Les antiquités de Nieborów (Musée National de Varsovie)." In *Actes du Colloque sur l'esclavage: Nieborów 1975, Prace Instytutu Historycznego Uniwersytetu Warszawskiego*, 7–21. Warsaw: University of Warsaw Press.

———. 1983. "L'histoire de deux pieces grecques dans la collection Radziwiłł au château de Nieborów." *Études et travaux* 13: 325–28.

Saliou, C. 2015. "Architecture and Society." In *A Companion to Ancient Aesthetics*, edited by P. Destée and P. Murray, 128–39. Chichester: Wiley Blackwell.

Salvemini, F., K. Sheedy, S. R. Olsen, M. Avdeev, J. Davis, and V. Luzin. 2018. "A Multi-Technique Investigation of the Incuse Coinage of Magna Graecia." *Journal of Archaeological Science: Reports Volume* 20: 748–55.

Salvesen, B. 2018. *3D: Double Vision*. Los Angeles: Los Angeles County Museum of Art.

Sapirstein, P. 2016. "The Columns of the Heraion at Olympia: Dörpfeld and Early Doric Architecture." *AJA* 120, no. 4: 565–601.

Şare, T. 2013. "The Sculpture of the Heroon of Perikle at Limyra: The Making of a Lycian King." *Anatolian Studies* 63: 55–74.

Schädler, U. 1991. "Attizismen an ionischen Tempeln Kleinasiens." *Istanbuler Mitteilungen*: 301–12.

Schenk, G. J. 2017. "Historical Disaster Experiences: First Steps Toward a Comparative and Transcultural History of Disasters across Asia and Europe in the Preindustrial Era." In *Historical Disaster Experiences: Towards a Comparative and Transcultural History of Disasters across Asia and Europe*, edited by G. J. Schenk, 3–44. Darmstadt: Springer.

Scherrer, P. 1999. "Bemerkungen zur Siedlungsgeschichte von Ephesos vor Lysimachos." In *100 Jahre Österreichische Forschungen in Ephesos, Akten des Symposions Wien 1995, AForsch 1*, edited by H. Friesinger, F. Krinzinger, 379–87. Vienna: Verlag der Österreichische Akademie der Wissenschaften.

Schiefsky, M. J. 2015. "*Technē* and Method in Ancient Artillery Construction: The *Belopoeica* of Philo of Byzantium." In *The Frontiers of Ancient Science: Essays in Honor of Heinrich von Staden*, edited by B. Holmes and K.-D. Fischer, 613–51. Berlin: De Gruyter.

Schlaifer, R. 1943. "The Cult of Athena Pallenis: (Athenaeus VI 234–235)." *Harvard Studies in Classical Philology* 54: 35–67.

Schmidt-Dounas, B. 2004. "Frühe Peripteraltempel in Nordgriechenland." *Mitteilungen des deutschen Archäologischen Instituts, Athenische Abteilung* 119: 107–41.

———. 2019. "Ionic or Doric." In *Listening to the Stones: Essays on Architecture and Function in Ancient Greek Sanctuaries in Honour of Richard Alan Tomlinson*, edited by E. Partida and B. Schmidt-Dounas, 11–19. Oxford: Archaeopress Archaeology.

Schneider, A. 1889. "Andokides." *Jahrbuch des Deutschen Archäologischen Instituts* 4: 195–207, pl. 4.

Scholten, J. B. 2000. *The Politics of Plunder: Aitolians and Their* Koinon *in the Early Hellenistic Era, 279–217 B.C.* Berkeley: University of California Press.

Schwandner, E.-L. 1985. *Der ältere Porostempel der Aphaia auf Aegina*. Berlin: De Gruyter.

Scott, M. C. 2014. *Delphi: A History of the Center of the Ancient World*. Princeton, NJ: Princeton University Press.

Seaford, R. 2004. *Money and the Early Greek Mind: Homer, Philosophy, Tragedy*. Cambridge: Cambridge University Press.

Seltman, C. 1949. "The Problem of the First Italiote Coinage." *Numismatic Chronicle and Journal of the Royal Numismatic Society* 9, no. 1/2: 1–21.

Sharpe, W. C. 2017. *Grasping Shadows: The Dark Side of Literature, Painting, Photography, and Film*. New

York: Oxford University Press.

Shaya, J. 2005. "The Greek Temple as Museum: The Case of the Legendary Treasure of Athena from Lindos." *AJA* 109, no. 3: 423–42.

Shear, T. L., Jr. 2016. *Trophies of Victory*. Princeton, NJ: Department of Art and Archaeology, Princeton University.

Sheedy, K. A., V. Luzin, F. Salvemini, P. Munroe, S. Olsen, U. Garbe, Max Avdeev, and T. Knowles. 2021. "Strange Objects and Strange Explanations: Understanding Incuse Coinages of South Italy by Non-Destructive Neutron Diffraction and Tomography." In *Interaction and Identity: Sicily and South Italy from the Iron Age to Late Antiquity*, edited by G. Shepherd, 253–74. Nicosia: Astrom Editions.

Shoe Meritt, L. S. 1982. "Some Ionic Architectural Fragments from the Athenian Agora." In "Studies in Athenian Architecture, Sculpture and Topography: Presented to Homer A. Thompson," supplement 20, *Hesperia*: 82–92, 204–205. Princeton, NJ: American School of Classical Studies at Athens.

———. 1993. "The Athenian Ionic Capital." *Symposium Papers XXII: Eius Virtutis Studiosi; Classical and Postclassical Studies in Memory of Frank Edward Brown*, edited by R. T. Scott and A. R. Scott, 314–25. Studies in the History of Art 43. Washington: National Gallery of Art.

———. 1996. "Athenian Ionic Capitals from the Athenian Agora." *Hesperia* 65, no. 2: 121–74.

Simpson, E. 1999. "Early Evidence for the Use of the Lathe in Antiquity." In *Meletemata: Studies in Aegean Archaeology Presented to Malcolm H. Wiener as He Enters His 65th Year*, edited by P. P. Betancourt, V. Karageorghis, R. Laffineur, and W.-D. Niemeier, 781–86. Aegaeum 20. Liège: University of Liège and the University of Texas at Austin.

Sioumpara, E. 2020. "Zerstörung und Wiederherstellung der Ordnung: Wiederverwendung von Baumaterialien in attischen Heiligtümern nach den Perserkriegen." In *Umgebaut: Umbau-, Umnutzungs- und Umwertungsprozesse in der antiken Architektur*, edited by K. Piesker, and U. Wulf-Rheidt, 91–110. Regensburg: Schnell and Steiner.

Sismanidis, K. 2012. "Ο υστεροαρχαϊκός ναός του Διός Σωτήρος και της Αθήνας Σώτειρας στα αρχαία Στάγειρα." In *ΘΡΕΠΤΗΡΙΑ*, edited by M. A. Tiverios, P. M. Nigdeles, and P. Adam-Veleni, 400–13. Thessaloniki: Α.Π.Θ.

———. 2021. "Μεταφέρθηκε ο υστεροαρχαϊκός ναός της Θεσσαλονίκης από τα αρχαία Στάγειρα;" In *25 années de recherches: Organisation de la ville et de la campagne dans les colonies du Nord de l'Égée VIIIᵉ–IIIᵉ siècles av. n.è. Actes du colloque de Thessalonique, 25-27 mai 2017*, 499–516. Athens: Canadian Institute in Greece.

Smith, A. E. 2010. "The Juxtaposition of Styles in the Metopes of the Athenian Treasury." MA thesis, University of North Carolina at Chapel Hill.

Smith, C. F. 1958. *Thucydides*. Loeb Classical Library. Cambridge, MA: Harvard University Press.

Sobak, R. 2015. "Sokrates among the Shoemakers." *Hesperia* 64, no. 4: 669–712.

Sourvinou-Inwood, C. 1979. "The Myth of the First Temples at Delphi." *Classical Quarterly* 29, no. 2: 231–51.

Spawforth, A.J.S. 2012. *Greece and the Augustan Cultural Revolution*. Cambridge: Cambridge University Press.

Stager, J. 2022. *Seeing Color in Classical Art: Theory, Practice, and Reception, from Antiquity to the Present*. Cambridge: Cambridge University Press.

Stanier, R. S. 1953. "The Cost of the Parthenon." *Journal of Hellenic Studies* 73: 68–76.

Stanton, G. R. 1984. "Some Attic Inscriptions." *Annual of the British School at Athens* 79: 289–306.

Stefanidou-Tiveriou, T. 2012. "Τα λατρευτικά αγάλματα του ναού του Διός και της Ρώμης στη Θεσσαλονίκη." In *Κλασική παράδοσηκαι νεωτερικά στοιχείαστην πλαστικήτης ρωμαϊκής Ελλάδας. Πρακτικά Διεθνούς Συνεδρίου Θεσσαλονίκη, 7–9 Μαΐου 2009*, edited by T. Stefanidou-Tiveriou, P. Karanastassi, and D. Damaskos, 273–86. Thessaloniki: University Studio Press.

Steimle, C. 2008. *Religion im römischen Thessaloniki: Sakraltopographie, Kult und Gesellschaft 168 v. Chr.–324 n. Chr. Studien und Texte zu Antike und Christentum 47*. Tübingen: Mohr Siebeck.

Steinbock, B. 2012. *Social Memory in Athenian Public Discourse*. Ann Arbor: University of Michigan Press.

Stevens, G. P., L. D. Caskey, J. M. Paton, and H. N. Fowler. 1927. *The Erechtheum: Measured, Drawn and Restored by Gorham Phillips Stevens*. Cambridge, MA: Harvard University Press.

Stewart, A. F. 2008. "The Persian and Carthaginian Invasions of 480 B.C.E. and the Beginning of the Classical Style: Part 2, the Finds from Other Sites in Athens, Attica, Elsewhere in Greece, and on Sicily; Part 3, the Severe Style: Motivations and Meaning." *AJA* 112, no. 4: 581–615.

———. 2013. "Die Invasionen der Perser und Karthager und der Beginn des Klassischen Stils." In *Zurück zur Klassik: Ein neuer Blick auf das alte Griechenland*, edited by V. Brinkmann, 132–43. Munich: Hirmer.

Stillwell, R. 1969. "The Panathenaic Frieze." *Hesperia* 38, no. 2: 231–41.

Stissi, V. V. 2002. "Pottery to the People: The Production, Distribution and Consumption of Decorated Pottery in the Greek World in the Archaic Period; (650–480 BC)." PhD diss., University of Amsterdam.

Stoyanova, D. 2022. *Строителна керамика и архитектурна теракота от Аполония Понтика (VI в. пр. Хр. — III в. пр. Хр.)*. Sofia: St. Kliment Ohridski University Press.

Stoyanova, D., and M. Damyanov. 2021. "Late Archaic and Early Classical Monumental Architecture on the Island of St. Kirik, Apollonia Pontike." In *Environment and Habitation around the Ancient Black Sea*, edited by D. Braund, V. F. Stolba, and U. Peter, 7–38. Berlin: De Gruyter.

Straub, N. 2019. *Studien zur ionischen Architektur auf der Peloponnes: Von den Anfängen in archaischer Zeit bis zum Ende der hellenistischen Epoche*. Wiesbaden: Harrassowitz.

Sutherland, C.H.V. 1948. "The 'Incuse' Coinages of South Italy." *Museum Notes (American Numismatic Society)* 3: 15–26.

Svenson-Evers, H. 1996. *Die griechischen Architekten archaischer und klassischer Zeit*. Archäologische Studien Bd. 11. Frankfurt: Peter Lang.

Tasia, A., Z. Lola, and O. Peltekis. 2000. "Θεσσαλονίκη – Ο υστεροαρχαϊκός ναός." *AEM Θ* 14: 227–46.

Theodorescu, D. 1968. "Un chapiteau ionique de l'époque archaïque tardive et quelques problèmes concernant le style, à Histria." *Dacia* 12: 261–303.

———. 1974. *Chapiteaux Ioniques de la Sicile Méridionale*. Naples: Centre Jean Bérard.

———. 1980. *Le Chapiteau Ionique Grec: Essai Monographique*. Hautes Études du Monde Gréco-Romain 11. Geneva: Droz.

Theodorescu, D., and H. Tréziny. 2000. "Le chapiteau ionique archaïque de Marseille." In *Les cultes des cités phocéennes*, edited by A. Hermary and H. Tréziny, 135–46. Aix-en-Provence: Edisud.

Thompson, H. A. 1960. "Activities in the Athenian Agora: 1959." *Hesperia* 29: 327–68.

Thonemann, P. 2016. *The Hellenistic World: Using Coins as Sources*. Cambridge: Cambridge University Press.

Threpsiades, J., and E. Vanderpool. 1965. "Themistokles' Sanctuary of Artemis Aristoboule." *AΔ* 19: 26–36, pls. 16–21, plans 1–2.

Tilia, B. 1978. *Studies and Restorations at Persepolis and Other Sites of Fārs*. Rome: ISMEO.

Tiverios, M. 1990. "Από τα απομεινάρια ενός προελληνιστικού ιερού ‹περί τον Θερμαίον Κόλπον.› " In *Πόλις και χώρα στην αρχαία Μακεδονία και Θράκη: Μνήμη Δ. Λαζαρίδη; Πρακτικά αρχαιολογικού συνεδρίου, Καβάλα 9 - 11 Μαϊου 1986*, 71–80. Thessaloniki: Hypourgeio Politismou, École française d'Athènes.

Tomlinson, R. A. 1963. "The Doric Order: Hellenistic Critics and Criticism." *Journal of Hellenic Studies* 83: 133–45.

Toner, J. 2013. *Roman Disasters*. Malden, MA: Polity Press.

Townsend, R. F. 2004. "Classical Signs and Anti-Classical Signification in 4th-Century Athenian Architecture." In *ΧΑΡΙΣ: Essays in Honor of Sara A. Immerwahr*, edited by A. P. Chapin, 305–26. Princeton, NJ: American School of Classical Studies at Athens.

Trell, B. L. 1942. "Architectura Numismatica Part II: Temples in Asia Minor." PhD diss., New York University.

Tuchelt, K. 1991. "Branchidai-Didyma: Geschichte, Ausgrabung und Wiederentdeckung eines Antiken Heiligtums." *Antike Welt* 22: 2–54.

———. 1994. "Notizen über Ausgrabung und Denkmalpflege in Didyma: Hubert Knackfuss in Erinnerung an seine Zeit der Tempelgrabung 1906 bis 1913." *Antike Welt* 25, no. 1: 2–31.

Tuplin, C. 2004. "Xenophon, Artemis and Scillus." In *Spartan Society*, edited by T. J. Figueira, 251–81. Swansea: Classical Press of Wales.

Tzochev, C. 2021. "The Architecture of the 4th Century B.C. Monumental Tomb at Starosel." *Archäologischer Anzeiger* 2021/2022: 1–120

Umholtz, G. 2002. "Architraval Arrogance? Dedicatory Inscriptions in Greek Architecture of the Classical Period." *Hesperia* 71, no. 3: 261–93.

Vallois, R. 1966. *L'architecture hellénique et hellénistique à Délos jusqu'à l'éviction des Déliens (166 av. J.-C.)*. Paris: E. de Boccard.

Vanhove, D. 1994. "The Laurion Revisited." In *Studies in South Attica 2*, edited by H. F. Mussche, 30–75. Ghent: Belgian Archaeological School in Greece.

Van Zanten, D. 1977. "Architectural Composition at the École des Beaux-Arts from Charles Percier to Charles Garnier." In *The Architecture of the École des Beaux-Arts*, edited by A. Drexler, 111–325. Cambridge, MA: MIT Press.

Velkov, V., and L. Domaradzka. 1994. "Kotys I (383/2-359 av. J.C.) et l'emporion Pistiros de Thrace." *BCH* 118: 1–15.

Vera, J. R. 2018. "How to Move a God: Shifting Religion and Imperial Identities in Roman Athens." PhD diss. University of Chicago.

Veyne, P. 1988. "Conduct without Belief and Works of Art without Viewers." Translated by J. Ferguson. *Diogenes* 36, no. 143: 1–22.

Vickers, M. 1972. "Hellenistic Thessaloniki." *Journal of Hellenic Studies* 92: 156–70.

Vieira, A. 2019. *On the Rock: The Acropolis Interviews*. Chicago: Soberscove Press.

Vince, J. H. 1930. *Demosthenes I: Olynthiacs, Philippics, Minor Public Speech against Leptines I–XVII, XX*. Loeb Classical Library 238. Cambridge, MA: Harvard University Press.

Vishwanath, D. 2006. "Coplanar Reflectance Change and the Ontology of Surface Perception." In *Visual Thought: The Depictive Space of Perception*, edited by L. Albertazzi, 35–70. Amsterdam: John Benjamins.

———. 2014. "Toward a New Theory of Stereopsis." *Psychological Review* 121, no. 2: 151–78.

Vitti, M. 1996. *Η πολεοδομική εξέλιξη της Θεσσαλονίκης από την ίδρυσή της έως τον Γαλέριο*. Athens: Archaeological Society of Athens.

Vokotopoulou, J. P. 1993. "Nouvelles données sur l'architecture archaïque en Macédoine centrale et en Chalcidique." In *Les Grands Ateliers d'architecture dans le monde égéen du VIe siècle av. J.-C. Actes du colloque d'Istanbul, 23–25 mai 1991*, edited by J. des Courtils and J.-C. Moretti, 89–95. Istanbul: Institut Français d'Études Anatoliennes-Georges Dumézil.

Voutiras, E. 1999. "Η λατρεία της Αφροδίτης στην περιοχή του Θερμαίου κόλπου" *6ο Διεθνές Συμπόσιο για την Αρχαία Μακεδονία 1996*: 1329–43.

Wallace, R. 2009. "Plato, Poikilia, and New Music in Athens." In *Poikilia: Variazioni sul tema*, edited by E. Berardi, F. L. Lisi, D. Micalella, 201–13. Acireale: Bonanno.

Walsh, J. 1986. "The Date of the Athenian Stoa at Delphi." *AJA* 90, no. 3: 319–36.

Waters, M. J. 2012. "A Renaissance without Order: Ornament, Single-Sheet Engravings, and the Mutability of Architectural Prints." *Journal of the Society of Architectural Historians* 71, no. 4: 488–523.

Welter, G. 1939. "Datierte Altare in Athen." *Jahrbuch des Deutschen Archäologischen Instituts* 54: 23–35.

Wescoat, B. D. 1987. "Designing the Temple of Athena at Assos: Some Evidence from the Capitals." *AJA* 91, no. 4: 553–68.

———. 2012a. *The Temple of Athena at Assos*. Oxford: Oxford University Press.

———. 2012b. "Coming and Going in the Sanctuary of the Great Gods, Samothrace." In *Architecture of the Sacred: Space, Ritual, and Experience from Classical Greece to Byzantium*, edited by B. D. Wescoat and R. G. Ousterhout, 66–113. Cambridge: Cambridge University Press.

———. 2018. *The Monuments of the Eastern Hill*. Samothrace 9. Princeton, NJ: American School of Classical Studies at Athens.

Wescoat, B. D., and R. Levitan. 2017. "Seeing the Parthenon Frieze: Notes from Nashville." In *Greek Art in Context: Archaeological and Art Historical Perspectives*, edited by Rodríguez Pérez, 57–72. London: Routledge.

White, D. 1971. "The Cyrene Sphinx, Its Capital and Its Column." *AJA* 75, no. 1: 47–55.

Williams, C. K., II. 1984. "Doric Architecture and Early Capitals in Corinth." *Athenische Mitteilungen* 97: 67–75.

Wilson Jones, M. 1991. "Designing the Roman Corinthian Capital." *Papers of the British School at Rome* 59: 89–151.

———. 2002. "Tripods, Triglyphs, and the Origin of the Doric Frieze." *AJA* 106, no. 3: 353–90.

———. 2014. *Origins of Classical Architecture: Temples, Orders, and Gifts to the Gods in Ancient Greece*. New Haven, CT: Yale University Press.

Winter, F. E. 2006. *Studies in Hellenistic Architecture*. Toronto: University of Toronto Press.

Witcombe, C.L.C.E. 2018. *Eye and Art in Ancient Greece: A Study in Archaeoaesthetics*. Turnhout: Harvey Miller Publishers.

Wölfflin, H. 1896. "Wie man Skulpturen aufnehmen soll." *Zeitschrift für Bildende Kunst* 7: 224–28.

Yegül, F. K. 2014. "A Victor's Message: The Talking Column of the Temple of Artemis at Sardis." *Journal of the Society of Architectural Historians* 73, no. 2: 204–25.

Yerkes, C. Y. 2017. *Drawing after Architecture: Renaissance Architectural Drawings and Their Reception*. Venezia: Marsilio.

Young, W. J., and B. Ashmole. 1968. "The Boston Relief and the Ludovisi Throne." *Boston Museum Bulletin* 66, no. 346: 124–66.

Zambas, K. 2002. *Οι εκλεπτύνσεις των κιόνων του Παρθενώνος*. Athens: YSMA.

Zhmud, L. 2012. *Pythagoras and the Early Pythagoreans*. Translated by K. Windle and R. Ireland. Oxford: Oxford University Press.

Zink, S. March. 2019. "Polychromy, Architectural, Greek and Roman." *Oxford Research Encyclopedia of Classics*: https://doi.org/10.1093/acrefore/9780199381135.013.8184.

Zink, S., M. Taschner, I. Reiche, M. Alfeld, C. Aibéo, E. Egel, K. Müller, A. Ristau, B. Neuhaus, W. Massmann. 2019. "Tracing the Colours of Hermogenes' Temple of Artemis: Architectural Surface Analysis in the Antikensammlung Berlin." *Techne* 48: 14–26.

Zuchtriegel, G. 2017. *Colonization and Subalternity in Classical Greece: Experience of the Nonelite Population*. New York: Cambridge University Press.

———. 2023. *The Making of the Doric Temple: Architecture, Religion, and Social Change in Archaic Greece*. Cambridge: Cambridge University Press.

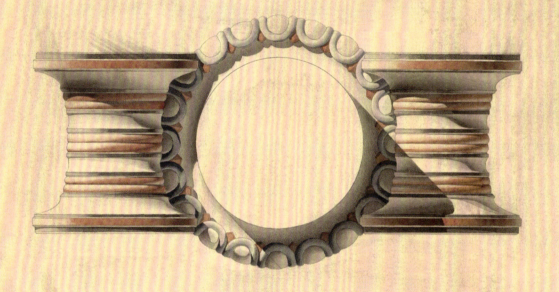

Index Locorum

Texts

Anth. Pal.
   7.441: 241n88

Aristophanes
  Ran.
    40
  Vesp.
    121–23: 245n12

Aristotle
  Cael.
    298a2–10: 108
  Rh.
    1398b: 32

Athenaeus
   6.26: 195
   8.62: 204

Cicero
  Academica
    2.7.20: 109

Demosthenes
   9.26: 130

Diodorus Siculus
   4.4.1: 247n56

Diogenes Laertius
   5.16: 133

Galen
  Simpl. Med.
    4.1: 241n95

Herakleitos
   Aet. ii.24 3: 100, 245n43

Herodotus
   1.29: 20
   1.49: 79
   1.52: 79
   1.62: 195
   1.64: 56
   1.92: 207
   2.48–49: 248n88
   2.121: 241n62
   4.99.5: 241
   5.7: 120
   5.51: 26
   6.43–45: 119
   6.46: 117, 247n26
   7.111: 247n57, 248n86
   9.28: 173

Hesiod
  Op.
    109–201: 239n13

Homer
  Od.
    7.88–90: 164

Hymn. Hom. Ap.
   43

Hypereides
   Fr. 80: 248n85

Livy
   40.4.9: 248

Lucian
  Iupp. trag.
    33: 241n102
  Hist. conscr.
    62: 241n62

Ovid
  Fast.
    1.305: 246n70

Pausanias
   3.18.4: 26
   4.31.8: 251
   5.10.3: 243n52
   5.20.6–7: 31
   10.11.6: 225
   10.15.4–5: 220
   10.15.2: 220, 222
   10.15.7: 220

Philo
  Bel.
    50.30: 12

Pindar
  Pae. 8: 164, 239n13

Plato
  Leg.
    955e–956a: 38, 242n107
  Phdr.
    260c: 246n65
  Resp.
    514a–520a: 107–108

Pliny
  HN
    7.198: 243n64
    35.40: 106
    35.29: 246n61
    36.90: 62
    36.95: 17, 20, 240n24, 241n95
    36.97: 20, 251n7
    36.179: 200

Plutarch
  Vit. Alex.
    1.3.5: 206

Vit. Them.
   22: 38
Vit. Thes.
   13: 195
Vit. Per.
   14.2: 207

[Plutarch]
  X orat.
    841f: 40

Porphyry
  Abst.
    2.18: 239n13

Ptolemy
  Geo.
    1.18: 241n95

Sappho
  fr.1: 164

Sophocles
  Phil.
    946: 246n65

Strabo
  4.1.4: 38, 232
  7.fr.24:130, 248n83
  7.4.2: 247n44
  14.1.4: 204
  14.1.20: 252n40
  14.1.21: 251n7
  14.1.22: 207, 252n39

Theophrastus
  Char.
    9.2: 247n46
  Hist. pl.
    5.4.2: 17

Thucydides
  1.10: 12
  1.25.4: 121
  2.15: 251n94
  3.104: 43, 56
  3.104.3–4: 42
  3.104.3: 199
  4.69: 26
  5.82: 26
  6.54: 153

Vitruvius
  1.1.2: 107
  1.1.12: 109
  1.2.2: 35, 100
  1.3.2: 24
  2.1.1–7:12
  3.4.4: 246n15
  3.5.7–10: 67
  3.5.8: 253n78
  3.5.10:68
  3.5.14: 79
  4.1.4–8: 2
  4.1.7–8: 12
  4.1.7: 200, 207
  4.1.8: 239n8
  4.2.1–5: 5
  4.2.2: 12, 15, 158
  4.3.1: 26
  4.4.2–3: 246n60
  4.4.2: 229
  4.4.3: 95, 245n48
  4.4.4: 101, 229
  7.praef.16: 202

Xenophanes
  fr.18: 12, 239n12

Xenophon
  An.
    5.3.7–13: 36, 241n104
    5.3.12: 38
  Hell.
    7.5.22: 242n106
  Oec.
    10.1: 242n106

Inscriptions

IEphesos
  1518: 207

IG I^3
  35: 27, 241n63
  46: 248n87
  101: 247n27
  476: 249n30
  948: 249n3
  1464: 243n55

IG II^2
  128: 119, fig. 4.9
  564: 27
  680: 253n99
  1672: 241n66
  1678: 28, 231, 241n68, 241n69

IG II/III^3 1,
  1007: 27

IG IV^2 1
  102: 240n51

IG VII
  3073: 27

IG XI 2
  161: 243n38, 243n48, 243n49
  287: 243n55

IG XII 5
  109: 247n32

IMylasa
  869: 244n84 (*see also* general index: *epiphanestatos topos*)

SEG
  34, 157: 251n100
  49, 911: 120 (*see also* general index: Pistiros Inscription)

General Index

abacus moldings, 167, 187, 235. *See also specific capitals; specific locations*
Achaemenid Empire, 206–7
Acharnai, 135, 196
acrolithic sculpture, 161
Acropolis (Athens): Asklepieion, 185; Ionic capitals from votive, 166, 189–90, 191, 192; korai, 166, 250n45; model for imitation, 226, 232, 233; Persian sack of, 153, 166, 185; Restoration Service, 85; site 35–36, 164, 166, 167. *See also* Akr. 135; Athena Nike, temple of; Erechtheion; Kallimachos Nike and its Ionic capital; Kekrops, tomb of; Parthenon; Propylaia; Thrasyllos, monument of
Aemilius Paullus, 212
Aeneas, 131, 248n92
Aeolian Greeks, 5
Aeolic capitals and "order," 2, 7, 45, 53, 76, 77, 79, 80, 81, 192
aesthetics, 12, 24, 33–34, 41, 101, 102. *See also* architecture: developmental narratives of; *poikilia*; proportions
Aetolians: and Delphi, 221–22, 225, 226; league (*koinon*) of, 220, 221, 222, 225; monuments of elite (Charixenos, Lykos), 217, 221–22, 225. *See also* Delphi; Delphi, Aristaineta Monument and its capitals
agency, distributed model of, 7, 26, 231
Agora (Athens): Enneakrounos fountain, 191–92; Ionic capitals from, 166, 167, 176; itinerant temples and, 131, 148, 193; Odeion of Agrippa, 148; romanization of, 148; Southeast Fountain House, 191–92; Southeast Temple, 148 (*see also* Sounion: temple of Athena); Southwest Temple, 148 (*see also* Thorikos, Stoa at); stoa of Attalos, 170, 192; temple of Ares, 131, 135, 142, 148, 194; 166, 167, 180–81 (*see also* Pallene (Attica): temple of Athena Pallenis); statues of the Tyrannicides, 148. *See also* Agora polychrome capitals; Agora A616; Inwood capital and Agora A3345
Agora A616, 178, 180, 189–92, 196
Agora A3345. *See* Inwood capital and Agora A3345
Agora polychrome capitals (A2972/A2973), 169–71 177, 189–90, 192, 193
Aigina, sanctuary of Aphaia. pediment sculpture of, 14; polychromy of temples, 157, 158, 159, 229; votive sphinx column, 81
Aineia, 129, 130
Aischylos, 40
Akr. 135, 166, 167, 244n3
Akr. 3776. *See* Kallimachos Nike and its Ionic capital
Akragas, temple of Zeus, 16–17
Alâzeytin, Karia 81
Alexander, Jeffrey, 206–7
Alexander the Great, 31, 129, 206
Altar of Apollo Pythios (Athens), 151, 154–55
Alzinger, Wilhelm, 9, 201, 202, 204, 205
Amandry, Pierre, 220
American School of Classical Studies, Athens, 182
Amphiareion, location of, 79, 245n12
Amphictyony: Delian, 28; Delphic, 220

Amphipolis, 106–7
Amyklai, throne of Apollo, 26, 27, 240n59
anachronism, 33. *See also* archaism
Anatolia, 131, 149. *See also* Karia; Lydia; Phrygia; *specific locations*
Anaxagoras of Klazomenai, 108
Andokides Painter, 9, 23
Androklos, 204
animal sacrifice, 120, 247n46
anthemion: carved molding, 133, 216; convex-concave alternation in, 229, 231, 91–93; frieze, 95–96; Samian type grave stelai, 92, 95
Antigonidon Plateia (Thessaloniki), 123, 127, 131, 133, 146, 248n60
Antissara, 116
Antoninus Pius, 205
Aphrodite: Aphrodite Aineias, 110, 129, 131–32, 134, 149; sailing and, 131, 205
Apollo. *See specific locations*
Apollodorus of Athens, 106
Apollonia (Mygdonia), 130
Apollonia Pontica, 91, 93
Apollonios of Perge, 104
archaeology of the past, defined, 6
archaeological reconstruction drawing, 9, 18, 56
Archaic style in Greek art, 12, 14
archaism: in architecture, 6, 39–40, 180–81, 192, 242n115; in relief sculpture, 6; in vase painting, 22
Archilochos capital (Paros), 32–34
Archilochos of Paros, 32, 33, 116
Archipenko, Alexander, 99–100, 245n39
architects: autonomy and collaboration, 26–28; drawings and specifications (*syngraphai*) by, 27, 35; education of, 109; fines for, 27–28; *hypoarchitekton* (assistant architect), 28; itinerancy of, 6–7, 25, 202; local origin, 26; as polymath, 246n73; oversight by, 28; salary of, 241n66. *See also* Vitruvius
architectural drawing, 12, 101. *See also* drawing
architectural energetics analysis, 245n26
architecture: copying in, 34–35; developmental narratives of, 12, 39–40; mathematics in, 103–4. *See also* architects; architectural drawing; regionalism in architecture
Archon Basileus, 195–96
Argead Dynasty, 129
Aristaineta. *See* Delphi, Aristaineta Monument and its capitals
Aristarchos of Samos, 108
Aristophanes, 40
Aristotle, 108
Arkadia, garden (Poland) 46–47
Artemis Ephesia: festival of, 43, 199; replication of cult statue, 36, 38, 231, 242n108. *See also* Ephesos, temple of Artemis Ephesia; Massalia: cult of Artemis Ephesia; Skillous, temple of Artemis Ephesia
Artemis Leukophryene, 26. *See also* Magnesia on the Maeander, temple of Artemis Leukophryene
Artemis Tauropolos, 120

Asklepios, sanctuary of, 27
Assos, temple of Athena, 24–25, 68-9, 240n50, 248n73
astragal, 167, 235
astronomical observation, 108–9, 246n70
Athenaeus, 195, 204
Athena Nike, temple of (Athens) 27, 68, 71, 73, 177, 182, 187, 189, 197
Athena Pallenis: league of, 196; *parasitoi*, 194–95. *See also* Agora (Athens): temple of Ares; Pallene (Attica): temple of Athena Pallenis
Athena Parthenos, 120, 246n7
Athena Trecheia, temple of, 1, 3, 22, 232
Athenodoros, 241n66
Athens: archaistic style in architecture in, 6; Assembly of, 117; capital preservation in, 165–66; committee of officials in, 40–41; conflicts of, 117; contrasting of, 12; defeat of, 40; destruction of, 6; Dipylon Gate of, 148; Empire of, 130, 152, 198; Hephaisteion, 104; invasion of, 194–95; Ionic order in, 150, 151–53, 192, 196; Long Walls, 27; painting at, 150, 152, 167; Pompeion, 167; reuse of architecture in, 6; Roman Agora, 11; stone-workers from, 26; temple of Artemis Aristoboule, 38–39; temple of Olympian Zeus, 16–17. *See also* Acropolis; Agora
Athens, National Archaeological Museum, 76, 182
Attica, 185, 194–95. *See also specific locations*
Attic style in Ionic architecture, 150, 152–54, 179, 182, 190, 218
Augustus, 129, 131, 133, 134

Baiae, 36
Bakalakis, Giorgos, 111, 112, 122–23, 130–31, 134, 145
Balandat, Luisa, 95
Baltes, Elizabeth, 148
balteus, 172, 177, 184, 188, 218, 235
Bammer, Anton, 9, 14, 95, 200, 202, 204, 205
Barker, Alfred Winslow, 102–3
base, column: Attic type, 150; Ephesian type, 124, 133, 146, 198; Samian type, 124, 146
Bassai: Ionic order at, 40, 49; temple of Apollo, 40
Bathykles of Magnesia, 26
Baxandall, Michael, 109
bead-and-reel motif, 124, 127, 145, 225, 235
Beazley, John, 22–23
Bendis, 110, 120
bicolumn monuments: at Delphi, 212–13, 221, 225, 226; at Olympia, 213; and Roman wall painting, 213. *See also* Delphi, Aristaineta Monument and its capitals
bilingual Attic vases, 9, 22–24, 28, 228
bilingual Ionic capitals: adornment of, 161; agency in production, 7, 26–27; Archaic elements on, 31; architectural tradition in, 6; bilingual, defined, 7; carving practices of, 7, 81–91 (*see also* carving); characteristics of, 10, 22, 41; charm of, 232–33; conditional visibility of, 7, 65–75 (*see also* visibility); copying of, 233; orientation of (inside/outside), 8, 228–31; origin of, 42, 228, 231; retrospective aspect of, 9–10, 231, 233; as transitional, 14; transmission of information regarding, 36; unfinished features of, 228, 229. *See also specific capitals; specific locations*
black-figure technique, 22, 23, 28
Boardman, John, 14
Boccioni, Umberto, 245n39
Boehm, Ryan, 130, 134–35, 145–46
Boeotian League, 27

bolster/pulvinus: comparison of, 51; illustration of, 97, 235; painting schemes for, 164; balteus patterns of, 162; variation of, 170, 188–89. *See also specific locations*
Brauron, 152
Brinkmann, Vinzenz, 169
building accounts, 25, 26, 161
buildings: in chronological sequence of styles, 6, 11; as heterogeneous, 14; looking at the past through, 31–41; proportion of, 12. *See also specific locations*
Burger, Wilhelm, 96
Burkert, Walter, 73

canalis, 51, 52, 166, 235. *See also specific locations*
canon, creation of, 40
capitals: Aeolic capitals, 2, 76, 79; carving of, 86, 142; center of gravity of, 44; corner capitals, 18, 20, 44, 46, 68; Doric capitals, 15–16, 25; echinus capitals (Ionic capitals without volutes), 18, 64; illustration of, 46, 47, 52, 57, 65, 70, 143, 234; inscriptions on, 32–33, 68, 143, 145; model (*paradeigma*), 28; proportional design of, 14, 24; transporting of, 142; *See also* Ionic capitals; *specific capitals; specific locations*
Carpo, Mario, 34
carving: experiment, 85–91, 228–29; illustration of, 82; of Ionic capitals, 81–91; master carver for, 231; prices for, 85; re-, 145; sanding process in, 90, 91; stealing the art of, 88; techniques of, 62–63; workflows for, 88–90. *See also* tools for stone carving; *specific locations*
caryatids, 35, 241n101. *See also* Erechtheion (Athens): caryatid porch of
Cassander, 129, 130, 135
casts. *See* plaster casts in antiquity
Çatallar Tepe, 64–65
Catania, 210
Catherine the Great of Russia, 47, 48
ceiling coffers, 157
Chaironeia, battle of, 40
Chalastre, 130
chiaroscuro, 100–101, 106, 107, 109; reflected light, 106. *See also* shadows
Chios, temple at Emporio, 160. See also Delphi: Chian Altar
chisels. *See* tools for stone carving
chronological sequence, 6, 11, 14
chryselephantine medium, 164, 250n40
Cicero, 109
clamps, 56, 135, 245n27, 251n82
Classical period, 152, 170, 185, 198, 202, 206, 221, 232
Claudius, 133
cloisonné jewelry, 162, 164
coinage, 29, 117–18, 119, 205
collaboration, in design, 23, 27–28
colonies (*apoikiai*), defined, 111, 246n1
colonnade: elements of, 234; painting of, 106–7; permeable boundaries and, 73; shadow design in, 101
color. *See* painting; pigments; polychromy, architectural
columns: as grave markers, 32, 151; historical value of, 32; illustration of, 234; inscription on, 20, 32, 33, 68; interior, 243n63; misalignment of roofs and, 146–47; optical illusions and, 103; peristyle, 44, 68, 229; polychromy of, 106–7, 156, 169; proportions of, 44, 67; shadow design of, 99–109; symbolic interpretations of, 32, 72; turning, 62–63, 243n64; variations of, 231; visibility and, 67, 68; votive, 2, 7, 14, 77, 79, 166, 185.

General Index 275

See also specific capitals; specific elements; specific locations

Composite order, 11

conditional visibility. *See* visibility

connoisseurship: in architecture, 241n71; in vase painting, 23

convex-concave elements: alternating of, 91, 96, 97; carving practices for, 82, 84, 85, 87–88; characteristics of, 42, 70, 71; coloristic use of, 99; defined, 1; depth, 248n73; in floral motifs, 92; in fluting, 103; illustration of, 97, 98, 126; in marble test, 85–91, 228–29; origin of, 6; in ornament, 91–99; overview of, 30; retrospective design and, 6; sanding process for, 90; sculptural styles of, 196; shading and, 99–109; workflows for carving of, 88–90. *See also specific locations*

Conze, Alexander, 96

copy: ancient accounts of, 36–37, 232–33; changing notions in Ancient, Medieval, and Renaissance architecture, 34–36; of cult statues, 36–38; of manuscript illustrations, 34–35; replacement pieces in architecture, 145, 204

Corinth: Peloponnesian War, 121; South Stoa Corinth, 172; temple of Apollo, 13, 104

Corinthian order, 11, 40, 73, 75

corner capital, 20, 44–45. *See also specific locations*

cornice, 157, 216. *See also specific locations*

Coulton, J. J., 26, 240n50, 245n44

Courby, Fernand, 213, 220

Courtils, Jacques de, 129

craft (*techne*), 88

crepidoma, 234

Crimean Peninsula, 120. *See also* Pantikapaion

cubism, 99, 100

cult: of Aeneas, 248n92; at Amyklai, 26; of Aphrodite Aineias, 130, 131, 132, 134; of Artemis, 38; of Artemis Ephesia, 38, 231, 232; of Athena Pallenis, 194, 195, 196, 204; of Athena Parthenos, 246n7; at Athenian Acropolis, 226; of Dionysos Thermaios, 130–31, 134, 248n86; features of, 164–65; hero/ancestor, 120; historical elements of, 7; Imperial, 110, 129; inscriptions and, 68, 120; of Mater Idaea, 131; mystery, 73; at Neapolis, 246n7; of Parthenos, 110, 112, 116, 117, 120, 121, 232; poliad/civic, 120, 121; syncretic, 7, 117; Thracian, 120; tomb, 120

cult statues, 6, 36, 38, 68, 71, 73, 119, 121, 131, 132, 134, 149, 165, 202, 231

Cyclades/Cyclades capitals, 14, 25, 44, 79, 109, 153, 178, 190

cyma reversa, 51, 182, 187, 216, 235

Daumet, Honoré, 112

Delian League, 117, 219

Delos: architecture of, 42, 218; Athens and, 28, 56; building inscription from, 28, 231; columns from, 32–33; corner capitals on, 8; Doric order from, 13; *dromos*, 53, 54; excavation of, 44, 45; festival of Apollo on, 43; inventory lists, 53; Ionic order and, 1, 8, 42, 73, 196; location of, 42; Museum, 44; *naopoioi* of, 28; Naxian quarter (*Quartier Naxien*), 54; Oikos of the Naxians, 53, 54, 56–61; pan-Ionian status of, 43; plan of, 54; *porinos naos*, 54, 55–56; Propylon (phases I, II, and III), 53–58, 61, 66; Stoa of Philip V, 49; votive Ionic columns at, 32, 56, 79, 81, 176

Delos, bilingual Ionic capitals from: attribution to *porinos naos*, 55–56; attribution to Propylon II, 53, 56–57; attachments of, 51, 52, 53; bilingualism of, 50; carving depth of, 87; comparison of capitals, 49–51, 52, 55; corner capital provenance, description of, 51–53, 230, 231, 243n34, 243n35–37; Henri-Paul Nénot's drawing of, 44, 45–47; high-relief sides of, 230; illustration of, 45, 48, 49, 50, 52, 70, 71; Ionic capitals and, 45–46; Nieborów capital provenance, 46–49; origin of bilingual type, 1, 8, 42, 196; overview of, 44–53; Pheia (Olympia Museum) capital provenance, 49; regional style unity in, 231; report regarding, 45; volute eye of, 52; votive dedication on, 56

Delphi: Chian altar, 225; column of Drusilla, 213; Daochos Monument, 216, 223–24; festivals at, 210, 221; museum, 213; Naxian Sphinx column, 79, 174, 175; oracle, 79, 204, 210, 221; pillar monuments, 212, 252n62; Pillar of Aemilius Paullus, 212; Pillar of Prusias II, 212, 220; sanctuary of Apollo, 210–11, 221; Siphnian treasury, 91, 92, 216; statue of Apollo Sitalkas, 220; Stoa of the Athenians, 188, 218, 225, 227, 232; temple of Apollo, 40, 199, 219, 239n13; temple terrace, 210–12, 217, 219; tripod of Gelon, 220. *See also* Aetolians; Delphi, Aristaineta Monument and its capitals

Delphi, Aristaineta Monument and its capitals: Aetolians and, 221; Aristaineta (patron), 199, 216, 232; archaistic features of, 225; attachment to capitals, 217; bolster design, 218, 225; comparison of, 217, 225, 226; contextual views of, 221, 223, 224; convex-concave features of, 217–18, 225; corner palmettes on, 203, 221; cornice of, 216; dating of, 220; dedications and, 221; description of, 210–13, 216–17, 221, 225, 227, 230; echinus of, 217; elements of, 214; elevation of, 215, 223; findspot of, 212; floral motifs of, 225; frieze of, 216; illustration of, 212, 214–19, 223–24; inscriptions on, 214, 216; location of, 220; overview of, 210–27; preservation of, 213; reconstruction of, 217, 220; restoration of, 219; significance of, 226; statue group on, 216, 222; topography of, 223–24; visibility of, 222–24; volutes of, 217, 25

Demosthenes, 130

dentils, 5, 165

Desypris, Giorgos, 85

Didyma: Archaic capitals from, 242n8; architect of, 202; naiskos of the temple of Apollo (late Classical dipteral), 216; sack by Persians, 198; temple of Apollo, Archaic dipteral, 17, 64, 231

Dillon, Sheila, 217, 222

Diogenes Laertius, 133

Dionysia, 40, 248n88

Dionysos, 35, 120, 129

Dionysos Thermaios, 110, 130–31, 132, 134, 149, 232. *See also* Thessaloniki, itinerant temple and its capitals

dipteral plan, 38, 62–63

disaster studies, 206–7

Dokimos, 33, 34

doors: Aeolic pilasters, 80–81; Ionic doorframes, 128–29

Doric order: architectural canon formation in, 40; Athens and, 151, 193; capitals, 49–51; changes to, 12; comparison of, 2, 13, 166; description of, 12; fluting in, 22, 61, 103–6, 229, 246n54, 248n73; Julien-David Le Roy and, 11–13; mixed Ionic features in, 26; origin stories of, 2, 5, 15; parallel of, 11, 46; polychromy of 157–58, 166, 172–73; proportions of, 11–12; Selinous and, 210, 226; stylistic chronology of, 11–12, 14. *See also* metopes; triglyphs; *specific monuments*

Dörpfeld, Wilhelm, 15

dovetailing, 187, 251n82

drawing: archaeological reconstruction, 9, 18, 56; architectural, 12, 101; perspective, 100; and Vitruvius, 35, 100
Drusilla, 212, 213

Early Iron Age, 117
East-Ionian style, 42, 43, 44, 61, 178
echinus: comparison of, 51, 182, 187; egg-and-dart, 50; fluted, 64, 65; illustration of, 235; painting of, 167, 168–69. *See also specific capitals; specific locations*
eclecticism, 111, 127, 131, 178, 225, 226
eclipses, 30, 100, 108
École des Beaux-Arts, 45, 46, 99
egg-and-dart motif, 50, 127, 157, 169, 175, 182, 192, 235. *See also specific capitals; specific locations*
Egypt: background of builder in Athens, 26; Egyptianizing style, 45, 192. *See also* Naukratis, temple of Apollo
Eleusis: building accounts, 241n66; Greater Propylaia, 35–37, 144; Telesterion, 249n4, temple of Artemis Propylaia, 36
Elgin, Lord, 48
encaustic painting, 156
entablature, 234
epiphanestatos topos ("the most visible location"), 102. *See also* visibility
Ephesos: Archaic form at, 199; development of, 203; festival of Artemis Ephesia in, 43, 199; foundation of, 206; grief in, 206–7; importance of, 199; location of, 198; myth regarding, 204; origin of, 204; origin of Ionic order at, 1, 8, 232; reorganization of, 206; Selçuk Museum, 200; temple burning at, 1; temple of Apollo Pythios, 204; temple of Artemis in, 1, 2; topography of, 204–5. *See also* Ephesos, temple of Artemis Ephesia; Ephesos, temple of Athena Trecheia and its capitals
Ephesos, temple of Artemis Ephesia (Artemision): anthemion, 95–97; bases, 18; capitals from, 1–3, 18–20, 63–64; column flutes, 18–19, 124; construction, 17–18; copies of, 36, 38; description of, 2, 17, 38, 200, 206; destruction of, 1, 198, 199, 206, 226; donations for, 20; eclecticism and, 17, 20, 24; 36, 38; excavation of, 124; illustrations of, 2–3, 18, 19, 20, 39; ornament of, 17–20, 24; sculpture of, 18
Ephesos, temple of Athena Trecheia and its capitals: bolster design of, 202, 204; carving depth of, 87; comparison of, 202, 204; convex-concave elements of, 200–201, 226–27; corner capital of, 204; dating of, 200, 202; description of, 200, 203, 230; discovery of, 204; distribution of, 202; identification with temple of Athena Trecheia, 1, 204–5, 207; illustration of, 3, 199, 201, 203; orientation of, 230; preservation of lost architectural forms, 1, 232; variations of, 200; volutes of, 201–2, 204; workshops and, 203
Epidauros: Abaton, 27; building accounts, 27–28, 241n66; propylon, 71; Tholos, 216
epigram, 33
Erechtheion (Athens): anthemion, 91; caryatid porch of, 35, 99, 241n101; column bases, 172; convex-concave elements in, 91–92, 99; copies, imitations, and quotations of, 36, 225, 233, 241n101; dating of, 153; gilding of, 161; glass inlays at, 162, 163, 177; north porch of, 99, 163, 172; ornamentation of, 161–62; photo of, 94–98; polychromy of, 156, 165, 167; porch of, 35; relief carving in, 153; repairs to, 144, 239n9, 251n82; workers at, 26, 240n56, 241n66

Eretria: Museum, 79–80, 150, 173, 175, 178; temple of Apollo Daphnephoros, 173
Eretria, bilingual Ionic capital from: attachments of, 177; bolster of, 175; carving depth of, 87; characteristics of, 153; comparison of, 176–77, 185; convex-concave elements of, 1, 176–77; description of, 161, 175, 177; embellishments of, 177; helix absence of, 178; identification of, 178; illustration of, 151, 173, 175, 176; influence of, 196; overview of, 173–79; polychromy of, 176–78, 230; volutes of, 175, 178
Eryx, Mt., 131
Étienne, Roland, 55–56
Euclid's *Optics*, 102
Euergus, 243n52
Euripides, 40
Eurydamos, 222
Eurymedon Palm, 219, 225
euthynteria, 234
Exchange of Populations and Thessaloniki, 122

Fenger, Ludvig Peter, 157
figure-ground contrast, 157
fillets, 61, 79, 90, 105, 113, 114, 125, 133, 152, 176, 177, 178, 182, 188, 190, 196, 217
floral motifs, 91, 92, 114, 203, 225. *See also specific capitals; specific locations*
fluting: chiaroscuro effect of, 103, 107; on column bases, 62, 63, 64, 99, 101; comparison of, 103, 104–5; concave, 103; in Doric order, 22, 103–4, 248n73; illustration of, 105; on Ionic capital echinus, 64, 65; in Ionic order, 22, 57, 61; optical illusion of, 102; prices for, 85; shadow design and, 101–6; tools for carving, 90; unfinished, 11, 16, variation in number or design, 18, 19, 21–22. *See also specific capitals; specific locations*
Fonseca, S. da, 222
foot units, 67, 148
Forum of Augustus (Rome), 36, 37, 233
frieze: archaistic style in, 6; of dancing Magnesians, 26; illustration of, 234; lotus-and-palmette, 91–92; origins of, 5; polychromy of, 157, 165; visibility and, 66. *See also* metopes; triglyphs; *specific temples; specific locations*

Gareskos, 130
Gargettos tribe (Aigeis), 196
Gauls, 221, 226
Gehl, Jan, 66
geison, 234
Gela, 208–9, 210
Georgopoulos, Petros, 85, 86, 87, 88
gilding, 8, 24, 161, 162, 164, 166, 177, 213, 219–20, 250n38, 252n66
glass attachments, 162, 163, 177
gold. *See* gilding
graffiti, 182
Greece, 1, 153
Greek architecture: archaism, 39–40 (*see also* archaism: in architecture); characteristics of, 8; developmental narratives of, 12, 40; history of research, 11–13; polychromy and, 153, 172; significance of, 7–8, 41
Gruben, Gottfried, 24, 44, 49, 53–6
guilloche, 99, 162, 163, 167, 172

General Index 277

Hadrian, 129, 133–34
Hagnous, 195
Halikarnassos, Mausoleum of, 96, 109, 162, 164, 167, 198, 203. *See also* Pytheos
Hanink, Johanna, 40
Hansen, Christian, 153, 155–56, 182, 183
hawks-beak molding, 157
heart-and-dart motif (Lesbian leaf), 50–51, 114, 127, 157, 169, 235. *See also specific capitals; specific locations*
Hébrard, Ernést, 146
Hekataios of Miletos, 130
helix, 230, 235. *See also specific capitals; specific locations*
Hellenistic period, 170, 198, 202, 206, 210, 232
Hellmann, Marie-Christine, 157–58
Hellner, Gösta, 50, 243n31
Hendrich, Christoph, 63–64
Hennemeyer, Arnd, 104
Herakleitos of Ephesos, 100, 108, 246n70
Hermes (statue), 241n102
Hermogenes, 26–27, 28. *See also* Magnesia on the Maeander, temple of Artemis Leukophryene
Hermokrates of Syracuse, 209
Herodotus, 20, 56, 61, 79, 119, 120
Herostratos, 198, 206
heterogeneous appearance: by circumstance, 14, 21, 22, 24–25, by design 14, 21, 22
Heuzey, Léon, 112
Himera, battle of, 220
Hipponion, 210
historic preservation in antiquity, 7, 31–32, 239n9
Homer, 121
Homolle, Théophile, 54
Hymettos, Mt. 195

identity, formation of, 7, 110, 117, 121, 199, 207, 221, 231–32, 246n1
Ignatiadou, Despina, 162
Ilissos River, temple on, 189, 192, 193
imitation, 34, 36, 38
Imperial cult, 110
incuse coins, 29–30
inscriptions: bilingual, 20; building accounts, 26–28; dedicatory, 20; painting letters of, 153; visibility of, 68, 69. *See also* Archilochos capital; Lindos: Lindian Chronicle
Inwood, Henry William, 192
Inwood capital and Agora A3345, 180–81, 192–93, 197
Ionia: and Athens 28, 152, 198; and Delos, 42, 43, 199; ethnic identity, 7; grave stelai, 92; influence in Athens, 191–92; Ionian Renaissance, 198; Ionian Revolt, 198; mythical origin, 2; science and 100; and Sparta, 26. *See also specific locations*
Ionic capitals: casts of, 36–37, 233; corner capitals, 18, 20, 44, 46, 68; gilding of, 161, 162; model (*paradeigma*), 28; normal capital, 44, 46, 68; polychromy of, 161–72; proportions of, 14, 44, 79, 111, 112, 124, 174–75; scatter plot of, 174; templates for, 24–25; wooden origins of, 5, 63. *See also* bilingual Ionic capitals
Ionic order: in Athens, 150, 151–53, 196; changes to, 12; comparison of, 166; cymation, 129, 132; dentils, 5, 101, 124, 165, 216, 246n13; description of, 12, 14; development of, 200; doorframes, 128–29; formation of canon, 40; history of, 2; meaning of, 5–6; origin story of, 2; overview of, 2–3; as parallel, 11; in the Peloponnese, 44; polychromy of, 8, 150, 153, 161, 165, 166, 172, 178; in Sicily, 26, 210; shadow design in, 101; streamlining of, 150; writings regarding, 2. *See also* Attic style in Ionic architecture; East-Ionian style; Island-Ionian style; *specific capitals*; *specific locations*
Island-Ionian style, 42, 43, 61
Island marble (Cycladic), 49, 77, 182, 185–86, 244n3. *See also* marble
Italy, 1. *See also specific locations*
itinerancy: of architects, 6–7, 25, 202; of sculptors, 26, 198, 210; of stone workers 25–26, 210
itinerant temples, phenomenon of, 148, 248n110. *See also* Agora (Athens): temple of Ares; Agora polychrome capitals; Sounion: temple of Athena; Thessaloniki, itinerant temple and its capitals; Thorikos, Stoa at

Jacquemin, Anne, 216, 220, 221, 222
Jeraka (Attica). *See* Pallene, bilingual Ionic capitals from; Yérakas
Johannes, Heinz, 62–63
Jong, Piet de, 169
Julius Caesar, 131

Kallithea, Attica, tomb monument of Nikeratos and Polyxenos, 187
Kallikrates (Athenian architect), 27
Kallikrates of Samos (Ptolemaic general), 213
Kallimachos Nike and its Ionic capital (Akr. 3776), 153, 154, 155, 166, 184, 188, 244n3
Kallimachos of Aphidna, 166
Kallipolitis, Vasilios, 173, 175
Kapoor, Anish, 161
Karadedos, Giorgos, 146, 248n60
Karaoli-Dimitriou St., 146
Karia: architecture of, 81; background of builder in Athens, 26
Karwiese, Stefan, 205
Katakolo, 49
Kaulonia, 29
Kavala, 112, 116, 196. *See also* Neapolis
Kekrops, tomb of (Kekropion), 35, 151
King's Law, 195–96
Kissos, 130
Kizilburun wreck, 185
Klaros: Ionic column monuments, 212, 213; temple of Apollo, 185
Klein, Yves, 161
Knell, Heiner, 39–40
Koch-Brinkmann, Ulrike, 169
Koldewey, Robert, 170, 172
Korkyra, 121
Korres, Manolis, 82, 193, 239n9, 240n48
Kotys I, 120
Koukouli-Chrysanthaki, Chaido, 118
Krastevich, Bulgaria, 10
Krautheimer, Richard, 34
Krischen, Fritz, 18
Kroisos (Lydian king), 20, 79, 207
Kroton, 29, 30, 79
Krousaians, 129–30

labor, 7–9, 66, 76, 84–85, 90–91, 116. *See also* workers

Ladstätter, Sabine, 205
Lansdowne Amazon, 133
Laroche, Didier, 216, 220, 225
lathe. *See* turning
leaf motifs, 96, 97, 157. *See also specific capitals; specific locations*
league of Athena Pallenis, 196
Lebadeia, temple of Zeus, 27
Leo Mathematicus (Bishop of Thessaloniki), 131
Leonardo da Vinci, 109
Le Roy, Julien David, 11–12, 46
Lesbian cyma, 114
Lesbos, temple at Messon, 21, 116, 160, 161, 170, 172, 206, 230
Leukas, 131
lewis iron, 209–10
lighting conditions, 7, 107, 109. *See also* shadows
limestone, 55, 56, 105, 132, 161, 173, 193, 208, 213. *See also* quarries
Limyra, Heroon of Perikles, 35, 36
Lindos: Lindian Chronicle, 31; sanctuary of Athena, 31
Livy, 131
Lohmann, Hans, 64
Lokroi Epizephyrioi, 26, 210
Lola, 132
lotus and palmette. *See* anthemion
Lucian, 241n102
Luynes, Duc de, 29–30
Lydia: background of builder in Athens, 26; patronage of Greek sanctuaries, 20, 79, 207
Lykourgos of Athens, 6, 40, 192, 242n116
Lysippides Painter, 9, 23
Lysippus, 133

Macedon: after Alexander, 129; and Athens, 40, 117, 130, 221; Roman province, 148. *See also* Macedonian tombs; *specific sites*
Macedonian tombs, 165, 166. *See also* Tomb of Eurydice; Tomb of Palmettes; Tomb, Rhomaios
Magna Graecia, 26, 209
Magnesia on the Maeander, temple of Artemis Leukophryene, 164–65, 170. *See also* Bathykles of Magnesia; Hermogenes
Mallwitz, Alfred, 50
Malten, Ludolf, 131
Marathon, battle of, 58, 194
Marathon Monument, 174
marble: carving experiment, 85–91, 228–29; carving practices for, 85; grain of, 86; Island/Cycladic, 77, 182, 185–86, 244n3; Parian, 25, 185, 213; patches, function of, 251n82; prices for, 85; quality of, 185; sanding of, 91; sourcing of, 185; as tool, 84. *See also* Naxos; Paros; Pentele, Mt.; Thasos
Marconi, Clemente, 67
Markopoulo, 195
Martin, Roland, 14
Massalia (Marseille): cult of Artemis Ephesia, 38, 231, 232; Ionic capital from, 38
materiality: of color, 250n34; deterioration, 33–34, 153; labor, value, and, 38, 162
materials. *See* marble; pigments; stone; wood
Maussollos (king of Karia), 198. *See also* Halikarnassos, Mausoleum of
Mayeux, Henri, 99
McGowan, Elizabeth, 166

meander, 167
Meiggs, Russell, 117
Messon. *See* Lesbos, temple at Messon
Metapontion (Metaponto): incuse coins, 29–30; Temple D, 170, 251
metics, defined, 26
metopes, 14, 67, 157, 230–31
metrology. *See* foot units
Mikocki, Tomasz, 47–48
Miletos, 202, 203
Möbius, Hans, 181–82, 185, 190, 192, 193
model, architectural (*paradeigma*), 25, 28
molding, 91, 157, 165. *See also specific capitals; specific locations*
Muss, Ulrike, 18
mutules, 5
Mygdones, 129–30
Mykale, Mt., 64
Mylonopoulos, Ioannis, 68

narrative reliefs, visibility of, 66
Naukratis, temple of Apollo, 92, 95
Naxos: Archaic period patron, 32, 56; innovator in Ionic style, 79; source of marble and emery 58, 79, 84; temple of Dionysos, Yria, 79, 131. *See also* Delos: Naxian Quarter; Delos: Oikos of the Naxians; Delphi: Naxian Sphinx Column; Stoa of the Naxians
Neapolis (Kavala): and Athens, 117, 119, 120; capital discovery in, 1; coinage of, 117–18, 119; conflicts with Thasos, 117; cult of Parthenos in, 119–20 246n7; description of, 116; founding of, 117; growth of, 121; location of, 25, 110, 112, 117; resources of, 117
Neapolis, temple of Parthenos and its capitals: bilingual capitals of, 25, 110, 114; capital variations at, 231–32; comparison of, 111, 124–25; convex-concave features of, 113–14, 149, 231–32; dating of, 111; description of, 230; discovery of, 112; features of, 112; illustration of, 52, 111, 115; inscriptions regarding, 118; mixed elements of, 122; origin of, 110, 118; overview of, 112–22; position of, 247n38; reconstructed columns of, 113; significance of, 117, 118; structure of, 112–13; volutes of, 231–32. *See also* Neapolis
necking drums, 91–92, 93
Neer, Richard, 23–24
Nemea, temple of Zeus, 104
Nénot, Henri-Paul, 44–46, 242n10&11
Nieborów Palace, 46–47. *See also* Delos, bilingual Ionic capitals from
Nikeratos, tomb monument of, 187
Nikias, 54
Niobe, 47
North Porch (Erechtheion), 99, 163, 172

Ohly, Dieter, 240n18
Ohnesorg, Aenne, 17–18, 63–64, 95–96
Oinomaos, column of (Olympia), 31–32
Oisyme, cave of the Nymphs, 116, 247n23, 247n47
Olympia: column of Oinomaos, 31–32; Leonidaion, 174; location of Pheia capital, 49; monument of Ptolemy II and Arsinoe II, 213; Nike of Paionios, 212; temple of Hera, 15–16, 20; temple of Zeus, 16, 104–5, 106, 157, 230–31
Omphalos (neighborhood of Thessaloniki), 130–31
orders, architectural: aesthetic conventions of, 220;

bicolumnar monuments as a "slice" of, 213, 226; contrasting combination of, 73, 74; origins of, 2, 5, 11–12, 15; parallels of, 11, 46. *See also* Corinthian order; Doric order; Ionic capitals; Ionic order

ornament: flexibility of, 24, 67; hierarchy of, 61, 210; interplay of convex and concave, 91–99, 109, 229; John Ruskin and, v, 99; of metal, 53, 135, 162, 177, 200, 217, 221; and observation of plants, 92, 245n29; and polychromy, 156, 161, 221; replication of, 36; standardization of, 25; variation in, 8, 127, 172, 173, 228 (see also *poikilia*; *Variationsfreude*); versus narrative relief, 66. *See also* anthemion; guilloche; meander

Oropos, 79–80. *See also* Amphiareion, location of

Oropos, Ionic capital from: bilingualism of, 81; bonding system of, 77–78; carving depth of, 79, 87; carving of, 81–91; coloring of, 77; comparison of, 79; description of, 76, 77, 244n8; discovery of, 1, 76; as freestanding monument, 80; as hybrid, 80; identification of, 76; image of, 77, 78, 80, 82, 83; overview of, 76–81; reuse of, 76; sculpture on top of, 76, 77, 79, 80

Ottoman power in the Aegean, 48

overseers of construction (naopoioi, epistatai), 27–28

ovolo, 51, 182, 235, 246n13

Paestum, temple of Athena, 208

Paga, Jessica, 192

painting (non-architectural): chiaroscuro (*skiagraphia*), 106, 246n61; of inscriptions, 153; oxidization of, 153, 156; panel painting, 156; of sculpture, 156, 166; three-tone system of, 246n61; wall painting, 107, 213. *See also* pigments; polychromy, architectural

Paionios of Ephesos, 202

Palermo Museum, 67, 209

Pallene (Attica): Antiochis (tribe), 196; league of Athena Pallenis, 196; location of, 185, 194, 195; *parasitoi*, 194–95; temple of Athena Pallenis, 135, 148, 181, 193–94

Pallene, bilingual Ionic capitals from (Stavro / Jeraka capitals): archaistic design of, 181; bonding system of, 186–87; carving depth of, 87; carving techniques of, 179–80; comparison of, 182, 185, 189–90; convex-concave elements of, 180, 184; dating of, 150, 180, 190–92, 197; description of, 230, 232; discovery of, 181–82; echinus of, 184; egg-and-dart motif of, 182, 185; excavation of, 193; experimentation of, 197; features of, 179–80; graffiti on, 182; helix of, 182, 184; influence of, 196; marble for, 185–86; orientation of, 230; overview of, 179–97; painting of, 185; palmettes of, 184; patching of, 180, 186–87; scale comparison of, 194; whorl of, 182, 184.

palmettes, 96, 97, 167, 203, 235. *See also specific capitals; specific locations*

Pangaion, Mt. (Thrace), 117

Panionion, 64–65

Pantikapaion, 167

parasemon (city insignia), 30

parasitoi, 195–96

Paros: 32–33, 79, capitals from, 32, 79; marble from, 25, 185, 213; Thasos and, 32, 112, 117, 120; workshops, 25, 32, 79. *See also* Archilochos capital

Parthenon (Athens): archaistic metope figures, 6, 239n8; column flutes, 103–4, 246n54; fluting in, 104; friezes at, 66; imitation of Doric order, 36; marble for, 185; painting at, 157; Parthenon Restoration Project, 85; Perikles and, 207; polychromy of, 157; pre-Parthenon, 103; visibility of frieze, 8, 66, 230

Parthenos, 112–13, 116, 119–20, 121, 149, 247n44, 247n47. *See also* Neapolis; Neapolis, temple of Parthenos and its capitals

Partida, Elena, 25, 216, 225

Pausanias, 26, 31, 220, 225

Pausias of Sicyon, 106

Peace of Nikias, 189

pediment sculpture, 14, 173, 175, 212, 222, 18n240

Peion, Mt., 204–5

Peisistratos (son of Hippias), 153

Peisistratos (tyrant of Athens), 43, 56, 192, 194–95

Peisistratos the Younger, 151

Pella, 167

Peloponnese, and Ionic architecture, 39, 44

Peloponnesian War, 26, 117, 225, 245n12

Peltekis, 132

Pentele, Mt., 185, 195

performance, of tragedies, 40

Pergamon, Great Altar of, 170

Perikles of Athens, 189, 207

Perikles of Limyra, 35–36

Perillos, 27

perception: of age, 33; and color, 153, 161, 196; solids and voids, 245n39; visual, 65, 66, 76, 99, 102, 107, 109

peripteral Ionic temples, 112

Persians: among builders in Athens, 26; spoils from, 219, 225

Persian Wars: destruction of sanctuaries, 6, 39, 119, 151, 153, 166, 173, 185, 194, 198, 239n10; fixed chronological point, 119, 173; Greek victory monuments, 39, 219, 220, 225, 226

perspective drawing (*scaenographia*), 100

Petrakos, Vasilios, 173, 175

petrification, 5. *See also* wood

Petropoulou, 245n12

phallic altars, 131

Phallos, 131

Pheidippides, 194

phialai: as attribute of Parthenos, 116, 119, 149; as ornament, 53, 114; as votives, 53, 56

Philip II, 40, 129, 130

Philip V, 31, 49, 54

Philolaos of Kroton, 30

Philo of Byzantion, 12

Phokians 220

photography, archaeological, 50, 96, 243n31

Phrygia: background of builder in Athens, 26; cult of Matar Idaea, 131; use of the lathe, 243n64

Piening, Heinrich, 169

pigments: azurite, 169; black, 158; cinnabar, 169, 171; discoloration of, 153; Egyptian blue, 156, 158, 169, 171; materiality of, 162, 250n34; scientific analysis of, 156, 164, 169; red, 156, 164; white, 164

Piraeus, 55, 56

Piraeus Museum, 187

Pistiros Inscription (Vetren, Bulgaria), 120

Pithos tribe (Kekropis), 196

plaster casts in antiquity, 36–37, 233

Plataia, battle of, 173, 211

Plato, 38, 88, 107

Pliny, 17, 20, 38, 62, 106, 200

Plutarch, 38–39, 195, 206, 207

Pnyx, 40

poikilia, 23–24, 228. See also *Variationsfreude*

Polichni, 123

polychromy, architectural: Athens and, 150–53;

280 General Index

bichrome, 156; bilingual Ionic capitals and, 177, 178, 196, 230; of ceiling coffers, 157; changes to, 164–65; chiaroscuro, 161; combination of different color stones, 161; of Doric order, 157–58, 161, 172–73; exterior/interior variation, 158; figure-ground contrast and, 157; illustration of, 167–68; imitation of precious materials, 164; importance of, 178; of Ionic order, 8, 150, 153, 161, 172–73, 178; of Ionic capitals, 7–8, 150, 196; oligochrome, 156; overview of, 153–73; preservation of, 165–66, 169; reconstructions of, 46, 170–71; trends in, 229, and visibility, 153. *See also* gilding; painting; pigments; *specific capitals*; *specific locations*

Polykleitos, 133
Polykrates, 42–43, 210. *See also* Samos: temple of Hera, dipteros II
Polyxenos (Kallithea), 187
pottery, 240n18
printing press and architectural drawing, 12, 34
pronaos columns, 21, 62–63. *See also* columns
proportions: and chronology, 12, 14; flexible design system, 24, 67; of Ionic capitals, 24, 44, 111, 175, 177, 190, 201, 240n15
Propylaia (Athens): capitals, 177, 180, 182, 188–90; imitation of, 35–37, 144
Prost, Francis, 56
Prusias II, 220
Psammis, 26
pseudoacrolithic sculpture, 161
Ptolemy II. *See* Samothrace, Sanctuary of the Great Gods: Propylon of Ptolemy II; Olympia: monument of Ptolemy II and Arsinoe II
Pydna, battle of, 212
Pythagoras of Samos, 29–30
Pythagoreans, 30
Pytheos, 109, 246n73

quarries: of *poros* limestone at Akte, Piraeus, 55, 56; of white marble from Pentele, Attica, 185; of other white marble in Attica (Agrileza, Thorikos, Agia Marina), 185; of limestone at Delphi, 213; initial stages of work done at, 27, 28, 29, 81, 86

Radziwiłłowa, Hélèna, 46–48
Rafina (Halai Araphenides), 185
red-figure technique, 22–23
regionalism in architecture, 7, 26, 42–43, 129, 184, 210, 231. *See also* Attic style in Ionic architecture; East-Ionian style; Island-Ionian style; itinerancy; workshops
repair: ancient accounts of, 41, 55; architectural, 6, 14–17, 110; clamps and pins, 51; committee overseeing repair in Athens, 41; Ephesos capital, 201, 204; to Ionic capitals, 248n110; Thessaloniki Ionic capitals, 110, 135–45; Stavro capital, 180, 187–88
replacements, replicas, and reproductions, 38, 40
Replat, Jean, 212, 225
retrospective design, 6, 9–10. *See also* archaism
Revett, Nicholas, 11
Rhamnous, temple of Nemesis, 185
Rheneia, 42, 48–49
Rheneian grave stele, 48–49
Rhoikos, 62. *See also* Samos: temple of Hera, dipteros I
Ridgway, Brunilde, 14
Riegl, Alois, 33

Rignanese, Giuseppe, 193
Roark, Howard, 28
Roma, 129, 133, 134
Rome: Column of Trajan, 66; Forum of Augustus, 36, 233, 241n101
rosettes, 53, 114, 127. *See also specific capitals*; *specific locations*
Ruskin, John, v, 99
Russian Empire, 48

Sabazios, 120
Samos: anthemion grave stelai, 92, 95; temple of Hera, dipteros I (Rhoikos Temple), 60, 61, 62, 63–64, 65; temple of Hera, dipteros II (Polykratean Temple), 60, 61, 63–64, 93, 95, 153; workshops, 26, 210
Samothrace, sanctuary of the Great Gods: Hall of Choral Dancers, 6; Ionic column monument, 213, mystery cult, 73; Propylon of Ptolemy II, 73, 74, 75, 96, 97; Theatral Circle, 73
sanding, in carving process, 90, 91. *See also* tools for stone carving
Sapirstein, Philip, 15
Sayer, Robert, 11
scale, 30, 38–39, 61, 66, 117, 122, 133
Schlaifer, Robert, 195, 196
scotia, 100
Scott, Michael C., 221
sculpture: acrolithic, 161; chronology and, 240n18; photographing of, 243n31; plaster casting and, 36; pseudoacrolithic, 161; restoration of, 32; solids and voids in, 100; style changes of, 18; trends in, 36. *See also specific locations*
Selinous (Selinunte): architectural sculpture from, 14, 67; Doric order and, 210, 232; Temple A, 210; Temple B, 158, 160–61; Temple C (Selinous), 67; Temple E, 14–15, 67, 230–31; Temple G, 16–17, 102; Temple Y, 67
Selinous, Ionic capitals: bolsters of, 208; carving depth of, 87; chronology of, 209; convex-concave elements of, 209; description of, 208; echinus of, 208; illustration of, 199, 209; palmettes of, 208; volute of, 208
Selinunte. *See* Selinous
Severe Style, 14
shadows, 99–109, 230–31. *See also* lighting conditions; vision
Shaya, Josephine, 31
Shoe Meritt, Lucy, 25, 180, 185, 190–91, 192, 193
Sicily, 26, 131, 210
sima block, 124, 143–44, 146–47, 148–49, 234
Sismanidis, Konstantinos, 133
skiagraphia, 106
Skias, Sparta, 26
Skillous, temple of Artemis Ephesia, 36, 38, 232, 241n105
slavery. *See* workers: enslaved
Smyrna, Old, 32
Snellen Eye Chart, 68
Sobak, Robert, 88
Socrates, 88
Sophokles, 40
Sostratos of Knidos, 241n62
Soteria, 221, 222
Sounion: temple of Athena, 148, 153, 156, 166, 168–69, 170, 175, 176–77, 185, 248n110; temple of Poseidon, 148, 185
South Italy, 26, 29, 30, 210. *See also specific locations*
Sparta, 12, 26, 221, 222, 225, 226
sphinxes, 45, 77, 79, 80, 81, 212, 244

spolia: find context of Ionic capitals, 76, 79, 124, 204–5, 209; imitation of style, 145; symbolic reuse, 6, 32, 233, 239n10
Stageira, 111, 129, 133
Stanton, G. R., 196
Starosel, tomb at, 160, 161, 230
statues, 161, 244n3. *See also specific locations; specific statues*
Stavro (Attica): Hagia Triada / Agios Ioannis Theologos church, 181. *See also* Pallene; Pallene, bilingual Ionic capitals from
Ste. Croix, G.E.M. de, 117
Stefanidou-Tiveriou, Theodosia, 133–34
Steimle, Christopher, 133
stelai, 49, 81, 86, 92, 95, 151
Stewart, Andrew, 14
Stoa of the Naxians, 53, 54
Stoa Poikile, 152
stoas, 58. *See also specific capitals; specific locations*
stone: emery, 84; grain of, 86; transportation of, 185. *See also* limestone; marble; quarries; tools for stone carving
St. Petersburg, 48
Strabo, 38, 130, 204, 207, 232
Stuart, James and Nicholas Revett, 11
stylobate, 234
syncretism, 110, 120, 130
synoecism, 131, 135, 145–46
Syracuse: Ionic architecture at, 26, 210; temple of Artemis, 210

Tegea, temple of Athena, 40
temples: building process of, 25–26; collapse of, 145; construction, 27; continuity, 40; as cultural instrument, 31; eye-level decoration of, 66–67; as museum, 31; scale comparison of, 39; significance of, 31. *See also specific locations*
Teos, temple of Dionysos, 27
Thales of Miletos, 108
Thasos: and Athens, 32, 111, 116, 117, 118–19, 178, 247n33; cave of Pan, 120; Ionic capitals from, 190; peraia of, 116–17; sanctuary of Artemis, 247n38; temple of Herakles (Herakleion), 112, 127–28, 147–49; workshops, 133, 148, 210
Themistokles, 38–39
Theodorescu, Dinu, 208, 209
Theodoros, 26, 62
Theophrastus, 17
Thermaic Gulf, 129 30
Therme, 129, 130. *See also* Thessaloniki; Thessaloniki, itinerant temple and its capitals
Theseus, 195
Thessaloniki: Antigonidon Plateia, 123, 127, 131, 133, 146, 248n60; "Area of Temples," 133; founding of, 129; Doubioti St. excavation (Byzantine peristyle), 124, 127, 142, 144; Museum of, 146; 1, 22, 122, 196, 246n2; Panagouda church, 123, 135; synoecism of, 131, 135, 145–46. *See also* Thessaloniki, itinerant temple and its capitals
Thessaloniki, itinerant temple and its capitals: carving depth of, 87; colonnade description of, 124; comparison of, 111, 125, 190; convex-concave elements of, 125–27, 135, 136, 142, 149; damage to, 143–44; dating of, 111, 131; description of, 161, 230; discovery of, 122; doorframes of, 128–29; excavations of, 123–24, 127, 132, 134, 144; foundation of, 132–33; illustrations of, 111, 145, 123, 125; inscriptions on, 127, 135, 142; as itinerant, 110; original deity, 129–33; original location of, 129–33, 134, 146, 147; redesign of, 146; repairs to, 110, 135, 137–41, 143–44, 149; replacement pieces, 143–44; sima block of, 143, 146–48; transport of, 134, 149; volute eyes of, 162; workshop, 148
Third Sacred War, 220
Thorikos, Stoa at, 11, 13, 185
Thrace: colonization of, 7, 117; conquest by Philip II, 129, 130; cult in, 120; natural resources of, 117; syncretism, 130. *See also* Bendis; Starosel
Thrasyllos, monument of (Athens), 35–36
Thucydides, 12, 26, 42, 43, 56, 121, 153, 199
Tiberius, 133
Tomb, Rhomaios (Vergina), 167
Tomb of Eurydice (Vergina), 161, 165, 167
Tomb of Palmettes (Lefkadia), 165, 167
Tomb of the Judgment (Mieza), 165
tongue-and-dart pattern, 114
tools for stone carving: bullnose chisels, 84, 88–90, 245n25; flat chisels, 82, 90; general toolbox, 25, 90; point chisels, 82; punch, 88, 245n23; rasps, 84; for sanding, 89. *See also* lewis iron; model, architectural; turning
torus elements, 18, 19
tragedies, 40
trauma, 206–7
treasuries, 210. *See also* Delphi: Siphnian treasury
Trell, Bluma, 205
triglyphs: block at Pallene, 193, 251n97; conjectural wooden origins of, 5; polychromy of, 157–61, 172, 229–30.
Turkey, 1. *See also specific locations*
Tuscan order, 11
turning (stone carving technique), 62–63, 243n64

unfinished: capital details, 228, 229; column flutes, 11, 16, 17, 102; temples 17, 122, 173, 198

Vallois, René, 56
value: Alois Riegl's model of age value (*Alterswert*) and historical value (*historischer Wert*), 33; archaism and, 22; cultural, 32; in materials and labor, 162
Vanderpool, Eugene, 182
Variationsfreude ("delight in variety"), 24, 228, 240n48. *See also poikilia*
vase painting. *See* archaism: in vase painting; bilingual Attic vases; black-figure technique; connoisseurship; red-figure technique
Venus Genetrix, 129, 131
Vergina: Rhomaios tomb, 167; Tomb of Eurydice, 161, 165, 167
Vienna, Ephesos Museum / Kunsthistorisches Museum, 200
visibility, 65–75, 229. *See also epiphanestatos topos*
vision: depth cues, 102; Euclid's *Optics*, 102; field of, 66; optical illusions, 102–3; Vitruvius and, 102, 105, 246n60. *See also* visibility
Vitruvius: on autonomy of architects, 26–27, 28; on chiaroscuro effects, 100–101, 105; on column fluting, 102, 105, 229, 246n60; on drawing, 35, 100; on education of the architect, 109; on Hermogenes, 26–27, 28; on Ionic order, 2, 11, 12, 14; on origin of the orders, 2, 5,

282 General Index

11–12, 15; on polychromy, 158; rules from, 67; on temple of Artemis, Ephesos, 199–200; on temple of Hera, Samos, 61; on terminology and proportions for Ionic capitals, 12, 79; on *venustas* (delight), 24

volute eyes: attachments to, 162, 163; comparison of, 51; embellishments for, 161; illustration of, 52, 162, 163, 235; painting of, 230. *See also specific capitals; specific locations*

volutes: carving process, 82, 88–90; on columns, 33; comparison of, 38; convex-concave elements of, 12, 14; on corner capitals, 44; description of, 5, 14; division of, 79; flat, 14; illustration of, 81, 235; painting of, 167; recarving of, 144–45. *See also* Ionic capitals; *specific capitals; specific locations*

votives: attachment to buildings, 53; imitation of cult statues for, 38; Ionic columns as part of, 2, 8, 14, 77, 81, 131. *See also* Acropolis (Athens), korai; Persians, spoils from; phialai; treasuries

Voutiras, Emmanuel, 131, 134

Warsaw, National Museum, 47
waterspout, 124, 143, 146, 149, 249n126
Wescoat, Bonna, 24–25
whorl, 196, 235. *See also* Ionic capitals; *specific capitals; specific locations*
Winckelmann, Johann Joachim, 12
Witcombe, Christopher, 38
wood: bracket (*Sattelholz*) as conjectural origin of Ionic volutes, 44, 64, 202; as building material, 17, 55, 61, 64, 175, 187; conjectural origin of architectural orders in, 5, 15, 176; as material for sculpture, 38. *See also* Olympia: column of Oinomaos; *xoana*
workers: enslaved, 26; foreign workers in Athens, 26; habits of, 24; itinerancy of, 25–26; organization of 27, 63; status of, 26
workshops, 26, 36, 91, 95, 111, 133, 148, 203, 210. See also itinerancy; Paros: workshops; regionalism in architecture

Xanthos, temple of Leto, 161
Xenophanes of Kolophon, 12
Xenophon, 36, 38, 39, 88, 231, 232, 242n106
xoana, 119–21, 149, 247n44

Yérakas (Attica) (also "Jeraka"): cemetery, 193; church of Agios Dimitrios, 181. *See also* Pallene; Pallene, bilingual Ionic capitals from

Zambas, Kostas, 103, 104
Zeus Eleutherios, 129, 133, 134
Zoster (Halai Aixonides), temple of Apollo, 249n1

Image Credits

© Aenne Ohnesorg (figs. 1.5, 2.2, 2.13)
American Excavations Samothrace (fig. 2.25)
Antike Kunst (fig. 4.12)
Archives of the American School of Classical Studies at Athens, Archives (figs. 1.19, Archaeological Photographic Collection AK 0010; 5.17; 5.29)
Art Resource, NY (figs. 2.3, 3.25)
Artist Rights Society (fig. 3.25)
© Beaux-Arts de Paris, Dist. RMN-Grand Palais (fig. 2.3)
Daniela Stoyanova (fig. 0.5)
Danish National Art Library (figs. 5.4, 5.5, 5.30)
© École française d'Athènes (figs. 2.11, 6.8, 6.12)
Ephesos Museum, Vienna (figs. 0.1, 6.1, 6.2, 6.5)
Ephorate of Antiquities of Athens (figs. 2.24, 3.22, 3.23, 5.37)
Ephorate of Antiquities of Cyclades (figs. 1.16, 2.12)
Ephorate of Antiquities of Ilia (figs. 2.6, 2.7, 2.22, 2.23)
Ephorate of Antiquities of Kavala-Thasos (figs. 2.10, 4.1, 4.2, 4.3, 4.4, 4.9, 4.17)
Ephorate of Antiquities of Phocis (figs. 2.18, 6.1, 6.11, 6.13, 6.16, 6.17, 6.18, 6.19, 6.20)
Ephorate of Antiquities of Samos-Icaria (figs. 2.15, 3.19, 3.16)
Ephorate of Antiquities of Serres (fig. 3.31)
Ephorate of Antiquities of West Attica, Piraeus & Islands (figs. 3.9, 5.26, 5.31, 5.32, 5.33, 5.35, 5.39)
Ephorate of Euboea (figs. 5.1, 5.24)
Ephorate of Macedonia (figs. 4.1, 4.12, 4.14, 4.16, 4.20, 4.23, 4.25, 4.26)
Epigraphic Museum, Athens (figs. 4.9, 5.3)
© Fitzwilliam Museum, Cambridge (fig. 3.25)
© Frank Hulek (fig. 2.19)
© Gabriel Moss (figs. 0.3, 4.18)
German Archaeological Institute, Athens (2.7, Gösta Hellner, D-DAI-ATH-1974/791, 792; 2.15, Hermann Wagner, D-DAI-ATH-Samos 2381; 2.18, Walther Wrede, D-DAI-ATH-Delphi 252; 3.16, Eva-Maria Czakó, D-DAI-ATH-Samos 5773; 3.17, Walter Hege, D-DAI-ATH-Hege 1852; 5.3, D-DAI-ATH-Athen Varia 23; 5.37, Hermann Wagner, D-DAI-ATH-Akropolis 854, 855)
German Archaeological Institute, Berlin (fig. 1.19, D-DAI-Z-FTT 8433)
© Hansgeorg Bankel (fig. 5.8)
Loïc Damelet (Centre Camille Jullian, CNRS) (fig. 3.15)
© Manolis Korres (figs. 3.6, 3.7)
Museo Archeologico Salinas, Palermo (figs. 2.20, 6.7)
© Museum of Fine Arts, Boston (figs. 0.4, 1.14)
National Archaeological Museum, Athens (figs. 3.1, 3.2, 5.25, 5.34)
National Museum, Warsaw (fig. 2.1)
Princeton University Library (figs. 1.9, 3.21, 3.24)
© Trustees of the British Museum, London (figs. 0.1, 5.14, 5.38)
Universitätsbibliothek Heidelberg (figs. 1.1, 1.3, 1.9, 1.11)
© Vinzenz Brinkmann, Ulrike Koch-Brinkmann, and Heinrich Piening (fig. 5.19)